D0216929

The Unpublished Opinions of the Warren Court

The Unpublished Opinions of the

WARREN
COURT

BERNARD SCHWARTZ

New York   Oxford
OXFORD UNIVERSITY PRESS
1985

Oxford University Press

Oxford   London   New York   Toronto
Delhi   Bombay   Calcutta   Madras   Karachi
Kuala Lumpur   Singapore   Hong Kong   Tokyo
Nairobi   Dar es Salaam   Cape Town
Melbourne   Auckland

and associated companies in
Beirut   Berlin   Ibadan   Mexico City   Nicosia

Published by Oxford University Press, Inc. 200 Madison Avenue
New York, New York 10016

Library of Congress Cataloging in Publication Data
Schwartz, Bernard, 1923-
The unpublished opinions of the Warren court.
1. Judicial opinions—United States.   2. United
States. Supreme Court. I. Title.
KF210.S3   1985   347.73'26   85-2915
ISBN 0-19-503563-1   347.30735

Printing (last digit): 9 8 7 6 5 4 3 2 1

Printed in the United States of America

FOR AILEEN

Abbreviations Used

CEW: Charles E. Whittaker

EW: Earl Warren

FF: Felix Frankfurter

FFH: Felix Frankfurter Papers, Harvard Law School

FFLC: Felix Frankfurter Papers, Library of Congress

HHB: Harold H. Burton

HHBLC: Harold H. Burton Papers, Library of Congress

HLB: Hugo L. Black

HLBLC: Hugo L. Black Papers, Library of Congress

JMH: John M. Harlan

JMHP: John M. Harlan Papers, Mudd Manuscript Library, Princeton University

PS: Potter Stewart

SR: Stanley Reed

TCC: Tom C. Clark

TCCT: Tom C. Clark Papers, Tarlton Law Library, University of Texas

WJB: William J. Brennan

WOD: William O. Douglas

Preface

For of all sad words of tongue or pen,
The saddest are these: "It might have been."
John Greenleaf Whittier, *Maud Muller*

One interested in the "might have been" in Supreme Court jurisprudence can find ample store for reflection in the work of the Warren Court. Many of the cases decided by that Court were close to having been decided differently. This was true both of leading cases and lesser-known ones—some of them now of interest only to Supreme Court specialists. In many, the vote the other way had already been taken, a draft opinion of the Court in accordance therewith prepared, and the decision ready to be announced. Then a switch in votes, a change in the grounds for decision, the illness or resignation of a Justice, or some other last-minute factor resulted in a changed decision and a new opinion explaining it.

So far as the public was concerned, all that was available to explain the Court's decision process were the published opinions; there was no indication that the Justices had almost decided the case differently or that the dissent was close to coming down as the draft opinion of the Court. Only those privy to the Court's internal workings were aware that the published opinions did not give anything like a true picture of the Court's decision process.

This book is an attempt to show what went on behind the scenes in eleven cases decided by the Warren Court. The cases themselves range in importance from *Brown* v. *Board of Education*, in many ways the watershed constitutional case of this century, and *Bell* v. *Maryland*, where a constitutional landmark was avoided only at the last minute, to cases that may be less important—though still of interest to Supreme Court aficionados. Most of the cases saw shifts in the Justices' votes, which made the decisions handed down different from those agreed upon earlier in conference. This was not true of the first case, *Alton* v. *Alton*, which became moot before the decision and opinions could be issued. In the second case, *Dayton* v. *Dulles*, the far-reaching draft opinion of the Court could not command a majority, and the decision was made on a narrower ground. In the seventh case, *Griswold* v. *Connecticut*, the original draft opinion of the Court was based on reasoning that was changed at the suggestion of a Justice, a change that made *Griswold* the foundation case in the constitutional protection of the individual right of privacy. The other cases, except *Brown*, saw vote switches that completely changed both the decisions and the opinions explaining them.

This book contains the draft opinions that were prepared by the Justices in the cases included. Such draft opinions are, of course, private Court papers. They have not heretofore been published, though extracts from them do appear in my judicial biography of Chief Justice Warren, *Super Chief: Earl Warren and His Supreme Court (1983)*.

I first became aware of these unpublished opinions when I was working on my Warren biography. It then occurred to me that it would be as worthwhile to publish these opinions as it was for Alexander M. Bickel to publish *The Unpublished Opinions of Mr. Justice Brandeis*. The opinions themselves were selected from hundreds that were made available to me while I was working on the Warren book. They were chosen both for their intrinsic interest and for what they tell us about the way in which the Supreme Court operates. The source of each opinion is given in a note at its beginning, except where it was made available to me on a confidential basis and is not in a collection to which scholars or the public have access. Reference is also made throughout the book to conference discussions and communications between the Justices. Their source is contained in the notes, except where conference notes or other documents were given to me in confidence. In the latter case, I have tried to identify the documents, usually by title and date. I have personally examined every document to which reference is made.

The draft opinions themselves are preceded by a brief history of each case, which presents the setting in which the drafts were circulated among the Justices. The draft opinions are followed by an analysis of what happened in the cases after the drafts were circulated. In particular, I try to explain why the drafts themselves did not ultimately come down as the opinions of the Court and dissents in the cases covered. In addition, there is an effort to show what might have happened if the draft opinions had been issued as they appear in this book. Insofar as possible, I try to contrast the "might have been" with the "was" in each case. The difference between the two made for a substantial difference in the law in the various areas involved.

The draft opinions in this book are at least as interesting for what they reveal about the decision process of the Warren Court as about the Justices who authored them. In addition, most of them played a crucial role in the decisions ultimately rendered, either because they were prepared as draft opinions of the Court or because they led directly to vote switches, which changed the decisions in the cases concerned. If the drafts in this book had come down as the ultimate majority and dissenting opinions, the law would have been very different in important areas of our public law. We can only imagine what the law and the society today would be like if *Griswold* v. *Connecticut* and *Shapiro* v. *Thompson* had been decided differently or if *Bell* v. *Maryland* had been decided on the merits against the claims of the civil-rights demonstrators.

Brown v. *Board of Education,* the last case, stands apart. The draft opinions there only became available when the Warren papers were opened in 1985. In addition, the *Brown* drafts are the only ones in this book that came down as Court opinions essentially in their original form. They are included for what they tell us about the drafting process in a truly historic case. They show that the opinions as well as the decisions in *Brown* were primarily the handiwork of the Chief Justice. Indeed, the changes made in the Warren drafts did anything but improve the final *Brown* opinions.

All but five of the draft opinions in this book are reproduced directly from the originals, as printed by the Supreme Court print shop. Two of the drafts are in typewritten and two in handwritten form and have been reset; the same is true of the *Griswold* opinion, as my copy of the original could not be reproduced.

I have been given generous access to papers of the Justices and am glad to acknowledge the help given by the Manuscript Division, Library of Congress, the University of Texas Law School, the Harvard Law Library, and the Mudd Manuscript Library, Princeton University. I am grateful to the latter two collections for their permission to quote from the papers of Justices Frankfurter and Harlan.

I should also acknowledge the generous support of Dean Norman Redlich and the New York University School of Law, the work of my tireless secretary, Mrs. Barbara Ortiz, as well as help for incidental research expenses by the Charles Ulrich and Josephine Bay Foundation (through Mrs. Raymonde Paul).

New York   B.S.
April 1985

Contents

The Unpublished Opinions of the Warren Court

Introduction: The Warren Court and Its Members

The United States Supreme Court is unique among governmental institutions in both size and power. "Alone among Government agencies," wrote Anthony Lewis in *The New York Times*, "the court seems to have escaped Parkinson's Law. The work is still done by nine men, assisted by eighteen young law clerks."[1]

When Earl Warren became Chief Justice, the Chief Justice's staff consisted of a mere handful of people. Warren himself later recalled his reaction on arriving at what one Justice liked to call "the marble mausoleum":[2]

> I remember well the day of my arrival at the Court. . . . I walked into the Supreme Court Building, and was ushered into the chambers of the Chief Justice by the marshal. There I was met by Mrs. McHugh, who had been the secretary of my predecessor, Chief Justice Vinson. . . . There were also there awaiting me two very elderly messengers . . . and there were three young law clerks recently out of law school. . . . That was my staff. Can you imagine the shock after the multiple secretariat and staff I had been accustomed to?[3]

But if the Supreme Court does not possess panoply, it certainly does possess power. "The Supreme Court," wrote Alexis de Tocqueville in 1835, "is placed higher than any known tribunal. . . . The peace, the prosperity, and the very existence of the Union are vested in the hands of the seven Federal judges."[4]

The U.S. Supreme Court is emphatically more than a law court, in the ordinary sense of that term. Before his elevation to the supreme bench, Benjamin N. Cardozo was for many years a distinguished member and chief of New York's highest court. With the perspective gained from judicial service in both Albany and Washington, Cardozo could note a basic difference between the highest courts of state and nation. The New York Court of Appeals, he said, "is a great common law court; its problems are lawyers' problems. But the Supreme Court is occupied chiefly with statutory construction—which no man can make interesting—and with politics." Of course, as Justice Jackson once pointed out, the word *politics* need not refer to a sense of partisanship but instead to a sense of policy making.[5]

When Cardozo came to Washington, he left what was then the greatest common-law court in the land; New York's Court of Appeals dealt essentially with the questions of private law that are the preoccupation and delight of most lawyers. The court to which he came was not, and has not been since the time of Chief Justice John Marshall, the usual type of law court. Public, not private, law is the stuff of Supreme Court litigation. Elevation to that tribunal requires the appointee to make the adjustment from preoccupation with the restricted, however novel, problems of private litigation to the most exacting demands of judicial statesmanship.

It is precisely that the Supreme Court *is* more than the usual law court that makes its work of vital significance to more than the relatively small number of litigants who appear before it. To the Supreme Court alone, in the final analysis, is assigned the function of guarding the ark of the Constitution. The Constitution itself is not a self-executing document. The *ought* laid down in 1787 must run the gantlet of judicial interpretation before it attains the practical status of an *is*. The Constitution, to paraphrase a statement by Chief Justice Charles Evans Hughes, must in practice be what the Supreme Court Justices say it is.[6] Or, as Bishop Hoadly observed in 1717, "[W]hoever hath an absolute authority to interpret written . . . laws; it is he who is truly the lawgiver to all intents and purposes and not the person who wrote . . . them."[7]

In another well-known statement de Tocqueville claims that "scarcely any political question arises in the United States that is not resolved sooner or later into a judicial question."[8] From this point of view, the Supreme Court is primarily a political institution. Since its decrees mark the boundaries between the great departments of government, and since on its actions depend the proper functioning of federalism and the scope to be given to the rights of the individual, a judge on such a tribunal has an opportunity to leave his imprint on the life of the nation as no mere master of the common law possibly could. Certainly, as an English writer recently noted, "in America, the Supreme Court is supreme. In no other democratic country do nine judges, none of them elected, tell the president and the legislature what each may or may not do."[9]

The Chief Justice and His Background

Of course, the Supreme Court is a collegiate institution whose collegiate nature is underscored by the custom the justices used to have of calling each other "Brethren." But each of the Brethren could only be guided, not directed. As Justice Felix Frankfurter once stated in a letter to Chief Justice Fred Vinson, ". . . good feeling in the Court, as in a family, is produced by accommodation, not by authority—whether the authority of a parent or a vote."[10]

The Court "family" is composed of nine individuals, who constantly bear out James Bryce's truism that "judges are only men."[11] "To be sure," Frankfurter once wrote Justice Stanley Reed, "the Court is an institution, but individuals, with all their diversities of endowment, experience and outlook determine its actions. The history of the Supreme Court is not the history of an abstraction, but the analysis of individuals acting as a Court who make decisions and lay down doctrines."[12]

Foremost among the individuals who made up the Warren Court was, of course, the Chief Justice himself. In many respects Earl Warren could have been a character out of Sinclair Lewis. Except for his unique leadership abilities, he was a rather typical representative of the Middle America of his day, with his bluff masculine bonhomie, his love of sports and the outdoors, and his lack of intellectual interests or pretensions.

In an interview Justice Stewart, himself a member of the Warren Court, told me that the Chief Justice had a "simple belief in the things we now laugh at: motherhood, marriage, family, flag, and the like." These furnished the foundation for Warren's scale of values throughout his professional life. If there was something of the Babbitt in this, it was also, as Justice Stewart put it to me, "a great source of strength, that he did have these foundations on which his thinking rested."

The early Warren was a direct product of his upbringing and surroundings. Born and raised in California, he grew up in a small town that was a microcosm of the burgeoning West itself. From a last vestige of the American frontier—with cowboys on horses, saloons, and gunfights—the town and state quickly came to be the paradigm of twentieth-century America. "All changed, changed utterly,"[13] as growth became the prime element of California life.

"Gentlemen, we have to plan for a whole new city of ten thousand people every Monday morning,"[14] Warren used to tell his council when he became Governor. In his later years the Chief Justice would recall proudly that during his years as governor of California his state had been able to absorb five million new arrivals "without any confusion or discord whatsoever."[15]

Like his state, Warren displayed a capacity for growth throughout his career. The popular conception of Warren's judicial career has, indeed, been one of a virtual metamorphosis—with the political grub suddenly transformed into the judicial lepidopteron. Certainly, Warren as Chief Justice appeared an entirely different person than he had been before his elevation to the Court. As his state's leading law-enforcement officer, Warren had been perhaps the foremost advocate of what a *Harper's* article was to term "Our Worst Wartime Mistake"[16]—the forced evacuation of persons of Japanese ancestry from the American West Coast after the Japanese attack on Pearl Harbor in December 1941. As

Chief Justice, Warren was the foremost proponent of racial equality. From his crucial role in the *Brown* segregation case[17] to the end of his Court tenure, he did more than any other judge in American history to ensure that the law, in W. H. Auden's phrase, "found the notion of equality."

As Governor, Warren strongly opposed reapportionment of the California legislature, even though, as he later conceded, "My own state was one of the most malapportioned in the nation."[18] As Chief Justice, Warren led the movement to bring the apportionment process within the equal protection guaranty, a movement that culminated in the Chief Justice's own opinion laying down the "one person, one vote" principle.[19]

Like John Marshall himself, Earl Warren had a political background. Soon after he had obtained his law degree from the University of California, Warren worked in the office of the District Attorney of Alameda County, across the bay from San Francisco. Five years later, in 1925, he was elected District Attorney himself, serving in that position until 1938. A 1931 survey of American district attorneys by Raymond Moley (later famous as a member of President Franklin D. Roosevelt's so-called Brain Trust) "declared without hesitation that Warren was the best district attorney in the United States."[20]

In 1938 Warren was elected Attorney General of California, and became Governor of that state in 1942. He was a most effective chief executive; he reorganized the state government and secured major reforming legislation, notably measures for a modern hospital system, improving the state's prisons and its correction system, providing an extensive highway program, and improving old-age and unemployment benefits. Warren proved an able administrator and was the only Governor of his state to be elected to three terms. He was, however, appointed to head the U.S. Supreme Court before he could serve out his third term, and resigned as Governor on October 3, 1953, so that he could take up his new duties as Chief Justice.

It *Was* the *Warren* Court

It is customary to designate a Supreme Court by the name of its Chief Justice. During Warren's tenure this was more than a mere formality. While Earl Warren was at its head, the Supreme Court bore the image of its Chief Justice as unmistakably as the earlier Courts of John Marshall and Roger B. Taney had reflected the unique leadership of those two men.

Many students of the Court dispute this. They claim that, while Chief Justice Warren may have been the nominal head of the Court that bears his name, the actual leadership was furnished by other Justices. Thus, a biography of Justice Hugo Black is based on the proposition that the Alabaman was really responsible for the "judicial revolution" that occurred during the Warren years.[21] More recently, one review of my biography of the Chief Justice asserts that, more than anything, it shows that the proper title of the Court while Chief Justice Warren sat in its center chair would be the *Brennan* Court.[22]

Justice Black himself always believed that he had led the judicial revolution that rewrote so much of the corpus of our constitutional law. Black resented the acclaim the Chief Justice received for leading what everyone looked on as the *Warren* Court. As Justice Black saw it, the Court under Chief Justice Warren had only written into law the constitutional principles that Justice Black had been advocating for so many years. When Warren retired as Chief Justice, the Justices prepared the traditional letter of farewell. The draft letter read, "For us it is a source of pride that we have had the opportunity to be members of the Warren Court." Justice Black changed this to "the Court over which you have presided."[23]

On the other hand, the other Justices who served with Chief Justice Warren all recognized his leadership role. Justice William O. Douglas, himself closest to Justice Black in his views, ranks Earl Warren with John Marshall and Charles Evans Hughes "as our three greatest Chief Justices."[24] Another member of the Warren Court told me that it was the Chief Justice who was personally responsible for the key decisions during his tenure. The Justices who sat with him have all stressed to me that Chief Justice Warren may not have been an intellectual like Justice Frankfurter, but then, as Justice Potter Stewart put it to me, "he never pretended to be one." More important, says Justice Stewart, he possessed "instinctive qualities of leadership." When Justice Stewart was asked by me about claims that Justice Black was the intellectual leader of the Court, he replied, "If Black was the intellectual leader, Warren was the *leader* leader."

Chief Justice Warren himself brought more authority to the position than had been the case for years. The most important work of the Supreme Court, of course, occurs behind the scenes, particularly at the conferences where the Justices discuss and vote on cases. The Chief Justice controls the conference discussion; his is the prerogative to call and discuss cases before the other Justices speak. All those who served with him stressed Chief Justice Warren's ability to lead the conference. "It is incredible," Justice William J. Brennan once said, "how efficiently the Chief would conduct the conferences, leading the discussion of every case on the agenda, with a knowledge of each case at his fingertips."[25]

Justice Stewart told me that at the conferences, "after stating the case, he [Warren] would very clearly and unambiguously state his position." The Chief Justice rarely had difficulty in reaching a decision, and once his mind was made up, he would stick tenaciously to his decision. As Justice White expressed it in an interview, Warren "was quite willing to listen to people at length . . . but, when he made up his mind, it was like the sun went down, and he was very firm, very firm about it." The others never had any doubt about who was the head of the Warren Court.

A reading of the conference notes of Justices on the Warren Court reveals that the Chief Justice was as strong a leader as the Court has ever had. As *The Washington Post* summarized my Warren biography it "shows Warren as even more of a guiding force in the landmark opinions of his court than some have previously believed. Chief Justice Warren helped steer cases from the moment they were first discussed simply by the way he framed the issues."[26] In almost all the important cases, the Chief Justice himself led the discussion toward the decision he favored. If any high bench can properly be identified by the name of one of its members, this high bench was emphatically the *Warren* Court and, without arrogance, he, as well as the country, knew it. After an inevitable initial period of feeling his way, Chief Justice Warren led the Supreme Court as effectively as any Chief Justice in our history. When we consider the work of the Warren Court, we are considering a constitutional corpus that was directly a product of the Chief Justice's leadership.

The Other Protagonists: The Activists

Of course, the Supreme Court is inevitably more than the judge who sits in its center chair. In many ways, the individual Justices operate, as some of them have said, like "nine separate law firms." Plainly, Chief Justice Warren was not going to be able to deal with the Brethren in the way he had directed matters as Governor of California. "I think," Justice Stewart affirmed to me, "he came to realize very early, certainly long before I came here [1958], that this group of nine rather prima donnaish people could not be led, could not be told, in the way the Governor of California can tell a subordinate, do this or do that."

What Justice Stewart says is true of any Supreme Court, but it was particularly true of the Justices on the Warren Court. The Court in the mid-1940s was characterized by Yale Law Professor Fred Rodell as "the most brilliant and able collection of Justices who ever graced the high bench together."[27] The stars of that Court were Justices Black, Frankfurter, Douglas, and Jackson, four of the greatest judges ever to serve on the highest bench, brilliant jurists, each possessed of a peculiarly forceful personality. In addition, Justices Black and Douglas, on the one side, and Justices Frankfurter and Jackson, on the other, represented polar views on the proper role of the Court in enforcing the Constitution. Their doctrinal differences, fueled by increasing personal animosity, erupted into the most bitter feud in Supreme Court history. All four were still serving when Warren was appointed—though Jackson died before he could make a real contribution to the Warren Court. The other three played important roles in the development of that Court's jurisprudence.

The senior among them was Justice Black, by then the recognized leader of the Court's liberal wing. Black never forgot his origins in a backward Alabama rural county. Half a century later, he described a new law clerk from Harvard as "tops in his class though he came from a God-forsaken place—worse than Clay County."[28] But his Alabama drawl and his gentle manners masked an inner firmness found in few men. "Many who know him," wrote Anthony Lewis when Black turned seventy-five, "would agree with the one-time law clerk who called him 'the most powerful man I have ever met.' "[29] Though of only slight build, Black always amazed people by his physical vitality. He is quoted in *The Dictionary of Biographical Quotation* as saying, "When I was forty my doctor advised me that a man in his forties shouldn't play tennis. I heeded his advice carefully and could hardly wait until I reached fifty to start again."[30]

Black's competitive devotion to tennis became legend. Until he was eighty-three, he continued to play several sets every day on the private court of his landmark federal house in the Old Town section of the Washington suburb of Alexandria. He brought the same competitive intensity to his judicial work. According to his closest colleague, Justice Douglas, "Hugo Black was fiercely intent on every point of law he presented."[31] Black was as much a compulsive winner in the courtroom as on the tennis court. "You can't just disagree with him," acidly commented his great Court rival, Justice Jackson, to *New York Times* columnist Arthur Krock. "You must go to war with him if you disagree."[32] Black would fight bitterly on the issues that concerned him, such as the First Amendment. His combative approach is well shown in the stands he took and the unusually strong drafts he wrote in two of the cases dealt with in this book, *Bell* v. *Maryland*[33] and *Time, Inc.* v. *Hill*.[34]

Yet if impact on the law is a hallmark of the outstanding judge, few occupants of the bench have been more outstanding than Black. It was Justice Black who fought for years to have the Court tilt the Constitution in favor of individual rights and liberties and who was, next to Chief Justice Warren himself, the leader in what Justice Fortas once termed "the most profound and pervasive revolution ever achieved by substantially peaceful means."[35] Even where Black's views have not been adopted literally, they have tended to prevail in a more general, modified form. Nor has his impact been limited to the Black positions that the Court has accepted. It is found in the totality of today's judicial awareness of the Bill of Rights and the law's newly intensified sensitivity to the need to apply its protection to all.

More than anything, Justice Black brought to the Supreme Court a moral fervor rarely seen on the bench. A famous passage by Justice Holmes has it that the black-letter judge will be replaced by the man of statistics and the master of economics.[36] Justice Black was emphatically a judge who still followed the black-letter approach in dealing with the constitutional text. "That Constitution," he said, "is my legal bible. . . . I cherish every word of it from the first to the last."[37] The eminent jurist with a dog-eared copy of the Constitution in his right coat pocket became a part of contemporary folklore. In protecting the sanctity of the organic word, Justice Black displayed all the passion of the Old Testament prophet in the face of graven idols. His ardor may have detracted from the image of the "judicial," but if the Justice did not bring to constitutional issues that "cold neutrality" of which Edmund Burke speaks,[38] his zeal may have been precisely what was needed in the Supreme Court. Anything less might have been inadequate to make the Bill of Rights the vital center of our constitutional law.

Before Chief Justice Warren's appointment, Justice Black's chief supporter on the Court had been Justice Douglas. "If any student of the modern Supreme Court took an association test," wrote Hugo Black, Jr., in his book about his father, "the word 'Black' would probably evoke the response 'Douglas' and vice versa."[39] Justice Black himself recognized this. Declining a 1958 invitation to write an article about Justice Douglas, Justice Black wrote, "You perhaps know without my stating it that I have the very highest regard for Justice Douglas as a friend and as a member of this Court. In fact, our views are so nearly the same that it would be almost like self praise for me to write what I feel about his judicial career."[40]

On the bench, as in his personal life, Justice Douglas always was a maverick, who went his own way regardless of the feelings of the other Justices. Justice Douglas would stick to his own views, and was quick to use his own method of deciding in concurrence or dissent. It made little difference whether he carried a majority or stood alone. He would rarely stoop to lobbying for his position and seemed more interested in making his own stand public than in working to get it accepted. As one law clerk put it to me, "Douglas was just as happy signing a one-man dissent as picking up four more votes." In *Dayton* v. *Dulles*,[41] as we shall see, Justice Douglas refused to tone down his far-reaching draft opinion of the Court, even though that meant losing his majority on the important constitutional issue involved in the case.

Though Justices Black and Douglas were regarded by the public as the leading activists, next to Warren himself, the Chief Justice always considered his most effective ally on the Court to be Justice Brennan. Soon after his appointment in 1956, the new Justice became Warren's closest colleague. The Chief Justice would turn to Justice Brennan when he wanted to discuss a case or some other matter on which he wanted an exchange of views. The two would usually meet on Thursdays, when the Chief Justice would come to the Brennan chambers to go over the cases that were to be discussed at the Court's Friday conference.

Justice Brennan's unassuming appearance and manner mask a keen intelligence. He was perhaps the hardest worker on the Warren Court. Unlike Justice Douglas, Brennan was always willing to mold his language to meet the objections of some of his colleagues, a talent that would become his hallmark on the Court and one on which the Chief Justice would rely frequently. It was Justice Brennan to whom the Chief Justice was to assign the opinion in some of the most important cases to be decided by the Warren Court.

Warren's Opponents

The activist position increasingly assumed by the Warren Court was opposed by what was usually called the Court's conservative wing. Its leader until his 1962 retirement, and the Chief Justice's strongest opponent until then, was Justice Frankfurter. Few members of the Court have been of greater interest both to the public and to Court specialists than Justice Frankfurter. In large measure, that has been true because his career posed something of a puzzle. Before his appointment to the bench, he was known for his interest in libertarian causes. He was also closely connected in the public mind with the New Deal, and it was generally expected that on the Court he would continue along a liberal path. Yet if one thing is certain, it is that it is risky to make predictions in advance of how new appointees will behave after they don the robe. "One of the things," Justice Frankfurter once said, "that laymen, even lawyers, do not always understand is indicated by the question you hear so often: 'Does a man become any different when he puts on a gown?' I say, 'If he is any good, he does.' "[42] Frankfurter himself seemed an altogether different man as a Justice than he had been off the bench. From academic eminence as an advisor to the New Deal to leader of the conservative Court cabal—that was the way students of the Court tended to see Justice Frankfurter's career.

During the first two years of Chief Justice Warren's tenure, he tended to vote with Justice Frankfurter more than with Justices Black and Douglas. The first case that follows, *Alton* v. *Alton*,[43] shows the early Warren-Frankfurter cooperation in action. As time went on, however, the Chief Justice tended more and more to assume the Black-Douglas activist posture, a posture more naturally congenial to one who had always been much more a man of action than reflection, and one more oriented toward results than process. With Justice Brennan's appointment, the activist wing had a firm core of four. *Time*, in its fashion, termed the new bloc on the Warren Court "B.B.D. & W."[44]

During the remainder of Justice Frankfurter's tenure, the Court remained split between the Warren and Frankfurter wings. The first expatriation cases—*Perez* v. *Brownell* and *Trop* v. *Dulles*[45]—in which the Chief Justice and the former professor divided the laurels, show how the balance shifted back and forth between the two wings of the Court.

The Court split was accompanied by increasing animosity between the two. The Chief Justice publicly charged Justice Frankfurter with "degrading this Court."[46] Justice Frankfurter, from his side, is said to have declared to Warren in conference, "You're the worst Chief Justice this country has ever had."[47] On another occasion, during a heated conference session, Justice Frankfurter was overheard screeching at the Chief Justice, "Be a judge, god damn it, be a judge!" Use of the verb *screeching* may not have been too much of an exaggeration. As a member of the Warren Court told me, once Frankfurter would "get going . . . his voice would rise to a pretty high decible content and pretty high on the scales."

In his private comments, the Justice was equally acerbic. In a letter to Judge Learned Hand, he referred to "the goulash of narrow minded prejudices of Earl & Black & Douglas & Douglas [*sic*]."[48] Not long before his retirement, Justice Frankfurter wrote to a colleague of a Warren opinion that "his crude, heavy-handed repetitive moralizing makes me feel like eating rancid butter. . . . I cannot help believing that E.W. has the bias of a sansculotte."[49]

With the retirement, in 1962, of Justice Frankfurter and his acolyte, Justice Charles E. Whittaker, the Court balance was completely altered. For the remainder of his tenure the Chief Justice had a solid majority. More than that, the personal recrimination that had characterized Chief Justice Warren's relationship with Justice Frankfurter was now a thing of the past. In an interview the Chief Justice later recalled that not a single voice had been raised in the Court conferences over a time period that began with Frankfurter's retirement.[50]

Of course, there were still opposing views among the Justices, but the Chief Justice's principal opponent had become the courtly Justice John Marshall Harlan, who had neither Frankfurter's abrasive personality nor his leadership abilities. Harlan's voice calling for judicial restraint was but a faint echo of that of his mentor and, in one reporter's phrase, "was now heard in a symbolic wilderness without the assured support of Frankfurter and Whittaker."[51] The balance of power had definitely shifted to the Chief Justice.

Justice Harlan looked like a Supreme Court Justice. Tall and erect, with sparse white hair, conservatively dressed in his London-tailored suits, with a gold watch chain across the vest under his robe, he exuded the dignity associated with high judicial office. Yet, underneath was a warmth that enabled him to be a close friend of those with whom he disagreed intellectually, notably Justice Black. Visitors could often see the two Justices waiting patiently in line in the Court cafeteria. The two were a study in contrasts: the ramrod-straight patrician with his commanding presence, and his slight, almost wispy colleague who looked like an old but cantankerous Southern farmer.

Justice Harlan was plainly one of the best, if not the best, lawyer on the Court and, next to Justice Frankfurter, the one most interested in the technical aspects of the Court's work. He became a sound, rather than brilliant, Justice who could be relied on for learned opinions that thoroughly covered the subjects dealt with, though they degenerated at times into law review articles of the type Justice Frankfurter too often wrote.

A word should also be said about two other Justices who tended to vote with Justice Frankfurter, Justices Tom C. Clark and Charles E.

Whittaker. The former is of particular interest, for, though his background and predilections were with the Frankfurter conception of judicial review, he did provide key votes for the Chief Justice in important cases, notably *Mapp* v. *Ohio*[52] and *Baker* v. *Carr.*[53] In the cases that follow, it was Justice Clark's switch in *Bell* v. *Maryland*[54] that enabled the Chief Justice and his supporters to prevent a decision that would have deprived the civil-rights movement of one of its most effective weapons. And in *Estes* v. *Texas,*[55] it was another Clark shift that permitted the Chief Justice's hostility to television in the courtroom to be translated into a constitutional prohibition.

Justice Clark could never shed his background as a prosecutor, which had culminated in his service as President Truman's Attorney General. As a Justice, Clark almost always followed the conservative pro-government position in criminal cases. This helps to explain the position he took in *Dayton* v. *Dulles,*[56] a point stressed in my discussion of that case, though it does not excuse the extreme language contained in the Clark draft dissent printed with that case. Nor does it justify the private phone call that the Justice made to FBI Director J. Edgar Hoover for help in his *Dayton* v. *Dulles* opinion.[57]

Justice Whittaker plays a part in three of the cases discussed—*Dayton* v. *Dulles*[58] and the first two expatriation cases[59]—largely because of his idiosyncratic switching of votes. He may have been the least talented Justice appointed during this century. Justice Whittaker, a member of the Warren Court told me, "used to come out of our conference literally crying. You know Charlie had gone to night law school, and he began as an office boy and he'd been a farm boy and he had inside him an inferiority complex, which . . . showed and he'd say, 'Felix used words in there that I'd never heard of.' "

More than any other member of the Warren Court, Justice Whittaker found it difficult to make up his mind. Chief Justice Warren's "great strength," the Justice just quoted told me, was "not to have to agonize. That was Charlie Whittaker's great problem, you know. He was a very, very conscientious man and a fine man, but he just didn't have the power of decision." According to Justice Douglas, "In Conference, Whittaker would take one position when the Chief or Black spoke, change his mind when Frankfurter spoke, and change back again when some other Justice spoke."[60] Then, after the conference, Justice Whittaker would often agonize and agonize over decisions, swinging back and forth in key cases, which would make it most difficult for the Chief Justice and the others.

Though Justice Whittaker would usually vote with the Frankfurter wing, he would often switch back and forth during the decision process. This Whittaker tendency may be seen in both *Dayton* v. *Dulles* and the first expatriation case—particularly in the latter, where the Justice changed his vote several times.

Justice Whittaker's difficulty in deciding led to a caustic Warren comment when the Justice retired. After he left the Court, Justice Whittaker took a highly paid legal post with General Motors. He then delivered widely reported attacks on the Court's decisions, notably in a 1964 speech before the American Bar Association. Whenever he heard about the Whittaker criticism, the Chief Justice used to say, "Charlie never could make up his mind about decisions until he left the Court."

Activism versus Self-Restraint

The differences between Chief Justice Warren and Justice Frankfurter were even more juristic than they were personal. Ultimately the division between them came down to a fundamental disagreement on the proper role of the judge in the constitutional system. In simplified terms, the division was between judicial activism and judicial self-restraint. The rule of restraint had been the handiwork of that seminal figure of modern American law, Justice Holmes.

In the years before Chief Justice Warren's appointment the Supreme Court had moved from judicial activism in cases involving economic regulation to the judicial restraint that Justice Holmes had advocated so vigorously in dissent. Before 1937, the Justices construed the Constitution to authorize them to pass on the wisdom of legislative policies in exercising review power. "There was a time when the Due Process Clause was used by this Court to strike down laws which were thought unreasonable, that is, unwise or incompatible with some particular economic or social philosophy."[61]

Critics contended that the Justices were arrogating for themselves a veto power never contemplated by the Constitution, what Theodore Roosevelt termed "the political function which American courts alone among the courts of the world possess."[62] The frequency with which the Supreme Court interposed the power to negate social legislation led to the famous charge by Justice Brandeis that it was exercising "the powers of a superlegislature."[63] Significantly, the leading French study of judicial review in the American system during this period was entitled *Government by Judiciary*.[64]

All this began to change in 1937 with the reversal in jurisprudence that Edward S. Corwin has characterized as "Constitutional Revolution, Ltd."[65] One strong impetus for the change was the repeated striking down by the Court of New Deal attempts to deal with the Great Depression. Franklin Roosevelt publicly referred to the justices as "nine old men" and spoke of changing the character of the Court by increasing the number of sitting justices; what has come to be called the Court-packing scheme. Although the threatened constitutional crisis was forestalled, the frustration of having presidential and Congressional emergency measures struck down by the Court engendered strong new liberal support for a policy of judicial restraint, the former minority opinion of Justice Holmes. It was at this time that Felix Frankfurter, then a professor at

Harvard Law School and one of the New Deal's prime movers, may have firmed up his own personal judicial philosophy that so strongly committed him to judicial restraint.

By the time Chief Justice Warren came to the Supreme Court, the Holmes approach had become established doctrine and had furnished the jurisprudential foundation for the transition from laissez faire to a government-regulated society. By mid-century, the regulated society had become an accepted fact, constitutionally as well as politically.

With the adoption of the Holmes restraint doctrine, the Supreme Court has come to accept governmental restrictions on the free exercise of property rights to an extent never before permitted in American law. At the same time, the Justices have seen that unless the rights of the person are correlatively expanded, the individual will virtually be shorn of constitutional protection; hence the recent shift in American public law to emphasis on the protection of personal rights. The Justices, like the rest of us, have been disturbed by the growth of governmental authority and have sought to preserve a sphere for individuality even in a society in which the individual stands dwarfed by the power concentrations that confront him.

In such a society the issues confronting the courts have also begun to change. Justices like Warren came to believe that even the Holmes canon could not suffice as the be-all and end-all of judicial review. The Chief Justice was willing to follow the rule of restraint in the economic area. It was, in truth, a 1963 decision of the Warren Court that "purported to sound the death knell for the doctrine of substantive due process"[66] in that area. Notwithstanding this judicial deference in the economic realm, however, the Chief Justice believed that restraint was not the proper posture in the cases involving claimed infringements on personal rights that increasingly came before the Court. In such cases, he advocated active intervention by the Justices to ensure enforcement of the guarantees for individual rights as they existed in the Bill of Rights. In the Warren view, the tenet of judicial self-restraint should not bind judges in cases involving restraints on life and liberty. In those cases, governmental acts must be scrutinized with greater care.

It was this activist approach that was opposed so strongly by Justice Frankfurter. The Justice remained true to the Holmes approach, insisting that self-restraint was the proper posture of a nonrepresentative judiciary, regardless of the nature of the asserted interests in particular cases. Though Warren was willing to follow the canon of judicial restraint in the economic area, he felt that the Bill of Rights provisions protecting personal liberties imposed on the judges an obligation of greater activism. When a law allegedly infringed on the personal rights guaranteed by the Bill of Rights, Warren refused to defer to the legislative judgment that the law was necessary to serve a legitimate end.

Warren rejected the Frankfurter philosophy of judicial restraint because he had come to feel that it thwarted effective performance of the

Court's constitutional role. Judicial abnegation, in the Chief Justice's view, all too often meant judicial abdication of the duty to enforce constitutional guarantees. "I believe," Warren declared in an interview on his retirement, "that this Court or any court should exercise the functions of the office to the limit of its responsibilities." Judicial restraint meant that, "for a long, long time we have been sweeping under the rug a great many problems basic to American life. We have failed to face up to them, and they have piled up on us, and now they are causing a great deal of dissension and controversy of all kinds." To Warren, it was the Court's job "to remedy those things eventually," regardless of the controversy involved.[67]

The differences between the Warren and Frankfurter approaches were anything but academic in their impact. They had a direct effect on the results in some of the cases to be discussed. It was Frankfurter's refusal to go along with the far-reaching constitutional holding in the draft opinion of the Court in *Dayton* v. *Dulles* that led to the Court's decision on a narrow nonconstitutional ground. Similarly, the Frankfurter doctrine of deference to the legislative judgment led him to take a broad view of Congressional expatriation power in *Perez* v. *Brownell* and *Trop* v. *Dulles*, while the Chief Justice was willing to strike down the federal statutes at issue in both cases. In *Kennedy* v. *Mendoza-Martinez*, the same differences in approach were manifested. Significantly, while Frankfurter was on the Court, he and his supporters had a bare majority in the case for upholding the expatriation law. As soon as he retired, however, and was replaced by Justice Arthur J. Goldberg, a firm supporter of the Warren approach, the final *Mendoza-Martinez* decision invalidating the law was reached.

The Warren Revolution

The Warren tenure on the highest bench lends substance to the Frankfurter comment that great men do make a difference, even in the law. Before Earl Warren's appointment, the Supreme Court was, like T. S. Eliot's True Church, "Wrapt in the old miasmal mist."[68] When Warren became Chief Justice, black Americans in the South were forbidden to drink from the same public water fountains as whites; rural America held the reins of state government and thus wielded disproportionate influence on the course of education, health, welfare, transportation, commerce, and communications; Senator Joseph R. McCarthy had reached his pinnacle of terror; and apathy characterized the intelligentsia and the poor alike.

By the time Chief Justice Warren retired, white patrimony had yielded to racial equality; political dominance had been transplanted to the urban and suburban areas in which most Americans lived; national paranoia had shifted from Communists to criminals; and civil disorder, sparked by poverty at home and warfare abroad, rocked both urban cores and college campuses.

In expanding civil liberties, broadening political freedom, extending the franchise, reinforcing freedoms of speech, assembly, and religion, limiting the power of the politicians in "smoke-filled rooms," and defining the limits of police power, the Warren Court had no equal in American history. And the Chief Justice who sat in its center was the principal catalyst for the all but unprecedented judicial revolution.

The main monument of the Warren leadership was, without a doubt, the decision in the *Brown* school segregation case.[69] Following the new Chief Justice's lead, the Court seized the vital constitutional issue by the bit (the same issue that had been meticulously avoided under Warren's predecessor) and unanimously outlawed school segregation.

The element of unanimity cannot be overemphasized. It was no mean feat for the Court's neophyte (as he then was), vested only with the moral prestige of his position as Chief Justice, to induce eight individualists, accustomed to arriving at decisions in their own ways and never hesitant about articulating their separate views, to create a consensus decision that was accepted unanimously, without a single dissenting or even separate voice to detract from the majesty and forthrightness of the opinion.[70]

The Warren Court's legal approach differed drastically from that of its predecessor. In cases involving conflicts between government and the individual, Chief Justice Vinson and the majority of his colleagues had usually been on the side of officialdom. Chief Justice Warren, on the other hand, started with a strong predisposition in favor of the individual. Under Warren's leadership, the Court was transformed into a tribunal inclined to look with a far more friendly eye on claims of violation of individual rights.

"When the generation of 1980 receives from us the Bill of Rights," Chief Justice Warren once said, "the document will not have exactly the same meaning it had when we received it from our fathers."[71] As interpreted by the Warren Court, the Bill of Rights had a very different meaning from that handed down by its predecessors. Freedom of speech, press, religion, the rights of minorities and those accused of crimes, and the rights of individuals subjected to legislative and administrative inquisitions all came under the Court's fostering guardianship. The Warren Court expanded the substantive content of personal rights, giving virtually all of them a wider meaning than they had theretofore had in American law. Protection of individual rights and liberties became the very focus of the contemporary Constitution.

In addition, the Chief Justice's leadership in the *Brown* case served as the starting point for a virtual egalitarian revolution in our law.[72] From the field of racial equality involved in *Brown*, the Warren Court spread the mantle of equal protection over an increasingly broad area, notably in the field of political rights and the rights of criminal defendants. Chief

Justice Warren himself has characterized the Reapportionment Cases,[73] holding that the equal protection clause lays down a judicially enforceable "equal population" principle for legislative apportionments, as the most important decided during his tenure.[74] Under them, the Court worked a reform comparable to that achieved by Parliament in translating the program of the English Reform Movement into the statute book. Implementation of these and other Warren Court decisions has demanded a new activist role for our judges, far removed from traditional limitations of the judicial function.

Indeed, the judicial activism that took place under the Warren Court's aegis was unprecedented in legal history. The Chief Justice and his colleagues led the movement to remake our law in the image of the evolving society. The result was one of the most creative periods in any legal system. During it, the law's task was to keep pace with the frenetic acceleration of societal change. In performing the task, the law virtually transformed itself. Not even in the days of John Marshall was there a period of such fundamental change in American public law.

The Supreme Court in Operation

Even close observers of the Supreme Court have rarely understood how that tribunal actually operates. Of course, even freshman law students are familiar with the formal mechanics of the Court's operation. They know that the Justices sit from October to late June or July in annual sessions called terms, with each term designated by the year in which it begins. Cases come to the Court from the U.S. Courts of Appeals and the highest state courts either by appeals or petitions for writs of certiorari. The Justices have discretion in deciding whether to take an appeal or grant certiorari. Each year the Justices decide to hear only a fraction of the cases presented to them. Thus, in the 1953 term, Chief Justice Warren's first, they heard only 170 cases out of 1,201 presented. In the 1968 term, the Chief Justice's last, of 3,117 cases presented, the Justices heard only 257 cases. By an unwritten rule, the Justices agree to take a case when at least four of the nine vote to do so.

If fewer than the required four vote to grant certiorari or take an appeal, the case in question is over and the decision of the lower court becomes the final decision. When the Court agrees to take a case, it is scheduled for both written and oral argument. Written briefs are filed by the opposing lawyers, and they then appear for oral argument. The arguments are presented publicly in the ornate courtroom.

Oral arguments before the Court are often dramatic events, participated in by the leaders of the American Bar. The Justices are rarely passive participants, but instead use the occasion to question the attorneys closely on any aspect of the case that interests them.

As far as the public is concerned, the postargument decision process is completely closed. The next knowledge the outside world has about a case occurs with the public announcement of the decision and the opinions filed by the Justices. It is known that the Justices discuss the cases argued at a conference session, which is totally private and attended only by them. When Warren became Chief Justice, these conferences were held on Saturdays. In 1955, the conference day was changed to Friday and they are still held on that day. The privacy of the conference is one of the most cherished traditions at the Court. In addition to the conference discussion, ideas are exchanged through memoranda and draft opinions. These, too, are completely private and almost none of them has ever been published. This book contains the first draft opinions of the Warren Court to be published.

For Supreme Court observers, the chief value of this book will be the insight it gives into the Court's hitherto unrevealed decision process. It is true that there have been accounts of that process in books like *The Brethren*,[75] but that book was based on hearsay and unnamed "secret sources." In addition, so far as my own research has paralleled the cases discussed in *The Brethren*, it has revealed to me that *The Brethren* account is both incomplete and inaccurate. An example of the difference in accounts can be found in the chapter of this book devoted to *Maxwell v. Bishop*,[76] which is also treated in detail in *The Brethren*.[77]

For students particularly, my discussion and the draft opinions reproduced will show what too few of them realize, that the decisions of the highest Court are basically collaborative efforts in which nine supreme individualists must cooperate to bring about the desired result. The burden is, of course, greatest on the Chief Justice, who must lead the majority when he is in it, and the Justice he calls upon to write the opinion—one who must command the support of at least four other strong-willed lawyers, each with his or her own definite views on the law and the Constitution.

The decision process in the Court is essentially a political process (in the nonpejorative use of that word). Yet all the "lobbying" and efforts at persuasion that go on—the sometimes petty infighting, the drafts and memoranda going back and forth among the Justices, the changes made in opinions as part of the bargaining process—all this is done for the purpose of reaching what the individual Justice considers the best result. There is, to be sure, politicking, compromises, and horsetrading in the often complex negotiations and compromises needed to attain a working majority, yet all for the purpose of advancing not the Justices themselves but the judicial doctrines in which they believe.

My intent was to use these draft opinions to provide clues to what actually happened behind the red velour curtain and let the chips fall where they may. In fact, however, they do fall in a way that reflects favorably on the Court. One is constantly impressed by the willingness of Justices to change their views upon consideration of the intellectual arguments made by their colleagues. No other governmental institution could be subjected to comparable scrutiny of its internal processes and come out so well.

Students may conclude from this book that the Court does not work at all in the cold, purely logical way that most people think it does; but it does work and, through the constant give and take between the Justices, in a way that ultimately serves the best interests of the country.

Notes

1. *New York Times*, April 21, 1962, p. 17.
2. Robert H. Jackson-FF, August 6, 1949. FFLC.
3. 109 *Congressional Record* 19848 (1963).
4. 1 de Tocqueville, *Democracy in America* 156 (Bradley ed. 1954).
5. The quotes in this paragraph are from Jackson, *The Supreme Court in the American System of Government* 54 (1955).
6. *2,000 Famous Legal Quotations* 197 (McNamara ed. 1967).
7. Id. at 10.
8. de Tocqueville, op. cit. supra note 4, at 290.
9. *The Economist*, July 2, 1983, p. 16.
10. FF-Fred Vinson, n.d. FFLC.
11. 1 Bryce, *The American Commonwealth* 274 (1917).
12. FF-SR, April 13, 1939. FFLC.
13. Yeats, "Easter 1916."
14. Weaver, *Warren: The Man, The Court, The Era* 147 (1967).
15. Pollack, *Earl Warren: The Judge Who Changed America* 105 (1979).
16. *Harper's* 193 (September 1945).
17. *Brown* v. *Board of Education*, 347 U.S. 483 (1954).
18. Warren, *The Memoirs of Earl Warren* 309 (1977).
19. *Reynolds* v. *Sims*, 377 U.S. 533 (1964).
20. Weaver, op. cit. supra note 14, at 44.
21. Dunne, *Hugo Black and the Judicial Revolution* (1977).
22. Hutchinson, "Hail to the Chief: Earl Warren and the Supreme Court," 81 *Mich. L. Rev.* 922, 923 (1983).
23. Dear Chief, June 23, 1969. HLBLC.
24. Douglas, *The Court Years 1939–1975* 240 (1980).
25. *N.Y. Times*, July 10, 1974, p. 24.
26. *Washington Post*, June 15, 1983, p. A16.
27. Rodell, *Nine Men: A Political History of the Supreme Courts from 1790 to 1955* 284 (1955).
28. Dunne, op. cit. supra note 21, at 85.
29. *The Supreme Court under Earl Warren* 135 (Levy ed. 1972).
30. *The Dictionary of Biographical Quotation* 79 (Klein and Winette eds. 1978).
31. Douglas, *Go East Young Man: The Early Years* 450 (1974).
32. Gerhart, *America's Advocate: Robert H. Jackson* 274 (1958).
33. Infra p. 149.
34. Infra p. 272.
35. Fortas, in *The Fourteenth Amendment Centennial* Volume 34 (Schwartz ed. 1970).

36. Holmes, "The Path of the Law," 10 *Harv. L. Rev.* 457, 469 (1897).
37. Dunne, op. cit. supra note 21, at 414.
38. 5 Burke, *Works* 67 (rev. ed. 1865).
39. Hugo Black, Jr., *My Father: A Remembrance* 239 (1975).
40. HLB-Alan Washburn, December 17, 1958. HLBLC.
41. Infra p. 73.
42. Frankfurter, *Of Law and Men: Papers and Addresses of Felix Frankfurter* 133 (1956).
43. Infra p. 22.
44. *Time,* July 1, 1957, p. 12.
45. Infra p. 77.
46. *N.Y. Times,* April 25, 1961, pp. 1, 27.
47. Pollack, op. cit. supra note 15, at 197.
48. FF-Learned Hand, February 13, 1958. FFLC.
49. FF-JMH, December 26, 1960. JMHP.
50. Dunne, op. cit. supra note 21, at 372.
51. Clayton, *The Making of Justice: The Supreme Court in Action* (1964).
52. 367 U.S. 643 (1961).
53. 369 U.S. 186 (1962).
54. Infra p. 188.
55. Infra p. 222.
56. Infra pp. 50–51.
57. Infra p. 51.
58. Infra p. 73.
59. Infra pp. 105–107.
60. Douglas, *The Court Years 1939–1975* 173 (1980).
61. *Ferguson* v. *Skrupa,* 372 U.S. 726, 729 (1963).
62. Theodore Roosevelt, Rochester, N.Y., speech (Sept. 27, 1913).
63. *Burns Baking Co.* v. *Bryan,* 264 U.S. 504, 534 (1924).
64. Lambert, *Le Gouvernement des Juges* (1921).
65. Corwin, *Constitutional Revolution, Ltd.* 64 (1941).
66. *Roe* v. *Wade,* 410 U.S. 113, 167 (1973), referring to *Ferguson* v. *Skrupa,* 372 U.S. 726 (1963).
67. *U.S. News & World Report,* July 15, 1969, p. 64.
68. Eliot, "The Hippotamus."
69. Supra note 17.
70. See Kluger, *Simple Justice* 657–747 (1976).
71. *The Public Papers of Chief Justice Earl Warren* 232 (Christman ed. 1959).
72. See Schwartz, *The Law in America* 240–244 (1974).
73. *Reynolds* v. *Sims,* 377 U.S. 533 (1964); *Baker* v. *Carr,* 369 U.S. 186 (1962).
74. Warren, op. cit. supra note 18, at 306.
75. Woodward and Armstrong, *The Brethren: Inside the Supreme Court* (1979).
76. Infra p. 394.
77. Woodward and Armstrong, op. cit. supra note 75, at 205–206.

1

Alton v. Alton (1954): Consensual Divorce Manqué

Had it not become moot before the Court's decision could be announced, *Alton* v. *Alton*[1] would have been a leading case in domestic relations law. The issue was the constitutionality of the Virgin Islands divorce law. Under it, where the plaintiff in a divorce action had spent six weeks in the islands, "this shall be prima facie evidence of domicile." In addition, where the defendant had been personally served or appeared in the action, "then the Court shall have jurisdiction . . . without further reference to domicile."

The law had been enacted in 1953; its effect was to make six weeks' physical presence, without more, a foundation on which to base a finding of domicile, even though there was no evidence of domiciliary intent. A person may have more than one residence, but only one domicile. *Residence* signifies living in a particular locality, while *domicile* means living in that locality with intent to make it a fixed and permanent home.[2] The Virgin Islands law was intended to capture some of the divorce business that had been attracted to Nevada since that state began granting "quickie" divorces in 1931. The new law's selling point was that it did not require a plaintiff to state any intention of continuing residence in the islands indefinitely.[3]

Alton v. *Alton* arose when Mrs. Alton sued for divorce in the Virgin Islands after six weeks' residence there. Her husband appeared but did not contest the action. The divorce petition came before the district judge just after the divorce law went into effect. The judge was apparently troubled by the new law's impact. He asked Mrs. Alton's counsel whether he had anything more than the fact of the six weeks' residence to present on the question of domicile. When the lawyer answered in the negative, the judge denied the divorce because the evidence was insufficient to prove domicile.

The divorce denial was affirmed by the court of appeals. That court ruled the statute unconstitutional on the ground that the Constitution

22

makes domicile a prerequisite to divorce jurisdiction. The statutory presumption that six weeks' residence was prima facie evidence of domicile was held unreasonable and hence violative of due process. The statute also eliminated domicile as a jurisdictional requirement if defendant was personally served or entered an appearance. This, too, was ruled violative of due process, since the Constitution makes domicile necessary before there can be divorce jurisdiction.

Though it did not so provide on its face, the Virgin Islands statute was, in effect, a provision for consensual divorce. This was pointed out by Chief Justice Warren in his statement opening the *Alton* conference on April 12, 1954: "of course the Virgin Islands legislation is in effect legislation to authorize consensual divorce, because the 6 week residence, if both parties agree . . . is merely a formality for getting a divorce."[4]

Justice Frankfurter stressed the same point. "In short," he summed up the statute later in the conference, "while . . . domicile is a jurisdictional requirement for the granting of divorce, the legislature of the Virgin Islands says that the parties by agreement may foist that jurisdiction on the court willy-nilly."

To be sure, by the time of the *Alton* case, the plaintiffs in so-called "quickie" divorce cases had been able to avoid the domicile requirement by falsely alleging that they had gone to Nevada, the Virgin Islands, or some other jurisdiction, intending to establish a domicile there. Since the Altons desired a divorce, the allegation of domiciliary intent was not challenged.

In a letter to the Chief Justice while the *Alton* opinions were being prepared, Justice Frankfurter asserted that the Justices would have to be blind, indeed, not to see and understand the true purpose of the Virgin Islands law. "To date," the Justice wrote, "fifteen judges have sat on the Virgin Islands statute. There isn't one of the fifteen who as a man would deny that the basis of the legislation and the litigation that followed, including the argument at the bar of this Court, is the avoidance of perjury; that, the statute was designed to save parties who want a consensual divorce from falsely swearing that they have abandoned their old domicile and have decided to become domiciled in the Virgin Islands."[5]

Under other "quickie' divorce statutes, as Justice Frankfurter put it at the *Alton* conference, there may still be "conscientious judges who exercise their responsibility in asking the lady plaintiff a few questions about her alleged domicil in Nevada." The Virgin Islands law, the Justice asserted, "seeks to plug that hole in consensual divorces by making the noncontestation of domicil as between the parties conclusively binding on the judge." From this point of view, Frankfurter explained, "the very purpose of the statute here, as I construe that purpose, is to take domicil out of the picture."

Could the legislature thus remove domicile as the sine qua non of divorce jurisdiction without violating due process? The court of appeals, as seen, had answered in the negative. The Supreme Court had never been squarely faced with the question. But its leading pre-*Alton* decision also implied a negative answer.

The case in question was *Williams* v. *North Carolina*.[6] Before *Williams*, the leading case was *Haddock* v. *Haddock*,[7] which held that a divorce granted against a wife in Connecticut did not have to be recognized by New York, the state of the wife's domicile, even though the husband had established a domicile in Connecticut, where there had been only service by publication but no personal service or appearance by the wife in the divorce action. *Williams* overruled *Haddock*, ruling that Nevada divorce decrees were entitled to full faith and credit where plaintiffs had resided in Nevada for more than six weeks, as prescribed by Nevada law, though the defendants were not personally served and had not entered an appearance.

But *Williams* did not change the requirement of domicile as a prerequisite to divorce jurisdiction. *Williams* was based on the assumption that the plaintiffs there had acquired a bona fide domicile in Nevada. The Court said that it could not assume "that petitioners' domicil was a sham and a fraud. Rather we must treat the present case . . . precisely the same as if petitioners had resided in Nevada for a term of years and had long ago acquired a permanent abode there." If no domicile had been acquired in Nevada, a different result would have been required. *Williams* did not "reach . . . the question as to the power of North Carolina to refuse full faith and credit to Nevada divorce decrees because . . . North Carolina finds that no bona fide domicil was acquired in Nevada."[8]

The implication is that without such a bona fide domicile, the Nevada decrees would be invalid. "If the actions of the Nevada court had been taken without 'due process of law,' the divorces which it purported to decree would have been without legal sanction in every state including Nevada."[9]

Alton v. *Alton* began where *Williams* v. *North Carolina* left off. The Virgin Islands divorce law substituted a presumption for the fact of domicile. It also provided that if there was personal service or an appearance by defendant, domicile was not necessary for the divorce court's jurisdiction. In practice, as already seen, the statute authorized consensual divorces, regardless of whether there was any domicile in the islands. Where both parties desired the divorce, the statute operated, in Justice Frankfurter's already quoted words, "to take domicil out of the picture."

The Justices gathered in conference on April 12, 1954, to consider the *Alton* case. From Justice Frankfurter's conference notes, all but Justices Douglas and Jackson were present. Chief Justice Warren started with a strong statement in favor of affirmance. In his view, domicile was an essential ingredient of divorce jurisdiction under the Constitution. Consensual divorce "was inadmissible under our constitutional scheme." Justice Frankfurter's notes summarized Warren's position: "He felt strongly that his conscience would not permit him to have this Court decide that one of the Territories could disregard the interests of all the States by having consensual divorces."

Justice Frankfurter strongly supported "the Chief's position that domicil is an essential prerequisite for the exercise of a State's power in terminating a marriage status in which other States were interested." As the Justice saw it, "if the issue of domicil is taken out of the case and therefore not contestable there is no basis of jurisdiction."

Except for Justice Frankfurter, however, there was no support at the conference for the Chief Justice's view. For Justice Black, with his literal view of the Constitution, the case was an easy one. "There is nothing in the Constitution to prohibit this legislation and he didn't think we are authorized to write anything into the Constitution to prohibit it."

Justice Frankfurter's notes indicate that he could not resist taking a jibe at his judicial rival. He interrupted Justice Black and "asked him if he would point out the clause which [prohibits][10] the President to seize the Steel companies." Nothing daunted, the Alabaman "replied, 'The constitution says the Congress shall make the laws' and went on to say that he never declared anything unconstitutional which was not clearly prohibited by the Constitution." As far as *Alton* was concerned, Black repeated that there was nothing in the Constitution to prohibit what the Virgin Islands statute did. "That's all there is to it and he does not think we have a right to amend the Constitution of the United States."

Justice Reed agreed that it was within the legislative power to enact the statute. "Domicil depends on intent and can sometimes be established by 30 seconds residence. The legislature . . . may lay down a presumptive mode of proving that requirement and he regarded 6 weeks as not an irrational prima facie basis on which to satisfy the requirement."

Justice Clark said that he also agreed with Black. In his view, "all the case would decide was that as far as the Virgin Islands was concerned if they wanted to live down there they were no longer husband and wife, and it is time enough to worry what may happen if what the Virgin Islands said comes in issue elsewhere."

Justices Burton and Minton took the same position. The former disagreed with Justice Frankfurter's view on the true meaning of the statute, saying that it "recognizes the requirement of domicil and makes it merely a prima facie rebuttable presumption." Justice Minton stressed that "The Constitution, as this Court has decided, left the determination of the civil status of marriage to the states. . . . this is simply a case of the legislature determining the requisites and what satisfies them."

At this, Justice Frankfurter's notes wryly state, "I discourteously interrupted to say I thought it was a little late, in view of *Marbury* v. *Madison*, to say that judicial review is barred by legislative action."

Justice Frankfurter may have had the better of the conference exchanges, but Justice Black and the others who supported the challenged statute had the votes. The conference indicated a strong majority in favor of upholding the Virgin Islands divorce law, with only the Chief Justice and Justice Frankfurter firmly opposed. Justice Black, the senior Justice in the majority, assigned the opinion to Justice Clark. The Texan circulated the opinion of the Court reprinted on page 32 on April 24, less than two weeks after the conference.

According to the Clark opinion, the key questions presented were the "reasonableness of inferring domiciliary intent from six weeks' residence, and the necessity of hinging divorce jurisdiction to domicil." The opinion upheld the presumption as "a reasonable exercise of . . . legislative authority." The Court was not prepared to say that the six weeks bore such a remote relationship to domiciliary intent that it had to find that "one has no 'rational connection' with the other." This holding, said Justice Clark, made it unnecessary to pass on the need for domicile as a prerequisite for divorce jurisdiction or any other issues.

The Chief Justice and Justice Frankfurter had voted to strike down the Virgin Islands statute. Chief Justice Warren prepared a dissent, which he sent to Justice Frankfurter for his comments. The copy in the Justice's papers is a typed memorandum.[11] It is probable (since this is the only copy in Justice Frankfurter's papers) that the dissent was not printed or circulated. Before that could be done, as we shall see, the case itself became moot and the Court's decision upholding the statute was never rendered.

The strong language in the proposed Warren dissent was out of character with the restrained position generally taken by the new Chief Justice in his first year on the Court,[12] but the issue, in the Chief Justice's view, involved the sanctity of the family—always near the top in Warren's hierarchy of values.[13] To Chief Justice Warren, the Court's decision would threaten what he termed at the conference "the very conception of the place of the family in our civilization." The Chief Justice's proposed dissent stresses this theme, asserting that "Marriage is our basic social institution. It is inherent in our civilization as well as throughout our colonial and national life."

Chief Justice Warren denied that divorce jurisdiction could constitutionally exist in the absence of domicile. Nor could domicile be established by "mere physical presence for a short period of time [without] satisfactory evidence that he or she intends to remain in the state of the divorce proceeding." The Chief Justice asserted that the statutory presumption was unreasonable. Nor was the clause "eliminating all requirement where both parties are represented" on firmer constitutional ground. Under it, the parties "have merely consented to domicile and, therefore, to jurisdiction. This is an intrusion on the judicial function because jurisdiction cannot be conferred by consent."

Justice Frankfurter indicated that he agreed with this last point. On the top of his copy of Chief Justice Warren's memorandum of dissent, he wrote, "*Klein:* 13 Wall 128." The Justice was referring to *United States v. Klein*,[14] the leading 1872 case holding that the legislature may not dictate the result in a particular case, even though the statute doing so is phrased in jurisdictional terms. Justice Frankfurter's notation suggests that he thought that *Klein* precluded any legislative attempt to do what the Virgin Islands statute did in requiring the divorce court to assume jurisdiction without any evidence of intent to establish domicile.

–MEMORANDUM

No. 531.—OCTOBER TERM, 1953.

Sonia Herrup Alton,
Petitioner,

v.

David Elie Alton.

On Writ of Certiorari to the United States Court of Appeals for the Third Circuit.

Memorandum by MR. CHIEF JUSTICE WARREN.

This case is particularly troublesome to me and primarily because from the beginning it has not been an adversary proceeding. It has been a cooperative if not "rigged" proceeding with the Bar of the Virgin Islands lending a helping hand. The importance and complexity of the case justify a full exposition before us which we have not had.

I do not profess to be entirely clear on the subject, but I am endeavoring, in my mind at least, to sustain the lower courts because I believe their conclusion is consistent with the American federal system and with the public welfare throughout the nation.

Instinctively, I feel this territorial statute constitutes a fraud on all the states. It is an attempt to disregard the institution of marriage as it is established, protected and preserved by each state for its own citizens. It brings us as close to the line of consensual divorces as it is possible to be without actually being there. There can be no reasonable dividing line between the two situations. If the act is sustained, I see no reason why we would not be compelled, on the authority of this case, to uphold consensual

---

* FFH. The original is a typed manuscript.

MEMORANDUM

divorce laws either in the Virgin Islands or in any of the states. I know there are others who believe we will eventually arrive at that situation regardless of what happens in this case, but even if that be true it seems to me that the Federal Government should not force it on the states through territorial law and a decision of this Court.

Marriage is our basic social institution. It is inherent in our civilization as well as throughout our colonial and national life. True, it is not mentioned specifically in the Constitution, but neither have many other problems that have been considered by this Court to be governed by the Constitution.

I have no doubt it was considered as being ingrained in American life by all of the makers of the Constitution. I imagine most of them would have considered the state interest and control of the marital status as much a matter of state sovereignty over its citizens as any other function of Government. Also, I doubt if at any time since the adoption of the Constitution any state would have been admitted to the Union if its provisional government had authorized consensual divorces for citizens of other states. I realize that what constitutes a republican form of government is a political and not a judicial question, but if I am correct in the assumption, it does represent a reliable concept of the American system and of what is inherent in it. The Constitution says nothing about polygamy, but I doubt if the Congress would admit a new state with a law authorizing it or that this Court would sustain a law to that effect thereafter.

It seems to me that this case revolves around the reciprocal rights of states which call forth a reciprocal duty on the part of every state to recognize the responsibility of sister states and their jurisdiction to guard as jealously as they desire the laws of marriage and the marital status of their own citizens. To me, it follows that domicile must, therefore, be inherent in the divorce laws of every state.

MEMORANDUM

In no other way, could each state give to the others the full faith and credit that the marriage laws are entitled to.

A divorce suit is not a two-party case as are actions on contracts and torts. In most states, it is recognized by judicial decision, if not by statute, that the state itself is always a silent party. In some states, the laws call for active intervention by the state when it is not a true adversary proceeding. It is only where the husband and wife have acquired separate domiciles that more than one state has ever been considered as having jurisdiction in a divorce proceeding and then only in the state of domicile of one or other of the parties. Therefore, it appears to me that the courts of any state or territory can have jurisdiction for divorce purposes over only those who reside there with the intention to remain. A person can have but one domicile and a new one cannot be acquired until the old one has been abandoned. Until a party or parties to the divorce proceeding offer satisfactory evidence that he or she intends to remain in the state of the divorce proceeding, there is no evidence therein of domicile. To say that mere physical presence for a short period of time without evidence of permanency constitutes proof of domicile is unreasonable.

Domicile can be acquired in six weeks or six days or six hours where there is an intention to do so, but six weeks or six years can make no prima facie case of domicile without the all-essential element of intent. This statute clearly attempts to accomplish this purpose, in one clause by making mere physical presence for the statutory period a prima facie domicile without any evidence of intent, and in the second clause by eliminating all requirement where both parties are represented. Under the first clause, it seems to me to be very doubtful if we have followed due process; under the second clause, the parties have merely consented to domicile and, therefore, to jurisdiction. This is an intrusion on the judicial function be-

MEMORANDUM

cause jurisdiction cannot be conferred by consent. In my opinion, it also fails to give full faith and credit to the statutes of other states of the Union. For either reason, I believe the statute is bad, particularly since there is no requirement of the statute to apply the law of domicile of the parties.

I would affirm the judgment of the court below.

SUPREME COURT OF THE UNITED STATES

No. 531.—OCTOBER TERM, 1953.

Sonia Herrup Alton, Petitioner, *v.* David Elie Alton.	On Writ of Certiorari to the United States Court of Appeals for the Third Circuit.

[April —, 1954.]

MR. JUSTICE CLARK delivered the opinion of the Court.

At issue is the constitutionality of § 9 (a) of the Virgin Islands Divorce Law. This section underlies petitioner's claim that the District Court has jurisdiction over her divorce action against respondent. The District Court, of its own initiative, dismissed the complaint for want of jurisdiction. The Court of Appeals for the Third Circuit, sitting *en banc,* held § 9 (a) unconstitutional and affirmed the judgment below in a 4–3 decision. 207 F. 2d 667. We granted certiorari. 347 U. S. 911.

Section 9 (a) of the Divorce Law provides:

> "Notwithstanding the provisions of sections 8 and 9 hereof, if the plaintiff is within the district at the time of the filing of the complaint and has been continuously for the six weeks immediately prior thereto, this shall be prima facie evidence of domicile, and where the defendant has been personally served within the district, or enters a general appearance in the action, then the Court shall have jurisdiction of the action and of the parties thereto without further reference to domicile or to the place where the marriage was solemnized or the cause of action arose."

This section was enacted by the Legislative Assembly of the Virgin Islands in order to avoid the interpretation of its 1944 Divorce Law by the Court of Appeals for the Third Circuit in *Burch* v. *Burch,* 195 F. 2d 799 (1952).

ALTON *v.* ALTON.

Section 9 of the 1944 Divorce Law required the plaintiff in a divorce action to be an "inhabitant of the district at the commencement of the action and for six weeks prior thereto, which residence shall be sufficient to give the Court jurisdiction." Since only physical presence for six weeks was thought adequate to satisfy the statute, it was not the practice in the Islands to submit proof of domiciliary intent in divorce actions. However, the Court of Appeals in the *Burch* case interpreted the statute as requiring the plaintiff to be a "domiciliary" of the Islands. Thereupon the District Court for the Islands refused to grant divorces in the absence of proof of domiciliary intent. Taking notice of this change in the traditional jurisdictional requirement of its Divorce Law, the Legislative Assembly passed § 9 (a) in 1953.

Petitioner, after six weeks' residence in the Virgin Islands, brought this action for divorce against respondent, a resident of Connecticut. Respondent appeared in the action and waived service of summons, but did not contest the allegations in the complaint. The case was heard by a District Court Commissioner who, in his Findings of Fact and Conclusions of Law, recommended a divorce. His only finding pertinent to the problem before us states "that the plaintiff is a resident of the Virgin Islands and has been for more than six weeks prior to the commencement of this action." Petitioner then moved the District Court for a confirmation of the Commissioner's recommendation that a divorce be granted. At a hearing on the motion, the District Judge asked petitioner's counsel "whether you have any more evidence to offer on the question of domicile." When counsel replied in the negative, the District Judge denied the motion and dismissed the complaint. His action in so doing was "because of the insufficiency of that procedure [§ 9 (a)] to prove a *prima facie* case of domicile."

ALTON *v.* ALTON.

The majority of the Court of Appeals adopted, and also expanded, the position taken by the District Judge in his unreported written opinion. The majority viewed § 9 (a) as containing alternative bases of jurisdiction. The first basis retained domicile as the operative jurisdictional fact, and made six weeks' residence *prima facie* evidence of domicile. They held this presumption of fact unreasonable and hence violative of the Due Process Clause of the Fifth Amendment: "A six-weeks' sojourn without proof of the intent with which one makes . . . [a domicile], we think, tends to establish nothing but the fact of six-weeks' physical presence." The court's willingness to hold the presumption unreasonable was reinforced, it said, by the fact that the presumption is related to the basis of jurisdiction rather than the merits of the cause and, secondly, because statistics showed that most divorces are not actually contested, so that the plaintiff would rarely be forced to submit proof of domiciliary intent to counter contrary evidence rebutting the presumption. The second basis for jurisdiction in § 9 (a), it reasoned, eliminates domicile as a jurisdictional fact if the plaintiff proves six weeks' physical presence and the defendant is personally served or enters a general appearance. This, too, the majority held a violation of due process. In their view, the Constitution makes domicile a prerequisite to divorce jurisdiction. The Court of Appeals dissenters thought the case controlled by the statutory presumption of domicile but, nevertheless, were of the opinion that both facets of § 9 (a) were constitutional.

This case presents three fundamental questions under the Due Process Clause of the Fifth Amendment. The first is reasonableness of inferring domiciliary intent from six weeks' residence, and the necessity of hinging divorce jurisdiction to domicile is another. Underlying both

ALTON *v.* ALTON.

questions is the issue of whether the Due Process Clause, which provides that "No person shall be . . . deprived of life, liberty, or property, without due process of law," authorizes the federal courts to invalidate a statute even though no "person"—petitioner or respondent—has complained of a deprivation.[1] The elementary question is the reasonableness of presuming domiciliary intent from six weeks' residence. We disagree with the courts below and hold the presumption a reasonable exercise of the legislative authority of the Virgin Islands Legislative Assembly. This view makes it unnecessary to pass on the other issues in the case at this time.[2]

The classic statement of the proper constitutional test of a statutory presumption was made by Mr. Justice Lurton in *Mobile, Jackson & Kansas City Railroad Co.* v. *Turnipseed,* 219 U. S. 35, 43 (1910), and has never been questioned by this Court.

> "[t]hat a legislative presumption of one fact from evidence of another may not constitute a denial of due process of law or a denial of the equal protection of the law it is only essential that there shall be some rational connection between the fact proved and the ultimate fact presumed, and that the inference of one fact from proof of another shall not be so unreasonable as to be a purely arbitrary mandate. So, also, it must not, under guise of presentation of evidence, operate to preclude the party from the right to present his defense to the main fact thus presumed.

---

[1] The application of the full faith and credit clause is not involved here.

[2] Avoiding the other issues in the case is particularly desirable because respondent has not, either here or in the court below, contested petitioner's position. Moreover, important constitutional questions should, whenever possible, be decided by the full Court.

ALTON *v.* ALTON.

"If a legislative provision not unreasonable in itself prescribing a rule of evidence, in either criminal
or civil cases, does not shut out from the party
affected a reasonable opportunity to submit to the
jury in his defense all of the facts bearing upon the
issue, there is no ground for holding that due process
of law has been denied him."

This test requires the courts to pay the greatest possible deference to the legislative judgment. If there be
"some rational connection between the fact proved and
the ultimate fact presumed," or if the inference is not
"wholly arbitrary," the courts must uphold the presumption. We cannot substitute our judgment for that of a
legislative body because we doubt the wisdom of, or if
some perceive a degree of artificiality in, a rule of evidence it has created. This definition of our limited role
perhaps explains why this Court has yet to invalidate on
due process grounds a rule of evidence of the type involved in this case—a local statutory presumption applicable to civil proceedings which merely creates an
inference of fact.

Mindful of our limited role in these cases, we consider
the reasonableness of presuming domiciliary intent from
residence. Physical presence and an intent to remain
indefinitely are the two elements that courts have held
must coincide for an individual to acquire a "domicile."
The duration of the physical presence may be twenty-four
hours, twenty-four days, or twenty-four years; there is
no minimum time implicit in the residence aspect of the
domicile doctrine, although local legislatures may impose
a minimum as a prerequisite for divorce jurisdiction in
its courts. And while "residence" and "intent" are con-
ceptually distinct requirements, there can be no doubt
that the duration of residence is relevant to the issue of
the individual's intent. Let us assume that in a jurisdiction with a six weeks' residence requirement for divorce

ALTON *v.* ALTON.

jurisdiction, a twenty-four year resident seeks to introduce evidence of the duration of her residence to support her claim to domiciliary intent. None could dispute that such evidence would be admissible to prove her intent. It is equally clear that if the local legislature were to provide that twenty-four years' residence shall be *prima facie* evidence of domiciliary intent, such a presumption would be held perfectly reasonable. Two important facts are clear: the duration of physical presence is relevant to the question of intent, and the fact that a jurisdiction's minimum residence requirement coincides with the residence period from which domiciliary intent may be inferred cannot alter the relevancy of duration of residence to intent. As a result, the issue before us narrows to the naked question of whether six weeks bears such a remote relationship to domiciliary intent that we must say that, on a constitutional level, one has "no rational connection" with the other. We are not prepared to say this.

We are mindful of the geographical mobility of our population and of a widespread desire for "quickie" divorces. To that extent there may be in certain cases some element of artificiality to the Virgin Islands' presumption. But artificiality *per se* does not condemn a statutory presumption. To the extent that we were to strike down statutory presumptions of fact because they contain an element of artificiality, we would violate the letter and spirit of the limitation on our power announced in the *Turnipseed* case; more than that, we would be ignoring the large body of precedent upholding statutory presumptions which were, at least in part, artificial. *E. g., Luria* v. *United States,* 231 U. S. 9 (1913); *Easterling Lumber Co.* v. *Pierce,* 235 U. S. 380 (1914). Of course, the artificiality of a presumption makes it all the easier to rebut. The Virgin Islands preserve the right of the defendant spouse to contest the plaintiff's claim to domicile. Nor does the pertinent part of § 9 (a) restrict.

ALTON *v.* ALTON.

the power of a District Judge to question the plaintiff
about her domiciliary intent. In short, this provision
does not substitute six weeks' presence in the Islands for
a requirement of domicile nor is there any limit on the
opportunity to inquire into the facts concerning the same.

The lower courts thought that because the presumption
relates to a jurisdictional fact it should be scrutinized
more carefully for its reasonableness. But we find no support for this view in the cases, see *Tot* v. *United States,*
319 U. S. 463 (1943); *Yee Hem* v. *United States,* 268
U. S. 178 (1925), nor do we think there is any basis for
the distinction. We also deem irrelevant to the question
of the reasonableness of a presumption the fact that in
many cases there is no active contest; the significant fact
under *Turnipseed* is that the opportunity to contest exists.

Reversed.

According to Justice Frankfurter's notes, Chief Justice Warren had concluded his conference presentation by stating that "[h]e felt strongly that his conscience would not permit him to have this Court decide" as the majority proposed. There is no doubt that, feeling as he did, the Chief Justice would have issued his memorandum as a dissent, if the opinion prepared by Justice Clark had come down as the *Alton* opinion of the Court.

Justice Frankfurter also would have been in dissent. On April 24, just after he had read Justice Clark's opinion, Frankfurter wrote to the Chief Justice, criticizing it: "The short of it is, I do not find anything under my oath of office that requires me to be a party to such conscious blindness."[15] When Justice Frankfurter received a copy of an April 29 letter from Justice Reed to Justice Clark saying, "I have decided to go along with your opinion," he wrote, "Do you suppose that those whom you respect most of those who sat here would have allowed such 'phony' stuff to go out?"[16]

But the majority felt just as strongly about their position. This is shown by what happened next in the *Alton* case. Before the Supreme Court decision could be announced, Abe Fortas, counsel for Mrs. Alton, sent a letter to the Supreme Court Clerk apprising him that Mr. Alton had just secured a divorce in Connecticut, where he was domiciled. When he was informed of this, Justice Frankfurter wrote to the Chief Justice "about the changed aspect of *Alton* v. *Alton,* in view of the now-disclosed Connecticut decree of divorce." The Justice asked, "Is not one conclusion clear: that in any event a reargument is called for on the question of mootness?"[17]

Justice Frankfurter then made a motion to have the case set for reargument. But the majority was so committed to deciding under the Clark opinion that it refused to adopt the motion (though it did apparently obtain four votes). At this, Justice Frankfurter animadverted to Justice Reed: "And this is the way you solved the problem—to disallow four of your colleagues to have a reargument to which, I am sure, Hughes, Holmes, Brandeis and Cardozo would surely have yielded!"[18]

But there was really no need for any argument to show that the Connecticut divorce rendered the *Alton* case moot, and that the case should now, as Justice Frankfurter wrote to the Chief Justice, be "thrown out by us."[19] On May 12, Justice Frankfurter sent a long letter to Justice Clark demonstrating that the case had clearly become moot.

What in Heaven's name—or that of the law—is there [Frankfurter asked] that this Court or the Virgin Islands court could decree as between the Altons that has not already been decreed in a definitive judgment of a court entitled to constitutional respect in every State of the Union, the District of Columbia and in every Territory subject to the jurisdiction of the United States?[20]

By then, even the majority had come to agree that "if this case isn't moot there never was and never will be a moot case."[21] On June 1, 1954, the Court issued a brief order dismissing the case as moot.[22] The Clark opinion of the Court and the Warren dissent were consequently never delivered, and no one outside the Court knew how close the Justices had come to upholding the Virgin Islands divorce law.

The Justices were given another opportunity to rule on the Virgin Islands divorce law the following year in *Granville-Smith* v. *Granville-Smith*.[23] The facts were similar to those in *Alton*. Once again a wife sued for divorce in the Virgin Islands, alleging residence there for forty-three days before the suit, and the husband appeared but did not contest the action. Once again the court of appeals affirmed denial of the divorce, relying on its decision in the *Alton* case.

If the Court had decided *Granville-Smith* on the merits of the Virgin Islands divorce law, a majority would have voted again to uphold the statute. The majority in favor of the law would, indeed, have been even greater than that in *Alton*. Justice Douglas, who had not participated in the *Alton* conference, indicated that he would go along with the *Granville-Smith* majority. A Douglas letter to Justice Frankfurter referred to the doubts expressed in the *Alton* discussions about the statute's constitutionality and declared, "I do not share the doubts on the constitutional issues, and I stated as much to the Conference."[24]

When Chief Justice Warren came to the February 5, 1955, *Granville-Smith* conference, he must have known that he could not obtain a majority for his view that the Virgin Islands law unconstitutionally dispensed with domicile as a prerequisite for divorce jurisdiction. Seeking to avoid a repeat of the *Alton* conference and vote, the Chief Justice urged that *Granville-Smith* should be decided on another ground entirely.

One of the problems involved in both *Alton* and *Granville-Smith* was the lack of genuine adversary proceedings at any stage in the cases, since both the wife and husband desired the divorces and would not try to make a strong case against the divorce law. In such a situation, the Supreme Court often follows the practice of appointing an eminent attorney to present the case against the result favored by the parties. In this case, the Court invited Dean Erwin N. Griswold of the Harvard Law School "to appear and present oral argument as *amicus curiae*" against the Virgin Islands statute.[25] Griswold argued that the statute was not within the power delegated by Congress to the Virgin Islands legislature to enact laws only on "all subjects of local application." He urged that the Court decide the case on this narrow ground "so as to avoid grave constitutional questions."[26]

At the *Granville-Smith* conference,[27] Chief Justice Warren stated that he was "greatly impressed" with the argument that the divorce law was not on a "subject of local application." According to Frankfurter's skimpy notes, the Chief Justice said this was a case of "Tail wagging law." By this he presumably meant that the statute, though ostensibly a divorce law for Virgin Islanders, was actually, as Griswold had argued, "designed for export."[28] Chief Justice Warren concluded that the Court should restrict the decision to the "local application" issue.

Though Justices Black, Reed, and Clark disagreed, Justices Frankfurter, Douglas, Burton, and Minton went along with the Chief Justice's approach—even though Justices Burton and Minton had voted to uphold the statute in *Alton* and Justice Douglas, as already seen, would have voted the same way had he been present at the *Alton* conference. (Presumably they did so out of deference to the principle that the Court should decide cases as narrowly as possible and avoid serious constitutional questions if at all feasible.) The vote was thus five to three (Justice Harlan, newly appointed to the Court, took no part in the case) in favor of affirming the invalidity of the Virgin Islands law, but on the ground that it was not legislation on a subject of local application since it was designed for people outside the islands.

The *Granville-Smith* opinion was assigned to Justice Frankfurter. He circulated an opinion in early March which spelled out the holding that the challenged statute was not of local application. In his written outline for the opinion, the Justice noted that the opinion should "state facts proving this is a statute for Export." He then posed what he considered the crucial question: "Would Congress if consciously called to give VI power to affect marriages on mainland for *mainland domiciliaries* have given it to VI?"[29]

Justice Frankfurter's first draft was essentially similar to his published *Granville-Smith* opinion on the issue of whether the divorce law was on a subject of local application. The Frankfurter draft was not, however, limited to the issue on which the case was ultimately decided. Instead, the Justice used the occasion to deal with the constitutional question bypassed after *Alton* became moot, and did so in a manner contrary to that voted by the *Alton* majority.

The Frankfurter draft began[30] by asserting, "The Virgin Islands enactment patently raises serious constitutional issues." It then questioned whether the statute did not violate the requirements of due process, as well as the requirement that full faith and credit be given to the domestic relations laws of the states. The draft stressed "that domicile of one party in the divorcing forum makes the substantive law of the forum controlling in the divorce proceedings. But no State has heretofore attempted to abandon 'domicile' of one of the parties as a prerequisite for divorce."

The draft concluded that there was a real question "whether § 9(a) impinges on the underlying assumption of our federal legal system." The "issues that are implicit in the Virgin Islands enactment would bring into judgment the ultimate limits on the power of a State to affect the domestic relations of persons permanently settled in other States."[31]

As already seen, the Court's decision in favor of the Virgin Islands divorce law was not rendered in *Alton* because the case became moot. Now Justice Frankfurter was attempting to elevate the minority view espoused in *Alton* by himself and the Chief Justice to the status of Supreme Court doctrine by including it in his draft *Granville-Smith* opinion of the Court.

The Justice's tactic was, however, immediately challenged. On March 11, Justice Douglas wrote to Frankfurter, "The majority vote on this case, as I understood it, concerned solely and simply a question of statutory construction. The opinion that you circulated has many due process emanations . . . that go counter to my convictions on due process." Douglas pointed out that his vote was necessary for a Court opinion. "But I cannot join a Court opinion that pushes me to the result for fear of constitutional difficulties."[32]

Since he needed Justice Douglas's vote, Justice Frankfurter revised his opinion. As he explained in a March 23 memorandum, "I have deleted all constitutional worries. It has been my endeavor, and I trust I have succeeded, not to convey the faintest whisper that any of us have any constitutional doubts."[33]

As it turned out, the only reference to the underlying constitutional issues in *Granville-Smith* was contained in Justice Clark's dissenting opinion, which was joined by Justices Black and Reed. But it gave an inaccurate picture of the division in the Court on that issue. The dissent stated, "While the Court's opinion makes no reference to any constitutional doubts, these may have motivated it in striking down the Islands' law on statutory grounds."[34] The Clark opinion indicated that the dissenters did not share the constitutional doubts and would have voted to uphold the law despite the "constitutional bugaboo"[35] of domicile.

The implication was that, while the three *Granville-Smith* dissenters would vote to reject the *Alton* court of appeals reasoning, the majority would accept it and vote to strike down the Virgin Islands divorce law as violative of due process. The actual division of the Court in the *Alton* case, which had considered the issue squarely only the year before, was, of course, the other way. This was, however, unknown outside the Court. If anything, *Granville-Smith* appeared to confirm the correctness of the court of appeals decision in *Alton*.[36] That decision continues to be cited as authority,[37] since there is no Supreme Court decision to the contrary.

There has, indeed, been no case in the highest Court raising the *Alton* issue since the *Alton* and *Granville-Smith* cases themselves. In the outline for his *Granville-Smith* opinion, Justice Frankfurter, after referring to the Virgin Islands law, noted, "There never having been such a statute passed by any State and therefore never before this Court."[38] Not surprisingly, there have been no such state statutes since *Granville-Smith*, for the *Alton* court of appeals decision has appeared to establish their unconstitutionality.

Had Mr. Alton not secured his Connecticut divorce, the legal picture might be entirely different today. The Clark opinion would then have been issued as the *Alton* opinion of the Court. It would have rejected the reasoning of the court of appeals and settled the constitutionality of the Virgin Islands divorce law. This would have filled in the gap left by *Williams* v. *North Carolina*[39] and permitted states such as Nevada virtually to remove the issue of domicile in "quickie" divorce cases.

Other states would doubtless also have enacted statutes patterned on the Virgin Islands law. Indeed, so far as divorce laws are concerned, there seems to be a legal counterpart of Gresham's law. State desire to share in the lucrative business of issuing "quickie" divorces might have led to increasing efforts to avoid the domicile requirement. The result could have been the widespread enactment of consensual divorce laws throughout the country.

If that development had occurred, the Supreme Court would, as Chief Justice Warren pointed out in his proposed *Alton* dissent, have upheld such laws "on the authority of this case."[40] In his draft dissent, the Chief Justice noted that "there are others who believe we will eventually arrive at that situation [i.e., of consensual divorce laws] regardless of what happens in this case." During the past decade and a half we have, in large part, arrived at the situation foreseen by the Chief Justice, with the recent proliferation of no-fault divorce laws. Critics of those laws argue that they have helped lead to a breakdown of marriage and the family as had been feared by Chief Justice Warren in the *Alton* case. One may wonder if the majority *Alton* decision might have helped to avoid this result by liberalizing the availability of divorce without going to the extreme of turning domestic relations law completely inside out.

Notes

1. 347 U.S. 610 (1954).
2. *Schreiner* v. *Schreiner*, 502 S.W.2d 840, 843 (Tex. Civ. App. 1973).
3. See Blake, *The Road to Reno: A History of Divorce in the United States* 157, 169 (1962).
4. The conference quotations are from *Summary of Conference on Alton v. Alton*, April 12, 1954. FFH.
5. FF-EW, April 24, 1954. FFH.
6. 317 U.S. 287 (1942).
7. 201 U.S. 562 (1906).
8. 317 U.S. at 292, 302.
9. Frankfurter, J., concurring, id. at 306.
10. The original is "permits," but this is plainly a misprint.
11. This is the version reprinted supra p. 28.
12. See Schwartz, *Super Chief: Earl Warren and His Supreme Court—A Judicial Biography* 151–155 (1983).
13. Id. at 139.
14. 12 Wall. 128 (U.S. 1872).
15. Loc. cit. supra note 5.
16. Handwritten comment at bottom of SR-TCC, April 29, 1954. FFH.
17. FF-EW, May 1, 1954. FFH.
18. Loc. cit. supra note 16.

19. Loc. cit. supra note 17.
20. FF-TCC, May 12, 1954. FFH.
21. Ibid.
22. *Alton* v. *Alton*, 347 U.S. 610 (1954).
23. 349 U.S. 1 (1955).
24. WOD-FF, March 11, 1955. FFH.
25. *Granville-Smith* v. *Granville-Smith*, 348 U.S. 885 (1954).
26. See 99 L. Ed. 775.
27. The conference quotations are from notes in FF's writing, headed "Granville." FFH.
28. 349 U.S. at 10.
29. Written notes, headed "Virgin Islands." FFH.
30. After stating the facts and history of the case. FF, *Opinion of the Court.*
31. No. 261—October Term, 1954. Elizabeth R. Granville-Smith, Petitioner *v.* Edward Granville-Smith [March ___, 1955]. Brackets in original. FFH.
32. Loc. cit. supra note 24.
33. FF, *Memorandum to the Conference,* March 23, 1955. FFH.
34. 349 U.S. at 26.
35. Id. at 27.
36. *Alton* v. *Alton*, 207 F.2d 667 (3d Cir. 1953).
37. E.g., *Carr* v. *Carr*, 46 N.Y.2d 207, 273 (1978).
38. Supra note 29.
39. Supra note 4.
40. Supra p. 28.

2

Dayton v. *Dulles* *(1958)*: "Faceless Informers" and Due Process

In *Dayton* v. *Dulles*,[1] Justice Douglas circulated a draft opinion of the Court that would have resolved one of the crucial legal issues presented during the cold-war period that followed World War II—that of the use of confidential information in proceedings allegedly involving national security. If the Douglas opinion had been issued as the Court's opinion in the *Dayton* case, such proceedings would have been subjected to the same requirements of confrontation and cross-examination that prevail in other administrative proceedings. Instead, the ultimate decision of *Dayton* on other grounds meant that, so far as the Supreme Court was concerned, the fitting of security procedures into the mold of due process was essentially a lost opportunity.

Dayton v. *Dulles* was one of two passport cases presented to the Court during the 1957 term. The other was *Kent* v. *Dulles*,[2] in which the artist Rockwell Kent had been denied a passport because he was a Communist, after having refused to submit an affidavit on Communist membership as required by the relevant regulations. Kent challenged the power given to the Secretary of State to issue passports without any standards limiting his discretion to grant or deny.

Dayton raised an even broader issue. He sought a passport to travel to India to accept a position as a research physicist. His application was denied on the ground that he was "going abroad to engage in activities that would advance the Communist movement." Dayton was given a hearing, but the decision was based not only on the evidence presented but also on "a confidential file composed of investigative reports from Government agencies" that Dayton was not allowed to examine. He was informed that the file contained information indicating his "association with various communists [and] with persons suspected of being part of the Rosenberg espionage ring." Dayton claimed that the procedure followed denied due process. The lower courts rejected his claim.

The issue raised by *Dayton* was one that had never been decided by

the highest Court. It arose out of the loyalty and security programs instituted as a major part of the government's response to the problems posed
by the cold war. The passport program involved in the *Dayton* case was
but a small facet of the federal loyalty-security apparatus that was set up
to deal with the threat of alleged subversion. Most far-reaching in their
impact were the various loyalty programs administered by governments
throughout the country. They were designed to weed out from government positions those who were allegedly disloyal or who otherwise constituted security risks. At the time of the *Dayton* case, the federal loyalty-
security program alone covered nearly six million employees in both
government and private industry; and this figure did not include the millions affected by comparable state measures.[3]

The loyalty-security programs were not limited to government employees. They were also applicable to government contractors and those
employed by them,[4] as well as to people who worked on government in-
stallations, such as military and naval bases.[5] In addition, as *Dayton* v.
Dulles shows, comparable measures were in force to ensure that passports
were not granted to those whose travel abroad was found contrary to the
national interest.

It may be argued that a loyalty program such as that inaugurated for
the federal civil service by Executive Order 9835 (the so-called loyalty
order promulgated by President Truman in March 1947) attempted to
achieve the impossible. During the first century and a half of the Republic, our people took it for granted that those whom they employed as
government servants were loyal to the United States. So far as their loyalty was concerned, civil servants were asked only to take the oath to support and defend the Constitution. During the cold-war period, it was felt
that this was not enough to ensure loyalty. Yet, paradoxically enough, this
concern itself was an indication that loyalty in this country was not what
it might have been in former days. While the Decii are rushing with devoted bodies on the enemies of Rome, what need is there of preaching
patriotism?[6] When loyalty is made a principal object of the state's concern, it has already sunk from its pristine condition.

Be that as it may, however, President Truman's 1947 order instituted
a broad loyalty program in the federal civil service, which was continued
in later administrations. Under that program, the loyalty of federal employees and would-be employees was inquired into. There was no real
doubt of the authority of the government to dismiss or refuse to hire employees who were disloyal or who constituted security risks. The existence of federal power in this respect was not directly decided by the
Supreme Court, but its decisions in the matter were based on the implicit
assumption that disloyal civil servants might be discharged in the national
interest.[7] And the Court expressly confirmed the authority of the states
to institute programs designed to eliminate disloyal employees from their
civil service systems.[8] The rationale was stated by Justice Frankfurter:

The Constitution does not guarantee public employment. City, State and Nation are not confined to making provisions appropriate for securing competent professional discharge of the functions pertaining to diverse governmental jobs. They may also assure themselves of fidelity to the very presuppositions of our scheme of government on the part of those who seek to serve it. No unit of government can be denied the right to keep out of its employ those who seek to overthrow the government by force or violence, or are knowingly members of an organization engaged in such endeavor.[9]

But if the authority of the federal government to bar disloyal employees from its service was not really open to question, the same was not true of the means used to implement the government's conceded power in this connection. This was particularly true of the procedural aspects of the government's loyalty-security program. It was, however, asserted that the loyalty-security program could not, by its very nature, be effectively executed if hearings under it were required to comply fully with all the procedural demands imposed upon administrative agencies in other cases. The right of cross-examination can serve to illustrate the point.

Every party to an administrative proceeding, reads the relevant section of the Federal Administrative Procedure Act, "shall have the right . . . to conduct such cross-examination as may be required for a full and true disclosure of the facts."[10] In the loyalty-security cases, it was claimed that to allow individuals to confront and cross-examine those who had given the Federal Bureau of Investigation information might impair the functioning of the investigative network that the FBI had built up. As one federal court said, "The Federal Bureau of Investigation has uniformly insisted that practically none of the evidential sources available will continue to be available to it if proper secrecy and confidence cannot at all times be maintained with respect to the original source of information."[11]

The point of view of the FBI in these cases is not difficult to understand. It was hardly to be expected that the Bureau would think it worthwhile to impair the usefulness of its undercover operatives by disclosing their identity.

At the same time, the failure to accord the full rights of confrontation and cross-examination tended too often to make the hearings accorded in loyalty-security cases a matter of empty form. What this could mean in practice was shown by *Peters* v. *Hobby*,[12] decided three years before *Dayton* v. *Dulles*. Dr. Peters, a professor of medicine, had been employed as a special consultant in the United States Public Health Service. Though he had twice been cleared of charges of disloyalty by the employing agency's loyalty board, he was barred from federal employment by the Civil Service Commission's Loyalty Review Board, which determined that there was a reasonable doubt as to his loyalty. Dr. Peters had been given a hearing on charges relating to alleged mem-

bership in the Communist Party, sponsorship of certain petitions, affiliation with various organizations, and alleged association with Communists
and Communist sympathizers. At the hearing, the sources of the information supporting the charges were not identified or made available to
Dr. Peters's counsel for cross-examination. In fact, the Board itself did
not even know the identity of all the informants against Dr. Peters.

In these circumstances, the situation confronting Dr. Peters was an
almost impossible one. Where the individual does not know the identity
of his accusers and cannot confront or cross-examine them, his task in
refuting their charges becomes all but insuperable. This was acutely
noted by Justice Douglas in the *Peters* case:

> Dr. Peters was condemned by faceless informers, some of whom were not
> known even to the Board that condemned him. Some of these informers
> were not even under oath. None of them had to submit to cross-examina-
> tion. None had to face Dr. Peters. So far as we or the Board know, they
> may be psychopaths or venal people, like Titus Oates, who revel in being
> informers. They may bear old grudges. Under cross-examination their
> stories might disappear like bubbles. Their whispered confidences might
> turn out to be yarns conceived by twisted minds or by people who,
> though sincere, have poor faculties of observation and memory.[13]

Confrontation and cross-examination under oath are essential elements in the American ideal of due process. How could condemnation by
"faceless informers" of the type involved in the *Peters* case be reconciled
with this ideal? Before *Dayton* v. *Dulles*, the Supreme Court had never
given anything like a satisfactory answer to this question. In the 1951
case of *Bailey* v. *Richardson*,[14] the Court did, it is true, uphold the kind
of procedure that prevailed in *Peters*, but it did so only by affirming, four
to four, the decision in favor of the government by the lower court; and,
as is customary in cases where there is an equal division in the highest
tribunal, the Court did not deliver any opinion in the *Bailey* case.

If there was a legal justification for the type of procedure followed
by the Loyalty Review Board in the *Peters* case, it was that relied on by
the lower court in *Bailey* v. *Richardson*. Its opinion turned on the view
that public employment was only a "privilege," not "a right." Where
such a privilege was involved, the government was not bound by the procedural requirements of due process. "Due process of law," declared the
lower *Bailey* court, "is not applicable unless one is being deprived of
something to which he has a right."[15] The same reasoning was presumably applicable in passport cases, such as *Dayton* v. *Dulles*, since a passport, too, was then considered a "privilege" beyond the procedural due
process pale.[16]

Before *Dayton* v. *Dulles*, the *Peters* case[17] itself had given the Warren Court the opportunity to deal with the issue of confidential information in loyalty-security cases. Dr. Peters claimed that the denial of opportunity to confront and cross-examine his accusers in his loyalty proceeding

violated due process. Indeed, in his argument before the Supreme Court, Thurman Arnold, appearing for petitioner, declared that he wanted to win on the constitutional right to confront and cross-examine.[18] But the Court decided *Peters* on another ground not even raised by Arnold in his argument. The Loyalty Review Board, which had ordered Peters removed from his position, had been set up under a presidential order giving it authority to review loyalty dismissals, but only in cases referred to it by the employing agency or the dismissed employee. The Board had taken Dr. Peters's case on its own motion after Peters had been cleared by his agency, and the Court held that this was beyond the Board's power. Once again the Court had been able to avoid the basic due process issue presented by the use of confidential information by government agencies.

In *Dayton* v. *Dulles*, the Justices appeared ready to seize the constitutional issue by the bit and make the decision that they had avoided in *Peters*. The conference on April 18, 1958, dealt with the two passport cases—*Dayton* v. *Dulles* and *Kent* v. *Dulles*—together. The Chief Justice had indicated his own view on the *Dayton* due process issue by his questioning of Solicitor General J. Ree Rankin during the April 10 oral argument:

> *The Chief Justice:* "Is it your position—do I understand correctly—that the Secretary can deny a pasport to an American citizen solely on the ground of confidential information?"
> *Mr. Rankin:* "If it is foreign affairs information."
> *Chief Justice:* "Who is going to say whether it is foreign affairs or domestic affairs? . . ."
> *Rankin:* "We must balance the interests involved. Sometimes the interest of the individual has to give way to the interest of the whole community."
> *Chief Justice:* "A person's right to get the information may have to give way, but does his right as a free American to travel have to give way? In what other field have we permitted the word of one officer of the government to deprive citizens of constitutional rights in peace time?"[19]

At the conference, Chief Justice Warren stated that he would discuss *Dayton* first and indicated that the confidential-information issue should be reached. Justice Clark's notes[20] summarized the Chief Justice's statement: "must decide whether Secy has power to prevent travel by citizen on grounds detrimental to foreign relations of U.S. on confidential evidence only." The Chief Justice thought that since there was "no express Congressional grant to Secy" to act as he had, "action of Secy is ultra vires."[21]

Justice Black noted that "in findings outside of confidential information, nothing against Dayton." Justice Frankfurter, according to Justice Clark's notes, then said, "No, as to Secretary's power to deny application for passport on grounds of national interest—based on confidential information— . . . not within authority under present law." Justices Douglas and Brennan expressed the same view, as did the Court's newly appointed member, Justice Whittaker.

Justices Burton, Clark, and Harlan voted to uphold the *Dayton* passport denial. That made for a six-to-three majority for striking down the denial. The Chief Justice assigned the opinion to Justice Douglas. This was the opportunity for which that Justice had been waiting. He had used every occasion to voice his constitutional condemnation of "faceless informers."[22] Now he was given the chance to elevate his view to the level of accepted Supreme Court doctrine. Despite the fact that the Chief Justice and others at the conference had based their votes on the theory that the Secretary had not been given the power by Congress to act on confidential information alone (and hence his action was beyond his statutory power), Justice Douglas did not limit himself to that approach. Instead, on May 9, he circulated the far-reaching draft opinion of the Court reprinted on p. 52.

The Douglas draft held squarely that Dayton's passport might not be denied on the basis of confidential information; due process required disclosure of all the facts upon which the Secretary of State relied: "The point of procedure is whether the hearing accorded petitioner satisfied the requirements of due process. We do not think it did."

Justice Douglas referred to *United States* v. *Nugent*,[23] where a selective service hearing was upheld even though the registrant was given only a "fair résumé" of the evidence against him. In particular, he was not permitted to see the FBI report on him, nor was he informed of the names of the persons interviewed by FBI investigators. The Douglas *Dayton* draft treats *Nugent* as an administrative law aberration and refuses "to extend it to cases involving rights under the Constitution," such as the right to travel abroad on which the passport applicant relies. In his companion opinion in *Kent* v. *Dulles*,[24] Justice Douglas had confirmed the right to travel abroad as one protected by due process; hence a passport, which was needed to make that right effective, could no longer be deemed a mere privilege. If the right to a passport is to be denied, "it should be done only on an open record and a fair hearing." By this Justice Douglas means a fair hearing according to the accepted administrative law principle that prohibits decisions "based on undisclosed facts."[25] Justice Douglas lays down the broad principle that a fair hearing requires "full disclosure of the facts upon which the administrative action is taken with an opportunity of the citizen to explain or rebut them." Evidence may not be used to deprive an individual of his rights unless it is disclosed: ". . . no hearing is fair where the decision rests on facts which are undisclosed and which the citizen has not been given an opportunity to challenge in the accepted ways."

Justice Clark had been Attorney General when President Truman's original Loyalty Order had been issued in March 1947 and continued in that post during the first two years of the loyalty programs's administration. On the Supreme Court, the Texan always took a strong position in favor of governmental efforts to deal with allegedly subversive activities. Justice Clark responded to the *Dayton* draft opinion of the Court by the forceful draft dissent reprinted on p. 64, which he circulated June 12. Justice Clark took sharp issue with Justice Douglas on due process. The majority decision, the draft dissent asserted, would place the Secretary of State "in the intolerable position of sacrificing the national interest no matter how he turned, either by issuing the passport or by disclosing the secret information." This, Justice Clark said, was the "incredible" majority solution and "it is paramount to advising the physician to curb the disease by killing the patient."

Justice Clark's extreme language shows how strongly he felt about what he termed the "Pyrrhic achievement reached for by the Court today." Indeed, the Texan felt strongly enough about the matter to telephone FBI Director J. Edgar Hoover for help on the case.[26] Justice Clark asked for something Hoover had said on the importance of passport control. Both the Clark draft *Dayton* dissent and the final dissent that the Justice issued in the *Kent* case[27] contained a footnote reference to a Hoover book, giving the Director's view on the subject.

It is perhaps unnecessary to say that such an *ex parte* contact with the FBI Director on a pending case raises a serious question of judicial propriety. Had the Clark phone call been known at the time *Dayton* v. *Dulles* was decided, it would certainly have subjected the Justice to much deserved criticism.

From: Douglas, J.

SUPREME COURT OF THE UNITED STATES

Circulated:

No. 621.—OCTOBER TERM, 1957. Recirculated:_____

Weldon Bruce Dayton, Appellant, *v.* John Foster Dulles.	On Appeal From the United States District Court for the District of Columbia.

[May —, 1958.]

MR. JUSTICE DOUGLAS delivered the opinion of the Court.

Petitioner, a native born citizen, is a physicist who has been connected with various federal projects and who has been associated as a teacher with several of our universities. In March 1954 he applied for a passport to enable him to travel to India in order to accept a position as research physicist at the Tata Institute of Fundamental Research, affiliated with the University of Bombay. In April 1954 the Director of the Passport Office advised him that his application was denied because the Department of State "feels that it would be contrary to the best interest of the United States to provide you passport facilities at this time."

Petitioner conferred with an officer of the Passport Office and as a result of that conversation executed an affidavit [1] which covered the wide range of matters inquired into and which stated in part:

> "I am not now and I have never been a member of the Communist Party.

---

[1] The Passport Regulations of the Secretary of State, as amended, 22 CFR § 51.142 provide:

"At any state of the proceedings in the Passport Division or before the Board, if it is deemed necessary, the applicant may be required, as a part of his application, to subscribe, under oath or

---

DAYTON v. DULLES.

"With the possible exception of a casual and brief association with the work of the Joint Anti-Fascist Refugee Committee for a few months in 1941 and 1942 (all as related below); I am not now and have never been a member of any of the organizations designated on the Attorney General's list (which I have carefully examined).

"I am not now engaged and I have never engaged in any activities which, so far as I know or at any time knew, support or supported the Communist movement.

"I wish to go abroad for the sole purpose of engaging in experimental research in physics at the Tata Institute of Fundamental Research in Bombay. I am not going abroad to engage in any activities which, so far as I know or can imagine, will in any way advance the Communist movement."

The Director of the Passport Office wrote petitioner's lawyer in reply that the Department had given careful consideration to the affidavit and added, "in view of certain factors of Mr. Dayton's case which I am not at liberty to discuss with him, the Department must adhere to its previous decision that it would be contrary to the best interests of the United States to provide Mr. Dayton with passport facilities at this time." Later the Director wrote again, saying:

"In arriving at its decision to refuse passport facilities to Mr. Dayton, the Department took into consideration his connection with the Science for Victory Committee and his association at that time with various communists. However, the determin-

---

affirmation, to a statement with respect to present or past membership in the Communist Party. If applicant states that he is a Communist, refusal of a passport in his case will be without further proceedings."

DAYTON *v.* DULLES.

ing factor in the case was Mr. Dayton's association
with persons suspected of being part of the Rosenberg espionage ring and his alleged presence at an
apartment in New York which was allegedly used
for microfilming material obtained for the use of a
foreign government."

Thereupon petitioner, pursuant to the Passport Regulations of the Secretary of State, as amended, 22 CFR
§ 51.135 *et seq.* filed a petition of appeal, with the Board
of Passport Appeals.[2]   He also requested, pursuant to
the Regulations,[3] information from the Board of particulars concerning three items: (1) petitioner's alleged "association with various communists"; (2) his "association
with persons suspected of being part of the Rosenberg

---

[2] "§ 51.138. *Appeal by passport applicant.* In the event of a
decision adverse to the applicant, he shall be entitled to appeal his
case to the Board of Passport Appeals provided for in § 51.139.

"§ 51.139. *Creation and Functions of Board of Passport Appeals.*
There is hereby established within the Department of State a Board
of Passport Appeals, hereinafter referred to as the Board, composed
of not less than three officers of the Department to be designated by
the Secretary of State. The Board shall act on all appeals under
§ 51.138. The Board shall adopt and make public its own rules
of procedure, to be approved by the Secretary, which shall provide
that its duties in any case may be performed by a panel of not less
than three members acting by majority determination. The rules
shall accord applicant the right to a hearing and to be represented
by counsel, and shall accord applicant and each witness the right
to inspect the transcript of his own testimony."

[3] "§ 51.162. *Supplementary information to applicant.* The purpose of the hearing is to permit applicant to present all information
relevant and material to the decision in his case. Applicant may,
at the time of filing his petition, address a request in writing to
the Board for such additional information or explanation as may
be necessary to the preparation of his case. In conformity with the
relevant laws and regulations, the Board shall pass promptly and
finally upon all such requests and shall advise applicant of its
decision. The Board shall take whatever action it deems necessary
to insure the applicant of a full and fair consideration of his case."

DAYTON *v.* DULLES.

espionage ring"; and (3) his "alleged presence at an apartment in New York which was allegedly used for microfilming material obtained for the use of a foreign government." The Board's reply contained some, but very little, of the information requested; and it stated:

"The file contains information indicating that the applicant was present at 65 Morton Street, New York City in the summer of 1949 (July or August) and at Apartment 61, 65 Morton Street, New York City, during the month of January 1950. The applicant's relationship, if any (past or present), with the following-named persons is considered pertinent to the Board's review and consideration of the case: Marcel Scherer, Rose Segure, Sandra Collins, Frank Collins, Bernard Peters, Kurt Fritz, Karl Sitte, Louis S. Weiss, Alfred Sarant, and William Perl."

A hearing was held [4] at which witnesses for petitioner and for the State Department testified. Pursuant to the

---

[4] Section 51.163 of the Regulations provide:

"The Passport file and any other pertinent Government files shall be considered as part of the evidence in each case without testimony or other formality as to admissibility. Such files may not be examined by the applicant, except the applicant may examine his application or any paper which he has submitted in connection with his application or appeal. The applicant may appear and testify in his own behalf, be represented by counsel subject to the provisions of § 51.161, present witnesses and offer other evidence in his own behalf. The applicant and all witnesses may be cross-examined by any member of the Board or its counsel. If any witness whom the applicant wishes to call is unable to appear personally, the Board may, in its discretion, accept an affidavit by him or order evidence to be taken by deposition. Such depositions may be taken before any person designated by the Board and such designee is hereby authorized to administer oaths or affirmations for the purpose of the depositions. The Board shall conduct the hearing proceedings in such manner as to protect from disclosure information affecting the national security or tending to disclose or compromise investigative sources or methods."

DAYTON *v.* DULLES.

Regulations [5] the Board announced, over petitioner's protest, that it would consider "a confidential file composed of investigative reports from Government agencies" which petitioner would not be allowed to examine. [6] Later petitioner was advised by the Acting Secretary of State that the Board had submitted its recommendation and that the Secretary, after "a review of the entire record and on the basis of all the evidence, including that contained in confidential reports of investigation," had denied the application. The denial was rested specifically upon § 51.135 of the Regulations. [7]

Petitioner then brought suit in the District Court for declaratory relief. The District Court entered summary

---

[5] *Supra.* note 4.

[6] The Regulations in providing for that contingency state:

"§ 51.170. *Probative value of evidence.* In determining whether there is a preponderance of evidence supporting the denial of a passport the Board shall consider the entire record, including the transcript of the hearing and such confidential information as it may have in its possession. The Board shall take into consideration the inability of the applicant to meet information of which he has not been advised, specifically or in detail, or to attack the creditability of confidential informants."

[7] That section provides:

"*Limitations on issuance of passports to persons supporting Communist movement.* In order to promote the national interest by assuring that persons who support the world Communist movement of which the Communist Party is an integral unit may not, through use of United States passports, further the purposes of that movement, no passport, except one limited for direct and immediate return to the United States, shall be issued to:

"(a) Persons who are members of the Communist Party or who have recently terminated such membership under such circumstances as to warrant the conclusion—not otherwise rebutted by the evidence—that they continue to act in furtherance of the interests and under the discipline of the Communist Party;

"(b) Persons, regardless of the formal state of their affiliation with the Communist Party, who engage in activities which support the Communist movement under such circumstances as to warrant the conclusion—not otherwise rebutted by the evidence—that they have

DAYTON *v.* DULLES.

judgment for the Secretary. 146 F. Supp. 876. The Court of Appeals reversed, 237 F. 2d 43, and remanded the case to the Secretary for reconsideration in the light of its earlier decision in *Boudin* v. *Dulles*, 235 F. 2d 532.

On remand the Secretary without further hearing denied the application under § 51.135 (c),[8] saying that "the issuance of a passport would be contrary to the national interest." The Secretary at this time filed a document called "Decision and Findings" which is reproduced as an Appendix to this opinion.

The District Court again granted summary judgment for the Secretary, 146 F. Supp. 876; and the Court of Appeals affirmed by a divided vote, —— ——. The case is here on a petition for a writ of certiorari. 355 U. S. 911.

The right to travel at home and abroad is a part of the "liberty" of which the citizen cannot be deprived without the due process of law of the Fifth Amendment. *Kent* v. *Dulles, ante,* p. ——, decided this day. It was not always necessary to have a passport to enjoy that right. *Id.* But now by force of § 215 of the Immigration and Nationality Act of 1952, 8 U. S. C. § 1185, a citizen must have "a valid passport" to depart from or enter the country.[9] Denial of a passport is today the denial of a consti-

---

engaged in such activities as a result of direction, domination, or control exercised over them by the Communist movement;

"(c) Persons, regardless of the formal state of their affiliation with the Communist Party, as to whom there is reason to believe, on the balance of all the evidence, that they are going abroad to engage in activities which will advance the Communist movement for the purpose, knowingly and wilfully of advancing that movement."

[8] *Supra,* note 7.

[9] Section 1185 provides in pertinent part:

"Travel control of citizens and aliens during war or national emergency—Restrictions and prohibitions on aliens.

"(a) When the United States is at war or during the existence of any national emergency proclaimed by the President, . . . and the President shall find that the interests of the United States require

DAYTON *v.* DULLES.

tutionally protected right.   It is only in that setting that
the point of procedure presented by this petition for certiorari can be evaluated.   The point of procedure is
whether the hearing accorded petitioner satisfied the
requirements of due process.   We do not think it did.

We put to one side cases like *Chicago & Southern Air
Lines* v. *Waterman Corp.*, 333 U. S. 103, where "political"
as distinguished from justiciable issues are involved.
There the Court dealt with matters in the discretion of
the President to grant or withhold and therefore concluded it was beyond the competence of courts to adjudi-
cate.   *United States* v. *Curtiss-Wright Corp.*, 229 U. S.
304, on which the Court of Appeals previously relied, concerned the power of the President, acting on confidential
information and pursuant to a Joint Resolution of Congress, to forbid the sale of munitions of war abroad.
That case, however, involved the special prerogatives of
the President in the field of foreign affairs, a domain in
which he has vast powers.   But as the Court of Appeals
stated, "The issuance of a passport is not the conduct of

---

that restrictions and prohibitions in addition to those provided
otherwise than by this section be imposed upon the departure of
persons from and their entry into the United States, and shall make
public proclamation thereof, it shall, until otherwise ordered by
the President or the Congress, be unlawful—

"(1) [There follow restrictions enumerated (1) through (7) not
here pertinent.]

.   .   .   .   .

"(b) After such proclamation as is provided for in subsection (a)
of this section has been made and published and while such proclamation is in force, it shall, except as otherwise provided by the
President, and subject to such limitations and exceptions as the
President may authorize and prescribe, be unlawful for any citizen
of the United States to depart from or enter, or attempt to depart
from or enter, the United States unless he bears a valid passport."

The Presidential Proclamation referred to is Proc. No. 3004, made
on January 17, 1953.   67 Stat. C.31.

DAYTON *v.* DULLES.

foreign affairs." It concerns the movement of the citizen from and to this country with all the values that inhere in that right of mobility. The right is cognate to the right to follow a profession or to earn a livelihood. See *Williams* v. *Frears,* 179 U. S. 270, 274; *Edwards* v. *California,* 314 U. S. 160. Cases like *Norwegian Nitrogen Co.* v. *United States,* 288 U. S. 294, are not in point, for the problem there was tariff making, a part of the legislative process. Hearings obviously are not necessary for the resolution of facts that are the basis of legislative action. We come closer to the present case when we reach *United States* v. *Nugent,* 346 U. S. 1. In that case a hearing under the Selective Service Act was held to be fair and to satisfy the requirements of due process where the registrant seeking his statutory exemption was given only a fair résumé of the adverse evidence against him. But *Gonzales* v. *United States,* 348 U. S. 407, qualified that ruling by requiring disclosure of the adverse information to the registrant, seeking the statutory exemption, when disclosure was a prime requirement of a fair hearing. Moreover the *Nugent* and *Gonzales* cases dealt with exemptions which have been considered to be matters of legislative grace, not constitutional right. See *Hamilton* v. *Regents,* 293 U. S. 245. Whatever the remaining scope of the *Nugent* ruling may be, we decline the invitation to extend it to cases involving rights under the Constitution.

The right of confrontation and cross-examination is, of course, deep-rooted in our criminal law. See *In re Oliver,* 333 U. S. 257. The Sixth Amendment indeed provides explicit standards. But as the Court said in *Wong Yang Sung* v. *McGrath,* 339 U. S. 33, 49, "The constitutional requirement of procedural due process of law derives from the same source as Congress' power to legislate and, where applicable, permeates every valid enactment of that body." In that case, the Court in

DAYTON *v.* DULLES.

holding that § 5 of the Administrative Procedure Act [10]
was applicable to deportation hearings, said:

> "When the Constitution requires a hearing, it
> requires a fair one, one before a tribunal which meets
> at least currently prevailing standards of impar-
> tiality. A deportation hearing involves issues basic
> to human liberty and happiness and, in the present
> upheavals in lands to which aliens may be returned,
> perhaps to life itself. It might be difficult to justify
> as measuring up to constitutional standards of
> impartiality a hearing tribunal for deportation pro-
> ceedings the like of which has been condemned by
> Congress as unfair even where less vital matters of
> property rights are at stake." *Id.*, pp. 50–51.

The right of the citizen to travel is certainly of no less
a magnitude than the right of the alien to remain here
unmolested. If that right is to be denied or curtailed,
it should be done only on an open record and after a fair
hearing. The right at stake is too precious for more
casual or informal treatment.

The law is prejudiced against administrative action
based on undisclosed facts. The Court said in *Morgan* v.
United States, 304 U. S. 1, 18–19:

> "The right to a hearing embraces not only the
> right to present evidence but also a reasonable oppor-
> tunity to know the claims of the opposing party and
> to meet them. The right to submit argument
> implies that opportunity; otherwise the right may
> be but a barren one. Those who are brought into
> contest with the Government in a quasi-judicial
> proceeding aimed at the control of their activities
> are entitled to be fairly advised of what the Govern-

---

[10] We do not consider the argument that the Administrative
Procedures Act applies to the issuance of passports as that question
was not raised in the petition for certiorari.

DAYTON v. DULLES.

ment proposes and to be heard upon its proposals before it issues its final command."

The Court in that case spoke of the prime requirement of fairness in hearings concerning property rights.[11] No less is required by due process where the liberty of the citizen is involved.

One prime requirement for a fair hearing seems to us to be an appropriately full disclosure of the facts upon which the administrative action is taken with an opportunity of the citizen to explain or rebut them. The Decision and Findings of the Secretary [12] disclose on their face no grounds for denying this citizen a passport. So far as the record shows, he is condemned for associations which

---

[11] In a rate case, Mr. Justice Cardozo wrote for the Court:

"The Commission had given notice that the value of the property would be fixed as of a date certain. Evidence directed to the value at that time had been laid before the triers of the facts in thousands of printed pages. To make the picture more complete, evidence had been given as to the value at cost of additions and retirements. Without warning or even the hint of warning that the case would be considered or determined upon any other basis than the evidence submitted, the Commission cut down the values for the years after the date certain upon the strength of information secretly collected and never yet disclosed. The company protested. It asked disclosure of the documents indicative of price trends, and an opportunity to examine them, to analyze them, to explain and to rebut them. The response was a curt refusal. Upon the strength of these unknown documents refunds have been ordered for sums mounting into millions, the Commission reporting its conclusion, but not the underlying proofs. The putative debtor does not know the proofs today. This is not the fair hearing essential to due process. It is condemnation without trial." *Ohio Bell Tel. Co.* v. *Commission*, 301 U. S. 292, 300.

"Notice, hearing and opportunity to answer," as stated by Chief Justice Taft in *Goldsmith* v. *Board of Tax Appeals*, 270 U. S. 117, 123, are the usual requirements of due process in administrative hearings. See *Bratton* v. *Chandler*, 260 U. S. 110, 114–115; *United States* v. *Abilene & So. R. Co.*, 265 U. S. 274, 289.

[12] See Appendix to this opinion.

DAYTON *v.* DULLES.

may have been wholly innocent. People of questionable character, some with criminal records, march through the episodes described in the findings. But there is not a shred of evidence attributing their unlawful or criminal projects to petitioner. He stands neither convicted nor accused of any crime. Congress has not made association with evil people or shady characters the basis for denial of a passport. As we said in *Kent* v. *Dulles, supra,* no standards have been written by Congress into the law which would permit the Secretary to deny a passport to a person because of his beliefs or his associations. Yet nothing more is disclosed on the face of these findings.

What the full record would disclose we do not know. The Secretary states in Part V of his Decision and Findings [13] that he has reason to believe that petitioner desires to go abroad to engage in activities "which will advance the Communist movement for the purpose, knowingly and wilfully of advancing that movement." He reaches that conclusion on "confidential information contained in the files of the Department of State, the disclosure of which might prejudice the conduct of United States foreign relations."

If the Secretary has a valid and lawful reason why petitioner should not receive a passport, the facts should be adequately disclosed to him. Perhaps they could be explained away. Perhaps they reflect untruths based on old grudges or prejudices. Perhaps they reflect errors in memory, faulty identifications, and the like. Perhaps they would dissolve upon explanation. It is the essence of a fair hearing that the citizen be given the right to be apprised of the evidence used to deny him his constitutional rights and to rebut it if he can. No hearing where he is denied that opportunity can be considered a fair one in the constitutional sense.

---

[13] See Appendix to this opinion.

DAYTON *v.* DULLES.

It is, however, argued that the undisclosed facts should be protected since they bear on delicate matters of foreign relations and internal security. There is no requirement that they be disclosed. The only requirement is that they not be used to deprive a citizen of his constitutional rights unless they are disclosed. The unfairness lies in keeping them secret and yet using them against the citizen. The point was put succinctly in *United States v. Andolschek,* 142 F. 2d 503, 506: "The government must choose; either it must leave the transactions in the obscurity from which a trial will draw them, or it must expose them fully." [14] That case dealt with evidentiary matters in a criminal trial. Cf. *Jencks v. United States,* 353 U. S. 657. But it states, we think, the controlling principle governing hearings on passport applications. Whatever may be the power of the Secretary of State to deny passports, there can be no denial without a hearing; and no hearing is fair where the decision rests on facts which are undisclosed, and which the citizen has not been given an opportunity to challenge in the accepted ways.

Reversed.

---

[14] Barth, The Loyalty of Free Men (1951), p. 117, states: "From the founding of this Republic—indeed from its earliest days as a colonial dependency—men accused of such petty crimes as pocket-picking have been granted the right to confront their accusers in open court and to require these accusers to testify under oath and to submit to cross-examination. The practice is rooted not in theory but in Anglo-Saxon experience running back to Magna Charta. It grew out of the knowledge that accusations are sometimes made falsely—perhaps out of malice, perhaps out of prejudice, perhaps out of innocent error. And confrontation affords the best means, is indeed an indispensable means, of uncovering this falsity."

SUPREME COURT OF THE UNITED STATES

M.:.

From: Cla

No. 621.—October Term, 1957.

Circu.

Recircu..

| Weldon Bruce Dayton, Appellant. *v.* John Foster Dulles. | On Appeal From the United States District Court for the District of Columbia. |

[June —, 1958.]

Mr. Justice Clark, dissenting.

At some point between No. 481, *Kent* v. *Dulles* and *Briehl* v. *Dulles,* also decided this day, and the present case, the majority has lost its zeal for avoiding constitutional problems. In *Kent* and *Briehl* the Court narrowly construed the authority of the Secretary of State to deny passports, limiting it to applicants who either do not owe allegiance to the United States or who seek a passport to facilitate the carrying on of criminal activity. The primary reason given for that restrictive interpretation was a desire to avoid a construction of the statute that would raise "serious constitutional questions." Petitioner in this case was denied a passport on neither of the above grounds, but rather because, in the determination of the Secretary, he was "going abroad to engage in activities which will advance the Communist movement for the purpose, knowingly and wilfully of advancing that movement." It is patent then that the decision in *Kent* and *Briehl* controls this case simply on the issue of authority, making wholly unnecessary the Court's resolution of the constitutional question posed by the Secretary's reliance on confidential information.

Be that as it may, my dissent to *Kent* and *Briehl* brings me to the constitutional issue which the Court decides here: The first and basic step in the majority's reason-

DAYTON *v.* DULLES.

ing is the belief that the right of confrontation, guaranteed in criminal cases by the Sixth Amendment, is secured in noncriminal proceedings by the Due Process Clause of the Fifth Amendment. That much may be taken as true. But once having stated that proposition, essential here because petitioner's passport denial admittedly was not a criminal proceeding, the Court proceeds to ignore the fact that confrontation is availed of here not directly—by way of the Sixth Amendment—but only indirectly, through the medium of Fifth Amendment Due Process. That distinction is vital. It is, indeed, dispositive of this case, for it necessitates a balancing process, of individual right against national interest, which the majority has refused to undertake.

Due process is above all else a fluid concept, capable of reflecting the felt necessities of a given time. In the words of Justice Holmes, "[I]t is familiar that what is due process of law depends on circumstances. It varies with the subject-matter and the necessities of the situation." *Moyer* v. *Peabody*, 212 U. S. 78, 84 (1909). More recently due process has been described as "not a mechanical instrument" and "not a yardstick," but rather a "delicate process of adjustment inescapably involving the exercise of judgment by those whom the Constitution entrusted with the unfolding of the process." *Joint Anti-Fascist Refugee Committee* v. *McGrath*, 341 U. S. 123 (1951) (concurring opinion of MR. JUSTICE FRANK-FURTER). The significance of all this was pointed up in the Court's analysis of due process in *Betts* v. *Brady*, 316 U. S. 455, 462 (1942):

> "The phrase formulates a concept less rigid and more fluid than those envisaged in other specific and particular provisions of the Bill of Rights. Its application is less a matter of rule. Asserted denial is to be tested by an appraisal of the totality of facts in a given case. That which may, in one setting, con-

DAYTON *v.* DULLES.

stitute a denial of fundamental fairness, shocking
to the universal sense of justice, may, in other circumstances, and in the light of other considerations,
fall short of such denial. In the application of such
a concept, there is always the danger of falling into
the habit of formulating the guarantee into a set
of hard and fast rules, the application of which in a
given case may be to ignore the qualifying factors
therein disclosed."

If the constant repetition of a given problem sometimes
results in what seems to be a fixed rule under the Due
Process Clause—such as the well-established maxim that
convictions obtained by use of coerced confessions violate
due process—that can hardly suffice to evade the responsibility of weighing all the circumstances of the
present case, admittedly one of first impression.

It is necessary then to balance on the one hand the
interest of the people as individuals, on the other the
interest of the people as a nation. In doing so, two factors
of great importance must be considered here: the war
power and the foreign affairs power of the Executive.
The confidential information utilized by the Secretary
in this case was of two sorts. The first was information
that could not be disclosed because in the considered judgment of the Secretary of State disclosure might "prejudice
the conduct of United States foreign relations." The
second was information that could not be fully disclosed
without injury to our national security. The general substance of the latter information was made known to petitioner, but details and sources were withheld on the
ground that disclosure, in the judgment of the Secretary,
would be "detrimental to our national interest by com-
promising investigative sources and methods and seriously
interfering with the ability of [the State] Department
and the Executive Branch to obtain reliable information
affecting our internal security. Moreover, it would have

DAYTON *v.* DULLES.

an adverse effect upon our ability to obtain and utilize information from sources abroad and interfere with our established relationships in the security and intelligence area."

A long series of cases in this Court has, until today, supported the right of the Government to act upon the basis of undisclosed information in noncriminal proceedings. See, *e. g., Jay* v. *Boyd,* 351 U. S. 345 (1956); *United States* v. *Nugent,* 346 U. S. 1 (1953); *Shaughnessy* v. *United States ex rel. Mezei,* 345 U. S. 206 (1953); *United States ex rel. Knauff* v. *Shaughnessy,* 338 U. S. 537 (1950); *Chicago & Southern Air Lines, Inc.,* v. *Waterman S. S. Corp.,* 333 U. S. 103 (1948); *United States* v. *Curtiss-Wright Corp.,* 299 U. S. 304 (1936); cf. *Williams* v. *New York,* 337 U. S. 241 (1949); *United States* v. *Reynolds,* 345 U. S. 1 (1953); *Duncan* v. *Cammell, Laird & Co.,* (1942) A. C. 624. Various factors in them, sometimes collectively but more often singly, tipped the balance in favor of nondisclosure. Not all of those factors, of course, are present here, but two of them are, the war power and the foreign affairs power.

However, in view of the manner in which the majority disposes of these cases nothing would be gained from repeating the many relevant quotations found in each that conflict with the action of the Court today. In *United States* v. *Nugent, supra,* this Court, in considering a claimed violation of constitutional confrontation in a statutory Selective Service hearing, denied a conscientious objector the right to inspect F. B. I. reports where he was furnished a "fair résumé" of the same. That, we said, was "a valid exercise of the war power." 346 U. S., at 9. But the Court brushes it aside with the declaration that "whatever [its] remaining scope . . . may be, we decline to extend it."

Likewise in *Curtiss-Wright, supra,* the Court recognized the power of the Executive to keep secret the con-

DAYTON *v.* DULLES.

fidential information used in matters affecting our foreign relations, quoting the well-known phrase of *Mackenzie* v. *Hare*, 239 U. S. 299. 311, that "We should hesitate long before limiting or embarrassing such power." But the majority puts it aside for the very reason that the Secretary resorted to nondisclosure here, namely, that it involved foreign affairs. In all fairness. I ask, in what field does this case fall? Surely the potential embarrassment to our foreign relations inherent in the disclosure of intelligence sources and activity in foreign countries involves foreign affairs. The Court seems to rely on a passing reference by the Court of Appeals that the *issuance of a passport* is not foreign affairs, but it fails to note that the Court of Appeals itself regarded the Secretary's *refusal to disclose* secret information, on the grounds certified here, as involving foreign affairs. It seems passing strange to me that when our top expert in foreign affairs— the Secretary of State—denies a request for disclosure on the express ground that it would embarrass our foreign affairs, this Court should decide that foreign affairs is not involved.

In *Waterman S. S. Corp., supra,* the Court declared that "The President . . . has available intelligence services whose reports are not and ought not to be published to the world. It would be intolerable that courts, without the relevant information, should review and perhaps nullify actions of the Executive taken on action properly held secret." 333 U. S., at 111. Today the Court excuses the force of those words by asserting that *Waterman* involved a political question. Yet the judgment of the Secretary here that disclosure involves potential injury to our foreign relations is just as much political in nature and therefore, under the majority's own view of the *Waterman* case, unreviewable.

I find no case involving either the war power or that of foreign affairs in which this Court previously has com-

DAYTON *v.* DULLES.

pelled disclosure. Certainly the Court cites none today. The majority opinion seems bottomed on two cases, *Wong Yang Sung* v. *McGrath,* 339 U. S. 33 (1950), and *Morgan* v. *United States,* 304 U. S. 1 (1938). The former case was a deportation proceeding and did not involve disclosure of confidential information. Moreover, Mr. Justice Jackson said there that failure to comply with the Administrative Procedure Act *might* involve, not that it *did* involve, constitutional questions. 339 U. S., at 50. Nor did the *Morgan* case, *supra,* involve confidential information. It had to do with the failure of the Secretary of Agriculture to consider the relevant record in passing on a stockyards case. Neither case supports reversal of the Secretary's use of secret information, under the war and foreign affairs powers, to deny a passport in time of national emergency.

The holding today flies in the face of the specific purpose for which the Congress enacted the travel-control statute, 8 U. S. C. § 1185. Congress clearly did not intend that the administrative operation of the travel-control system during war or national emergency be subject to the procedural protections of a criminal trial. No case by an appellate court requires such protection. Rather the Act was adopted precisely because prior thereto evidentiary requirements such as the Court now imposes prevented the effective restriction of travel found necessary by the Congress. The Court says that petitioner is condemned "for associations which may have been wholly innocent. People of questionable character, some with criminal records, marched through the episodes . . . but there is not a shred of evidence attributing their unlawful conduct to petitioner. He stands neither convicted nor accused of any crime." But the Congress intended that the Secretary not be bound by the substantial-evidence

DAYTON *v.* DULLES.

rules that would justify criminal prosecution. The Committee Report of the House Foreign Affairs Committee, H. R. Rep. No. 485, 65th Cong., 2d Sess. 2–3, declared:

> "One case was mentioned of a United States citizen who recently returned from Europe after having, to the knowledge of our Government, done work in a neutral country for the German Government. There was strong suspicion that he came to the United States for no proper purpose. Nevertheless, not only was it impossible to exclude him but it would now be impossible to prevent him from leaving the country if he saw fit to do so. The known facts in his case are not sufficient to warrant the institution of a criminal prosecution, and in any event the difficulty of securing legal evidence from the place of his activities in Europe may easily be imagined.

> .   .   .   .   .

> "It is essential to meet the situation that the Executive should have wide discretion and wide authority of action . . . . There have recently been numerous suspicious departures for Cuba which it was impossible to prevent. Other individual cases of entry and departure at various points have excited the greatest anxiety. This is particularly true in respect of the Mexican border, passage across which can not legally be restricted for many types of persons reasonably suspected of aiding Germany's purposes."

And when the bill came up for debate on the House floor, the Committee's representative stated:

> ". . . the Government is very much hampered by lack of authority to control the travel to and from this country, even of people suspected of not being

DAYTON *v.* DULLES.

loyal, and even of those whom they suspect of being in the employ of enemy governments. [56 Cong. Rec. 6029.]

> .   .   .   .   .

"There are [persons] whose loyalty is suspected, but there is not enough evidence to convict them in a court of justice. [*Id.*, at 6064.]

> .   .   .   .   .

". . . Our ports are open, so far as the law is concerned, to alien friends, citizens, and neutrals, to come and go at will and pleasure, and that notwithstanding the Government may suspect the conduct and the intention of the individuals who come and go. [*Id.*, at 6065.]" *

Once it is established that either national security or foreign relations—and certainly when both together—may suffer from disclosure, then I think it clear the balance must tip in favor of the public as against the individual right. Any other result would place the Secretary in the intolerable position of necessarily sacrificing the national interest no matter how he turned, either by issuing the passport or by disclosing the secret information. Incredible as it may seem, that is the solution offered by the majority: it is paramount to advising the physician to curb the disease by killing the patient. The same national security preserved by keeping secret the confidential information will be jeopardized by the cost of doing so, namely, issuance of the passport to one whose travel abroad it is known will be inimical to the best interests of the country.

I am aware that implicit in my position is the necessity of relying on the good faith of the Secretary to speak

---

*For authoritative coverage of the necessity for travel control, see Masters of Deceit by J. Edgar Hoover.

DAYTON *v.* DULLES.

the truth when he determines that disclosure may injure
national security or foreign relations.   This, until today,
we have always done.   And I am sure the concept of due
process is such as to permit it.   There are those who are
equally sure that faith in any authority is the certain end
of freedom.   Yet what is the freedom for which we
strive?   Surely not the freedom of one to endanger the
liberty of all.   Such "freedom" sounds wondrously like
the pitch of tyranny to me.   I have been far too long
in the conflicting, adjusting, necessarily accommodating
world of men, to contribute to the sort of Pyrrhic achievement reached for by the Court today.   I would affirm.

Neither the Douglas draft opinion of the Court nor the Clark draft dissent were delivered when *Dayton* v. *Dulles* was finally decided. After the Douglas and Clark drafts were circulated, Justice Whittaker changed his vote and joined the dissenters. Justice Frankfurter continued to vote for reversal, but the Douglas opinion, with its wide-ranging due process holding, went too far for him. On May 12, Frankfurter wrote to Douglas that he would have to file a concurring opinion in order "to respect . . . my rigorous feeling against reaching constitutional issues when non-constitutional disposition is adequate."[28] On May 15, the following Frankfurter concurrence was circulated:

> I concur in the judgment. In refusing to issue petitioner a passport on the avowed ground taken by him, the Secretary of State exceeded his statutory powers, as the Court, with my agreement, has held in *Kent* v. *Dulles,* decided this day. Accordingly, I ought not reach the constitutional issues canvassed by the Court in this case, however much I might find myself in agreement with the Court's conclusions.[29]

Justice Douglas at first refused to alter the constitutional basis on which his draft opinion rested.[30] He wanted to make his far-reaching condemnation of confidential information even if it meant an opinion supported by only four Justices. At this point, however, the Chief Justice intervened. He persuaded Douglas that it would be undesirable to have the Court appear so divided that it could not agree on a majority opinion. On June 13, Douglas sent around a memorandum that stated, "There are only four for the opinion in this case as last circulated—namely, the Chief Justice, Justice Black, Justice Brennan, and myself. Since we are in the minority and since this is a constitutional issue, we have decided to defer to the majority of the Court and accordingly not to reach the constitutional question."[31]

The Douglas memo said that he was consequently eliminating the constitutional holding from his *Dayton* opinion. The opinion as finally issued indicated that the Court had decided not to reach the constitutional issue and was reversing on the same ground as in the *Kent* case, decided the same day. That ground was that Congress had not given the Secretary of State the power to deny passports on substantive grounds such as those relied on in the *Kent* and *Dayton* cases. Justice Clark still dissented, joined by Justices Burton, Harlan, and Whittaker. The Clark dissent contained only a short paragraph on the issue that had evoked such strong language in his original draft. Since the majority did not consider the constitutional question, Justice Clark's final *Dayton* dissent stated, "I would affirm on the question of authority without reaching any constitutional issue."[32]

Had the original Douglas draft come down as the *Dayton* opinion of the Court, it would have had far-reaching consequences. The Court would not have invalidated the pervasive loyalty-security programs that cut across American society during the period, so far as their substantive aspects were concerned. But the Douglas draft would have stricken down the essential element of loyalty-security procedure: the use of confidential information in reaching decisions. The heresy that a lower level of due process was permitted when administrative action was based on security grounds would have been repudiated. Instead, the basic principle would have been upheld for all administrative proceedings that the full case against him must be disclosed to the individual concerned, with the right in him to rebut. "No hearing where he is denied that opportunity" the Douglas draft declared, "can be considered a fair one in the constitutional sense."

If this principle had been established in loyalty-security cases by the *Dayton* opinion of the Court, the government would have been left only with the choice summarized by Justice Clark in his draft dissent: Either drop the loyalty-security proceeding or disclose the secret information. This might not have been tantamount to "curb[ing] the disease by killing the patient,"[33] but it might well have resulted in "killing" the loyalty-security programs. *Dayton* could have meant that no loyalty-security proceeding could have been brought without full disclosure and confrontation. That game, the government might have concluded, was plainly not worth the candle.[34]

As it turned out, the Supreme Court never did decide the constitutionality of the use of confidential information in cases involving alleged impact upon national security. In *Cafeteria Workers Union* v. *McElroy*,[35] three years after *Dayton* v. *Dulles*, the Court (over the vigorous dissent of Justice Brennan, joined by Chief Justice Warren and Justices Black and Douglas) went out of its way to confirm the already discussed *Bailey* v. *Richardson*[36] reasoning. "The Court," states the *Cafeteria Workers* opinion, "has consistently recognized that . . . the interest of a government employee in retaining his job, can be summarily denied. It has become a settled principle that government employment, in the absence of legislation, can be revoked at the will of the appointing officer."[37] The clear implication was that, at least where government employees were concerned, loyalty-security decisions could be made without procedural requirements, including that of disclosure of confidential information.

It is true that in *Green* v. *McElroy*[38] the opinion of the Court, delivered by Chief Justice Warren, contained strong language on the importance of confrontation and cross-examination.[39] But the statements of the Chief Justice were delivered by way of obiter. The *Greene* decision, like those in *Peters* v. *Hobby*[40] and *Dayton* v. *Dulles*, was able to shun the due process issue by disposing of the case on other grounds. The Department of Defense was held without authorization, in the absence of express delegation from Congress or the President, to conduct a security proceeding without confrontation and cross-examination.

In addition, more recent cases have gone far to undermine the *Bailey–Cafeteria Workers* foundation for the loyalty-security-type procedure.[41] The Supreme Court has specifically repudiated the notion that because there is no right to a government benefit, such as public employment, the benefit may be denied without due process procedural requirements:[42] "the Court now has rejected the concept that constitutional rights turn upon whether a governmental benefit is characterized as a 'right' or as a 'privilege.' "[43] If that is true, the principle "against administrative action based on undisclosed facts" that Douglas stressed in his draft *Dayton* opinion should apply as fully to proceedings allegedly involving national security as it does to ordinary administrative proceedings.

But no case has yet so held. Despite the more recent decisions undermining the *Bailey–Cafeteria Workers* rationale for use of "faceless informers" in loyalty-security cases, the constitutionality of their use is still a legal lacuna. The question that *Dayton* v. *Dulles* failed to answer remains an open one. Because of this, the loyalty-security apparatus could continue in existence well past the cold-war period and its ghost may even now walk in governmental corridors.

Notes

1. 357 U.S. 144 (1958).
2. 357 U.S. 116 (1958).
3. See Brown, *Loyalty and Security: Employment Tests in the United States* 61–118 (1958).
4. *Greene* v. *McElroy*, 360 U.S. 474 (1959).
5. *Cafeteria Workers Union* v. *McElroy*, 367 U.S. 886 (1961).
6. Compare Carlyle, *Characteristics*, in 25 Harvard Classics 345.
7. See, e.g., *Cafeteria Workers Union* v. *McElroy*, 367 U.S. 886 (1961); *Cole* v. *Young*, 351 U.S. 536 (1956); *Peters* v. *Hobby*, 349 U.S. 331 (1955).
8. See *Garner* v. *Los Angeles Board*, 341 U.S. 716 (1951); *Adler* v. *Board of Education*, 342 U.S. 485 (1952). But see *Keyishian* v. *Board of Regents*, 385 U.S. 589 (1967) (state law in *Adler* case ruled unduly vague and overbroad).
9. Concurring, in *Garner* v. *Los Angeles Board*, 341 U.S. 716, 724–5 (1951).
10. 5 U.S.C. § 556(d).
11. *Parker* v. *Lester*, 227 F.2d 708, 718 (9th Cir. 1955).
12. 349 U.S. 331 (1955).
13. Concurring, id. at 350–1.
14. 341 U.S. 918 (1951).
15. 182 F.2d 46, 58 (D.C. Cir. 1950).
16. See Schwartz, *Administrative Law* § 5.14 (2d ed. 1984).
17. Supra note 14.
18. 23 *U.S. Law Week* 3266 (1955).
19. 26 *U.S. Law Week* 3295 (1958).
20. TCCT.
21. The quotes are from Justice Clark's notes, ibid.
22. Loc. cit. supra note 13.
23. 346 U.S. 1 (1953).

24. Supra note 2.
25. See Schwartz, *Administrative Law* § 7.13 for discussion of this so-called principle of *exclusiveness of the record.*
26. J. Edgar Hoover, TCC, June 9, 1958. TCCT.
27. 357 U.S. at 140.
28. FFLC.
29. FFLC.
30. See WOD-FF, May 13, 1958. FFLC.
31. WOD, *Memorandum to the Conference,* June 13, 1958. JMHP.
32. 357 U.S. at 154.
33. I.e., Justice Clark's phrase, supra.
34. Compare Barth, *The Loyalty of Free Men* 133 (1951).
35. 367 U.S. 886 (1961).
36. Supra note 15.
37. 367 U.S. at 896.
38. 360 U.S. 474 (1959).
39. Id. at 497–9.
40. Supra note 12.
41. *Board of Regents* v. *Roth,* 408 U.S. 564, 571, n. 9 (1972).
42. *Elrod* v. *Burns,* 427 U.S. 347, 360 (1976).
43. Id. at 361.

3

Perez v. Brownell and Trop v. Dulles (1958): Expatriation and Congressional Power

Few cases gave the Warren Court as much difficulty as *Perez* v. *Brownell*[1] and *Trop* v. *Dulles*,[2] the two expatriation cases decided in 1958. As Justice Frankfurter explained it a few months after they were disposed of, "The problems there were new, difficult and of far-reaching import in our national life. More than that, not only was the Court divided, but within the narrow majority there were those who had doubts and uncertainties."[3] When the cases were finally decided, the two decisions appeared inconsistent, leaving the extent of Congressional power to declare citizenship forfeit uncertain, despite the Court's lengthy consideration of the subject.

All this would have been avoided had the draft opinions of the Court originally prepared by Chief Justice Warren in *Perez* and *Trop* come down as the final opinions in the two cases. The Warren opinions gave a simple—almost simplistic—answer to the question of Congressional expatriation authority. As the cases were finally decided, there were conflicting opinions of the Court, which left the law on the subject confused, a condition that continued until the original Warren view finally prevailed almost a decade later.

The governing statute in the expatriation cases was the Nationality Act of 1940. Section 401(e) of that law provided for the loss of nationality by American citizens who voted in foreign elections. Section 401(g) stated that the citizenship of an American citizen convicted by a court-martial of deserting the military or naval forces in time of war, and dishonorably discharged, could also be taken away. Section 401(j) provided for loss of nationality by citizens who departed from or remained outside the United States in time of war or declared national emergency for the purpose of evading military service.

Perez was a native-born American who resided in Mexico during most of World War II. When he sought admission to the United States in 1947, he stated that he had stayed outside the country to avoid the draft and had voted in Mexico. He was excluded on the ground that he had expatriated himself under Sections 401(e) and (j) of the Nationality Act. He then brought an action for a declaratory judgment (i.e., a judgment declaring his rights) affirming that he was still a citizen.

Trop was an Army private confined in a stockade in Casablanca in 1944 for a breach of discipline. He escaped but was then convicted of desertion by a court-martial and sentenced to three years at hard labor and a dishonorable discharge. In 1952 Trop's application for a passport was denied on the ground that he had lost his citizenship under Section 401(g). An action for a declaratory judgment that Trop was a citizen then followed. The lower courts in both *Perez* and *Trop* had decided in favor of the government, holding that Sections 401(e), (g), and (j) were within Congressional power on their face.

In the Supreme Court, the expatriation cases furnished the occasion for a sharp difference in judicial philosophy. The split was between the doctrine of judicial restraint espoused by Justice Frankfurter and the increasingly activist approach of Chief Justice Warren. To Justice Frankfurter, the crucial question was, "who is to judge" on what acts should terminate citizenship.

> Is it the Court or Congress? Indeed, more accurately, must not the Court put on the sack cloth and ashes of deferring humility in order to determine whether the judgment that Congress exercised, judged as it must be under the Due Process Clause, is so outside the limits of a supportable judgment by those who have the primary duty of judgment as to constitute that disregard of reason which we call an arbitrary judgment[?][4]

At the May 5, 1957, conference on the cases, Justice Frankfurter expressed the same view. According to Justice Burton's notes, Frankfurter stated, "Ultimate determinant is not what find in Constitution but our conception of what is job of the judges."[5] For Justice Frankfurter the governing doctrine was that of deference to the Congressional judgment.

Chief Justice Warren, in leading the conference, rejected this canon of judicial restraint. As Justice Burton's notes summarized the Chief Justice's statement, "Govt. has right to provide for denationalization when he makes the claim to dual citizenship," but not in other cases. Above all, government "can't impose it as punishment[;] if so has right to jury trial." In a letter soon afterwards, Justice Frankfurter wrote, "I'm quoting the Chief" for the view "that citizenship by birth can come to an end only by 'renunciation.' "[6]

For the Chief Justice that was all there was to the cases. If Congress had no power to take away citizenship unless it had been renounced, then the Nationality Act provisions were invalid and it was the job of the Court so to hold. In his conception of the expatriation power, notions of deference and restraint were irrelevant. The Court's decision should depend, not on any deference to Congress, "but on the Court's honest judgment as to whether the law was within the competence of the Congress."[7]

The conference vote was sharply divided. Justices Black, Douglas, Harlan, and Brennan agreed with Chief Justice Warren and voted to reverse in both *Perez* and *Trop*. Justices Frankfurter, Burton, Clark, and Whittaker voted to affirm. As will be seen, however, the votes were anything but firm. Justice Harlan, who had voted with the majority, wrote to Justice Frankfurter on May 13, "Frankly, I havent yet reached any firm conclusion, although my instinct still is that the expatriation power is a narrow one."[8]

After the Justices have voted on a case in conference, the Chief Justice assigns the opinion of the Court, unless he is not in the majority (in which case the senior majority Justice assigns the opinion). The power to assign the opinion has been called the most important that pertains to the highest judicial office. In discharging it, a Chief Justice is similar to a general deploying his army: It is he who determines what use will be made of the Court's personnel; his employment of the assigning power will both influence the growth of the law and his own relations with his colleagues.

Chief Justice Warren assigned the *Perez* and *Trop* opinions to himself. His simple view on expatriation—that citizenship by birth could be ended only by renunciation—enabled him to prepare the draft opinions of the Court reprinted on pages 81 and 99. They were circulated to the other Justices on June 8.

The principal opinion of the Court prepared by Chief Justice Warren was written for the *Perez* case. It was based on the expatriation concept he had stated at the conference—that "of expatriation as voluntary renunciation." This limited view led the opinion to reject the assertion of

> a broad power in Congress, implied from the very fact of national sovereignty, to make loss of nationality follow from acts which Congress may reasonably think constitute an unwarranted participation in the sovereign affairs of a foreign nation or which are inconsistent with gravest obligations of American citizenship. We do not believe the decisions of this Court sustain the existence of any such broad implied power.

Instead the only power recognized in Congress to take away citizenship contrary to the will of the citizen was one "no broader than is necessary to prevent the acquisition of dual nationality."

Having laid down this restricted concept of the expatriation power, it was easy for the Warren draft opinions to conclude that the challenged provisions of the Nationality Act went beyond Congressional authority. The acts that had been committed by Perez and Trop were plainly not intended by them lead to loss of citizenship; hence, there was no voluntary renunciation by them. Nor had their acts led to acquisition of dual nationality. That being the case, Congress was without power to take away their citizenship.

Voting in a foreign election did not necessarily amount to a transfer of allegiance; yet the statute was based on a virtually conclusive presumption to that effect. Nor could Congress prescribe loss of citizenship "for avoidance of even 'a fundamental obligation of citizenship'" such as draft evasion. If Congress considered certain acts wrongful, it could prescribe sanctions that would become "the business of the criminal courts." But there was "no power in Congress to take away citizenship for the acts described by §401(e) and (j)."

In the short companion *Trop* draft, the Chief Justice stated that what he had said in his *Perez* draft "is largely dispositive of the issue here." If Congress had "no power to prescribe loss of citizenship as the consequence of conduct inconsistent with fundamental obligations of citizenship," such as draft evasion, the same was true of conduct such as Trop's "desertion." The basic principle was, "The Fourteenth Amendment leaves no authority in Congress to decide who among the United States citizens are deserving of continued citizenship, no matter what their shortcomings may be." The Congressional power was only that "to regulate citizenship in the interest of preventing the acquisition or retention of dual nationality." There was no rational relation between the operative effect of the statute as applied to Trop and this limited power.

Had the *Perez* and *Trop* cases been decided under the Chief Justice's draft opinions of the Court, it would have settled the law on expatriation in accordance with the simple Warren view on the limited nature of Congressional power—that expatriation power was restricted to cases involving voluntary acquisition of dual nationality. Under this approach, Congress had no authority to condition continued citizenship upon compliance with prescribed canons of conduct. Citizenship could not be taken away for misconduct. Hence it followed that Sections 401(e),(g), and (j) were unconstitutional.

The Chief Justice's *Perez* draft would have decided the constitutionality of Section 401(j), as well as 401(e). That would have made it unnecessary for the Court to decide the *Mendoza-Martinez* case (the next case in this book), which was to give the Justices so much trouble during the next few terms. And it would have avoided the doctrinal difficulties which critics have noted in the opinions finally issued by the Court in these cases.

The Warren drafts would also have resolved the issue of expatriation power in 1958, rather than a decade later in *Afroyim* v. *Rusk*,[9] when the Chief Justice's view finally prevailed. In the interim, the extent of Congressional authority to take away citizenship remained unclear, both because of the seemingly inconsistent decisions finally rendered in *Perez* and *Trop* and the difficulties caused by the *Mendoza-Martinez* case and the decision made by the Court there.

Circulated: _____ JUN 5

SUPREME COURT OF THE UNITED STATES

Decided: _____

No. 572.—OCTOBER TERM, 1956.

Clemente Martinez Perez, Petitioner,

v.

Herbert Brownell, Jr., Attorney General of the United States of America.

On Writ of Certiorari to the United States Court of Appeals for the Ninth Circuit.

[June —, 1957.]

MR. CHIEF JUSTICE WARREN delivered the opinion of the Court.

This case presents the question of the constitutionality of two subsections, (e) and (j), of § 401 of the Nationality Act of 1940. These subsections provided:

"A person who is a national of the United States, whether by birth or naturalization, shall lose his nationality by:

. . . . .

"(e) Voting in a political election in a foreign state or participating in an election or plebiscite to determine the sovereignty over foreign territory; or

. . . . .

"(j) Departing from or remaining outside of the jurisdiction of the United States in time of war or during a period declared by the President to be a period of national emergency for the purpose of evading or avoiding training and service in the land or naval forces of the United States." [1]

---

[1] 54 Stat. 1168, as amended, 58 Stat. 746. The provisions were recodified by the Immigration and Nationality Act of 1952, 66 Stat. 267. Section 401(e) is unchanged as § 348 (a)(5) of the 1952 Act, 8 U. S. C. § 1481 (a)(5). Section 348 (a)(10) of the 1952 Act, 8

---

* JMHP.

PEREZ *v.* BROWNELL.

Petitioner was born in El Paso, Texas, in 1909, a fact of which he was apprised in 1928. His parents were Mexican-born, and he went with them to Mexico in 1919 or 1920. He resided there, with interruptions which we

U. S. C. § 1481 (a) (10), is a substantial re-enactment of § 401 (j), with this addition:

"For the purposes of this paragraph failure to comply with any provision of any compulsory service laws of the United States shall raise the presumption that the departure from or absence from the United States was for the purpose of evading or avoiding training and service in the military, air, or naval forces of the United States."

Section 401 of the Nationality Act of 1940, 54 Stat. 1168, as amended, 58 Stat. 4, 58 Stat. 677, 58 Stat. 746, provided in full:

"Sec. 401. A person who is a national of the United States, whether by birth or naturalization, shall lose his nationality by:

"(a) Obtaining naturalization in a foreign state, either upon his own application or through the naturalization of a parent having legal custody of such person: *Provided, however,* That nationality shall not be lost as the result of the naturalization of a parent unless and until the child shall have attained the age of twenty-three years without acquiring permanent residence in the United States: *Provided further,* That a person who has acquired foreign nationality through the naturalization of his parent or parents, and who at the same time is a citizen of the United States, shall, if abroad and he has not heretofore expatriated himself as an American citizen by his own voluntary act, be permitted within two years from the effective date of [t]his Act to return to the United States and take up permanent residence therein, and it shall be thereafter deemed that he has selected to be an American citizen. Failure on the part of such person to so return and take up permanent residence in the United States during such period shall be deemed to be a determination on the part of such person to discontinue his status as an American citizen, and such person shall be forever estopped by such failure from thereafter claiming such American citizenship; or

"(b) Taking an oath or making an affirmation or other formal declaration of allegiance to a foreign state; or

"(c) Entering, or serving in, the armed forces of a foreign state unless expressly authorized by the laws of the United States, if he has or acquires the nationality of such foreign state; or

"(d) Accepting, or performing the duties of, any office, post, or employment under the government of a foreign state or political

PEREZ *v.* BROWNELL.

shall note, until 1952. In 1932 petitioner married a Mexican national, by whom he has seven children. Petitioner applied for admission to the United States in July 1943 as a railroad laborer. He stated in his application

subdivision thereof for which only nationals of such state are eligible; or

"(e) Voting in a political election in a foreign state or participating in an election or plebiscite to determine the sovereignty over foreign territory; or

"(f) Making a formal renunciation of nationality before a diplomatic or consular officer of the United States in a foreign state, in such form as may be prescribed by the Secretary of State; or

"(g) Deserting the military or naval forces of the United States in time of war, provided he is convicted thereof by court martial and as the result of such conviction is dismissed or dishonorably discharged from the service of such military or naval forces: *Provided,* That notwithstanding loss of nationality or citizenship or civil or political rights under the terms of this or previous Acts by reason of desertion committed in time of war, restoration to active duty with such military or naval forces in time of war or the reenlistment or induction of such a person in time of war with permission of competent military or naval authority, prior or subsequent to the effective date of this Act, shall be deemed to have the immediate effect of restoring such nationality or citizenship and all civil and political rights heretofore or hereafter so lost and of removing all civil and political disabilities resulting therefrom; or

"(h) Committing any act of treason against, or attempting by force to overthrow or bearing arms against the United States, provided he is convicted thereof by a court martial or by a court of competent jurisdiction; or

"(i) Making in the United States a formal written renunciation of nationality in such form as may be prescribed by, and before such officer as may be designated by, the Attorney General, whenever the United States shall be in a state of war and the Attorney General shall approve such renunciation as not contrary to the interests of national defense; or

"(j) Departing from or remaining outside of the jurisdiction of the United States in time of war or during a period declared by the President to be a period of national emergency for the purpose of evading or avoiding training and service in the land or naval forces of the United States."

PEREZ *v.* BROWNELL.

that he was a native-born citizen of Mexico. He was permitted to enter the United States on a temporary basis as a laborer and returned to Mexico about March 1944. Within a month he asked and received permission to re-enter the United States to continue his employment as a railroad laborer. In November 1944 he returned to Mexico. Although aware of the duty of United States citizens to register for the World War II draft, he did not register. In 1947 petitioner sought, for the first time, to enter the United States as a citizen. Upon his statement in an administrative exclusion proceeding that he had stayed outside the United States to avoid the draft and had voted in Mexico, he was held to have expatriated himself and was excluded. In 1952 petitioner, reverting to his claim of Mexican citizenship, entered the United States as a farm laborer. The following year he surrendered himself to immigration authorities in San Francisco as an alien in the United States illegally, although he claimed United States citizenship. After a hearing petitioner was ordered deported.

Thereupon he brought this action for a judgment declaring that he is a citizen of the United States, alleging his birth in this country.[2] Respondent's answer admitted that petitioner was native born but asserted that he had lost his citizenship by the acts of expatriation he had admitted in the 1947 exclusion proceeding. The District Court found as a fact that petitioner remained outside the United States from November 1944 until July 1947 for the purpose of avoiding or evading military service and that he voted in a political election in Mexico in July 1946. Petitioner was held therefore to have lost his nationality under § 401 (e) and (j) and the relief he prayed for was denied. The Court of Appeals for the Ninth Circuit affirmed, sustaining the statute against

---

[2] The action was brought under 28 U. S. C. § 2201 and 8 U. S. C. § 1503.

PEREZ *v.* BROWNELL.

petitioner's constitutional attack.[3] We granted certiorari. 352 U. S. 908.[4] No issue is raised concerning the crucial findings of the District Court as to expatriation nor the other findings which we have paraphrased in stating the case.

I.

A consideration of the power of Congress to declare American citizenship forfeit must begin with the first sentence of § 1 of the Fourteenth Amendment.[5] It is there provided that "All persons born or naturalized in the United States, and subject to the jurisdiction thereof, are citizens of the United States and of the State wherein they reside." United States citizenship, thus, was petitioner's constitutional birthright as it is that of every person born in this country. Congress is without power to alter the effect of birth in the United States. *United States* v. *Wong Kim Ark,* 169 U. S. 649. In speaking of petitioner's citizenship by birth we do not mean to imply that the naturalized citizen stands on any different footing. We do wish to emphasize that we are not concerned with the power to denaturalize for fraud or illegality in the procurement of naturalization.[6]

---

[3] 235 F. 2d 364.

[4] We subsequently granted petitioner's motion to waive payment of Clerk's costs and to print petitioner's brief and record at public expense. 352 U. S. 959.

[5] The fact that the statute speaks in terms of loss of nationality does not mean that it is not petitioner's citizenship which is sought to be forfeited. He is a national by reason of being a citizen, Nationality Act of 1940, § 101 (b), 54 Stat. 1137, now 8 U. S. C. § 1101 (a)(22). Hence he can lose his status as a national of the United States only by losing his citizenship. In the context of this opinion, the terms nationality and citizenship can be used interchangeably. Cf. *Rabang* v. *Boyd,* 353 U. S. —.

[6] See *Knauer* v. *United States,* 328 U. S. 654; *Baumgartner* v. *United States,* 322 U. S. 665; *Schneiderman* v. *United States,* 320 U. S. 118; *Tutun* v. *United States,* 270 U. S. 568; *Luria* v. *United States,* 231 U. S. 9.

PEREZ *v.* BROWNELL.

That an American citizen may voluntarily abandon his "cherished status," *Knauer* v. *United States,* 328 U. S. 654, 658, was established by Congress in 1868. In the preamble to a statute of that year Congress declared that "the right of expatriation is a natural and inherent right of all people." 15 Stat. 223. Although the operative provisions of that statute were directed primarily toward protecting our citizens by adoption from the claims of their countries of origin, the language was properly regarded as establishing the reciprocal right of American citizens to abjure their allegiance.[7] In the early days of the Republic the right of expatriation was a matter of controversy. The common-law doctrine of perpetual allegiance influenced the opinions of this Court.[8] And, although impressment of British seamen who had become Americans was one of the causes of the War of 1812, the executive officials of the Government were not unwavering in their support of the right of expatriation.[9] Prior to 1868 all efforts to obtain congressional enactments concerning expatriation failed.[10] The doctrine of perpetual allegiance, however, was so ill-suited to the growing nation whose doors were open to immigrants from abroad that it could not last. Nine years before Congress acted

---

[7] See *Savorgnan* v. *United States,* 338 U. S. 491, 498 and n. 11; Foreign Relations, 1873, H. R. Exec. Doc. No. 1, 43d Cong., 1st Sess., Pt. 1, Vol. II, pp. 1186–1187, 1204, 1210, 1213, 1216, 1222 (Views of President Grant's cabinet members) ; 14 Op. Atty. Gen. 295; Tsiang, The Question of Expatriation in America prior to 1907, pp. 97–98, 108–109. But see H. R. Doc. No. 326, 59th Cong., 2d Sess. 160–162.

[8] See *Shanks* v. *Dupont,* 3 Pet. 241, 246; *Inglis* v. *Trustees of Sailor's Snug Harbour,* 3 Pet. 99, 125. But see *The Santissima Trinidad,* 7 Wheat. 283, 347–348.

[9] 3 Moore, Digest of International Law, §§ 434–437; Tsiang, 45–55, 71–86, 110–112.

[10] Tsiang, 55–61.

PEREZ *v.* BROWNELL.

Attorney General Black stated the American position in a notable opinion:

> "Here, in the United States, the thought of giving it [the right of expatriation] up cannot be entertained for a moment. Upon that principle this country was populated. We owe to it our existence as a nation. Ever since our independence we have upheld and maintained it by every form of words and acts. We have constantly promised full and complete protection to all persons who should come here and seek it by renouncing their natural allegiance and transferring their fealty to us. We stand pledged to it in the face of the whole world." [11]

Congress, however, did not immediately define the manner in which a citizen of the United States could exercise his "natural and inherent right" to expatriate. The question was left to be decided judicially and administratively on a case-by-case basis.[12]

This unsatisfactory state of affairs lasted until 1907. The previous year Congress received from a Board of three State Department officials recommendations for legislation dealing with citizenship, expatriation and protection of American citizens abroad.[13] Most of the Board's recommendations were enacted into law. 34 Stat. 1228. Section 2 of the Act of 1907 provided that "any American citizen shall be deemed to have expatriated himself" by being naturalized in a foreign country or by taking an oath of allegiance to a foreign country.[14]

---

[11] 9 Op. Atty. Gen. 356, 359.

[12] Tsiang, 97–100, 101–103, 108–109.

[13] H. R. Doc. No. 326, 59th Cong., 2d Sess.

[14] Section 2 also created a rebuttable presumption that a naturalized citizen residing for two years in the country from which he came

PEREZ v. BROWNELL.

Section 3 declared that an American woman marrying a foreigner should take her husband's nationality, but provided that she could resume her American citizenship upon termination of the marital relation by registering with a United States consul or returning to reside in this country, if abroad, or by continuing to reside in this country if she was already here. It was litigation arising under § 3 that led to this Court's leading decision on expatriation, *Mackenzie* v. *Hare*, 239 U. S. 299, which will be discussed below.

In 1938 a Cabinet Committee, consisting of the Secretaries of State and Labor and the Attorney General, came forward with its proposals for revision and codification of the Nationality Laws.[15] These proposals were the foundation of the Nationality Act of 1940, which added new grounds of expatriation, including § 401 (e), voting in a foreign political election. The draft evasion provision, § 401 (j), was added in 1944. 58 Stat. 746. Section 401 was recodified with some changes by § 348 (a) of the Immigration and Nationality Act of 1952, 66 Stat. 267, and new grounds for expatriation were added by the Expatriation Act of 1954, 68 Stat. 1146.[16]

---

or five years in any other foreign country had ceased to be an American citizen. In addition, it provided that no American citizen should be allowed to expatriate himself when his country was at war.

[15] Codification of the Nationality Laws of the United States, H. R. Committee Print, 76th Cong., 1st Sess.

[16] See note 1, *supra*, for the text of § 401. All the grounds for expatriation provided by § 401 were carried forward, with a few modifications, by the 1952 Act. In addition, § 348 (a)(9) of the 1952 Act, the successor to § 401 (h), provides for loss of nationality by "committing any act of treason against, or attempting by force to overthrow, or bearing arms against, the United States, *violating or conspiring to violate any of the provisions of section 2383 of Title 18, or willfully performing any act in violation of section 2385 of Title 18, or violating section 2384 of Title 18 by engaging in a conspiracy to overthrow, put down, or to destroy by force the Govern-*

PEREZ *v.* BROWNELL.

II.

The whole course of statutory development outlined above represents an ever greater departure from the traditional concept of expatriation as "the voluntary renunciation or abandonment of nationality and allegiance," *Perkins* v. *Elg*, 307 U. S. 325, 334.[17] Today loss of nationality has been made the consequence of conviction of a number of criminal offenses as well as of the acts involved in this case and its companions.[18]

The Government does not attempt to argue from the fictitious premise that by voting in a Mexican election or by staying in Mexico to dodge the draft petitioner manifested an intent voluntarily to transfer or abandon his American citizenship. Rather, it asserts a broad power in Congress, implied from the very fact of national sovereignty, to make loss of nationality follow from acts which Congress may reasonably think constitute an unwarranted participation in the sovereign affairs of a foreign nation or which are inconsistent with the gravest obligations of American citizenship.

We do not believe the decisions of this Court sustain the existence of any such broad implied power. To begin

ment of the United States, or to levy war against them, if and when he is convicted thereof by a court martial or by a court of competent jurisdiction; . . . ." 66 Stat. 267, as amended, 68 Stat. 1146, 8 U. S. C. (Supp. IV) § 1481 (a)(9). (1954 amendment in italics.)

[17] The statement quoted from *Perkins* v. *Elg* is relied upon by petitioner as indicating a total want of congressional power to provide for "involuntary" expatriation. The Court, however, stated elsewhere in the opinion that "citizenship must be deemed to continue unless she [respondent] has been deprived of it through the operation of a treaty or congressional enactment or by her voluntary action in conformity with applicable legal principles." 307 U. S., at 329. See also *id.*, at 334; *Kawakita* v. *United States*, 343 U. S. 717, 728; *Mandoli* v. *Acheson*, 344 U. S. 133, 136.

[18] See note 16, *supra*.

PEREZ *v.* BROWNELL.

with, the Court has held that the power of naturalization, U. S. Const., Art. I, § 8, cl. 4, "is a power to confer citizenship, not a power to take it away." *United States* v. *Wong Kim Ark, supra,* at 703. See also *Osborn* v. *Bank of the United States,* 9 Wheat. 738, 827. No other express provision of the Constitution can be cited.

Mackenzie v. *Hare, supra,* is the keystone of the Government's argument for a broad implied power. In that case an American woman married an Englishman after the passage of the Act of 1907. She continued to reside here with her husband. The right to register as a voter was denied her on the ground that she had lost her American nationality by taking on the English nationality of her husband. She sought a writ of mandamus to compel her registration and from the California Supreme Court's denial of the writ she came to this Court on a writ of error. The Court first rejected her contention that § 3 of the 1907 Act did not apply to her, as a woman who had never left the country. Then the Court reached her constitutional claim, that Congress could not take from her the citizenship that was hers by birth under the Fourteenth Amendment. Because of the significance of the case to the problem at hand, it is worthwhile to quote at length the concluding paragraphs of Mr. Justice McKenna's opinion for the Court disposing of this contention.

> "It would make this opinion very voluminous to consider in detail the argument and the cases urged in support of or in attack upon the opposing conditions. Their foundation principles, we may assume, are known. The identity of husband and wife is an ancient principle of our jurisprudence. It was neither accidental nor arbitrary and worked in many instances for her protection. There has been, it is true, much relaxation of it but in its retention as in its origin it is determined by their intimate relation

PEREZ *v.* BROWNELL.

and unity of interests, and this relation and unity may make it of public concern in many instances to merge their identity, and give dominance to the husband. It has purpose, if not necessity, in purely domestic policy; it has greater purpose and, it may be, necessity, in international policy. And this was the dictate of the act in controversy. Having this purpose, has it not the sanction of power?

"Plaintiff contends, as we have seen, that it has not, and bases her contention upon the absence of an express gift of power. But there may be powers implied, necessary or incidental to the expressed powers. As a government, the United States is invested with all the attributes of sovereignty. As it has the character of nationality it has the powers of nationality, especially those which concern its relations and intercourse with other countries. We should hesitate long before limiting or embarrassing such powers. But monition is not necessary in the present case. There need be no dissent from the cases cited by plaintiff; there need be no assertion of very extensive power over the right of citizenship or of the imperative imposition of conditions upon it. It may be conceded that a change of citizenship cannot be arbitrarily imposed, that is, imposed without the concurrence of the citizen. The law in controversy does not have that feature. It deals with a condition voluntarily entered into, with notice of the consequences. We concur with counsel that citizenship is of tangible worth, and we sympathize with plaintiff in her desire to retain it and in her earnest assertion of it. But there is involved more than personal considerations. As we have seen, the legislation was urged by conditions of national moment. And this is an answer to the apprehension of counsel

PEREZ *v.* BROWNELL.

that our construction of the legislation will make every act, though lawful, as marriage, of course, is, a renunciation of citizenship. The marriage of an American woman with a foreigner has consequences of like kind, may involve national complications of like kind, as her physical expatriation may involve. Therefore, as long as the relation lasts it is made tantamount to expatriation. This is no arbitrary exercise of government. It is one which, regarding the international aspects, judicial opinion has taken for granted would not only be valid but demanded. It is the conception of the legislation under review that such an act may bring the Government into embarrassments and, it may be, into controversies. It is as voluntary and distinctive as expatriation and its consequences must be considered as elected." 239 U. S., at 311–312.

The Court thought to keep the case within the bounds of the historical concept of expatriation as voluntary renunciation by speaking of "a condition voluntarily entered into, with notice of the consequences," and the marital relation as "tantamount to expatriation." But because the voluntary performance of an act with notice of its consequences is obviously different from express, voluntary renunciation or abandonment of citizenship, the Court also adverted to the implied powers of the Federal Government in its relations with foreign nations;[19] it described the statute as "urged by conditions of national moment," of Congress' power to avoid international "embarrassments" and "controversies."

The nature of those "embarrassments" and "controversies" which Congress may act to avoid by prescribing reasonable regulations for the loss of citizenship was made

---

[19] For a general discussion of the implied powers of the National Government in international affairs, see *United States* v. *Curtiss-Wright Export Corp.*, 299 U. S. 304, 314–322.

PEREZ *v.* BROWNELL.

more explicit in *Savorgnan* v. *United States,* 338 U. S. 491. An American woman who wished to marry an Italian vice-consul in this country was informed that in order to do so she must first become an Italian citizen. To this end she applied for and was granted Italian citizenship. Thereafter she signed an instrument, which contained an oath of allegiance to the King of Italy and an expression of renunciation of American citizenship. The oath was in Italian, which she did not understand, and it was not read to her. In her suit for a judgment declaring her to be a United States citizen the District Court found as a fact that she had no intention of renouncing her American citizenship. This Court held that she had nevertheless expatriated herself under § 2 of the Act of 1907 by taking on Italian nationality.[20] "The United States has long recognized the general undesirability of dual allegiance . . . . There is nothing . . . in the Act of 1907 that implies that, after an American citizen has performed an overt act which spells expatriation under the wording of the statute, he, nevertheless, can preserve for himself a *duality of citizenship* by showing his intent or understanding to have been contrary to the usual legal consequences of such an act." (Emphasis supplied.) 338 U. S., at 500. The same point had been made 40 years before by the State Department Board which recommended the legislation of 1907.

"It is true that because of conflicting laws on the subject of citizenship in different countries a child

---

[20] Her marriage did not *ipso facto* result in expatriation because § 3 of the Act of 1907 had been repealed in 1922 by the Cable Act, 42 Stat. 1022. Actually, the Court did not need to decide whether naturalization alone resulted in expatriation. By administrative interpretation of § 2 of the Act of 1907 and by § 403 (a) of the Nationality Act of 1940, 54 Stat. 1169, residence in the country of naturalization was required for expatriation. The Court held that the woman's subsequent residence in Italy satisfied the requirement.

PEREZ *v.* BROWNELL.

may be born to a double allegiance; but no man
should be permitted to place himself in a position
where his services may be claimed by more than one
government and his allegiance be due to more than
one." [21]

Our decisions, then, establish a power of Congress to
declare citizenship forfeit contrary to the will of the citizen no broader than is necessary to prevent the acquisition
of dual nationality. Whether there is also power to prevent the retention of dual nationality in certain circumstances, see *Nishikawa* v. *Dulles, post,* p. ——; or whether
there is power to make the loss of United States citizenship follow from acts of abandonment of citizenship which
prove adherence to a foreign country even though technically its nationality is not acquired, we do not need now to
decide.[22] We do conclude, however, that whatever implied power there may be in Congress to regulate citizenship does not warrant either of the statutory provisions
involved in this case.

III.

Section 401 (e). The Government contends:

"Since voting is one of the highest duties of a citizen, it normally connotes an intimate participation
in the public affairs of the foreign country and a
strong attachment to that state. Indeed, in most
countries only nationals (or those who have indicated their intention to become nationals) can vote.
The connection with foreign political processes and
with foreign obligations is very close; a form of

---

[21] H. R. Doc. No. 326, 59th Cong., 2d Sess. 23.

[22] Taking an oath of allegiance to a foreign state, made to result
in loss of United States nationality by § 401 (b) of the Nationality
Act of 1940, need not result in acquiring the nationality of the
foreign state. See Flournoy, Naturalization and Expatriation, 31
Yale L. J. 702, 848, 858.

PEREZ *v.* BROWNELL.

political allegiance to the other state is shown by the very act of voting.   Congress could therefore reasonably declare that Americans who voted abroad should cease to be Americans."

The difficulty with this argument is that because of the breadth of the statute and its absolute effect we cannot be concerned merely with what voting "normally" connotes.   The statute is not limited to voting in countries where only nationals can vote.   We note that the 1928 presidential election was the first in this country in which no alien was eligible to vote.[23]   Voting in a foreign political election is not made merely evidence of expatriation but is made conclusive of the question.   Congress has painted with so broad a brush that our inquiry must be what voting *necessarily* connotes.   So inquiring, we find that voting in a foreign election may be a most equivocal act and one which need not raise any of the international complications through dual claims of allegiance with which Congress is empowered to deal.   The implication of foreign allegiance is too slight,[24] the possibilities of international embarrassments too suppositious to permit any voting in a foreign political election to result automatically in expatriation and, so far as the record shows for the petitioner in the case at bar, statelessness.[25]   In terms of the

---

[23] Aylsworth, The Passing of Alien Suffrage, 25 Am. Pol. Sci. Rev. 114.

[24] If the statute is viewed as establishing a conclusive presumption from the fact of foreign voting that the voter intended to renounce his United States citizenship or cast his lot with a foreign country, it is subject to the defect stated by this Court in *Manley* v. *Georgia*, 279 U. S. 1, 7. "The connection between the fact proved and that presumed is not sufficient." See also *Tot* v. *United States*, 319 U. S. 463; *Bailey* v. *Alabama*, 219 U. S. 219.

[25] The Government suggests that petitioner is also a citizen of Mexico. This fact does not appear of record, and if it is true, it is a mere fortuity since the statute is not so limited in its operation.

PEREZ *v.* BROWNELL.

Due Process Clause of the Fifth Amendment, a limitation on congressional power in this as in all other areas, there is not the requisite relationship between § 401 (c) and the interest legitimately to be served by expatriation legislation.

Section 401 (j). The Government contends:

> "[A] statute prescribing loss of nationality for one who remains out of the country to avoid military service is a reasonable exercise of the power of Congress. The problem of draft evaders who remain out of the country in a period of war or national emergency in order to avoid a fundamental obligation of citizenship—service in defense of the nation—is manifestly a serious one. It is rendered peculiarly grave by the fact that, in remaining out of the country, such persons put themselves out of the reach of ordinary criminal sanctions which apply to draft evaders within the country. Moreover, these men present a problem in international relations since, so far as other countries are concerned, they remain United States citizens, while, so far as this nation is concerned, they have rejected the obligations of citizenship."

We do not agree that for avoidance of even "a fundamental obligation of citizenship" there is power in Congress to prescribe loss of citizenship. The power with which we have heretofore dealt derives from this nation's sovereignty, the necessities of its place among the family of nations. The Government urges with respect to the broader power for which it contends that "the act of expatriation must have such a close relation to the cardinal elements of United States nationality and allegiance that it is reasonable, with due consideration for the 'cherished status' of American citizenship . . . , for Congress to impose loss of nationality as a result of the commission

PEREZ *v.* BROWNELL.

of the act." We do not believe that the Fourteenth Amendment guarantee of citizenship allows any such balancing of interests. Under our system sanctions against anti-social acts, including violations of the obligations of citizenship, are the business of the criminal courts. The draft evader as well as the tax evader is subject to criminal prosecution and such penalties as Congress may prescribe, limited, of course, by the Eighth Amendment's ban on cruel and unusual punishment.

We can appreciate the seriousness of the offense which led Congress to enact § 401 (j). The citizen who plays fast and loose with the obligations of his citizenship by remaining away from his native land in her hour of need and then attempting to re-enter to resume the benefits of his citizenship is deserving of no sympathy and calls for adequate punishment. And the same can be said for the man who evades military service while remaining in this country. We cannot hold that the problems of extradition and the statute of limitations justify rendering the one stateless (as well as liable to criminal prosecution) while punishing the other only by a prison term.[26] This branch of the Government's argument suggests— though elsewhere a penal intent for § 401 is expressly disavowed—that § 401 (j) might be regarded as a penal sanction in aid of the congressional power to raise and equip armies. So regarded, the statute of course has the fatal defect that punishment would be imposed without any of the substantive and procedural safeguards of a criminal trial. This defect alone is all that is needed to dispose of the Government's appeal to history for sup-

---

[26] The only tolling statute is 18 U. S. C. § 3290, providing that "No statute of limitations shall extend to any person fleeing from justice." At bar Government counsel expressed doubt that the statute would apply to one *remaining* outside the country to avoid the draft or prosecution for draft evasion. But if it does not so apply it could easily be made to do so.

PEREZ *v.* BROWNELL.

port of § 401 (j). The Act of March 3, 1865, 13 Stat.
490, provided for forfeiture of "rights of citizenship" of
deserters and those who, enrolled for the draft, departed
from the district of their enrollment or the United States
with intent to avoid the draft. Whatever else may be
said of that statute,[27] it was in terms penal,[28] and, although
it was never construed as to draft evaders, this Court said
by way of dictum in *Kurtz* v. *Moffit,* 115 U. S. 487, 501,
that a deserter's rights of citizenship could be forfeited,
if at all, only upon conviction by a court-martial.

We recognize that only the most compelling considerations should lead to the invalidation of an Act of Congress, and where it is a matter of legislative judgment
this Court will not intervene. But the Court also has its
duty—that of protecting the fundamental rights of individuals. That duty is imperative when the very citizenship of an individual is at stake—that status which is his
birthright and which alone assures him of the continued
enjoyment of the precious rights conferred by our Constitution. Finding no power in Congress to take away
citizenship for the acts described by § 401 (e) and (j),
we reverse the judgment of the Court of Appeals and
remand to the District Court for proceedings in conformity
with this opinion.

It is so ordered.

---

[27] See *Trop* v. *Dulles, post,* p. ——.

[28] See 1 Codification of the Nationality Laws of the United States,
H. R. Committee Print, 76th Cong., 1st Sess. 68.

Circulated: JUN 5 19

SUPREME COURT OF THE UNITED STATES

Recirculated:_____

No. 710.—October Term, 1956.

Albert L. Trop, Petitioner,
v.
John Foster Dulles, as Secretary of State of the United States, et al.

On Writ of Certiorari to the United States Court of Appeals for the Second Circuit.

[June —, 1957.]

Mr. Chief Justice Warren delivered the opinion of the Court.

In this case, a companion to *Perez* v. *Brownell, ante,* p. ——, there are presented questions of the construction and validity of § 401 (g) of the Nationality Act of 1940.

"A person who is a national of the United States, whether by birth or naturalization, shall lose his nationality by:

. . . . .

"(g) Deserting the military or naval forces of the United States in time of war, provided he is convicted thereof by court martial and as the result of such conviction is dismissed or dishonorably discharged from the service of such military or naval forces: *Provided,* That notwithstanding loss of nationality or citizenship or civil or political rights under the terms of this or previous Acts by reason of desertion committed in time of war, restoration to active duty with such military or naval forces in time of war or the reenlistment or induction of such a person in time of war with permission of competent military or naval authority, prior or subsequent to the effective date of this Act, shall be deemed to have the immediate effect of restoring such nationality or

* JMHP.

TROP *v.* DULLES.

citizenship and all civil and political rights heretofore
or hereafter so lost and of removing all civil and
political disabilities resulting therefrom . . . ." [1]

Petitioner is a native born citizen of the United States.
As an Army private serving in French Morocco in 1944,
he was confined in Casablanca for a breach of discipline.
He escaped and surrendered himself the next day. He
was charged with desertion, tried by a general court-
martial, convicted and sentenced to three years at hard
labor, forfeiture of all pay and allowances and a dishonorable discharge. In 1952, having returned to this country,
petitioner applied for a passport. It was denied him
on the ground that he had lost his nationality under
§ 401 (g). There followed this action for a declaratory
judgment that petitioner is a citizen. The District Court
granted respondent's motion for summary judgment, and
the Court of Appeals for the Second Circuit affirmed,
Chief Judge Clark dissenting.[2] We granted certiorari.
352 U. S. 1023.

I.

Petitioner first urges that we construe the statute so
that it would not be applicable to him. He suggests a
construction which would limit the operation of the
statute to those who desert to the enemy. The only reason he assigns for such a reading of the subsection is to
avoid serious constitutional questions. We are, of course,
fully cognizant of the obligation of this Court, when a
serious constitutional question is raised, "first [to] ascertain whether a construction of the statute is fairly possible by which the question may be avoided." *Crowell*
v. *Benson*, 285 U. S. 22, 62. See *United States* v. *Wit-*

---

[1] 54 Stat. 1168, as amended, 58 Stat. 4. The current provision is
§ 348 (a)(8) of the Immigration and Nationality Act of 1952, 66 Stat.
267, 8 U. S. C. § 1481 (a)(8).

[2] 239 F. 2d 527.

TROP *v.* DULLES.

kovich, 353 U. S. ——, for a recent example of our following that principle. But here we do not believe the limited construction of the statute suggested by petitioner is fairly possible. First, the plain language of the subsection is directed toward the military crime of desertion, of which going over to the enemy is not a necessary element.[3] Secondly, the proviso added in 1944, 58 Stat. 4, for possible restoration of nationality by restoration to duty strongly suggests that Congress viewed the statute as applicable to any kind of deserter; the restoration to duty of one who deserts to the enemy would be an extraordinary occurrence. Finally, § 403 (a) of the Nationality Act of 1940, 54 Stat. 1169, excepted only subsections (g) and (h) from the rule it established that the acts specified by § 401 must take place outside the United States or be followed by residence abroad to result in expatriation. Desertion to the enemy within the United States, while not impossible, is an unlikely event.

II.

We come then to the constitutional issue, and what we have said in *Perez v. Brownell, supra,* is largely dispositive of the issue here. We hold here in connection with § 401 (g) as we did there in connection with § 401 (j) of the Nationality Act of 1940, that Congress has no power to prescribe loss of citizenship as the consequence of conduct inconsistent with fundamental obligations of citizenship. The Fourteenth Amendment leaves no authority in Congress to decide who among United States citizens are deserving of continued citizenship, no matter what their shortcomings may be. Furthermore, it seems clear that

---

[3] At the time of petitioner's conviction, the offense was defined by the Articles of War as follows:

"Any person subject to military law who quits his organization or place of duty with the intent to avoid hazardous duty or to shirk important service shall be deemed a deserter." 41 Stat. 792.

TROP *v.* DULLES.

there is no rational relation between the operative effect of this statute as applied to a deserter who does not go over to the enemy and the congressional power to regulate citizenship in the interest of preventing the acquisition or retention of dual nationality. The Government stated in argument that if its position is sustained a young Army draftee in a camp in this country would automatically become stateless if he were tried as a deserter, convicted and sentenced to be dishonorably discharged.

The Government does not attempt to sustain the statute as a punitive sanction in aid of Congress' power to make rules for the government and regulation of the land and naval forces. U. S. Const., Art. I, § 8, cl. 14. We accept the contention that Congress intended only to exercise whatever power it possesses independently to prescribe conditions for the loss of citizenship. The phraseology of the subsection, its placement with other provisions that are clearly not penal,[4] point in this direction. It is true that the Cabinet Committee which proposed the 1940 Nationality Act referred to the Act of 1865 punishing deserters by forfeiture of their rights of citizenship as a precedent for § 401 (g).[5] But the committee went on to say that § 401 (g) "technically is not a penal law."[6] The indication that Congress meant to override this view or envisaged § 401 (g) as creating an additional penalty which could be imposed upon deserters

---

[4] See *Perez* v. *Brownell, ante.* p. ——, n. 1.

[5] I Codification of the Nationality Laws of the United States, H. R. Committee Print, 76th Cong., 1st Sess. 68.

[6] *Ibid.* In a letter of submittal, Secretaries Hull and Perkins and Attorney General Cummings said:

"None of the various provisions in the Code concerning loss of American nationality . . . is designed to be punitive or to interfere with freedom of action. They are merely intended to deprive persons of American nationality when such persons, by their own acts, or inaction, show that their real attachment is to the foreign country and not to the United States." *Id.,* at VII.

TROP *v.* DULLES.

by a court-martial is too nebulous to serve as the basis for finding a penal intent.[7]

Thus, we need not consider petitioner's further contention that expatriation, at least when it leads to statelessness, constitutes cruel and unusual punishment in violation of the Eighth Amendment. That this claim is not far-fetched is evidenced by the fact the Chief Judge of the court below took it as the ground for his dissent.[8] Nor need we consider whether the affirmative grant of citizenship by § 1 of the Fourteenth Amendment in and of itself precludes the use of expatriation as a punishment for a criminal act. We entertain the gravest doubts about the power of Congress to authorize a military or civil tribunal to condemn an American citizen to statelessness as punishment. It will be time enough to resolve these doubts should Congress manifest a purpose to exercise such a purported power.

A further word should be said about the Act of 1865. The Government contends that the long existence of this statute puts a gloss of many years of history on § 401 (g).[9] But the statute was, as we have said, obviously penal; the phrase "rights of citizenship" is ambiguous and was never

---

[7] The only such indication is found in the Report of the Senate Committee, which said:

"Desertion from the military or naval service of the United States in time of war would, as under present law, result in loss of citizenship after conviction by court martial. A new section provides for loss of citizenship through the commission of any act of treason against the United States, or attempting by force to overthrow it, or to bear arms against it. Because the penalty is so drastic, it would follow only after conviction by court martial or a court of competent jurisdiction." S. Rep. No. 2150, 76th Cong., 3d Sess. 3.

[8] 239 F. 2d, at 530. See also Comment, The Expatriation Act of 1954, 64 Yale L. J. 1164, 1187–1194, 1199–1200.

[9] The statute, 13 Stat. 490, was amended in 1912 to make it inapplicable in times of peace, 37 Stat. 356, and repealed by § 504 of the Nationality Act of 1940, 54 Stat. 1172.

TROP *v.* DULLES.

authoritatively construed by this Court; [10] and, most
significantly, this Court never passed upon the validity
of the Act.   There is only the passing reference to it in
Kurtz v. *Moffitt,* 115 U. S. 487, 501, where the Court, in
quite a different context—holding that a state peace officer
had no authority to arrest an alleged deserter without a
warrant—stated in dictum its agreement with a number
of state courts that conviction by court-martial must pre-
cede the forfeiture imposed by the Act.[11]

The judgment of the Court of Appeals is reversed and
the cause remanded to the District Court for proceedings
in conformity with this opinion.

It is so ordered.

---

[10] It appears that administratively the phrase "rights of citizenship"
was taken to mean "citizenship." See Foreign Relations 1873, H. R.
Exec. Doc. No. 1, 43d Cong., 1st Sess., Pt. 1, Vol. II, p. 1187 (View
of Secretary of State Fish) ; H. R. Doc. No. 326, 59th Cong., 2d Sess.
159 (State Department Board) ; Hearings before the House Committee on Immigration and Naturalization on H. R. 6127, superseded
by H. R. 9980, 76th Cong., 1st Sess. 132–133 (testimony of Mr.
Flournoy, State Department representative).   However, in 1924
President Coolidge granted amnesty and pardon to persons convicted
of deserting after the Armistice of November 11, 1918, but while
the United States was still technically at war. He "fully remitted
as to such persons any relinquishment or forfeiture of their rights
of citizenship" and spoke of many of them as having "reestablished
themselves in the confidence of their *fellow citizens.*" (Emphasis
supplied.) 43 Stat. 1940. See Roche, The Loss of American
Nationality, 99 U. of Pa. L. Rev. 25, 60–62.

[11] See *State* v. *Symonds,* 57 Me. 148; *Severance* v. *Healey,* 50 N. H.
448; *Goetchens* v. *Matthewson,* 58 Barb. 152, rev'd on other grounds,
61 N. Y. 420; *Huber* v. *Reily,* 53 Pa. 112.

At the *Perez-Trop* conference, as already seen, the Chief Justice had five votes in favor of his view for reversal. It was, however, too late in the term for the cases to be decided on the basis of the Warren draft opinions of the Court. Even some in the bare majority had what Justice Frankfurter termed "doubts and uncertainties"[10] about the decisions and the Warren drafts. Thus, Justice Harlan's already quoted comment to Justice Frankfurter (p. 79), a week after the conference on the cases, indicated that his vote with the majority was anything but firm.[11] And a memorandum of another majority Justice stresses the weaknesses of the *Perez* draft opinion.[12] The draft does not really explain why the denationalization power was beyond the power of Congress. It analyses the prior cases that upheld voluntary renunciation of citizenship and then asserts, without supporting reasoning or authority, that Congress could not provide for involuntary expatriation in this case.

The minority Justices would, of course, not agree to the Warren drafts, but they also complained about the lack of time to deal adequately with such important cases. In a *Memorandum for the Conference* circulated June 7, 1957, two days after receiving Chief Justice Warren's *Perez* draft, Justice Frankfurter stated that he would prepare a dissent. However, he wrote,

> The issues at stake are too far-reaching and the subject matter calls for too extensive an investigation, let alone the time necessary for writing an adequate opinion, that I shall not attempt the preparation of such an opinion before the Term closes. I shall content myself with noting my inability to agree and the promise of filing an opinion at the next Term of Court.[13]

With the cases in this posture, the Justices decided to hold the expatriation cases for the following term. On June 24, the Court issued an order setting the cases for reargument in October.[14] In a letter a year later, Justice Frankfurter explained that the conference had yielded to his claim that more time was needed: "There are situations when the feeling of a Brother that he needs the summer, as it were, to work on setting forth his views in a case should delay handing down a decision. Such a situation was presented by the *Expatriation Cases* at the end of last Term." With this factor and the doubts about the cases already noted, "Nothing could have been more appropriate to the circumstances of that situation than to set the cases down for reargument."[15]

The *Perez* and *Trop* cases were reargued on October 28, 1957. At the conference the next day, most of the Justices adhered to the positions they had taken at the May 5 conference on the cases. But there were crucial vote changes. Justice Harlan, who had voted originally to reverse, was now for affirmance in both cases. Justice Brennan changed his *Perez* vote to affirmance, though he was still for reversal in *Trop*. Justice Whittaker stuck to his vote to affirm in *Perez*, but had changed his mind and voted to reverse in *Trop*.

The October 29 conference left the Chief Justice with his bare *Trop* majority. However, since Justices Harlan and Whittaker had switched positions, the vote for reversal was now Chief Justice Warren and Justices Black, Douglas, Brennan, and Whittaker, with the remaining four for affirmance. In *Perez*, the decision itself had changed. Since Justices Harlan and Brennan had altered their votes, there was now a six-to-three decision for affirmance, with only Chief Justice Warren and Justices Black and Douglas still for reversal.

Justice Frankfurter was now the senior majority Justice in *Perez*, and he assigned the opinion to himself. He soon prepared a draft opinion of the Court essentially similar to his final opinion in the case. Justice Frankfurter also tried to persuade Justice Whittaker to change his *Trop* vote again and, during the next month, Justice Whittaker did switch his vote once more. This now gave Justice Frankfurter a bare majority in *Trop* and he circulated a draft opinion of the Court similar to his ultimate dissent in the case.

The change in the *Perez* decision meant a narrowing in the scope of the case. The Frankfurter opinion sustained the divestiture of citizenship because Perez had voted in a foreign election, holding that Section 401(e) of the Nationality Act was a valid exercise of Congressional expatriation power. The decision to that effect made it unnecessary to determine whether Perez's citizenship could also be taken away because he had been outside the country to avoid the draft during World War II. Hence, the *Perez* opinion no longer dealt with the question of the constitutionality of Section 401(j),[16] which the Warren draft opinion of the Court in June had also answered in the negative.

The changed votes in *Perez* and *Trop* left the Chief Justice with a minority in both cases. He circulated draft dissents on March 14, 1958, that were more elaborate than the draft opinions of the Court he had circulated the previous June. They were basically similar to the final Warren opinions in the cases. Like the Frankfurter *Perez* opinion, the Warren dissent did not go into the constitutionality of Section 401(j). That issue was left for the *Mendoza-Martinez* case, which is the subject of the next chapter.

Chief Justice Warren's redrafted *Trop* opinion was now based on another theory that the Chief Justice had stated at the October 29 conference: that loss of citizenship was a punishment that Congress had no power to impose. The redraft asserted that taking away citizenship for Trop's desertion was imposition of cruel and unusual punishment, a point that had been mentioned, though expressly left open, in the June 1957 Warren *Trop* draft.

After Chief Justice Warren circulated his draft *Trop* dissent, Justice Whittaker once more changed his vote and joined the Chief Justice's opinion. This meant that Chief Justice Warren again had a bare majority for reversal in *Trop*. But the Chief Justice had to deliver his *Trop* opinion as that of a plurality only, since Justice Brennan wrote him on March 12, 1958, that he could not join and was filing his own opinion.[17]

The *Perez* decision was announced by Justice Frankfurter on March 31, with an opinion of the Court based on the Justice's already-referred-to draft. The opinion was supported by only a bare majority (Justices Frankfurter, Burton, Clark, Harlan, and Brennan). Justice Whittaker had written to Justice Frankfurter on March 5 that he had reconsidered the case and now concluded that Section 401(e) "is broader than was within the constitutional power of Congress to declare."[18] Justice Whittaker switched his vote here also and joined the Warren *Perez* dissent.

As already indicated, had Chief Justice Warren's original June 5 drafts been issued as the *Perez* and *Trop* opinions of the Court, the law on expatriation would have been settled in favor of the Chief Justice's restricted view on Congressional power in the matter. Further case law on the subject would have been unnecessary. Instead, the *Perez* and *Trop* decisions that were finally handed down reached inconsistent results on the extent of expatriation authority. The confusion in the matter was compounded when the Court decided the *Mendoza-Martinez* case. The result was that, as the Court itself was to admit almost ten years later with regard to *Perez*, "That case . . . has been a source of controversy and confusion ever since."[19]

In 1967, however, the confusion was eliminated when the Court finally adopted the approach to expatriation power taken in the original Warren *Perez-Trop* draft opinions of the Court. That occurred in *Aroyim* v. *Rusk*,[20] where the constitutionality of Section 401(e) of the Nationality Act was again at issue. Aforyim had been denied a passport on the ground that he had lost his citizenship under Section 401(e) by voting in an election in Israel. He brought a declaratory judgment action and urged the Court to reconsider the *Perez* case, adopt the view of the Warren dissent there, and overrule the *Perez* decision.

The Court, by a bare majority, agreed and overruled *Perez*. Justice Black's *Afroyim* opinion of the Court struck down Section 401(e) on essentially the same theory of expatriation which Chief Justice Warren had asserted in his original *Perez-Trop* drafts, that citizenship could only be lost voluntarily, which meant that Congress had no power to take away citizenship for acts that did not amount to a voluntary renunciation. As summarized in *Afroyim*, "Our holding does no more than to give to this citizen that which is his own, a constitutional right to remain a citizen in a free country unless he voluntarily relinquishes that citizenship."[21] The Court thus finally adopted the position taken in the May 5, 1957, *Perez-Trop* conference and the original Warren draft opinions of the Court in those cases.

Notes

1. 356 U.S. 44 (1958).
2. 356 U.S. 86 (1958).
3. FF-HHB, TCC, JMH, WJB, CEW, June 25, 1958. FFLC.
4. FF-JMH, May 9, 1957. FFH.
5. HHBLC.
6. Loc. cit. supra note 4.
7. HLB-Fred Rodell, Sept. 5, 1962. HLBLC.
8. Handwritten at top of loc. cit. supra note 4.
9. 387 U.S. 253 (1967).
10. Loc. cit. supra note 4.
11. Supra note 8.
12. WJB, No. 44, The *Perez* Opinion.
13. FF, *Memorandum for the Conference Re: No. 572—*Perez v. Brownell, June 7, 1957. FFH.
14. 354 U.S. 934 (1957).
15. Loc. cit. supra note 3.
16. See 356 U.S. at 62.
17. WJB-EW, March 12, 1958.
18. CEW-FF, March 5, 1958. FFH.
19. *Afroyim* v. *Rusk,* 387 U.S. 253, 255 (1967).
20. Supra note 9.
21. 387 U.S. at 268.

4

Kennedy v. Mendoza-Martinez (1963): Expatriation as Punishment

The discussion of the *Perez* and *Trop* cases[1] in the last chapter presented two possible scenarios for the Supreme Court's resolution of the issue of the constitutional extent of expatriation power. The first was presented by Chief Justice Warren's original draft opinions of the Court. They would have settled the law in favor of the restricted view ultimately taken nine years later in *Afroyim* v. *Rusk*.[2] The second was that written by the opinions ultimately issued in the *Perez* and *Trop* cases. They left the law on the subject in a confused state that was not cleared up for almost a decade by the *Afroyim* decision.

But a third scenario was also possible. That was the case because *Kennedy* v. *Mendoza-Martinez*,[3] which followed the *Trop* approach in further limiting expatriation power, had at first been decided the other way. Had the draft opinion that Justice Stewart originally wrote been issued as the *Mendoza-Martinez* opinion, it might have led to an expansive view of expatriation power. In that case, *Afroyim* v. *Rusk* might not have been decided as it was and the view on expatriation power that would have prevailed might have been the broad one espoused by Justice Frankfurter in the *Perez* and *Trop* cases.

It will be recalled that *Perez* v. *Brownell* originally involved a challenge to two sections of the Nationality Act: Section 401(e), providing for loss of nationality for voting in a foreign election, and Section 401(j), providing for loss of nationality for departing from or remaining outside the United States in time of war or declared national emergency to evade the draft. In his June 1957 *Perez* draft opinion of the Court,[4] the Chief Justice had ruled that both sections were unconstitutional. However, as we saw in the last chapter, the final *Perez* opinion of the Court found it unnecessary to deal with the validity of Section 401(j).

The issue thus avoided in *Perez* was the principal issue presented in the *Mendoza-Martinez* case. *Mendoza-Martinez*, a citizen by birth, had left the country to escape the draft during World War II. On his return, he was convicted of draft evasion. He was later ordered deported as an alien. He then sought a declaratory judgment that he was still a citizen. The lower court found that he had lost his citizenship under Section 401(j). On April 7, 1958, the Supreme Court remanded the case for reconsideration in light of the decision in *Trop* v. *Dulles*.[5] On remand, the lower court held that Section 401(j) was unconstitutional. The case came once more to the Supreme Court on direct appeal during the 1959 term.

The December 11, 1959, conference on *Mendoza-Martinez* voted in favor of reversal, with the Chief Justice and Justices Black and Douglas strongly dissenting on the basis of their positions in the *Perez* and *Trop* cases. Justice Frankfurter, the senior Justice in the tentative majority, assigned the opinion to Justice Stewart. He circulated a draft opinion of the Court in January 1960. Stewart's chief problem was to distinguish the case from *Trop*. The draft found that Section 401(j) was appropriate to the accomplishment of vital objectives under the war power and that it did not impose "punishment" that would call the Eighth Amendment into play. Stewart also wrote that the conduct described in Section 401(j) could rationally be viewed as an abnegation of allegiance, so that Mendoza-Martinez's action could be viewed as a voluntary expatriation.

Justice Brennan refused to join the Stewart draft. Instead, he circulated a draft concurrence stating that Congress could conclude that a dual national who fled to his other country to escape the draft had transferred his allegiance to the other country. That still made six votes for reversal, with Stewart's draft still speaking as the opinion of the Court for five Justices.

At this point the Chief Justice raised a new issue, which sent back the case to the district court again. Chief Justice Warren suggested the possibility that the conviction for draft evasion collaterally estopped the government from impeaching Mendoza-Martinez's citizenship. Since a nonresident alien could not be guilty of draft evasion, the conviction necessarily was based on his continued citizenship, and the government could not now deny that he was still a citizen. If Warren was correct on the estoppel issue, that would make decision of the constitutional issue unnecessary and the Justices agreed that the issue should be explored further by the lower court. Even Justice Frankfurter, who strongly supported the Stewart draft, stated, "I do not think that this new matter—a claim of collateral estoppel—should be considered here as though this were a court of first instance."[6] On April 18, 1960, the Court issued a *per curiam* remanding the case for consideration of the issue.[7]

On remand, the lower court held that the government was not estopped from now asserting the loss of citizenship and, on the merits, reaffirmed its earlier ruling that Section 401(j) was unconstitutional. The case again came back to the Supreme Court for reargument in the 1961 term. At the October 13, 1961, conference, there was once more a majority (this time composed of Justices Frankfurter, Clark, Harlan, Whittaker, and Stewart) in favor of reversing and holding Section 401(j) constitutional.

In addition, another new issue was discussed by the Justices, whether the single district judge had jurisdiction or whether, since a judgment of unconstitutionality had been entered, a special three-judge district court was necessary. The issue had been raised for the first time in a *Memorandum to the Conference* circulated by Justice Brennan on October 5, 1961, a few days before the reargument on the case.[8]

Brennan had raised the issue as a delaying tactic to avoid a decision in favor of constitutionality. But the conference majority voted in favor of the district judge's jurisdiction. An October 10 memorandum by Justice Frankfurter pointed out that the statute requiring a three-judge court[9] applied only to an injunction suit against a federal statute on the ground of unconstitutionality, not to a suit for a declaratory judgment such as that brought by Mendoza-Martinez. Frankfurter stressed the difference, saying,

> I do not subscribe to the view that the mischief of ill-considered restraint on governmental operations at which Congress was aiming will be set loose by our refusing to extend §2282 to declaratory judgments. The unavailability of an immediate contempt sanction, coupled with the balancing of convenience that a three-judge court would undertake if asked to translate a declaration into an injunction, seems to me a sufficient distinction and, if need be, safeguard.[10]

Once again, Justice Stewart was assigned the majority opinion. In January 1962 he circulated the draft opinion of the Court printed (in a version recirculated January 25) on p. 113. The Stewart draft rejected the estoppel argument and followed the Frankfurter view that no three-judge court was necessary. On the constitutional merits, the Stewart draft was similar to his January 1960 draft, which has been mentioned. The draft noted the government's argument that Section 401(j) had a direct relationship to foreign affairs. It was, however, unnecessary to decide whether the foreign affairs power could justify denationalization for the conduct in question. "For it is apparent that Congress in enacting the statute was drawing upon another power, broad and far-reaching"—namely, the war power. Congress was relying on this power in its enactment of Section 401(j). "The desire to end a potential drain upon the country's military manpower . . . constituted a purpose having sufficient rational nexus to the exercise of the war power."

In addition, the Stewart draft stressed the legitimacy of Congressional concern with the effect on wartime morale of the existence of a group who had fled the country to avoid the draft. Expatriation was a reasonable measure to deal with this problem. "The declaration that those in this separate and clearly identifiable class had permanently relinquished their citizenship constituted a solution to the problem which was both rational and efficacious."

The *Trop* case was distinguished on the ground that "the deprivation of citizenship effected by this statute is not 'punishment' in the constitutional sense." Instead it "dealt with a basic problem of wartime morale reaching far beyond concern for any individual affected." Mendoza-Martinez's actions "involved conduct inconsistent with undiluted allegiance to this country." The statute was thus a rational "exercise of power [by] Congress to recognize an abandonment of citizenship by those who have abandoned this nation to avoid defending it in time of need."

In terms of the developing law on expatriation power, the Stewart draft would have gone far toward establishing broad Congressional authority if it had come down as the *Mendoza-Martinez* opinion of the Court. Justice Stewart started his discussion of the constitutional issue with the basic "proposition that Congress may make expatriation the consequence of the voluntary conduct of the citizen, irrespective of the citizen's subjective intention to renounce his nationality, and irrespective too of his awareness that denationalization may be the result of his conduct." This would have done away with the Warren conception of expatriation power as limited to cases involving voluntary acquisition of dual nationality. Instead, denationalization could be imposed for specified acts that did not amount to willing renunciations of citizenship. All that was needed to sustain expatriation laws was that "the deprivation of citizenship [for the acts specified] must bear a rational relationship to an affirmative power possessed by Congress under the Constitution."

SUPREME COURT OF THE UNITED STATES

No. 19.—OCTOBER TERM, 1961.

Robert F. Kennedy, Attorney General of the United States, Appellant,	On Appeal From the United States District Court for the Southern District of California.
v.	
Francisco Mendoza-Martinez.	

[February —, 1962.]

MR. JUSTICE STEWART delivered the opinion of the Court.

Section 401 of the Nationality Act of 1940, as amended in 1944, provided that:

> "A person who is a national of the United States, whether by birth or naturalization, shall lose his nationality by: . . . (j) Departing from or remaining outside of the jurisdiction of the United States in time of war or during a period declared by the President to be a period of national emergency for the purpose of evading or avoiding training and service in the land or naval forces of the United States." [1]

The facts in the present case are not in dispute, having been stipulated by the parties. The appellee was born in this country in 1922, and was therefore a citizen of the United States by birth. Under the laws of Mexico, appellee has also been a citizen of that Republic all his life. During 1942 he left the United States and went to Mexico for the single purpose of evading and avoiding training and service in the armed forces of the United

---

[1] 54 Stat. 1168, as amended by the Act of September 27, 1944 (58 Stat. 746). This provision has now been incorporated into § 349 of the Immigration and Nationality Act of 1952, 66 Stat. 163, 267–268, 8 U. S. C. § 1481.

KENNEDY *v.* MENDOZA-MARTINEZ.

States. He remained in Mexico continuously from 1942 until November 1946 for that sole purpose. In 1947, upon his plea of guilty in the United States District Court for the Southern District of California, he was convicted of violating § 11 of the Selective Training and Service Act of 1940, and was sentenced to imprisonment for one year and a day. In 1953 he was served with a warrant of arrest in deportation proceedings. Pursuant to this warrant, a deportation hearing was held before a Special Inquiry Officer, who thereafter ordered the appellee to be deported from the United States as an alien. An appeal from this decision was dismissed by the Board of Immigration Appeals.

The appellee then brought suit in a United States District Court for a judgment declaring him to be a national of the United States. The sole basis of his action was the claim that § 401 (j) of the Nationality Act, under which he had been found by the administrative authorities to have lost his United States citizenship, was unconstitutional. The court rejected the appellee's claim of unconstitutionality, and its judgment was affirmed by the United States Court of Appeals for the Ninth Circuit, 238 F. 2d 239. This Court (356 U. S. 258) granted a petition for a writ of certiorari, summarily vacated the judgment of the Ninth Circuit, and remanded the cause to the District Court for reconsideration in the light of our intervening decision in *Trop* v. *Dulles,* 356 U. S. 86.

On remand the trial court in an unreported opinion rendered a judgment declaring that § 401 (j) was unconstitutional. The case came here again, this time on direct appeal.[2] After oral argument the Court *sua sponte* raised the possibility of a dispositive nonconstitutional

---

[2] 28 U. S. C. § 1252: "Any party may appeal to the Supreme Court from an interlocutory or final judgment, decree or order of any court of the United States . . . holding an Act of Congress unconstitutional

KENNEDY *v.* MENDOZA-MARTINEZ.

question, and again remanded the case to the District Court, with permission to the parties to amend their pleadings to put in issue the question of whether the indictment and conviction of the appellee for draft evasion in 1947 operated collaterally to estop the Government from later claiming that he had lost his United States citizenship while in Mexico. 362 U. S. 384. On remand the District Court in an unreported opinion again entered judgment in favor of the appellee, holding that the Government was not estopped from asserting that the appellee had lost his United States citizenship, and reaffirming its prior ruling that § 401 (j) was unconstitutional. The case is now here for the third time.

Although the basic issue which has from the outset been tendered by this litigation is the constitutionality of § 401 (j) of the Nationality Act, that issue cannot be reached in this case if, as the appellee contends, the United States is estopped from asserting that he has lost his citizenship. Nor can we reach the underlying constitutional issue, if, as has now been suggested, the appellee's suit should have been presented *nisi prius* to a statutory three-judge District Court, rather than, as it was, to a single judge. We therefore turn to these two nonconstitutional questions.

I.

It is the appellee's position that his 1947 prosecution and conviction for draft evasion necessarily amounted to a judicial determination that he had not lost his American citizenship. To understand his argument it is necessary to examine the indictment and judgment in that criminal proceeding, as well as the provisions of the law under which the prosecution was brought.

---

in any civil action, suit, or proceeding to which the United States or any of its agencies, or any officer or employee thereof, as such officer or employee, is a party."

KENNEDY *v.* MENDOZA-MARTINEZ.

The single count of the indictment to which the appellee pleaded guilty in 1947 alleged that he had been "a male person within the class made subject to selective service under the Selective Training and Service Act of 1940;" that he had registered with his Draft Board in Kern County, California; and that:

> ". . . on or about November 15, 1942, in violation of the provisions of said act and the regulations promulgated thereunder, the defendant did knowingly evade service in the land or naval forces of the United States of America in that he did knowingly depart from the United States and go to a foreign country, namely: Mexico, for the purpose of evading service in the land or naval forces of the United States and did there remain until on or about November 1, 1946."

The indictment contained two additional counts. One charged the appellee with failure to report for induction on December 11, 1942, as ordered; the other charged him with failure to keep his draft board advised where mail would reach him.

The judgment of conviction on his plea of guilty recited that he had:

> ". . . on or about November 15th 1942, knowingly departed from the United States to Mexico, for the purpose of evading service in the land or naval forces of the United States and . . . remained there until on or about November 1st 1946."

The judgment further ordered:

> ". . . that the second and third counts be dismissed, it appearing to the court that the offenses charged therein arose out of the same circumstances."

The Selective Training and Service Act of 1940, under which the appellee was prosecuted, provided in pertinent part that "every male citizen of the United States, and

KENNEDY *v.* MENDOZA-MARTINEZ.

every other male person residing in the United States
[of a specified age group] . . . shall be liable for training
and service. . . ."[3] By its terms the statute thus
imposed the duty of military service upon citizens and
resident aliens, but not upon nonresident aliens.

The appellee points out that on September 27, 1944,
when Congress enacted § 401 (j), he was not in the
United States, but in Mexico. He says that the provisions of § 401 (j) purported on that date to strip him of
his citizenship and thus to make him a nonresident alien.[4]
Since a nonresident alien could not be guilty of draft
evasion, and since, he argues, both the indictment and the
judgment rested on a charge of draft evasion from 1942
to and including 1946, his conviction necessarily amounted
to a government admission and a judicial determination
that he remained a citizen after the enactment of § 401 (j)
in 1944. In other words, he argues that the judgment
finding him guilty of draft evasion after September 27,
1944, necessarily comprehended a determination that he
continued to be a citizen after that date.

The District Court rejected this argument, ruling "that
the prior criminal proceedings against [the appellee] did
not necessarily or in actual fact make any determination
as to [the appellee's] citizenship and, therefore, the doctrine of collateral estoppel is not applicable." The court
pointed out that in 1942 the appellee was liable for induction, whether he was a United States citizen or only a
resident; that, in either event, if he left the United States
to avoid the draft, he was subject to prosecution upon

---

[3] 54 Stat. 885, as amended; 55 Stat. 844 *et seq.*

[4] The Government points out that though the appellee was then in
Mexico, there is nothing to show that he did not still "reside" in the
United States. It argues that the word "residing" in the Selective
Service Act referred to legal residence and not mere geographic
location. In the view we take of the case, this inquiry need not be
pursued.

KENNEDY *v.* MENDOZA-MARTINEZ.

his return; and that, therefore, the 1947 prosecution did not involve the issue of his nationality. We agree with that conclusion.

We accept the appellee's premise that collateral estoppel "may arise from a criminal proceeding to estop a party in a subsequent civil action." *Emich Motors Corp.* v. *General Motors Corp.,* 340 U. S. 558. We accept also the contention that collateral estoppel may operate to bar the United States from relitigating a party's status, even though the first court's determination of status was erroneous. *United States* v. *Moser,* 266 U. S. 236. But the doctrine of collateral estoppel, as distinguished from *res judicata,* operates to preclude relitigation only of those factual questions which were actually put in issue in the prior proceedings or necessarily comprehended in the prior judgment. *Cromwell* v. *County of Sac,* 94 U. S. 351, 352–353, 369; *Frank* v. *Magnum,* 237 U. S. 309, 334.

In the present case, the appellee's citizenship was certainly not an issue actually litigated in the 1947 proceedings. The indictment and judgment make clear that the gravamen of the appellee's offense was leaving the country to escape induction into the armed forces in 1942. The indictment alleged that the appellee was then "a male person within the class made subject to selective service," a class which included both citizens and noncitizens. There was nothing in the indictment nor in the judgment, therefore, which alleged or determined that he was a citizen at the time he became criminally liable for draft evasion. As the Government correctly points out, a resident alien who fled the country to escape induction was liable to prosecution upon his return. A citizen who departed to evade the draft and returned as an alien was in no different position.

Nor was the issue of appellee's citizenship necessarily determined by the judgment of conviction. The basic fallacy in appellee's position is the assumption that he was

KENNEDY *v.* MENDOZA-MARTINEZ.

indicted and convicted of an offense continuing until 1946. The factual recitals in the indictment and judgment that the appellee remained in Mexico "until on or about November 1, 1946," do not sustain that interpretation. We may assume that draft evasion can properly be considered a single, continuing offense. See *Fogel* v. *United States,* 162 F. 2d 54. This concept would become relevant in protecting a defendant against multiple prosecutions, in determining proper venue, or in assessing the effect of a statute of limitations. See *United States* v. *Cores,* 356 U. S. 405; *Goodman* v. *United States,* 289 F. 2d 256, vacated and remanded, — U. S. —. None of those questions was involved in the prosecution of the appellee in 1947. There is nothing whatever to indicate that the words in the indictment and judgment upon which the appellee so heavily relies were anything more than what they purported to be—a simple statement of fact. If the appellee had been a resident alien instead of a citizen when he left this country in 1942, the indictment and judgment recitals that he remained in Mexico until 1946 would not have operated to determine his citizenship status. The same factual recitals in the actual circumstances of the present case were equally colorless. In either case the statements at most would go to show the period during which the defendant had been a fugitive from justice, tolling the otherwise applicable three-year statute of limitations.[5]

In sum, the 1947 judgment of conviction was not based in any respect upon the appellee's citizenship status either before or after September 27, 1944. It follows that the District Court was correct in concluding that the Government in the present proceeding was not estopped from asserting that the appellee had lost his citizenship under the provisions of § 401 (j) of the Nationality Act.

---

[5] 18 U. S. C. (1946 ed.) §§ 582, 583. See 18 U. S. C. § 3290.

KENNEDY *v.* MENDOZA-MARTINEZ.

II.

This proceeding was brought under § 360 (a) of the
Immigration and Nationality Act of 1952, which authorizes an individual within the United States to bring an
action in a District Court for a declaratory judgment of
citizenship against the head of any government agency
or department which has denied him a right or privilege
of citizenship upon the ground that he is not a national
of the United States.[6] Without objection the cause was
decided by a single district judge—in the first instance
and after each remand by this Court. The belated suggestion has now been made that 28 U. S. C. § 2282 is
applicable to this controversy. Section 2282 forbids the
granting, except by a three-judge District Court, of any
"interlocutory or permanent injunction restraining the
enforcement, operation or execution of any Act of Congress for repugnance to the Constitution of the United
States. . . ." If that section was applicable, the District Court which determined this controversy had no
jurisdiction to do so, and we should be compelled once
again to remand the case, this time for consideration by
a three-judge District Court. See *Federal Housing*

---

[6] 66 Stat. 163, 273–274, 8 U. S. C. § 1503 (a):

"If any person who is within the United States claims a right or
privilege as a national of the United States and is denied such right or
privilege by any department or independent agency, or official thereof,
upon the ground that he is not a national of the United States, such
person may institute an action under the provisions of section 2201 of
Title 28 against the head of such department or independent agency
for a judgment declaring him to be a national of the United States
[with exceptions not here relevant] . . . . An action under this
subsection may be instituted only within five years after the final
administrative denial of such right or privilege and shall be filed in the
district court of the United States for the district in which such
person resides or claims a residence, and jurisdiction over such officials
in such cases is conferred upon those courts." Compare § 503 of
the Nationality Act of 1940, 54 Stat. 1137, 1171–1172.

KENNEDY *v.* MENDOZA-MARTINEZ.

Administration v. *The Darlington, Inc.*, 352 U. S. 977. But we have concluded, for the reasons which follow, that the parties are correct in their view that this case was properly decided by a single district judge.[7]

No injunction was granted by the District Court, and a review of the circumstances disclosed by the record leaves us satisfied that no injunction was in fact requested. The first two judgments of the District Court were rendered upon a complaint which prayed only for declaratory relief, as the records in this Court clearly reveal.[8] At the October 1959 Term we remanded the cause to the District Court for a third trial "with permission to the parties to amend the pleadings, if they so desire, to put in issue the question of collateral estoppel and to obtain an adjudication upon it." 362 U. S. 384, 387. In the trial court the complaint was amended so as to include the claim of collateral estoppel. In addition, a clause was added to the original prayer for declaratory relief, asking for an order "that defendants herein are enjoined and restrained henceforth from enforcing . . . any and all orders of deportation directed against the plaintiff. . . ." Before trial, however, an amended trial stipulation was signed by the parties and approved by the district judge, who ordered that the stipulation should "govern the course of the trial. . . ." This stipulation set out the agreed facts and specified in detail the issues of law to be decided. Completely unmentioned was any issue of law or fact even remotely suggesting that there existed a question of whether an injunction should be allowed.

From these circumstances three conclusions may fairly be drawn. First, the complaint was amended to include a prayer for an injunction against deportation solely in

---

[7] Both parties argued here the inapplicability of § 2282.

[8] On April 17, 1961, we granted a motion for permission to use in the present case the record which was before us on the prior appeal. 365 U. S. 876.

KENNEDY *v.* MENDOZA-MARTINEZ.

connection with the addition of a nonconstitutional claim—the claim of collateral estoppel. Secondly, even as so limited, the addition of a prayer for an injunction exceeded the specified bounds of the permission to amend the pleadings contained in this Court's judgment on remand. This amendment was, therefore, unauthorized and improper. Rule 15 (a) Fed. Rules Civ. Proc. Thirdly, the prayer for an injunction was in any event abandoned prior to trial, as is made manifest by the pretrial stipulation and the court's order approving it. For these reasons we are satisfied that there was no prayer for an injunction in this case at the time it went to trial.[9] See *Healy* v. *Ratta,* 289 U. S. 701.

It is suggested, however, that § 2282 was applicable even though all that was sought was a declaratory judgment. Without pausing to consider when, if ever, an action asking only declaratory relief might require the invocation of a three-judge District Court, we think it is clear that this was not such a case.

The judicial history of the several three-judge court statutes has been a history of strict construction. These statutes are not measures of broad social policy. Rather, they are enactments "technical in the strict sense of the term, and to be applied as such." *Phillips* v. *United States,* 312 U. S. 246, 251. The three-judge court requirement of § 2282 is, by the statute's terms, made applicable only to injunctions, and then only when the injunction has the effect of "restraining the enforcement, operation or execution" of a federal statute. What prompted the enactment of § 2282 was a history of broadside attacks by private litigants upon federal legislation, in which the

---

[9] This conclusion is borne out by the fact that there was not even a reference to a request for an injunction in the District Court's memorandum opinion, findings of fact and conclusions of law, or judgment.

KENNEDY *v.* MENDOZA-MARTINEZ.

equity powers of the federal courts had been invoked to paralyze governmental action by the issuance of broad injunctions.[10] Two particularly harmful effects of such litigation which were emphasized during the congressional debates were the monetary costs of unforeseen and debilitating interruptions in the administration of federal law and the difficulty of coping with litigation which struck repeatedly and often repetitiously wherever jurisdiction over government officials could be acquired.[11] The background of this legislation was thus not unlike that of 28 U. S. C. § 2281, which imposes a requirement of three judges for similar injunctive suits affecting state legislation. When speaking of the earlier statute, we said,

> "By [§ 2281] . . . Congress provided an exceptional procedure for a well-understood type of controversy. The legislation was designed to secure the public interest in 'a limited class of cases of special importance.' *Ex parte Collins*, 277 U. S. 565, 567. It is a matter of history that this procedural device was a means of protecting the increasing body of state legislation regulating economic enterprise from invalidation by a conventional suit in equity."
> *Phillips* v. *United States*, 312 U. S. 246, ——.

The action to determine citizenship in the present case was of an entirely different order. The complaint invoked the specialized review procedure expressly authorized by § 360 (a) of the Nationality and Immigration Act of 1952. The precise purpose of this provision is to afford judicial review of administrative decisions concerning citizenship status. Although the operation of a federal statute may

---

[10] See 81 Cong. Rec. 479, 2142–2143; see generally S. Doc. No. 42, 75th Cong., 1st Sess.

[11] 81 Cong. Rec. 479–481, 2142–2143.

KENNEDY *v.* MENDOZA-MARTINEZ.

pro tanto be restricted by a judicial order issued in such a proceeding, the restriction is imposed only after a litigant has complied with well-defined administrative proceedings and has invoked a judicial review procedure expressly provided by Congress. The review proceeding is itself a built-in part of the statutory scheme.

The inapplicability of § 2282 to statutory review proceedings of this nature is confirmed by our decisions. In *Fleming* v. *Nestor*, 363 U. S. 603, the plaintiff had brought an action in a Federal District Court to review an administrative order denying him Social Security benefits.[12] Challenging the constitutionality of the statute under which the payments had been terminated, his complaint asked the District Court to "order the defendant to withdraw his order suspending the payment of benefits to the plaintiff, to pay the plaintiff accrued benefits as may be due him, plus interest, and all Social Security benefits that may accrue to him in the future, and grant such other relief and further relief as may be just and proper under the circumstances."[13] We held that a three-judge court was not required. After observing that the plaintiff's complaint had drawn the constitutionality of a federal statute into question, we stated: "However, the action did no more. It did not seek affirmatively to interdict the operation of a statutory scheme. A judgment for appellee would not put the operation of a federal statute under the restraint of an equity decree; indeed, apart from its effect under the doctrine of *stare decisis*, it would have no other result than to require the payment of appellee's benefits." 363 U. S. 603, at 607. Last Term the Court summarily and unanimously decided the same basic

---

[12] The proceeding was authorized by § 205 (g) of the Social Security Act, 53 Stat. 1370, as amended, 42 U. S. C. § 405 (g).

[13] See record in No. 54, October Term, 1959, p. 2.

KENNEDY *v.* MENDOZA-MARTINEZ.

issue in *Thompson* v. *Whittier*, 365 U. S. 465. There the plaintiff had sought a judgment declaring that a federal statute under which he had been administratively denied veterans' benefits was unconstitutional. His complaint also asked for a judgment "ordering the . . . [Administrator] to pay the veterans' benefits due or which become due. . . ." [14] A three-judge court, which had been convened at the plaintiff's request, upheld the constitutionality of the statute. 185 F. Supp. 306. The plaintiff thereupon appealed to this Court under 28 U. S. C. § 1253, which permits such a direct appeal in all cases to which § 2282 is applicable. We dismissed the appeal, holding that "[t]he case does not arise under 28 U. S. C. § 2282, requiring the convening of a three-judge court."

Both reason and authority thus support the conclusion that jurisdiction in the present case was properly exercised by the District Court, and we come, therefore, to the underlying constitutional issue—whether § 401 (j) of the Nationality Act of 1940 was beyond the power of Congress to enact.

III.

In *Perez* v. *Brownell*, 356 U. S. 44, and *Trop* v. *Dulles*, 356 U. S. 86, this Court gave thorough consideration to the basic constitutional problems presented by expatriation legislation.[15] Those decisions serve both to limit and to illuminate the area of relevant inquiry here. Thus we start with the proposition that Congress may make expatriation the consequence of the voluntary conduct of a United States citizen, irrespective of the citizen's subjective intention to renounce his nationality, and irrespective too of his awareness that denationalization may be

---

[14] See original record in No. 500, October Term, 1960, p. 3.

[15] In this opinion the terms "expatriation" and "denationalization" are used synonymously, as are "citizenship" and "nationality."

KENNEDY *v.* MENDOZA-MARTINEZ.

the result of his conduct.[16] *Perez* v. *Brownell, supra.* See *Mackenzie* v. *Hare,* 239 U. S. 299; *Savorgnan* v. *United States,* 338 U. S. 491.

As with any other exercise of congressional power, however, deprivation of citizenship must bear a rational relationship to an affirmative power possessed by Congress under the Constitution. By the same token, the action of Congress in this area, as in any other, is open to challenge as violative of specific provisions of the Bill of Rights, whether generally or with particularized reference to the law's impact in an individual case. *Trop* v. *Dulles, supra.* Moreover, previous decisions of this Court concerning expatriation have suggested the existence of other limitations peculiarly applicable to the employment of this measure by Congress. We must determine, therefore, whether the legislative action before us falls within these relevant constitutional metes and bounds.

The first branch of the inquiry is enlightened by a review of the statute's history. Unlike the two sections of the Act at issue in *Perez* v. *Brownell* and *Trop* v. *Dulles,* § 401 (j) did not have its genesis in the Cabinet Committee's draft code which President Roosevelt submitted to Congress in 1938.[17] Indeed, § 401 (j) was the product of a totally different environment—the experience of a nation at war.

---

[16] In *Perez* v. *Brownell,* the Court pointed out that the provision of the Fourteenth Amendment that "All persons born or naturalized in the United States, and subject to the jurisdiction thereof, are citizens of the United States. . . ." does not restrict the power of Congress to enact denationalization legislation. It was there stated that "there is nothing in the terms, the context, the history or the manifest purpose of the Fourteenth Amendment to warrant drawing from it a restriction upon the power otherwise possessed by Congress to withdraw citizenship." 356 U. S., at 58, n. 3.

[17] See *Perez* v. *Brownell,* 356 U. S., at 52–57; *Trop* v. *Dulles,* 356 U. S., at 94–95; Codification of the Nationality Laws of the United States, H. R. Comm. Print, Pt. 1, 76th Cong., 1st Sess. 68–69.

KENNEDY *v.* MENDOZA-MARTINEZ.

On February 16, 1944, Attorney General Biddle addressed a letter to the Chairman of the Senate Immigration Committee, calling attention to circumstances which had arisen after the institution of the draft in World War II, and suggesting the legislation which subsequently became § 401 (j). The Attorney General's letter stated in part:

> "I invite your attention to the desirability of enacting legislation which would provide (1) for the expatriation of citizens of the United States who in time of war or during a national emergency leave the United States or remain outside thereof for the purpose of evading service in the armed forces of the United States and (2) for the exclusion from the United States of aliens who leave this country for the above-mentioned purpose.
>
> .   .   .   .   .
>
> "The files of this Department disclose that at the present time there are many citizens of the United States who have left this country for the purpose of escaping service in the armed forces. While such persons are liable to prosecution for violation of the Selective Service and Training Act of 1940, if and when they return to this country, it would seem proper that in addition they should lose their United States citizenship. Persons who are unwilling to perform their duty to their country and abandon it during its time of need are much less worthy of citizenship than are persons who become expatriated on any of the existing grounds.
>
> "Accordingly, I recommend the enactment of legislation which would provide (1) for the expatriation of citizens of the United States who in time of war or during a national emergency leave the United States or remain outside thereof for the purpose of evading service in the armed forces of the United

KENNEDY *v.* MENDOZA-MARTINEZ.

States and (2) for the exclusion from the United States of aliens who leave this country for that purpose. Any person who may be deemed to have become expatriated by operation of the foregoing provision would be entitled to have his status determined by the courts pursuant to the above-mentioned section of the Nationality Act of 1940.

"Adequate precedent exists for the suggested legislation in that during the First World War a statute was in force which provided for the expatriation of any person who went beyond the limits of the United States with intent to avoid any draft into the military or naval service (37 Stat. 356). This provision was repealed by section 504 of the Nationality Code of 1940 (54 Stat. 1172; U. S. C., title 8, sec. 904)." [18] S. Rep. No. 1075, 78th Cong., 2d Sess. 2.

---

[18] The statute in force "during the First World War" was originally enacted almost a century ago. By the Act of March 3, 1865, § 21 (13 Stat. 490) Congress provided for forfeiture of the rights of citizenship of deserters from the armed forces and of enrolled draftees who departed from their district or from the United States with intent to avoid service in the armed forces. Although the statute spoke in terms of forfeiture of "rights of citizenship," apparently it was administratively considered a loss-of-nationality-law. See *Trop v. Dulles,* 356 U. S., at 89, note 3. By denationalizing draftees who remained in the United States but simply departed from the jurisdiction of their district with intent to avoid military service, this law was substantially different from the statute at issue in the present case.

The 1865 legislation antedated by three years formal enunciation of the principle that it is "the natural and inherent right of all people" to divest themselves of their allegiance to any state. 15 Stat. 223, R. S. § 1999. And it antedated by more than 40 years the formulation of a more detailed denationalization policy expressed in the Expatriation Act of 1907. 34 Stat. 1228. See *Perez v. Brownell,* 356 U. S., at 48–51.

In 1912 the 1865 statute was amended to make it inapplicable in time of peace (Act of August 22, 1912, 37 Stat. 356). As so amended, the law remained in effect through the First World War

KENNEDY *v.* MENDOZA-MARTINEZ.

The bill was passed unanimously by both the House and the Senate and became Public Law No. 471 of the Seventy-Eighth Congress. Neither the committee reports nor the limited debate on the measure in Congress add any substantial gloss to the legislative action.[19]

Against this background of history, the appellant submits that the Congress, in enacting this statute, could rationally have been drawing on three sources of recognized constitutional power: the implied power to enact legislation for the effective conduct of foreign affairs; the express power to wage war, to raise armies, and to provide for the common defense; and the inherent attributes of sovereignty.

The appellant argues that § 401 (j), like § 401 (e), sustained in *Perez* v. *Brownell, supra,* has a direct relationship to foreign affairs. He points out that international complications could arise if this country attempted to effect the return of citizen draft evaders by requests to a foreign sovereign which that nation might be unwilling to grant. The appellant insists that the possibility of international embroilments resulting from problems caused by fugitive draft evaders is not fanciful, pointing

---

and until repealed by the Nationality Act of 1940 (54 Stat. 1172). The Nationality Act of 1940 as originally passed provided for loss of citizenship by those deserting the armed forces in time of war (a provision subsequently invalidated in *Trop* v. *Dulles, supra*). It contained no provision with respect to draft evaders.

[19] The House Committee Report does contain some particularization of the problem to which the legislation was addressed: "It is, of course, not known how many citizens or aliens have left the United States for the purpose of evading military service. The Department of Justice discovered that in the western district of Texas, in the vicinity of El Paso alone, there were over 800 draft delinquents recorded in the local Federal Bureau of Investigation office, born in this country and, therefore citizens, who had crossed the border into Mexico for the purpose of evading the draft, but with the expectation of returning to the United States to resume residence after the war." H. R. Rep. No. 1229, 78th Cong., 2d Sess. 1–2.

KENNEDY *v.* MENDOZA-MARTINEZ.

to the background of international incidents preceding the
War of 1812, and the long history, later in the nineteenth
century, of this country's involvement with other nations
over the asserted liability of our naturalized citizens to
military obligations imposed by their native countries.[20]
Expatriation of those who leave the United States with
draft evasion as their purpose, the appellant says, might
reasonably be attributed to a congressional belief that
this was the only practical way to nip these potential
international problems in the bud. Compare *Perez* v.
Brownell, 356 U. S., at 60; *Trop* v. *Dulles,* 365 U. S., at
106 (concurring opinion).

In the view we take of this case, it is unnecessary to
pursue further an inquiry as to whether the power to regulate foreign affairs could justify denationalization for the
conduct in question.[21] For it is apparent that Congress

---

[20] See III Moore, Digest of International Law, §§ 434, 436–438, 440
(1906); Tsiang, The Question of Expatriation in America Prior to
1907, 44–55, 71–72, 78–84 (1942).

[21] The House Committee Report indicates that the interest of the
State Department in the legislation was a negative one: "A representative of the State Department appeared and indicated that his
Department had no objection to the bill." H. R. Rep. No. 1229,
78th Cong., 2d Sess. 2. In explaining the bill to the House Committee
of the Whole, Representative Dickstein, the Chairman of the House
Committee on Immigration, made no mention of international complications: "I would classify this piece of legislation as a bill to
denaturalize and denationalize all draft dodgers who left this country
knowing that there was a possibility that they might be drafted in
this war and that they might have to serve in the armed forces,
in the naval forces, or the marines, and in an effort to get out of such
service. We are all American citizens and our country has a great
stake in this war; nevertheless, we have found hundreds of men who
have left this country to go to certain parts of Mexico and other
South American countries with the idea of evading military service
and of returning after the war is over, and taking their old places
in our society." 90 Cong. Rec. 3261.
  In explaining the bill to the Senate, Senator Russell, the Chairman
of the Senate Committee on Immigration also indicated no purpose

KENNEDY *v.* MENDOZA-MARTINEZ.

in enacting the statute was drawing upon another power, broad and far-reaching.

A basic purpose of the Constitution was "to provide for the common defence." To that end, the Framers expressly conferred upon Congress a compendium of

to avoid international complications: "The . . . bill relates to the class of persons, whether citizens of the United States or aliens, who departed from the United States in order to avoid service in the armed forces of the United States under the Selective Service Act. Information before the committee indicated that on one day several hundred persons departed from the United States through the city of El Paso, Tex., alone, in order to avoid service in either the Army or the Navy of the United States, and to avoid selection under the selective-service law. This bill provides that any person who is a national of the United States, or an American citizen, and who in time of national stress departed from the United States to another country to avoid serving his country, shall be deprived of his nationality.

"It further provides that any alien who is subject to military service under the terms of the Selective Service Act, and who left this country to avoid military service, shall thereafter be forever barred from admission to the United States.

"Mr. President, I do not see how anyone could object to such a bill. An alien who remains in the country and refuses to serve in the armed forces in time of war is prosecuted under our laws, and if found guilty he is compelled to serve a term in the penitentiary. Under the terms of the Selective Service Act an American citizen who refuses to serve when he is called upon to do so is likewise subject to a prison term. Certainly those who, having enjoyed the advantages of living in the United States, were unwilling to serve their country or subject themselves to the Selective Service Act, should be penalized in some measure. This bill would deprive such persons as are citizens of the United States of their citizenship, and, in the case of aliens, would forever bar them from admission into the United States. Any American citizen who is convicted of violating the Selective Service Act loses his citizenship. This bill would merely impose a similar penalty on those who are not subject to the jurisdiction of our courts, the penalty being the same as would result in the case of those who are subject to the jurisdiction of our courts." 90 Cong. Rec. 7628–7629.

KENNEDY *v.* MENDOZA-MARTINEZ.

powers which have come to be called the "war power." [22]
Responsive to the scope and magnitude of ultimate
national need, the war power is "the power to wage war
successfully." See Charles Evans Hughes, War Power
under the Constitution, 42 A. B. A. Rep. 232, 238. "It
extends to every matter and activity so related to war as
substantially to effect its conduct and progress. The
power is not restricted to the winning of victories in the
field and the repulse of enemy forces. It embraces every
phase of the national defense, including the protection of
war materials and the members of the armed forces from
injury and from the dangers which attend the rise, prosecution, and progress of war." *Hirabayashi* v. *United
States*, 320 U. S. 81, 93. See *Lichter* v. *United States*,
334 U. S. 742.

It is evident that Congress was drawing upon this power
when it enacted § 401 (j). To be sure, the underlying
purpose of this statute can hardly be refined to the point
of isolating one single, precise objective. The desire to
end a potential drain upon this country's military manpower was clearly present in the minds of the legislators
and would itself have constituted a purpose having sufficient rational nexus to the exercise of the war power.

---

[22] "The Congress shall have Power. . .

"To declare War, grant Letters of Marque and Reprisal, and make
Rules concerning Captures on Land and Water;

"To raise and support Armies, but no Appropriation of Money to
that Use shall be for a longer Term than two Years;

"To provide and maintain a Navy;

"To make Rules for the Government and Regulation of the land
and naval Forces;

　　　　.　　　　　.　　　　　.　　　　　.　　　　　.

"To make all Laws which shall be necessary and proper for carrying into Execution the foregoing Powers, and all other Powers vested
by this Constitution in the Government of the United States, or
in any Department or Officer thereof." Art. I, § 8, cls. 11, 12, 13,
14, 18.

KENNEDY v. MENDOZA-MARTINEZ.

Indeed, there is no more fundamental aspect of this broad power than the building and maintaining of armed forces sufficient for the common defense. *Selective Draft Law Cases,* 245 U. S. 366; see *Falbo* v. *United States,* 320 U. S. 549. But the limited and clearly identifiable class to which this legislation was applied, and the fact of its enactment in addition to existing deterrent sanctions, indicate that Congress may well have been dealing primarily with an even more pervasive problem.

The Act applies only to those who have left this country or remained outside of it for the purpose of avoiding the draft. Congress can reasonably be understood to have been saying that those who flee the country for such express purposes do more than simply disobey the law and avoid the immediate imposition of criminal sanctions. They disassociate themselves entirely from their nation, seeking refuge from their wartime obligations under the aegis of another sovereign. Congress could reasonably have concluded that the existence of such a group, who voluntarily and demonstrably put aside their United States citizenship "for the duration," could have an extremely adverse effect upon the morale and thus the war effort not only of the armed forces, but of the millions enlisted in the defense of their nation on the civilian front. During the consideration of § 401 (j) in Congress there were repeated references to the expectation that fugitive draft evaders then living abroad would return to this country after the war to resume citizenship and to enjoy the fruits of victory. The effect upon wartime morale of the known existence of such a group, while perhaps not precisely measurable in terms of impaired military efficiency, could obviously have been considered substantial. We cannot say that expatriation was not a reasonable measure to meet the problem with which Congress was confronted. The declaration that those in this separate

KENNEDY v. MENDOZA-MARTINEZ.

and clearly identifiable class had permanently relinquished their citizenship constituted a solution to the problem which was both rational and efficacious.

Thus § 401 (j) is quite different from the statute held invalid in *Trop* v. *Dulles, supra*. In that case there were not five members of the Court who were able to find the "requisite rational relation" between the war power of Congress and § 401 (g) of the Act imposing denationalization upon wartime deserters from the armed forces. The concurring opinion adopted the view that the effect of § 401 (g) was simply to impose an addditional punishment upon a soldier convicted of desertion in time of war—an offense already punishable by the maximum penalty of death. Moreover, the statute was "not limited in its effects to those who desert in a foreign country or who flee to another land." 356 U. S., at 107. Indeed, "[T]he Solicitor General acknowledged that forfeiture of citizenship would have occurred if the entire incident had transpired in this country." 356 U. S., at 92. It was therefore said that "[A]s a deterrent device this sanction would appear of little effect, for the offender, if not deterred by thought of the specific penalties of long imprisonment or even death, is not very likely to be swayed from his course by the prospect of expatriation." 356 U. S., at 112. It was emphasized, finally, that conduct far short of disloyalty could technically constitute the military offense of desertion, 356 U. S., at 112, 113, and that the harshness of denationalization for conduct so potentially equivocal was "an important consideration where the asserted power to expatriate has only a slight or tenuous relationship to the granted power." 356 U. S., at 110.[23]

---

[23] Indeed, four members of the Court found the imposition of "statelessness" in the circumstances of that case a cruel and unusual punishment within the meaning of the Eighth Amendment. 356 U. S., at 93–104.

KENNEDY *v.* MENDOZA-MARTINEZ.

Section 401 (j), on the other hand, does not represent an attempt by Congress to impose an additional punishment upon one convicted of a military or civil offense. The statute by its terms is completely inapplicable to those criminally convicted of draft evasion who have remained in the United States; it is exclusively aimed at those, whether or not ever criminally convicted, who have gone to or remained in another land to escape military service. Moreover, the conduct which the statute reaches could never be equivocal in nature, but is always and clearly a "refusal to perform this ultimate duty of American citizenship," *Trop* v. *Dulles,* 356 U. S., at 112 (concurring opinion).

The argument is made that even though § 401 (j) may be constitutionally legitimate in terms of general congressional power, the provision nevertheless runs afoul of a specific prohibition of the Eighth Amendment by imposing a cruel and unusual punishment, and that it violates the Fifth Amendment guarantee of due process by imposing punishment without the requisite safeguards of a criminal trial. The answer to both these contentions is that the deprivation of citizenship effected by this statute is not "punishment" in the constitutional sense.

A large part of the answer to the question of whether or not a statute is punitive is to be found by looking to the purpose of the legislation. The question in its traditional form has been whether a disability is imposed for the purpose of vengeance or deterrence, or whether the disability is but an incident to some broader regulatory objective. A finding of punitive intent, or lack of it, has often rested on an investigation of specific legislative history. See *Cummings* v. *Missouri,* 4 Wall. 277, 320, 322; *United States* v. *Lovett,* 328 U. S. 303, 308–312; *Trop* v. *Dulles,* 356 U. S., at 107–109 (concurring opinion). Thus the plurality opinion in *Trop* v. *Dulles* relied on an inability to discern behind the statute there

KENNEDY *v.* MENDOZA-MARTINEZ.

involved any nonpunitive purpose. *Id.,* at 97. See generally, *Fleming* v. *Nestor,* 363 U. S. 603, 613–617; cf. *De Veau* v. *Braisted,* 363 U. S. 144, 160; *Communist Party* v. *Subversive Activities Control Board,* 367 U. S. 1, 83–88. In commenting on this general mode of inquiry, we said in *Fleming* v. *Nestor,* "We observe initially that only the clearest proof could suffice to establish the unconstitutionality of a statute on such a ground. Judicial inquiries into congressional motives are at best a hazardous matter, and when that inquiry seeks to go behind objective manifestations it becomes a dubious affair indeed. Moreover, the presumption of constitutionality with which this enactment, like any other, comes to us forbids us lightly to choose that reading of the statute's setting which will invalidate it over that which will save it." *Id.,* at 617.

Examination of the present statute convinces us that it cannot be characterized as punitive. In the light of the decisions in *McKenzie, Savorgnan,* and *Perez, supra,* it can hardly be said that denationalization is a measure which is inherently penal. Nor in the light of what was said in *Nestor* can we find clear proof that the prime purpose of this legislation was a punitive one. We are met at the outset by the same indefiniteness of purpose emphasized in *Nestor.* The attitude of many members of Congress towards those whom the statute was intended to reach was obviously far from neutral.[24] Moreover, there is evidence that the deterrent effect of the legislation was considered. But these putative indicia of punitive intent are overbalanced by the fact that this statute dealt with a basic problem of wartime morale reaching far

---

[24] The fact that the word "penalty" was used in the congressional debate on the legislation is, of course, not controlling. "How simple would be the task of constitutional adjudication and of law generally if specific problems could be solved by inspection of the labels pasted on them!" *Trop* v. *Dulles,* 356 U. S., at 94.

KENNEDY *v.* MENDOZA-MARTINEZ.

beyond concern for any individual affected. Moreover, § 401 (j) does not represent the imposition of an additional disability upon conviction of a criminal offense, as was true of the statute found penal in *Trop* v. *Dulles.* The statute applies to a class consisting of those who leave this country or remain outside of it for the express purpose of avoiding military service in a time of urgent national need.

Nor do we find a lack of procedural due process in the operation of § 401 (j). While the initial determination of loss of nationality under the statute was an administrative one, that determination was a mere preliminary. In the appellee's declaratory judgment action to establish his citizenship, he was entitled to a *de novo* judicial hearing. *Ng Fung Ho* v. *White,* 259 U. S. 276; *Kessler* v. *Strecker,* 307 U. S. 22, 35. Had not all the essential facts been stipulated, the Government would have been charged with the heavy burden of proving by clear, convincing, and unequivocal evidence that he had voluntarily fled or remained away from his country in time of war or national emergency for the purpose of evading his duty to serve in its defense. *Gonzales* v. *Landon,* 350 U. S. 920; *Nishikawa* v. *Dulles,* 356 U. S. 129.

Previous decisions have suggested that congressional exercise of the power to expatriate may be subject to a further constitutional restriction—a limitation upon the kind of activity which may be made the basis of denationalization. Withdrawal of citizenship is a drastic measure. Moreover, the power to expatriate endows government with authority to define and to limit the society which it represents and to which it is responsible. This Court has never held that Congress' power to expatriate may be used unsparingly in every area in which it has general power to act. Our previous decisions upholding involuntary denationalization all involved conduct inconsistent with undiluted allegiance to this coun-

KENNEDY *v.* MENDOZA-MARTINEZ.

try.   *Perez* v. *Brownell,* 356 U. S., at 60–61; *Savorgnan* v. *United States,* 338 U. S., at 502, and n. 18; *McKenzie* v. *Hare,* 329 U. S., at 311–312; compare *Trop* v. *Dulles,* 356 U. S., at 107 (concurring opinion).

The statute before us comes so clearly within the compass of these decisions as to make unnecessary in this case an inquiry as to what the ultimate limitation upon the expatriation power may be.   The conduct to which § 401 (j) applies, involving not only the attribute of flight from this country in time of war or national emergency, but flight for the express purpose of evading military service, amounts to an unequivocal and conspicuous manifestation of nonallegiance to this nation, whether considered objectively or subjectively.   Ours is a tradition of the citizen soldier.   As this Court has said, "[T]he very conception of a just government and its duty to the citizen includes the reciprocal obligation of the citizen to render military service in case of need and the right to compel it." *Selective Draft Law Cases,* 245 U. S. 366, at 378.   It is hardly an irrelevant exercise of power for Congress to recognize an abandonment of citizenship by those who have abandoned this nation to avoid defending it in time of need.

Judgment reversed.

Once again the Stewart *Mendoza-Martinez* draft did not become the opinion of the Court. Though Justices Frankfurter, Clark, and Harlan quickly agreed to join the draft, Justice Whittaker indicated that he would concur only in the result. He refused to agree with Justice Stewart's view that involuntary expatriation might be used by Congress in pursuance of the war power.

The Stewart *Mendoza-Martinez* draft now commanded only a plurality on the merits, since Justice Whittaker was only willing to concur on a different theory. As expressed in a *Memorandum to the Conference on Mendoza-Martinez* circulated by him, this was that Section 401(j) could be sustained on the narrow ground of Congressional power to anticipate what amounted to an abnegation of allegiance and prescribe expatriation as a consequence regardless of subjective intent concerning retention or loss of citizenship.

The other four Justices (the Chief Justice and Justices Black, Douglas, and Brennan) adhered to their October 13, 1961, conference votes. Justice Douglas circulated a draft dissent, which Justice Black quickly joined, arguing that expatriation statutes were invalid for the reasons stated in his *Perez* dissent[11] and also because they amounted to bills of attainder. Justice Brennan also sent around a draft dissent stating that Section 401(j) was unconstitutional, but urging the Court to refrain from deciding the constitutional issue by holding that a three-judge district court should have been convened.

When he read Justice Brennan's draft, Justice Frankfurter wrote that the Brennan view on the substantive issue only fortified the views stated in the Stewart draft opinion of the Court. To Justice Frankfurter, the division among the Justices only emphasized their differing views on the proper scope of judicial review. In his view, Justice Brennan was acting more like a legislator than a judge, identifying desire with constitutionality and voting against legislation he did not like.

"The whole course of his [Brennan's] argument," Frankfurter wrote,

> emphasizes to a striking degree the difference in conceptions of the judicial function when sitting in judgment upon the constitutionality of an Act of Congress. If Bill had been Senator from New Jersey, he wouldn't have to change a word in what he has written in a speech voting against the wisdom of the legislation or the weight of arguments, pro and con, for enacting these provisions. What in effect he is doing is to pass *de novo* judgment on the propriety or wisdom, or even fairness, of the legislation.[12]

It was now the end of February 1962, four and a half months after the reargument in the case. At this point, Justice Whittaker became ill and could no longer participate in the decision, since his illness forced his resignation from the Court. This left the Court evenly divided on the constitutionality of Section 401(j), with Justices Frankfurter, Clark, Harlan, and Stewart for upholding the section, and Chief Justice Warren and Justices Black, Douglas, and Brennan against. With the Court thus divided, it was decided once again to hold the *Mendoza-Martinez* decision for the following term. On April 2, 1962, an order was issued restoring the case once more to the calendar for reargument.[13]

What happened next well illustrates the importance of changes in the Justices to the Court's decision process. With Justice Frankfurter and Whittaker on the bench the vote had been in favor of the constitutionality of Section 401(j). When *Mendoza-Martinez* was reargued on December 4, 1962, the composition of the Court had changed. Justice White had replaced Justice Whittaker and Justice Goldberg had taken Justice Frankfurter's seat. At the December 9 conference, the votes of the new Justices shifted the balance. Justice White voted to uphold Section 401(j), but Justice Goldberg voted the other way. That made for a bare majority in favor of striking down Section 401(j).

The opinion for the new majority was assigned to Justice Goldberg. He delivered the opinion of the Court on February 13, 1963, holding Section 401(j) unconstitutional on the ground that Congress had employed the sanction of expatriation as a punishment—for the offense of leaving the country to avoid military service—without affording the procedural safeguards guaranteed by the Fifth and Sixth Amendments. Justice Stewart, joined by Justice White, issued a dissent[14] similar to the draft opinions of the Court he had circulated in 1960 and 1961. Justices Harlan and Clark also dissented.[15]

The Goldberg *Mendoza-Martinez* opinion is based on the Chief Justice's opinion of the Court in *Trop* v. *Dulles;* but it goes much further in its reasoning. According to the *Mendoza-Martinez* opinion, the Framers "intended to safeguard the people of this country from punishment without trial by duly constituted courts," in which the tested safeguard of trial by jury would be observed.[16]

There are, however, many cases in our system in which penalties are imposed by nonjudicial officials. And even though we limit ourselves to power over the person, it is not accurate to assume that penalties may be inflicted only by courts sitting with a jury under the Sixth Amendment. Even if we leave aside cases involving petty offenses, contempts, and military trials, we can take deportation as an obvious example. Deportation is a penalty against the person of the most severe type. Yet it is not considered a "criminal" proceeding embraced by the constitutional guaranty of a jury trial.[17]

It is hard to see why what is true of divestment of citizenship is not also true of deportation. Indeed, the very language the *Mendoza-Martinez* opinion uses to point up the rigor of the sanction employed by Congress— that it results in a "deprivation 'of all that makes life worth living' "[18]—is taken from a famous statement of Justice Brandeis in a case involving not denationalization, but deportation.[19] It may be that the Court's distinction between the denationalization and deportation cases is based on the view expressed in some cases that deportation is not punishment.[20] That may be true as a matter of Supreme Court doctrine, but it might be somewhat difficult to explain to an alien whose physical expulsion after years of residence in this country "may result also in loss of both property and life, or of all that makes life worth living."[21]

The *Mendoza-Martinez* opinion was confusing the notion of punishment with that of criminal punishment under the Sixth Amendment. If, as the opinion implies, there is a flat prohibition against the imposition of any punishment without a judicial trial, conducted in conformity to the Fifth and Sixth Amendments, that would make for a drastic revision of existing law. Aside from the acknowledged exceptions to the Sixth Amendment already discussed, which clearly involve impositions of punishment, there are the innumerable instances in which administrative agencies in this country are authorized to impose sanctions (including even the imposition of monetary fines[22]) as punishment, subject only to limited judicial review.

Whether subject to these criticisms or not, the *Mendoza-Martinez* opinion builds on *Trop* in delimiting expatriation power. After the *Mendoza-Martinez* decision, *Perez* v. *Brownell* appeared as an anomaly in its upholding of an expatriation statute. The *Perez* exception, now standing alone, could not maintain its position for long in the face of the new Court majority that had rejected Congressional power in *Mendoza-Martinez*.

The situation would have been different had the original Stewart draft come down as the *Mendoza-Martinez* opinion of the Court. Then *Trop* v. *Dulles* would have been the exception to the broad Congressional power of expatriation recognized in both the *Perez* and *Mendoza-Martinez* cases. If that had been the case, it may be doubted that, even with the retirement of Justices Frankfurter and Whittaker, the Court would have repudiated both *Perez* and *Mendoza-Martinez* and swept away virtually all expatriation authority, as it did in 1967 in *Afroyim* v. *Rusk*.[23] The law on expatriation that ultimately prevailed might have been that urged by Justice Frankfurter in the 1957 term expatriation cases and not that espoused by Chief Justice Warren.

Notes

1. *Perez* v. *Brownell*, 356 U.S. 44 (1958); *Trop* v. *Dulles*, 356 U.S. 86 (1958).
2. 387 U.S. 253 (1967).
3. 372 U.S. 144 (1963).
4. Supra p. 81.
5. 356 U.S. 258 (1958).
6. *Mackey* v. *Mendoza-Martinez*, 362 U.S. 384, 387 (1960).
7. 362 U.S. 384 (1960).
8. FFH.
9. Under 22 U.S.C. § 2282.
10. FF, *Memorandum for the Conference Re: No. 19*, Kennedy v. Mendoza-Martinez, Oct. 10, 1961. FFH.

11. 356 U.S. at 79.
12. FF-PS, Feb. 28, 1962. FFH.
13. 369 U.S. 832 (1962).
14. 372 U.S. at 201.
15. Id. at 197.
16. Id. at 166.
17. *Zakonaite* v. *Wolf*, 226 U.S. 272 (1912).
18. 372 U.S. at 166.
19. *Ng Fung Ho* v. *White*, 269 U.S. 276, 284 (1922).
20. See *Harisiades* v. *Shaughnessy*, 342 U.S. 580, 594–595 (1952).
21. *Ng Fung Ho* v. *White*, 259 U.S. 276, 284 (1922).
22. See Schwartz, *Administrative Law* § 2.25 (2d ed. 1984).
23. Supra note 2.

5

Bell v. Maryland (1964):
Civil Rights versus Property Rights

Though the Warren Court did more for the vindication of civil rights than any other governmental institution, that tribunal came close to handing down a decision that would have deprived the civil-rights movement of one of its most effective weapons. The decision would have occurred in *Bell* v. *Maryland*,[1] where an opinion of the Court drafted by Justice Black would have come down as the majority opinion if its opponents had not ultimately succeeded in having the case decided on another, narrower ground. Had the Black opinion prevailed, *Bell* v. *Maryland* would have taken away from civil-rights demonstrators their most dramatic means of drawing attention to racial discrimination, the sit-in, which spread through the South after the first sit-in demonstration in Greensboro, North Carolina, at the beginning of 1960. The sit-in demonstrators were met with arrests and convictions, which slowly worked their way up to the Supreme Court.

The sit-ins were then a recent manifestation of the problem that civil disobedience had posed for the law throughout American history. From the time of the Boston Tea Party to the era of Prohibition, Americans had felt free to disobey laws they considered unjust. Perhaps the greatest use of the civil disobedience technique in this country occurred in the years before the Civil War when those opposed to slavery condemned the Mexican War as an immoral plot to extend slavery, participated in the "underground railway," and defied laws passed by the slave-owning interests. It was then, in 1849, that Thoreau wrote his seminal essay justifying civil disobedience.[2]

Thoreau was too much the theorist to put civil disobedience to more than a token test. A prison, he wrote, may be "the only house in a slave State in which a free man can abide with honor."[3] But when he refused to pay his poll tax in protest against slavery, he was satisfied to spend a single symbolic night in Concord jail, leaving in the morning after his aunt paid the tax for him.

Thoreau's doctrine, however, has served to justify Americans more activist than he, from the abolitionists of his day to the sit-in demonstrators of the 1960s. The sit-in cases presented the Supreme Court with a particularly difficult problem. Civil disobedience as such does not pose troublesome legal issues. To be sure, it raises philosophic problems. The duty of the individual to obey what he may consider an unjust law, in the face of what he may deem the higher duty not to lend obedience to public power exerted for unjust ends, may pose for the individual a crisis of conscience that is not readily resolved.

From a purely legal point of view, nevertheless, there can be no such problem. A law must be treated by the courts as laying down a binding legal norm until such time as its validity is successfully challenged. Thoreau's question, "Must the citizen . . . resign his conscience to the legislators?"[4] must remain legally irrelevant. "Civil disobedience," Martin Luther King himself conceded, "can never be legal. These would certainly be contradictory terms. In fact, civil disobedience means that it is not legal."[5] That is, indeed, the whole point about civil disobedience, that its practitioner fully expects to be prosecuted for his actions, but that, through his prosecution and conviction, the injustice of the law would be exposed to the public.

The sit-in cases that came before the Supreme Court were more complex than most cases involving disobedience of the law on moral grounds. The sit-in cases raised the issue of whether a state could use its power to help a private owner to discriminate against blacks. Of course, if a state uses its authority to discriminate on racial grounds, its action patently violates the Fourteenth Amendment. But the amendment's Equal Protection Clause prohibits only discriminatory "state action"; it does not reach purely private discrimination.[6] What happens, however, if the police act in aid of a private store owner who is following his private policy of discrimination? When the police answer the owner's call and arrest the sit-in demonstrators, is that "state action" subject to the Equal Protection Clause? And when a state court convicts the demonstrators for trespassing or breach of the peace, is the state acting to enforce the store owner's decision to discriminate?

The case law on the matter began with *Shelley* v. *Kraemer*,[7] decided in 1948. The decision there ruled that enforcement by a state court of a covenant restricting use or occupancy of property to whites denied equal protection to a black against whom the covenant was enforced. The covenant alone may have been only an instrument of private discrimination, since it was an agreement between individuals respecting the control and disposition of their property, but enforcement by the courts was "state action" that would violate the Equal Protection Clause. Is the same reasoning applicable to the sit-in cases?

Some of the sit-in cases were relatively easy for the Court to decide. Where the state is involved directly in the given discriminatory practice, the discrimination itself is "state action" violative of the equal protection guaranty. That is the case where the discrimination is required by state or local law or administrative direction. In three sit-in cases that came to the Supreme Court during the 1962 term, city ordinances required racial separation in restaurants.[8] Though the discussion in the Court's conference dealt with the broader constitutional issues involved in sit-ins,[9] the Justices agreed with Chief Justice Warren, who urged that the cases should be decided on the narrow ground that the sit-in convictions should be reversed because they had the effect of enforcing the ordinances: "When a state agency passes a law compelling persons to discriminate against other persons because of race, and the State's criminal processes are employed in a way which enforces the discrimination mandated by that law, such a palpable violation of the Fourteenth Amendment cannot be saved."[10] The same approach was followed in a fourth 1962 term sit-in case, where statements of the mayor and police chief opposing restaurant desegregation were treated as having the same effect as an ordinance not permitting desegregated service.[11]

Penalties may also not be imposed upon sit-in demonstrators where they have a legal right to the service that they demand. That is now the case in public accommodations covered by the Civil Rights Act of 1964. That law contains a broad Congressional provision for racial equality in public accommodations that "affect commerce." In *Hamm* v. *Rock Hill*,[12] the Court dealt with the effect of the 1964 statute on sit-in convictions. In its opinion, the Court emphasized that Congress had created a statutory right to racial equality in public accommodations, backed by a prohibition against racial discrimination or any effort to punish any person seeking to exercise this statutory right. The statute, according to the Court, "prohibits prosecution of any person for seeking service in a covered establishment, because of his race or color."[13]

Bell v. *Maryland* was decided by the Court during the 1963 term, before the Civil Rights Act of 1964 became law. Indeed, had the opinion of the Court originally drafted by Justice Black, with the strong support of four other Justices, been issued as the *Bell* opinion, it is possible that there would have been neither the broadside provision for racial equality in the 1964 statute nor the *Hamm* holding of immunity for sit-in demonstrators seeking to vindicate their rights.

The *Bell* case itself and three companion cases[14] involved fact patterns essentially similar to the other sit-in cases of the period. In each, blacks sat down in restaurants or lunch counters and refused to leave without being served. They were arrested and convicted of violating state trespass laws.

The Solicitor General, who had been permitted to intervene *amicus curiae*, urged the Court to dispose of *Bell* on the narrow ground that reversal was required because the demonstrators had not been told to leave until after they had entered the premises, and the statutes applied only to entry on land after notice not to enter. At their October 18, 1963, conference, the Justices rejected that approach as only a legalistic excuse to avoid decision. They decided to follow the lead of the Chief Justice, who urged them to "get to the 'raw' of the problem" and reach the basic issue of whether the convictions of the sit-in demonstrators violated the Fourteenth Amendment. Warren argued that equal protection had been denied. He said that, where public accommodations were concerned, "as long as they [the demonstrators] behave themselves, the owner can't have police to help to throw them out. The state then unconstitutionally enforces discrimination."

The Justices were sharply divided on the constitutional issue. Justices Douglas, Brennan, and Goldberg supported the Chief Justice's view that the convictions should be reversed as contrary to the Fourteenth Amendment. But the other five Justices, led by Justice Black, voted the other way. Justice Black delivered an emotional statement in favor of his view at the conference, declaring that he could not believe that his "Pappy," who operated a general store in Alabama, did not have the right to decide whom he would or would not serve.

The conference vote was five to four to affirm the sit-in convictions on the merits. Justice Black, the senior in the majority, assigned the majority opinion to himself. The Alabaman prepared a draft opinion of the Court, which he first sent to Justices Clark, Harlan, Stewart, and White, the other members of the conference majority.[15] After the draft was approved by them, it was circulated to all the Justices on March 12, 1964.

The Black draft opinion of the Court in *Bell* v. *Maryland* is reprinted on page 149. It is substantially similar to the dissent that Justice Black later issued in the case, except for two sections added to meet points made in the opinion written by Justice Brennan, which became the opinion of the Court in *Bell*, as well as a concurrence issued by Justice Goldberg.

Justice Black had, of course, been a leader in the judicial enforcement of the rights guaranteed by the Equal Protection Clause, but the relatively simple cases involving vindication of civil rights, such as *Brown* v. *Board of Education*,[16] had given way to cases such as the sit-in cases, where the civil rights asserted conflicted with other constitutional rights.

Justice Black refused to go along with his erstwhile allies when rights that he recognized were being vindicated by direct action he considered incompatible with the rule of law upon which all rights ultimately rested. In the conflict of interests involved in the sit-in cases, Black came down on the side of property and preservation of public order.

The first opinion of the Court, drafted by Justice Black, contains a straightforward exposition of his view on the constitutional relationship between civil rights and property rights. The Fourteenth Amendment, it states, does not forbid a state to prosecute for crimes committed against a person, no matter how discriminatory against others that person may be. "It would betray our whole plan for law and order" to say that a citizen cannot call for the aid of the police because of his personal prejudices. The mere judicial enforcement of the trespass law is not enough to impute to the state the restaurant's refusal to serve blacks.

The basic holding of the majority who had voted for affirmance of the *Bell* convictions was stated as follows in the Black draft opinion of the Court (in a passage not contained in the *Bell* dissent that Justice Black ultimately issued):

> We hold that the Fourteenth Amendment does not bar Maryland from enforcing its trespass laws so long as it does not do so with an evil eye and a prejudiced heart and hand. We do not believe that the Amendment was written or designed to interfere with a property owner's right to choose his social or business associates, so long as he does not run counter to a valid state or federal regulation. It would overturn the whole history of this country to take away a man's property or any part of it except by taking it for a public use and paying him just compensation as the law provides.

A week after he received Justice Black's draft opinion of the Court, Justice Douglas circulated a *Bell* dissent. A month later, on April 20, Justice Goldberg also sent around a dissent, and on May 7 the Chief Justice circulated his own draft dissent. The Douglas and Goldberg drafts need not be discussed, since they were basically the same as the *Bell* concurring opinions they finally issued. The Warren draft, however, was ultimately withdrawn and the Chief Justice did not publish any opinion of his own in the *Bell* case. The unpublished Warren draft dissent is reprinted on p. 164.

The Chief Justice's draft dissent was prepared in *Barr* v. *Columbia*,[17] one of the companion cases to *Bell* v. *Maryland*. It was an atypically emotional opinion, demonstrating the Chief Justice's depth of feeling against a practice that to him was just as repugnant as school segregation.[18] The Chief Justice indignantly refers to the policy of the luncheonette concerned, to sell food to blacks to take out provided they did not sit at the lunch counter. This, Warren declared,

> was founded on a right to compel Negroes to stand up to buy their food solely for the reason that they were Negroes. The store might as well have offered to feed only Negroes who would crawl in on their hands and knees, or, as in other caste systems, who would purchase food under conditions that would not cause their shadow to fall on the food of whites. It saddens me deeply to think that this Court, which has so far advanced the notion of the equal dignity of all men before the law, would sanction the right so publicly to first shame and then punish one who merely seeks that which any white man takes for granted.

The Warren draft rejected the notion that only the property owner's private right was involved: "[I]t is the policy of the State that is being enforced as well as that of the private entrepreneur." To the Chief Justice, the constitutional balance clearly tilted in favor of the sit-in demonstrators: "[T]he important civil right of equal access to public places is a right which the Constitution forbids a State to deny in the name of private property."

The majority decision the other way took from the black "that little bit of humanity which he loses each time a state-sanctioned inferior status is publicly thrust upon him. I cannot in conscience be a part of a return to a tradition which so belongs to the past."

There is a third unpublished opinion in *Bell* v. *Maryland* reprinted on page 173. This is the opinion that Justice Clark drafted. This Clark draft, written as an opinion reversing on the constitutional merits, served as the final catalyst to induce the Court to decide *Bell* v. *Maryland* as it did. The Clark draft will be discussed in the summary of the later history of *Bell* v. *Maryland*, which follows the Black, Warren, and Clark opinions, starting on page 187.

SUPREME COURT OF THE UNITED STATES

From: Black,

No. 12.—October Term, 1963.   Circulated:_

Recirculated

Robert Mack Bell et al., Petitioners, *v.* State of Maryland.   On Writ of Certiorari to the Court of Appeals of the State of Maryland.

[March —, 1964.]

Mr. Justice Black delivered the opinion of the Court.

The petitioners were convicted in a Maryland state court on a charge that they "unlawfully did enter upon and cross over the land, premises, and private property" of the Hooper Food Co., Inc., "after having been duly notified by Alfred Warfel, who was then and there the servant and agent for Hooper Food Co., not to do so," in violation of Maryland's criminal trespass statute.[1] The conviction was based on a record showing in summary that:

> A group of fifteen to twenty Negro students, including petitioners, went to Hooper's Restaurant to engage in what their counsel describes as a "sit-in protest" because the restaurant would not serve Negroes. The hostess, on orders of Mr. Hooper, the owner, told them, "solely on the basis of their color," that she would not serve them. Petitioners refused to leave when requested by the hostess and the manager; instead they went to tables, took seats, and refused to leave, insisting that they be served. On orders of the owner the police were called, but they advised the manager that a warrant would be necessary before they could arrest petitioners. The manager then went to the police station and swore

[1] Md. Code, Art. 27, § 577.

BELL *v.* MARYLAND.

out the warrants. Petitioners had remained in the restaurant in all an hour and a half, testifying at their trial that they had stayed knowing they would be arrested—that being arrested was part of their "technique" in these demonstrations.

The Maryland Court of Appeals affirmed the convictions, rejecting petitioners' contentions urged in both courts that Maryland had (1) denied them equal protection and due process under the Fourteenth Amendment by applying its trespass statute to enforce the restaurant owner's policy and practice of racial discrimination, and (2) denied them freedom of expression guaranteed by the Constitution by punishing them for remaining at the restaurant, which they were doing as a protest against the owner's practice of refusing service to Negroes.[2] Because constitutional questions of a similar nature have been raised in a series of cases involving "demonstrations" and "sit-ins," we granted certiorari in this case and set it for argument along with a group of the others.[3] The Solicitor General has filed *amicus* briefs and participated in oral argument in these cases; while he joins in asking reversal of all the convictions, his arguments vary in significant respects from those of the petitioners. For reasons to be stated, we reject the contentions of the petitioners and of the Solicitor General in this case and affirm the judgment of the Maryland court.

I.

We consider first the contention that the Maryland statute is void for vagueness under the Due Process Clause of the Fourteenth Amendment because its lan-

[2] 227 Md. 302, 176 A. 2d 771 (1962).

[3] 374 U. S. 805 (1963); see also *Griffin* v. *Maryland*, 370 U. S. 935 (1962); *Barr* v. *City of Columbia*, 374 U. S. 804 (1963); *Bouie* v. *City of Columbia*, 374 U. S. 805 (1963); *Robinson* v. *Florida*, 374 U. S. 803 (1963) (probable jurisdiction noted).

BELL *v.* MARYLAND.

guage gave no fair warning that "sit-ins" staged over a restaurant owner's protest were prohibited by the statute. The challenged statutory language makes it an offense for any person to "enter upon or cross over the land, premises or private property of any person or persons in this State after having been duly notified by the owner or his agent not to do so . . . ." Petitioners say that this language plainly means that an entry upon another's property is an offense only if the owner's notice has been given before the intruder is physically on the property; that the notice to petitioners that they were not wanted was given only after they had stepped from the street into the restaurant; and that the statute as applied to them was void either because (1) there was no evidence to support the charge of entry *after* notice not to do so, or because (2) the statute failed to warn that it could be violated by remaining on property after having been told to leave. As to (1), in view of the evidence and petitioners' statements at the trial it is hard to take seriously a contention that petitioners were not fully aware, before they ever entered the restaurant, that it was the restaurant owner's firmly established policy and practice not to serve Negroes. The whole purpose of the "sit-in" was to protest that policy. (2) Be that as it may, the Court of Appeals of Maryland held that "the statutory references to 'entry upon or crossing over,' cover the case of remaining upon land after notice to leave," and the trial court found, with very strong evidentiary support, that after unequivocal notice to petitioners that they would not be seated or served they "persisted in their demands and, brushing by the hostess, took seats at various tables on the main floor and at the counter in the basement." We are unable to say that holding this conduct barred by the Maryland statute was an unreasonable interpretation of the statute or one which could have deceived or even surprised petitioners or others who

BELL *v.* MARYLAND.

wanted to understand and obey it. It would certainly
be stretching the rule against ambiguous statutes very
far indeed to hold that the statutory language misled
these petitioners as to the Act's meaning, in the face of
evidence showing a prior series of demonstrations by
Negroes, including some of petitioners, and in view of
the fact that the group which included petitioners came
prepared to picket Hooper and actually courted arrest,
the better to protest his refusal to serve colored people.

We reject the contention that the statute as construed
is void for vagueness. In doing so, we do not overlook
or disregard the view expressed in other cases that statutes which, in regulating conduct, may indirectly touch
the areas of freedom of expression should be construed
narrowly where necessary to protect that freedom.[4]   And
we do not doubt that one purpose of these "sit-ins" was
to express a vigorous protest against Hooper's policy of
not serving Negroes.[5]   But it is wholly clear that the
Maryland statute here is directed against conduct which
States have traditionally prohibited in this country,
namely, remaining on the premises of another after having been warned to leave.[6]   And none of our prior cases
has held that a person's right to freedom of expression
carries with it a right to force a private property owner
to furnish his property as a platform to criticize the
property owner's use of that property. Cf. *Giboney* v.
Empire Storage & Ice Co., 336 U. S. 490 (1949). We
hold that the statute as construed and applied is not void
for vagueness.

---

[4] *Winters* v. *New York,* 333 U. S. 507, 512 (1948); *Cantwell* v.
Connecticut, 310 U. S. 296, 307–308 (1940).

[5] See *Garner* v. *Louisiana,* 368 U. S. 157, 185 (1961) (HARLAN, J.,
concurring).

[6] See *Martin* v. *City of Struthers,* 319 U. S. 141, 147, n. 10 (1943).

BELL *v.* MARYLAND.

II.

Section I of the Fourteenth Amendment provides:

> "No State shall . . . deprive any person of life,
> liberty, or property without due process of law; nor
> deny to any person within its jurisdiction the equal
> protection of the laws."

This section of the Amendment, unlike other sections,[7]
is a prohibition against certain conduct only when done
by a State—"state action" as it has come to be known—
and "erects no shield against merely private conduct, however discriminatory or wrongful." *Shelley* v.
Kraemer, 334 U. S. 1, 13 (1948).[8] This well-established
interpretation of section 1 of the Amendment—which all
the parties here, including the petitioners and the Solicitor General, accept—means that this section of the
Amendment does not of itself, standing alone, in the
absence of some cooperative state action, forbid property
holders, including restaurant owners, to ban people from
entering or remaining upon their premises, even if the
owners act out of racial prejudice.   But "the prohibitions
of the Amendment extend to all action of the State denying equal protection of the laws" whether "by its legislative, its executive, or its judicial authorities." *Virginia*
v. *Rives*, 100 U. S. 313, 318 (1880).   The Amendment
thus forbids all kinds of state action, by all state
agencies and officers, that discriminate against persons
on account of their race.[9] Petitioners, but not the
Solicitor General, contend that their conviction for tres-

---

[7] *E. g.*, § 5: "The Congress shall have power to enforce by appropriate legislation, the provisions of this article."

[8] Citing *Civil Rights Cases*, 109 U. S. 3 (1883); *United States* v.
Harris, 106 U. S. 629 (1883); *United States* v. *Cruikshank*, 92 U. S.
542 (1876).

[9] See *Shelley* v. *Kraemer*, *supra*, 334 U. S. 1, 14–15 (1948), particularly notes 13 and 14.

BELL *v.* MARYLAND.

pass under the state statute was by itself the kind of discriminatory state action forbidden by the Fourteenth
Amendment. This contention, on its face, has plausibility when considered along with general statements to
the effect that under the Amendment forbidden "state
action" may be that of the Judicial as well as of the Legislative or Executive Branches of Government. But a
mechanical application of the Fourteenth Amendment to
this case cannot survive analysis. The Amendment does
not forbid a State to prosecute for crimes committed
against a person, however prejudiced or narrow the victim's views may be. Nor can the prejudice and bigotry
of the victim of a crime be automatically attributed to
the State that prosecutes. Such a doctrine would not
only be based on a fiction, it would also severely handicap
a State's efforts to maintain a peaceful and orderly society.
Our society has put its trust in a system of criminal laws
to punish lawless conduct. To avert personal feuds and
violent brawls it has led its people to believe and expect
that wrongs against them will be vindicated in the courts.
Instead of attempting to take the law into their own
hands, they have been taught to call for police protection
to protect their rights wherever possible.[10] It would

---

[10] The use in this country of trespass laws, both civil and criminal,
to allow people to substitute the processes of the law for force and
violence has an ancient origin in England. Land law was once
bound up with the notion of "seisen," a term connoting "peace and
quiet." 2 Pollock and Maitland, The History of English Law Before
the Time of Edward I (2d ed. 1909), 29, 30. As Coke put it, "he
who is in possession may sit down in rest and quiet . . . ." 6 Co.
Rep. 57b. To vindicate this right to undisturbed use and enjoyment of one's property, the law of trespass came into being. The
leading historians of the early English law have observed the constant
interplay between "our law of possession and trespass" and have
concluded that since "to allow men to make forcible entries on
land . . . is to invite violence," the trespass laws' protection of
possession "is a prohibition of self-help in the interests of public
order." 2 Pollock and Maitland, *supra*, at 31, 41.

BELL *v.* MARYLAND.

betray our whole plan for law and order to say that a citizen, because of his personal prejudices, is cast outside the law's protection and cannot call for the aid of officers sworn to uphold the law and preserve the peace. None of our past cases justifies reading the Fourteenth Amendment in a way that might well penalize citizens who are law-abiding enough to call upon the law and its officers for protection instead of using their own physical strength or dangerous weapons to preserve their rights.

In contending that the State's prosecution of petitioners for trespass is state action forbidden by the Fourteenth Amendment, petitioners rely chiefly on *Shelley* v. *Kraemer, supra.* That reliance is misplaced. *Shelley* held that the Fourteenth Amendment was violated by a State's enforcement of restrictive covenants providing that certain pieces of real estate should not be used or occupied by noncaucasians, Negroes, or orientals, either as owners or tenants, and that in case of use or occupancy by such proscribed classes, the title of any person so using or occupying it should be divested. Many briefs were filed in that case by the parties and by *amici curiae.* To support the holding that state enforcement of the agreements constituted prohibited state action even though the agreements were made by private persons to whom, if they act alone, the Amendment does not apply, two chief grounds were urged: (1) This type of agreement constituted a restraint on alienation of property, sometimes in perpetuity, which, if valid, was in reality the equivalent of and had the effect of state and municipal zoning laws, accomplishing the same kind of racial discrimination as if the State had passed a statute instead of leaving this objective to be accomplished by a system of private contracts, enforced by the State. See *Marsh* v. *Alabama,* 326 U. S. 501 (1946); *Terry* v. *Adams,* 345 U. S. 461 (1953); cf. *Yick Wo* v. *Hopkins,* 118 U. S. 356 (1886); *Nashville, C. & St. L. R. Co.* v.

BELL *v.* MARYLAND.

Browning, 310 U. S. 362 (1940).[11]   (2) Nearly all the
briefs in *Shelley* which asked invalidation of the restrictive covenants iterated and reiterated that judicial
enforcement of this system of covenants was forbidden
state action because the right of a citizen to own, use,
enjoy, occupy, and dispose of property is a federal right
protected by the Fourteenth Amendment and by valid
federal statutes passed pursuant to congressional power
authorized by section 5 of the Amendment.[12]   This argument was buttressed by citation of many cases, some of
which are referred to in this Court's opinion in *Buchanan*
v. *Warley,* 245 U. S. 60 (1917).   In that case this Court
struck down, under the Fourteenth Amendment and federal statutes, a city ordinance which zoned property on
the basis of race, stating, 245 U. S., at 81, "The right
which the ordinance annulled was the civil right of a white
man to dispose of his property if he saw fit to do so to a
person of color, and of a colored person to make such disposition to a white person."   In *Shelley* this Court rested
heavily on the holding and opinion in *Buchanan* v. *Warley, supra,* quoting this statement from it: "The Fourteenth Amendment and these statutes [1866 and 1870]
enacted in furtherance of its purpose operate to qualify
and entitle a colored man to acquire property without

---

[11] On this subject the Solicitor General, in his brief, says: "The
series of covenants becomes in effect a local zoning ordinance binding
those in the area subject to its restrictions without their consent.
Cf. *Buchanan* v. *Warely,* 245 U. S. 60. Where the State has delegated to private persons a power so similar to lawmaking authority,
its exercise may fairly be held subject to constitutional restrictions."

[12] 14 Stat., § 1, p. 27 (1866), now 8 U. S. C. § 42, provides: "All
citizens of the United States shall have the same right in every State
and Territory, as is enjoyed by white citizens thereof, to inherit, purchase, lease, sell, hold and convey real and personal property." 15
Stat., § 16, p. 144 (1870), now 8 U. S. C. § 41, provides that "all
persons shall have the same right . . . to make contracts . . . as is
enjoyed by white citizens . . . ."

BELL *v.* MARYLAND.

state legislation discriminating against him solely because of color." 334 U. S., at 11–12. And the Court in *Shelley* went on to cite with approval two later decisions of this Court which, relying on *Buchanan* v. *Warley,* had invalidated other city ordinances.[13]

It seems pretty clear that the reason judicial enforcement of the restrictive covenants in *Shelley* was deemed state action was the conclusion, 334 U. S., at 19, that the State had there made available "the full coercive power of government to deny to petitioners, on grounds of race or color, the enjoyment of property rights in premises which petitioners are willing and financially able to acquire and which the grantors are willing to sell." In other words, state enforcement of the covenants had the effect of denying to the parties their constitutional and statutory rights to own, occupy, enjoy, and use their property as they wished. But the contention of petitioners here would require us to hold that the owner of Hooper's restaurant in Baltimore had no constitutional or statutory right to occupy, enjoy, and use his property by excluding persons from it at his own discretion and for his own reasons. We cannot subscribe to such a one-sided interpretation of a constitutional provision, the very heart of which is a guarantee of equal treatment under law to all.

In holding that mere judicial enforcement of the trespass law is not sufficient to impute to Maryland Hooper's refusal to serve Negroes, we are in accord with the Solicitor General's views as we understand them. He takes it for granted

"that the mere fact of State intervention through the courts or other public authority in order to provide sanctions for a private decision is not enough

---

[13] *Harmon* v. *Tyler,* 273 U. S. 668 (1927); *Richmond* v. *Deans,* 281 U. S. 704 (1930).

BELL *v.* MARYLAND.

to implicate the State for the purposes of the Fourteenth Amendment. . . . Where the only State
involvement is color-blind support for every property-owner's exercise of the normal right to choose
his business visitors or social guests, proof that the
particular property-owner was motivated by racial
or religious prejudices is not enough to convict the
State of denying equal protection of the laws."

The Solicitor General also says:

"The preservation of a free and pluralistic society
would seem to require substantial freedom for private choice in social, business and professional associations. Freedom of choice means the liberty to be
wrong as well as right, to be mean as well as noble,
to be vicious as well as kind. And even if that view
were questioned, the philosophy of federalism leaves
an area for choice to the States and their people,
when the State is not otherwise involved, instead of
vesting the only power of effective decision in the
federal courts."

We, like the Solicitor General, reject the argument that
the State's protection of Hooper's desire to choose his
customers on the basis of race by prosecuting trespassers
on his premises is enough, standing alone, to deprive
Hooper of his right to operate his property in his own
way. But we disagree with the contention that there are
other circumstances which, added to the State's prosecution for trespass, justify a finding of state action. There
is no Maryland law, no municipal ordinance, and no
official proclamations or actions of any kind that show
the slightest state coercion of, or encouragement to,
Hooper to bar Negroes from his restaurant.[14] Neither
the State, the city, nor any of their agencies has leased

---

[14] Compare *Peterson* v. *Greenville,* 373 U. S. 244 (1963); *Lombard* v. *Louisiana,* 373 U. S. 267 (1963).

BELL *v.* MARYLAND.

publicly owned property to Hooper.[15] It is true that
the State and city regulate the restaurants—but not as
to whether their customers shall be of one race or another. License fees are collected, but this licensing has
no relationship to race. Under such circumstances, to
hold that a State must be held to have participated in
prejudicial conduct of its licenses is too big a jump for us
to take. Businesses owned by private persons do not
become agencies of the State because they are licensed;
to hold that they do would be completely to negate all
our private ownership concepts and practices. And the
mere fact that a privately owned business serves a large
segment of the public does not mean that it is constitutionally required to serve all. One of the most distin-
guishing characteristics of a privately owned business is
that, in the absence of statutory or common-law regulations, it conducts its business according to its own judgment as to what is in its best interests. And it should
not need to be said that common law or statutory ideas
of a duty of "public utilities" to serve the public are not
of constitutional dimensions. *Nebbia* v. *New York,* 291
U. S. 502 (1934), served to clarify much of the past
confused thinking on this subject.

Neither the parties nor the Solicitor General, at least
with respect to Maryland, has been able to find the present existence of any state law or local ordinance, any state
court or administrative rulings, or any other official state
conduct which could possibly have had any coercive
influence on Hooper's racial practices. Yet despite a
complete absence of any sort of proof or even respectable
speculation that Maryland in any way instigated or
encouraged Hooper's refusal to serve Negroes, it is argued
at length that Hooper's practice should be classified as
"state action." This contention rests on a long narrative

[15] Compare *Burton* v. *Wilmington Parking Authority,* 365 U. S.
715 (1961).

BELL *v.* MARYLAND.

of historical events, both before and since the Civil War, to show that in Maryland, and indeed in the whole South, state laws and state actions have been a part of a pattern of racial segregation in the conduct of business, social, religious, and other activities. This pattern of segregation hardly needs historical references to prove it. The argument is made that the trespass conviction should be labeled "state action" because the "momentum" of Maryland's "past legislation" is still substantial in the realm of public accommodations. To that extent, the Solicitor General argues, "a State which has drawn a color line may not suddenly assert that it is color blind." We cannot accept such an *ex post facto* argument to hold the application here of Maryland's trespass law unconstitutional. Nor can we appreciate the fairness or justice of holding the present generation of Marylanders responsible for what their ancestors did in other days—even if we had the right to substitute our own ideas of what the Fourteenth Amendment ought to be for what it was written and adopted to achieve.

There is another objection to accepting this argument. If it were accepted, we would have one Fourteenth Amendment for the South and quite a different and more lenient one for the other parts of the country. Present "state action" in this area of constitutional rights would be governed by past history in the South—by present conduct in the North and West. Our Constitution was not written to be read that way, and we will not do it.

We hold that section 1 of the Fourteenth Amendment does not bar Maryland from enforcing its trespass laws so long as it does so with impartiality. We do not believe that this section of the Amendment was written or designed to interfere with a property owner's right to choose his social or business associates, so long as he does not

BELL *v.* MARYLAND.

run counter to a valid state or federal regulation. This Court has done much in carrying out its solemn duty to protect people from discrimination. It is destined to do more as cases and controversies involving racial questions are brought before it. But we decline to say that the Amendment of itself compels either a black man or a white man running his own private business to trade with anyone else against his will. The case before us does not involve the power of the Congress to pass a law compelling privately owned businesses to trade with all if they trade with any. We express no views as to such a law. We simply decline to construe the Fourteenth Amendment as embodying such a drastic change in what has until very recently been accepted by all as the right of a man who owns a business to run the business in his own way so long as some valid regulatory statute does not tell him to do otherwise. If free enterprise means anything, it means that.

III.

Petitioners, but not the Solicitor General, contend that their convictions for trespass deny them the right of freedom of expression guaranteed by the Constitution. They argue that their

> "expression (asking for service) was entirely appropriate to the time and place at which it occurred. They did not shout or obstruct the conduct of business. There were no speeches, picket signs, handbills or other forms of expression in the store possibly inappropriate to the time and place. Rather they offered to purchase food in a place and at a time set aside for such transactions. Their protest demonstrations were a part of the 'free trade in ideas' (*Abrams* v. *United States*, 250 U. S. 616, 630, Holmes, J., dissenting)."

BELL *v.* MARYLAND.

Their argument comes down to this: that since petitioners did not shout, obstruct Hooper's business (which
the record refutes), make speeches, or display picket
signs, handbills, or other forms of expression, they had a
perfect constitutional right to assemble and remain in
the restaurant, over the owner's continuing objections,
for the purpose of expressing themselves by language and
"demonstrations" bespeaking their hostility to Hooper's
refusal to serve Negroes.   Our prior cases do not support
such a privilege growing out of the constitutional rights of
speech and assembly.   Unquestionably petitioners had
a constitutional right to express these views wherever
they had an unquestioned legal right to be.   Cf. *Marsh*
v. *Alabama, supra.*   But there is the rub in this case.
The contention that petitioners had a constitutional right
to enter or to stay on Hooper's premises against his will
because, if there, they would have had a constitutional
right to express their desire to have restaurant service
over Hooper's protest is a boot-strap argument.   The
right to freedom of expression is a right to express views—
not a right to force other people to supply a platform or
a pulpit.   It is argued that this supposed constitutional
right to invade other people's property would not mean
that a man's home, his private club, or his church could
be forcibly entered or used against his will—only his store
or place of business which he has himself opened to the
public.   This argument assumes that Hooper *had* opened
his restaurant to the public.   But the whole quarrel of
this group with Hooper was that, instead of opening to all,
he refused service to Negroes.   Moreover, the Fourteenth
Amendment protects "life, liberty and property," not just
some people's "life," some people's "liberty," and some
kinds of "property."

A great purpose of freedom of speech and press is to
provide a forum for settlement of acrimonious disputes
peaceably, without resort to intimidation, force, or vio-

BELL *v.* MARYLAND.

lence. The experience of ages points to the inexorable fact that people will fight, sometimes to the death, to protect that which the law recognizes as theirs from forcible invasion or occupancy by others. Trespass laws are born of this experience. They have been, and doubtless still are, important features of any government dedicated, as this country is, to a rule of law. Whatever power it may allow the States or grant to the Congress to regulate the use of private property, the Constitution does not confer upon any group the right to substitute rule by force for rule by law. Force leads to violence, violence to mob conflicts, and these to the rule by the strongest groups with control of the most deadly weapons. Our Constitution, noble work of wise men, was designed— all of it—to chart a quite different course: to "establish Justice, insure domestic Tranquility . . . and secure the Blessings of Liberty to ourselves and our Posterity." Sometimes the Rule of Law seems too slow to some for the settlement of their just grievances. But it is the plan of our Government. On it we have put our trust and staked our future. This constitutional Rule of Law has served us well. Maryland's trespass law does not depart from it. Nor shall we.

The judgment of the Court of Appeals of Maryland is

Affirmed.

From: The Ch:

Circulated:__

Recirculated:

SUPREME COURT OF THE UNITED STATES

No. 9.—October Term, 1963.

Charles F. Barr et al., Petitioners, *v.* City of Columbia.	On Writ of Certiorari to the Supreme Court of South Carolina.

[May —, 1964.]

Mr. Chief Justice Warren, dissenting.

In this and companion cases, the Court has interposed principles of privacy and the protection of property rights between Negro petitioners and the right to equal treatment in public places. Its decision will stand in sharp contrast to the traditional fate in this Court of narrow and technical arguments which are offered as the excuse for denying fundamental human rights. More important, unfortunately, will be the effect which the decision will have on the future development of basic American principles of equality. But we need not reach into the future to examine the effects of the decision. To me, the facts of this case precisely illustrate the extremes to which the doctrine on which the Court bases its opinion can be extended.

The scene of the activity in this case was the Taylor Street Pharmacy in Columbia, South Carolina. As described by its manager, it advertises itself as a complete department store. It is divided essentially into two areas, a "front" area and a luncheonette department. Each area operates under a license from the city, and the two are divided by a shoulder-high partition. Within the luncheonette department are three half-moon shaped counters with stools appropriately spaced along the counter area. Access to the store is through a door leading into the front area, and to get to the luncheonette

* JMHP.

BARR *v.* CITY OF COLUMBIA.

department, one must pass by other counters which dispaly the varied products of a modern department store.

The front area openly caters to all races, and in fact would seem to a significant extent economically dependent upon the patronage of Negroes. In any event, as the manager testified,[1] the store stood with open arms to get the Negro dollar. Both of the petitioners who testified stated that they had on previous occasions entered the front area without objection for the purpose of making a purchase, and in fact, one of them made a purchase in the front area on his way to the rear of the store on the occasion which gave rise to his arrest.

The luncheonette department is a different story, however. Although the manager pointed out that the store was advertised as a complete department store, like the normal department store no advertising significance was placed on the fact that it had a lunch department. And

---

[1] Specifically:

"Q. . . . You in the operation of your store, cater to the public generally, don't you?

"A. That's correct.

"Q. Irrespective of race?

"A. In the front area, that's correct, the Taylor Street Pharmacy department."

And later:

"Q. Do you have Negroes trading in your store?

"A. Yes.

"Q. One or two, or in large numbers?

"A. I think quite large numbers.

"Q. So quite a bit of the income from your store comes from Negroes?

"A. Quite a bit.

"Q. You don't hesitate to give them service do you?

"A. In the front area, definitely not.

"Q. As a matter of fact, you invite them in don't you?

"A. That's correct.

"Q. Just like any other member of the public, you invite them in?

"A. That's correct."

BARR *v.* CITY OF COLUMBIA.

although it is not clear where, a notice was posted to the effect that the management reserved the right to refuse service to anyone.[2]   The manager testified that it was the store's policy not to serve Negroes in the lunch department, and that although they were invited into the store, they were not wanted in the lunch area.

But they were not completely excluded.   The words of the manager make this clear:

> "Q. You don't invite them into the luncheon area. I mean Negroes?
>
> "A. We do not.
>
> "Q. Under any circumstances?
>
> "A. If they request it, we will fix an order to go for them, at their request.
>
> "Q. So Negroes can then come into the back area, I guess I'll call it, the luncheon area, and receive food service?
>
> "A. Food service to go."

The store, in other words, invited the food patronage of Negroes, but not on the same terms as that of other races. What the Taylor Street Pharmacy tells these petitioners and other Negroes, then, is that they are welcome to come in and spend their money, both on food and other items, so long as they do not sit down at empty stools which line the counter where they await their food to take out.

The Court's justification for the State's enforcement of the Pharmacy's *right* to say this is that otherwise the

---

[2] How one unfamiliar with the policies of the store was to tell the difference between the open invitation into the front of the store and the lack of an invitation into the lunch area remains a mystery.   The only indication was this notice, which presumably stated merely that the management reserved the right to refuse service to anyone.   Although the exact wording of the sign is not in the record, what is in the record is open to interpretation as a reservation of the right to exclude people whose behavior was thought unsatisfactory.   In any event, the notice did not state as such that Negroes were not welcome.

BARR *v.* CITY OF COLUMBIA.

Court would be required "to hold that . . . [the store], despite the absence of statutory regulation, had no constitutional or statutory right to occupy, enjoy, and use . . . [its] property by excluding persons for reasons satisfactory to the owner. We cannot subscribe to such a one-sided interpretation of a constitutional provision and federal statutes, the very heart of which is a guarantee of equal treatment under law to all." *Bell* v. *Maryland, ante,* at ——. The Court has thus elevated to the status of constitutional protection a claimed property right which is at best the right to solicit the patronage of Negroes at a lunch counter if they stand up, but to deny it if they sit down. What possible purpose the State advances by enforcing and protecting such a narrow and impersonal right completely escapes me, lest it be the right to perpetuate a custom of systematic segregation in public eating facilities. That this is a legitimate State objective cannot, of course, be argued.

When this case is examined from the perspective of the actual events leading up to the arrest of these petitioners, with a particular eye to the manner in which this highly theoretical "property right" was sought to be protected, the difficulty of concluding, as the Court has done, that "the officers here did nothing which would justify a holding that they were acting for the State in any capacity except to arrest people who violated the trespass statute," *ante,* at ——, becomes apparent. For not only in this case has the State expressed an unusual benevolence for a bizarre right to issue deceptive invitations to service in public places, but the right was enforced by its police with a particular fervor which one would hope could be directed at the more serious criminal offenses which plague our day. Here, as we shall see, the police initiated and carried to fruition the entire affair which resulted in the arrest and punishment of these petitioners.

BARR *v.* CITY OF COLUMBIA.

The events which occurred on Tuesday, March 15, 1960, were presaged by a telephone call *from the police to the store manager* the day before. In the manager's own words, "I was informed on Monday that they would be there at 12:35 Tuesday . . . ." That the informants were the police is made clear by testimony which followed:

"Q. . . . Now on March 15, 1960, you testified that you knew that these defendants or some others would come into your store?

"A. I didn't know that. I was informed on Monday, that a demonstration was planned for the Taylor Street Pharmacy at 12:35. Didn't say what date.

"Q. Based upon your information you then asked the assistance of the police department and other police officers?

"A. That's correct.

"Q. And the police officers who were in your store on March 15, 1960, were there at your request?

"A. Well, I would say yes or no. I mean they came and informed me of the demonstration and we were working as a group. I'll put it that way. I didn't call them to come around and inform me. They informed me in advance."

And what were "we working as a group" to prevent? Again in the manager's words:

"A. . . . Any type of violence could erupt or anything, against my store policy. It could create violence.

"Q. Anything against your store policy, you then wished the officers to assist you in preventing?

"A. That's correct."

The Court has pointed out in part of its opinion, and with that I agree, that there was no evidence to support a

BARR *v.* CITY OF COLUMBIA.

conviction for breach of the peace. The petitioners, college students, were quiet, cleanly, and in all respects orderly. With elements of violence thus removed, the arrest, although technically for the crime of trespass, can solely be justified as for the purpose of enforcing the store's policy, a policy which, as noted, was founded on a right to compel Negroes to stand up to buy their food solely for the reason that they were Negroes. The store might as well have offered to feed only Negroes who would crawl in on their hands and knees, or, as in other caste systems, who would purchase food under conditions that would not cause their shadow to fall on the food of whites. It saddens me deeply to think that this Court, which has so far advanced the notion of the equal dignity of all men before the law, would sanction the right so publicly to first shame and then punish one who merely seeks that which any white man takes for granted. Irrespective of the activity of other branches of our Government, the courts, and particularly this Court, cannot escape the responsibility imposed by the Constitution to assure to all Americans the basic right of equal protection under the laws.

The extent of police involvement in enforcing the store policy is further evidenced by the scene when the five petitioners arrived at the store. They came in two groups, three in one group and two in another.[3] As one

---

[3] Although there is much talk of a planned demonstration, actually there is little evidence in the record to support the conclusion that these five petitioners were part of an organized plan to converge on the Taylor Street Pharmacy. The two petitioners who testified each stated that they had independently formed the conclusion to go to the pharmacy to get their lunch. One of them, David Carter, would only say in response to questioning on this score that the trip of his group to the store was prearranged only to the extent that the idea was formed prior to departing for the store. But in any event, that the petitioners' or the storeowners' rights should be ele-

BARR *v.* CITY OF COLUMBIA.

of the petitioners testified, when they arrived at the store, "we saw the newsmen and the policemen on the outside." Waiting inside for them were the store manager and Officer Stokes, a member of the South Carolina Law Enforcement Division and apparently not in uniform. At least one other policeman, a Deputy Sheriff, was also waiting for them inside, as was the manager of the luncheonette department. The petitioners entered the store, and apparently some lingered in the front of the store to make a purchase of cigarettes or cards while the others proceeded to the rear and into the lunch department. They sat on vacant stools, and before they asked for service, the manager made a statement to the group that he was not going to serve them, and that they would have to leave.[4] He did not even know at this point whether they wanted to be served there or whether they wanted food to take out. All he knew was that, being Negroes, they sat on stools which were reserved for white customers.

Petitioners did nothing in response to the manager's request to leave, and it was Officer Stokes who was the next to move. *He* then requested that the manager go to each individual and ask him in his presence to leave.[5]

---

vated or diminished by the fact alone that five people may have decided the day before to eat lunch at the pharmacy is not suggested by respondents or the Court.

[4] The record is not clear as to what the manager actually said. Both he and Officer Stokes testified that he told the petitioners to leave, although the petitioners each testified that they interpreted the manager's statement as leaving them the option to stay although it would do them no good to stay since they would not be served.

[5] There is no indication that the manager asked the officer's assistance at this point. Stokes testified that:

"Q. . . . After he [the manager] requested them to leave, did they get up and leave?

"A. No, sir, they never turned around. They just sat there at the counter.   [*Footnote 5 continued on p. 8*]

BARR *v.* CITY OF COLUMBIA.

This the manager did, and then left the department to the police officers for the purpose of enforcing the store policy. For as the manager said, "[*w*]*e had a previous agreement* to that effect, that if they did not leave, they would be placed under arrest for trespassing."[6]

It is thus apparent that not only was the State, now with the full support of a majority of this Court, seeking

---

"Q. In other words, they didn't pay any attention to his request?

"A. They didn't do anything.

"Q. What happened then?

"A. *I requested* that Mr. Terry [the store manager] go to each individual and ask him to leave, in my presence, . . ."

The manager's testimony is equally explicit:

"Q. What did they do when they came in?

"A. Well, just the same testimony as Mr. Stokes gave, they went back to the lunch department, through the store and back to the lunch department. Four of them sat at the first counter and one at the second counter, and I went back and asked them, or told them I would not serve them and asked them to leave, *and Mr. Stokes then requested* that I ask each one individually, which I did, all but one, and the luncheonette manager asked him and they refused to leave, and I left the department, with the law enforcement officers there."

[6] The last question asked of the manager was whether it was his idea to have petitioners arrested, or the idea of the police department. His reply:

"I'll put it that it was the both of us' idea, that if they were requested to leave and failed to leave, and given time to leave, that they would be arrested."

Stokes' testimony on this point is also revealing:

"Q. [D]id . . . [the manager] request that you arrest these defendants?

"A. No.

"Q. Did he request that you evict them from his premises?

"A. You mean at that time?

"Q. At any time?

"A. No. He did state before that he didn't want them in his store.

"Q. Did he go further and say: 'If they come in my store, I want you to arrest them' or words to that effect?

"A. No, I won't say he said that."

BARR *v.* CITY OF COLUMBIA.

to protect and enforce a narrow and technical right to serve Negroes standing up but not sitting down, but it was doing so in a manner which hardly befits the neutrality which the Court describes.   An officer of the State Police, a Deputy Sheriff, and local police were all present beforehand, and the police had suggestively informed the manager that a demonstration was forthcoming.   The cooperation of the State and local enforcement authorities in this case, together with the overreaching of the police, serves to accentuate a fact true in all of these cases, that it is the policy of the State that is being enforced as well as that of the private entrepreneur.   To say that the policy is merely "private" ignores the fact that without the State it could not survive.

What this leads to is illustrated by the testimony of David Carter, one of the petitioners.   He testified that he took his seat next to a white lady who was eating her lunch.   The luncheonette manager, according to Carter's version of the events, came up to the lady and told her to "get up, we'll get them out of here."   Prior to the arrival of the manager, Carter testified, the lady gave no indication of getting up: "She sat there and began eating *just as if I was a human being sitting beside her, which I was."*   As my Brothers DOUGLAS and GOLDBERG have convincingly demonstrated, the important civil right of equal access to public places is a right which the Constitution forbids a State to deny in the name of private property. The Constitution can mean no less if it is to restore to the Negro, as the Civil War Amendments intended, that little bit of humanity which he loses each time a state-sanctioned inferior status is publicly thrust upon him.   I cannot in conscience be a part of a return to a tradition which so belongs to the past.

SUPREME COURT OF THE UNITED STATES.

: Clark,

No. 12.—OCTOBER TERM, 1963.

Circulated: JU

Recirculated:

Robert Mack Bell et al., Petitioners, *v.* State of Maryland.

On Writ of Certiorari to the Court of Appeals of the State of Maryland.

[June —, 1964.]

MR. JUSTICE CLARK.

This case presents questions under the Fourteenth Amendment as to the validity of a conviction for the crime of trespass arising out of the refusal of the petitioners, who are Negroes, to leave a public restaurant in Baltimore City upon the request of the management based solely upon the ground of their color. The basic question on the merits is whether the conviction is proscribed by the Fourteenth Amendment.[1] The Court of Appeals held that the trespass was upon the privately owned premises of respondent and was the result of its policy not to serve Negroes. It, therefore, concluded *inter alia* that, absent local laws requiring segregation, there was no state action present and affirmed the conviction. 227 Md. 302. In view of the recurring importance of the question we granted certiorari. 374 U. S. 805. We have concluded that the State is involved to such a "significant extent," *Burton* v. *Wilmington Parking Authority*, 365 U. S. 715, 722 (1961), that the case must be reversed.

1. THE FACTS.

On June 17, 1960, at about 4:15 p.m. 12 Negro students entered the lobby of respondent's Hooper restaurant. Upon reaching the top of the four steps leading from

---

[1] In view of our disposition we do not reach any other questions presented.

BELL *v.* MARYLAND.

the entrance lobby to the dining room one of the students
asked the hostess that they be seated. She replied, "I'm
sorry, but we have not integrated yet." The manager
of the restaurant soon approached the group and said
that it was "company policy" not to serve them. Some
of the students brushed by while the manager was talking and seated themselves at various tables in the dining
room. The president of the restaurant corporation soon
appeared and instructed the manager to call the police.
Two officers came to the restaurant, after which the
manager read the Maryland trespass statute to the students, requested them to leave, and some left the premises.
The names of those remaining were taken and the president went to the courthouse and secured warrants for
their arrest. Upon his return, no arrests were made and
all agreed to appear for trial on the following Monday.

The record indicates that the restaurant is owned by
a corporation, Hooper Food Company, Inc. The president testified that he was in the rear of the restaurant,
where there is a bar and lounge, when he was attracted
by "the commotion up front"; that he reasoned with
some of the students as to why the restaurant's policy
was not yet one of integration.

> "I set at the table with him and two other people . . .
> and told him that I had two hundred employees and
> half of them were colored. I thought as much of
> them as I did the white employees. I invited them
> back in my kitchen if they'd like to go back and talk
> to them. I wanted to prove to them it wasn't my
> policy, my personal prejudice, we were not, that
> I had valuable colored employees and I thought just
> as much of them. I tried to reason with these
> leaders, told them that as long as my customers were
> deciding who they want to eat with, I'm at the mercy
> of my customers. I'm trying to do what they want.
> If they fail to come in, these people are not paying

BELL *v.* MARYLAND.

my expenses, my bills. They didn't want to go back and talk to my colored employees because every one of them is in sympathy with me and that is we're in sympathy with what their objectives are, and what they are trying to abolish, but we disapprove of their methods of force and pushed their way in."

The testimony was that the students, aside from the original pushing their way in, were peaceful, sat at the tables reading books and caused no disturbance. At their trial the students raised Fourteenth Amendment due process and equal protection objections, including free speech and association, as well as racial discrimination claims. These were all rejected by the trial court and on appeal.

2. The Factual Setting of the Claims.

It is well that we first orient ourselves as to the factual background presented. It involves an asserted trespass upon the premises of a public restaurant and bar which is licensed and regulated by the State. The premises are open to the public and, as far as the record shows, the corporation holds out a standing invitation for all to enter and be served. Under Maryland law the term "restaurant" is defined to be "an establishment for the accommodation of the public, equipped with a proper and adequate dining room, tables, chairs, and sufficient facilities for preparing and serving regular meals, as may be approved by the liquor control board." Art. 2.B § Z, Annotated Code of Maryland, 1957. The claim asserted, therefore, concerns only a public place not private premises or personal associations.

Nor do petitioners claim any "social rights." Their suit has nothing to do with matters of purely private concern, such as the right of a homeowner to close his door on whosoever he chooses. As Mr.. Justice Douglas stated it in *Lombard* v. *Louisiana,* 373 U. S. 267, 274

BELL *v.* MARYLAND.

(1963): "If this were an intrusion of a man's home or
yard or farm or garden, the property owner could seek
and obtain the aid of the state against the intruder."
Nor does this case concern the use of the property of a
private membership club. It has to do only with equal
civil rights not with equal social privileges. The petitioners make no claim to the latter. In this framework
we pass on to the precedents of this Court in regard to
Fourteenth Amendment claims of equal protection.

3. EVOLVEMENT OF THE DOCTRINE OF "STATE ACTION."

The "state action" doctrine was evolved in the *Slaughter House Cases,* 16 Wall. 36 (1873), where Mr. Justice
Miller, speaking for the Court, held that the Fourteenth
Amendment was directed at "action of a state . . . by
way of discrimination against the Negroes as a class
or on account of their race." And, seven years later, in
Ex parte Virginia, 100 U. S. 339 (1880), the Court
held that the Fourteenth Amendment "was to secure
equal rights to all persons" and that it "must mean that
no agency of the State or of the officers or agents by whom
its powers are exerted, shall deny to any person within
its jurisdiction the equal protection of the laws" or take
any action which deprives them "of property, life or liberty without due process of law, or denies or takes away
the equal protection of the laws." Three years later the
Civil Rights Cases, 109 U. S. 3 (1883), pounded home the
same doctrine. Mr. Justice Bradley, speaking for the
Court, struck down convictions based on denial to persons
of color of accommodations and privileges of an inn or
hotel (Civil Rights Act of 1875). He placed several
significant passages in his opinion in this regard:

> "The only question under the present head . . . is
> whether the reprisal to any persons of the accommo-
> dations of an inn or public conveyance or a place of
> public amusement *by an individual and without any*

BELL *v.* MARYLAND.

sanction or support from any state law or regulation
does inflict upon such persons any manner of servi-
tude . . . ." At p. 23. (Emphasis supplied.)

And in discussing this question with respect to denial of
public accommodations because of color the Court specifically carved out of its holding: "Whether it might not
be a denial of a right which, *if sanctioned by state law,*
would be obnoxious to the prohibitions of the Fourteenth
Amendment is another question." At p. 21. (Emphasis
supplied.) Finally, in discussing the grant of power
under the Amendment the Court held:

> "Under the 14th Amendment, it [Congress] has
> power to counteract and render nugatory all state
> laws and proceedings which have the effect to abridge
> any of the privileges and immunities of citizens of
> the United States, or to deprive them of life, liberty
> or property without due process of law, or to deny to
> any of them the equal protection of the laws." At
> p. 23.

The overriding criteria of those cases, *i. e.,* the presence
of state sanctions, was put in clearer focus when it was
determined that rules of law declared by a state's judiciary are just as much subject to the restraints of the
Fourteenth Amendment as are rules embodied in legislation. This Court has long found denial of Fourteenth
Amendment rights in judicially erected substantive rules.
Cantwell v. *Connecticut,* 310 U. S. 296 (1940); *Bridges* v.
California, 314 U. S. 252 (1941); *Edwards* v. *South Carolina,* 372 U. S. 22 (1963). And it came to pass, pursuant
to this ruling, that *de facto* segregation by private choice,
enforced by court decree, was stricken down in *Marsh* v.
Alabama, 326 U. S. 501 (1946), through the denial of the
use of criminal trespass statutes to control speech on private company-owned streets; and the civil injunctive
process to enforce private restrictive covenants to keep

BELL *v.* MARYLAND.

the Negro from owning real property was denied in *Shelly v. Kraemer*, 334 U. S. 1 (1948); and, in the political field, *Terry* v. *Adams*, 345 U. S. 461 (1953), struck down the private Jaybird primary which sought to take away the effectiveness of the Negro vote; and, in *Barrows* v. *Jackson*, 346 U. S. 249 (1953), *Shelly* v. *Kraemer, supra*, was revisited and damages arising from the breach of a private restrictive covenant on land, based upon color, were declared to be nonrecoverable. Finally, and only last Term, prosecutions under the trespass laws of the State based upon sit-ins were found to be state action proscribed by the Fourteenth Amendment. *Lombard* v. *Louisiana*, 373 U. S. 267 (1963). Also *Peterson* v. *Greenville*, 373 U. S. 244 (1963); *Shuttlesworth* v. *Birmingham*, 373 U. S. 262 (1963), and *Wright* v. *Georgia*, 373 U. S. 284 (1963).

Likewise significant limitations were placed on places of public accommodation, operated by a State or its lessee, in a series of holdings that patrons could not be excluded therefrom because of color. *Watson* v. *City of Memphis*, 373 U. S. 526 (1963); *New Orleans City Park Improvement Assn.* v. *Detiege*, 358 U. S. 54 (1958); *Mayor and City Council of Baltimore* v. *Dawson*, 350 U. S. 877 (1955); *Holmes* v. *City of Atlanta*, 350 U. S. 879 (1955); *Muir* v. *Louisville Park Theatrical Assn.*, 347 U. S. 971 (1954); *Derrington* v. *Plummer*, 240 F. 2d 922, and *Burton* v. *Wilmington Parking Authority*, 365 U. S. 715 (1961). And in *Boynton* v. *Virginia*, 364 U. S. 454 (1960), prosecution of a Negro who sought service in a privately operated restaurant (not connected with any transportation facility) in an interstate bus terminal was struck down on the ground of the Interstate Commerce Act's requirement that a carrier serve its passengers without regard to color.

And so it is crystal clear today that the State cannot require a private establishment to segregate its customers. Nor is the mere presence of a Negro in an estab-

BELL *v.* MARYLAND.

lishment segregating or refusing to serve Negroes a criminal offense. *Garner* v. *Louisiana,* 368 U. S. 157 (1961). The choice of the State to discriminate is completely foreclosed. The teaching of these cases is that if discrimination in a private establishment is to survive it must be clearly established that the State has not been involved in the discrimination to any "significant extent." The question is "whether the character of the state's involvement in an arbitrary discrimination is such that it should be held responsible for the discrimination." Mr. Justice Harlan, concurring in *Peterson* v. *Greenville, supra,* at p. 249. We turn to an application of these teachings.

4. The Application of the Fourteenth Amendment.

There can be no question but what the Fourteenth Amendment under our cases creates a constitutional right in all Americans, regardless of color, to be treated equally by all branches of the Government. Indeed, President Johnson only recently stated this national policy in these words:

> "Today Americans of all races stand side by side in Berlin and Viet Nam. They died side by side in Korea. Surely they can work and eat and travel side by side in America." State of the Union Message, January 8, 1964.

Previous Presidents enunciated the same doctrine in no unmistakable terms. Likewise the States have responded at a quickened pace and today we find 31 States with public accommodation statutes on their books.[2] In addition, some 143 cities [as of July 1963] of 10,000 or

---

[2] Those States not having public accommodation laws are: Alabama, Arizona, Arkansas, Georgia, Florida, Hawaii, Kentucky, Louisiana, Mississippi, Nevada, Missouri, North Carolina, Oklahoma, South Carolina, Tennessee, Texas, Utah, Virginia, West Virginia.

BELL *v.* MARYLAND.

more population in North and South Carolina, Georgia,
Alabama, Mississippi, Florida, Texas, Maryland, West
Virginia, Oklahoma, and Kentucky have voluntarily
removed restrictions in public accommodations. See
Thomas P. Lewis, The Sit In Cases: Great Expectations.
The Supreme Court Review, 1963, p. 139, n. 89.   Indeed,
the City of Baltimore itself has an ordinance prohibiting
owners and operators of places of public accommodation,
including restaurants, from denying this service or facilities to any person because of color.   Ordinance No. 1249,
June 8, 1962, § 10 (a).   And Maryland itself enacted a
similar statute effective June 1, 1963, applicable to
Baltimore City and Baltimore County.   § 4913 Md.
Code Ann. (1963 Supp.).   As we have seen the definition of "restaurant" in the Maryland Annotated Code
declares it to be an "establishment for the accommodation of the public" and the regulations of the Board of
Liquor License Commissioners of Baltimore City describes it for license purposes as "any lunchroom, cafe
or other establishment located in a permanent building
with ample space and accommodations wherein hot meals
are habitually prepared, sold and served *to the public*
during the hours it is regularly open for business . . .
equipped with a kitchen having complete facilities and
utensils for preparing and serving hot and cold meals *to
the public.*
   Moreover, it is firmly established throughout the
United States, regardless of statutes and ordinances such
as exist in Maryland, that the common usages of restaurant facilities places them in the same category as the
innkeeper, as described by Justice Story in his Law of
Bailments: "An innkeeper is bound . . . to take in all
travellers and wayfaring persons and to entertain them,
if he can accommodate them, for a reasonable compensation; . . ." § 476 (Schouler, 9th ed., 1878).   And as

BELL *v.* MARYLAND.

the requirement was stated by Blackstone over a hundred years earlier as:

> "If an innkeeper, or other victualler, hangs out a sign and opens his house for travellers, it is an implied engagement to entertain all persons who travel that way; and upon this universal *assumpsit* an action on the case will lie against him for damages if he, without good reason, refuses to admit a traveler." 3 Blackstone Commentaries 166.

While, as Mr. Justice McLean stated in *United States* v. *McDaniel,* 7 Pet. 1, 15 (1833): "Usage cannot alter law, but it is evidence of the construction given to it; . . . usages . . . which have become a kind of common law . . . regulate the rights and duties of those who act within their respective limits." We know of no usage that has grown any more into "a kind of common law" than that recognized by all men with respect to public restaurants. Indeed, the universality of the understanding "has become a piece of the fabric of society," Thomas P. Lewis, *supra,* at 144, and has led to a common dependence of our people upon the accommodations of public eating places day in and day out. As a result, thousands of establishments of this type are in operation and millions of our people go to them with the expectation and realization of service. Nothing has stronger support in experience. The well-behaved are always welcome. In some communities the only exceptions are those of color. This customary treatment has, therefore, in some communities, grown into a standard, foreign to the Equal Protection Clause.

In such a totality of circumstances as those we conclude that the rationale of *Shelly* v. *Kraemer, supra; Marsh* v. *Alabama, supra; Buchanan* v. *Worley,* 245 U. S. 60 (1917), and *Harmon* v. *Tyler,* 273 U. S. 668 (1927), apply. In

BELL *v.* MARYLAND.

Shelly, as we have seen, the Court forbids the enforcement
of private restrictive covenants on land because of color.
The Court analogized the restrictions to municipal zoning
laws, proscribed by the Fourteenth Amendment. Hence
the State violated its "neutral" position when its courts
enforced the covenants. Here the Hooper restaurant
turned away the Negro students from its establishment
entirely because of color. This could not have been
accomplished under a statute or ordinance and, on the
basis of *Shelly,* the State could not enforce the discrimination. It is said that in *Shelly* the purchaser was able
and willing to buy and the owner willing to sell and that
to enforce the covenant would destroy their federally
secured right. But this argument was demolished in
Barrows v. *Jackson,* 346 U. S. 249 (1953), where there
was no such relationship. In fact, one of the covenantors
to the discrimination sued another for damages on the
breach of a restrictive covenant against a sale to non-Cau-
casians entered into between them. The Court refused
to allow any damages. It held

> "It sufficiently appears, that mulcting in dam-
> ages . . . will be solely for the purpose of giving
> vitality to the restrictive covenant, that is to say, to
> punish the respondent for not continuing to discrim-
> inate . . . . This Court will not permit or require
> California to coerce respondent to observe a restric-
> tive covenant that this Court would deny California
> the right to enforce in equity *Shelly, supra;* or that
> this Court would deny California the right to incor-
> porate in a statute; *Buchanan* v. *Worley,* 245 U. S.
> 60; or that could not be enforced in a federal juris-
> diction because such a covenant would be contrary to
> public policy." At p. 258.

In short, the Court said, the effect of its decision was to
"close the gap to the use of the covenant, so universally

BELL *v.* MARYLAND.

condemned by the courts." Mrs. Jackson, the co-covenantor, neither claimed nor had been denied any constitutional right. The fact is that Mr. Barrows claiming the constitutional right—nonimpairment of his contract. There was no non-Caucasian before the Court. Still the Court permitted her to rely on the invasion of the constitutional rights of others, [the non-Caucasian] to defend successfully this damage suit. We believe the rationale of the case controls here. The practice of discrimination is likewise "universally condemned"; the State cannot engage in it. The students here—like Mrs. Jackson—must be allowed to "close the gap."

Much is made of the fact here that this is private property. But a similar situation was present in *Marsh* v. *Alabama, supra,* where a suburb of Mobile, Alabama, Chickasaw, was owned by the Gulf Shipbuilding Corporation. Marsh, a Jehovah's Witness, "came onto the sidewalk . . . stood near the Post Office and undertook to distribute literature." At p. 503. There was a posted notice "This is Private Property, and Without Written Permission No Street or House Vender, Agent or Solicitation of Any Kind Will be Permitted." Marsh was warned that she could not distribute the literature and was asked to leave. Refusing, she was prosecuted for entering and remaining on the premises of another. As Mr. Justice Black said for the Court:

> "Ownership does not always mean absolute dominion. The more an owner, for his advantage, opens up his property for use by the public in general, the more do his rights become circumscribed by the statutory and constitutional rights of those who use it." At p. 506.

Hooper's restaurant was in an analogous position. The property in neither case had been dedicated to the pub-

BELL *v.* MARYLAND.

lic but its usage was of a public character. The opinion
clearly draws this distinction:

> "We do not think it makes any significant consti-
> tutional difference as to the relationship between
> the rights of the owner and those of the public that
> here the State, instead of permitting the corporation
> to operate a highway, permitted it to use its prop-
> erty as a town, operate a 'business block' in the town
> and a street and sidewalk on that business block."
> At p. 507. " . . . The 'business block' serves as the
> community shopping center and is freely accessible
> and open to the people in the area and those passing
> through. The managers appointed by the corpora-
> tion cannot curtail the liberty of press and religion
> of these people consistently with the purposes of the
> Constitutional guarantees, and a state statute, as the
> one here involved, which enforces such action by
> criminally punishing those who attempt to distribute
> religious literature clearly violates the First and
> Fourteenth Amendments to the Constitution." At
> p. 508.

And in the case of *Harmon* v. *Tyler, supra,* an ordinance of New Orleans provided that a white person wishing to reside in a Negro community or a Negro wishing
to do so in a white community must secure the written
consent of a majority of the persons of the opposite race
inhabiting such community. It was stricken down on
the authority of *Buchanan* v. *Worley,* 245 U. S. 60 (1917),
which was a zoning ordinance based on race. *Harmon* is
particularly apposite here for, it will be remembered, that
Hooper's reason for turning back the students was not
because of *his* policy but because of *his customers*—"as
long as my customers were deciding who they wanted to
eat with—he would continue segregation. This was

BELL *v.* MARYLAND.

tantamount to a vote of his customers, just as it was in *Harmon*, and was not his personal choice. Hence it must not be given sanction by the State.

In sum, we believe that the State is involved here to a significant extent; that the customary usages to which restaurants are devoted has become "a kind of common law" within legal purview; that the State here is doing directly what it cannot do indirectly; and, that the imposition of the criminal trespass sanction, therefore, violates the Equal Protection Clause. As was said in *Strauder* v. *West Virginia,* 100 U. S. 303 (1879), as to the intent of the Fourteenth Amendment:

> "It was designed to assure to the colored races the enjoyment of all of the civil rights that, under the law, are enjoyed by white persons, and to give that race protection of the general government in that enjoyment, whenever it should be denied by the state . . . . What is this but declaring that the law in the states shall be the same for the black as for the white . . . . Its language is prohibitory; but every prohibition implies the existence of rights . . . . Any state action that denies this immunity to a colored man is in conflict with the Constitution." At p. 307.

It is said that our conclusion will bring on violence and disrespect for law because parties will resort to self help, not being able to enforce their prejudices through state channels. This is, we believe, somewhat fantastic. We cannot believe that a public establishment would use force to eject those who come to trade. In addition, since there would be no violation of law one resorting to self help would do so at his own peril. The obvious answer, of course, is that the Congress has the authority to implement the Fourteenth Amendment as well as our decision,

BELL *v.* MARYLAND.

drawing the guidelines necessary to practical administration.   This we cannot do since we only pass on justiciable
issues coming here on a case-to-case basis.   Moreover, the
Congress is better advised as to the necessary steps to be
taken and in the give and take ofthe legislative process
can fashion an Act that will meet the necessities of the
situation.

Reversed.

If the Black draft had become the final opinion of the Court in *Bell* v. *Maryland*, it might have done more than deprive the civil-rights movement of its most dramatic means of protest; it might also have had a serious negative impact upon the civil-rights bill then being debated in Congress. During the *Bell* conference on October 18, 1963, the Chief Justice and Justice Brennan expressed the fear that affirmance of the sit-in convictions might have a crippling effect on the prospects for Congressional passage. Justice Brennan declared that the minority would do their utmost to delay the decision as long as possible in the hope that Congress would meanwhile act favorably on the bill or that some member of the majority might be led to change his vote.

The same view was expressed in strong language by Justice Brennan in a May 5, 1964, revised draft of a dissent that he circulated urging the Court to avoid deciding *Bell* on the constitutional merits. The Brennan draft's introduction referred to the Congressional debate on Title II of the civil-rights bill, which by then had degenerated into the longest filibuster in the Senate's history. "We of this Court," Justice Brennan wrote, "are not so removed from the world around us that we can ignore the current debate over the constitutionality of Title II if enacted." The Brennan draft then declared that

> we cannot be blind to the fact that today's opposing opinions on the constitutional question decided will inevitably enter into and perhaps confuse that debate. My colleagues thus choose the most unfortunate time to commit the error of reaching out to decide the question. In doing so they unnecessarily create the risk of dealing the Court a "self-inflicted wound"— because the issue should not have been decided at all.

Justice Brennan's draft dissent was ultimately to become the opinion of the Court in *Bell* v. *Maryland*, but with the above-quoted language deleted. After the Brennan draft was circulated, Justice Black sought to soften the damaging implications for the civil-rights bill that Justice Brennan had drawn from the Black draft opinion of the Court. A recirculation of the Black draft on May 15 contained a new opening statement:

> The issue in this case is whether the Fourteenth Amendment, of itself, forbids a State to enforce its trespass laws to convict a person who comes into a privately owned restaurant, is told that because of his color he will not be served, and over the owner's protest refuses to leave. The case does not involve the constitutionality of any existing or proposed state or federal legislation requiring restaurant owners to serve people without regard to color.[19]

The Black disclaimer would scarcely have blunted the negative consequence that the Court's affirmance of the sit-in convictions might have had on passage of the civil-rights bill. That result was not to happen, however, as the Justices ultimately decided not to dispose of *Bell* v. *Maryland* on the constitutional merits. The key factor in this resolution of *Bell* was the circulation by Justice Brennan on April 27 of a draft dissent that argued for reversal of the convictions on a new ground.

The Brennan draft relied on Maryland laws, passed in 1962 and 1963 after the *Bell* convictions, prohibiting discrimination in public accommodations in Baltimore, where the *Bell* case arose. Justice Brennan concluded that these public accommodations laws required reversal of the *Bell* convictions. He relied on the common-law rule that repeal or other legislative nullification of a criminal statute had the effect of vacating convictions still pending under the statute. This was the rule that the Court was to apply in the already-referred-to case of *Hamm* v. *Rock Hill*,[20] after enactment of the Civil Rights Act of 1964.

The Brennan opinion was agreed to by the Chief Justice and Justice Goldberg. Only Justice Douglas, of the minority at the *Bell* conference, refused to join, since he stubbornly insisted on a decision on the constitutional merits. At this point, Justice Clark also agreed to join the Brennan opinion, announcing in a May 27 memorandum, "As I advised Brother Black this morning, I am joining the opinion of Brother Brennan."

The Clark switch from the Black opinion brought the Court to an impasse. There were now four votes for Justice Brennan's opinion, reversing without considering the constitutional merits, and four for Justice Black's opinion, upholding the constitutionality of the sit-in convictions. Justice Douglas continued to vote for reversal, but only on the ground that the convictions violated the Fourteenth Amendment.

The impasse continued until June 11, when Justice Clark circulated the opinion reprinted on p. 173. This Clark draft was written as a reversing opinion that could serve as the opinion of the Court in *Bell* v. *Maryland*. It is of particular interest because it was written by the only Southern member of the Court aside from Justice Black and took a view diametrically opposed to that of the Alabaman. The Clark draft adopts the minority conference view that the state was "involved to such a significant extent" in the case that the "convictions are proscribed by the Fourteenth Amendment."

Justice Clark's draft details "the character of the State's multifold involvement [that] makes it responsible for the discrimination here." The state, wrote Justice Clark, was giving "substance, force, and effect" to the restaurant owner's private discrimination, thus accomplishing by indirection the type of discrimination it was prohibited from doing directly. "It would to us seem strangely inconsistent to hold that although no legislature may authorize a court to prohibit Negroes the use of public restaurants for a moment that the owner through the use of the State's processes can prevent its use by Negroes forever."

The Clark adherence to the minority conference view on the constitutional merits now made for a bare majority in favor of striking down the sit-in convictions as violative of the Fourteenth Amendment. Justice Clark did, however, indicate that, while he was prepared to issue his opinion as the potential opinion of the Court, he still was of the view that the

Brennan draft's disposition of *Bell* was preferable. From this point of view, the Clark opinion may have represented less a conversion on the merits than a tactic designed to assure a majority for the Brennan opinion avoiding decision on the merits.

The Clark opinion did lead to a majority behind Justice Brennan's opinion. Justice Stewart changed his vote and agreed to join the Brennan draft. If Justice Stewart had not joined the Brennan opinion, Justice Clark's opinion would have meant a majority decision reversing the sit-in convictions as violative of the Fourteenth Amendment. Justice Stewart told his clerks that, to prevent the Clark opinion from being issued as the *Bell* opinion of the Court, he was joining Justice Brennan.[21]

The Brennan opinion was now recirculated as the *Bell* opinion of the Court. When it was announced on the last day of the term, June 22, 1964, it was joined by Justices Stewart, Clark, and Goldberg, and the Chief Justice. As it turned out, six of the Justices expressed their view on the constitutional merits. Justices Douglas and Goldberg, joined by the Chief Justice (who had withdrawn his own draft opinion on the merits, supra page 164), issued concurrences arguing that the sit-in convictions violated the Fourteenth Amendment. Justice Black, joined by Justices Harlan and White, issued a revised version of his draft opinion of the Court, supra page 149, asserting that the convictions were constitutional.

So far as the public record was concerned, three Justices had expressed a view each way on the merits and three (Justices Brennan, Clark, and Stewart) had expressed no view. Only those privy to the Court's deliberations realized how close the Justices had come to deciding the constitutionality of the sit-in convictions, and to do so under Justice Black's draft opinion of the Court. If they had decided *Bell* that way, the history of the civil-rights movement might have been different. Perhaps, as some of the Justices feared, the negative *Bell* decision on the sit-ins would have weakened, if not defeated, the civil-rights bill before Congress. Instead, soon after the decision, on July 2, the Civil Rights Act of 1964 was enacted. Its prohibition of racial discrimination in restaurants and other public accommodations elevated the goal of the sit-in demonstrators to the law of the land. The underlying issue that had so sharply divided the Justices in *Bell* v. *Maryland* thus became moot and the Court never did decide the constitutional issue that it ultimately avoided in *Bell*.

Notes

1. 378 U.S. 226 (1964).
2. Thoreau, *On the Duty of Civil Disobedience.*
3. Thoreau, *Unjust Laws.*
4. Ibid.
5. King, "The Civil Rights Struggle in the United States Today," 20 *The Record of the Assn. of the Bar, City of N.Y.* [Supplement] No. 5, 21 (1965).

6. Civil Rights Cases, 109 U.S. 3 (1883).

7. 334 U.S. 1 (1948).

8. *Peterson* v. *Greenville,* 373 U.S. 244 (1963); *Avent* v. *North Carolina,* 373 U.S. 244 (1963); *Gober* v. *Birmingham,* 373 U.S. 244 (1963).

9. See Schwartz, *Super Chief: Earl Warren and His Supreme Court—A Judicial Biography* 480–481 (1983).

10. *Peterson* v. *Greenville,* 373 U.S. 244, 248 (1963).

11. *Lombard* v. *Louisiana,* 373 U.S. 267 (1963).

12. *Hamm* v. *Rock Hill,* 379 U.S. 306 (1964).

13. Id. at 311.

14. *Barr* v. *Columbia,* 378 U.S. 146 (1964); *Bouie* v. *Columbia,* 378 U.S. 347 (1964); *Robinson* v. *Florida,* 378 U.S. 153 (1964).

15. Note, n.d. TCCT: "Mr. Justice Black has sent copies of this to Justices Harlan, Stewart, White and yourself," attached to HLB draft opinion, supra page 149.

16. 347 U.S. 483 (1954).

17. 378 U.S. 146 (1964).

18. See *Brown* v. *Board of Education,* 347 U.S. at 494.

19. HLB, opinion of the Court, *Bell* v. *Maryland,* recirculated May 15, 1964, JMHP.

20. Supra note 12.

21. See Schwartz, op. cit. supra note 9, at 524.

6

Estes v. *Texas* (1965): Television in the Courtroom

The legal problems posed by the newer communications media were among those that came before the Supreme Court during Chief Justice Warren's tenure. In particular, it was then that the Justices first had to deal with the issue of television in the courtroom. In resolving the conflict between the First Amendment right of access to news and the Sixth Amendment right to a fair trial, the Warren Court came down squarely on the side of the latter. But the Court had originally decided that TV in the courtroom did not violate due process and had come close to issuing a Stewart opinion of the Court to that effect. Once again, a switch by Justice Clark changed the result, though the final decision did not go as far as either he or the Chief Justice wished in banning the video camera from criminal trials.

The television-in-the-courtroom issue came before the Warren Court in *Estes* v. *Texas*.[1] At that time, only two states (Texas and Colorado) allowed television cameras in the courtroom, and both the federal rules and the American Bar Association Canons of Judicial Ethics excluded them. The *Estes* trial was notorious and received national attention. Defendant moved to exclude television and other cameras. A two-day hearing on the motion was itself televised. Twelve cameramen jostled for position in the courtroom. Their activities, even Justice Stewart's dissent concedes, "led to considerable disruption of the hearings."[2] For the trial itself, a booth was constructed at the rear of the courtroom. An opening permitted four TV cameras, clearly visible to all in the courtroom, to photograph the proceedings. The Texas courts rejected defendant's claim that the televised hearing and trial had deprived him of due process.

From the time it first considered *Estes* v. *Texas*, the Supreme Court was sharply split on the case. Only four Justices (Warren, Douglas, Harlan, and Brennan)—the bare minimum required—voted to grant certiorari, with the other five voting to deny. The conference on the case after oral argument, on April 2, 1965, showed that the Court was as closely divided on the merits, though the lineup was not the same as on the certiorari vote.

The conference case against televised trials was led by the Chief Justice, who firmly believed that allowing TV was, in the words of his unissued draft *Estes* dissent, "allowing the courtroom to become a public spectacle and source of entertainment."[3] In his conference presentation, the Chief Justice stated that it contravened due process to stage a trial in this way; the "decorum of the courtroom" was violated. Chief Justice Warren saw no violation of the First Amendment. The press, including television, had the right to be in the courtroom only as part of the public, but to do what was done in the *Estes* trial was violative of the right of fair trial. The Chief Justice indicated he would exclude TV in all circumstances, and even with the consent of the accused and his lawyers, he said, "I'd be against it."

The strongest statement in support of the Chief Justice was made by Justice Douglas. "A trial is not a spectacle," he declared, and it makes no difference whether defendant objected or not. According to Justice Douglas, this type of proceeding "is the modern farce—putting the courtroom into a modern theatrical production."

Justices Harlan and Goldberg agreed. The right to a public trial, said Justice Harlan, did not mean that the public had a right to a public performance. To Justice Goldberg, "the shambles" deprived defendant of a fair trial. What was involved here was an obtrusive intervention of the outside into defendant's trial.

Justices Clark, Stewart, and White opposed a flat ban on TV in the courtroom. Justice Clark stressed the trial judge's finding that no prejudice had been shown. Justices Brennan and Black were more doubtful, but voted to affirm the conviction. Justice Brennan concluded that this trial was "no sham"; the jury was sequestered and there was no showing that the witnesses, the judge, or others were affected in a prejudicial way. Justice Black said that, though he personally was against television in the courts, this was something new that was working itself out. He noted that some day the technology might improve so as not to disturb the actual trial. Even with the disturbance here, Justices Brennan and Black cast their votes to make a bare majority for affirmance.

The senior member of the conference majority, Justice Black, assigned the case to Justice Stewart. He circulated a draft opinion of the Court on May 13. This is the opinion reprinted on page 195. It would have affirmed the decision below holding that the televising of the *Estes* trial did not involve any constitutional violation. This draft was essentially similar to the *Estes* dissent that Justice Stewart eventually issued. If the draft had come down as the *Estes* opinion, it would have adopted the reasoning of the ultimate Stewart dissent as that of the Court and substantially changed the legal picture with regard to TV in the courtroom.

The Stewart draft starts by rejecting the claim that the introduction of cameras into a criminal trial, over defendant's objection, violates the

Fourteenth Amendment. "On the record of this case," the draft states, "we cannot say that any violation of the Constitution occurred." It points (much as Stewart's final dissent does) to the facts, saying that, while the situation during the pretrial hearing was plainly disruptive, there was nothing to indicate that the conduct of anyone in the courtroom during the trial was influenced by the television.

This meant, according to Justice Stewart, that the Court was

> presented with virtually an abstract question. We are asked to pronounce that the United States Constitution prohibits all television cameras and all still cameras from every courtroom in every State whenever a criminal trial is in progress. . . . We are asked to hold that the Constitution absolutely bars television and cameras from every criminal courtroom, even if they have no impact upon the jury, no effect upon any witness, and no influence upon the conduct of the judge.

This, the Stewart draft concluded, the Court could not do and the judgment below was affirmed.

Two interesting points are made in the draft's last footnote that are not contained in Justice Stewart's *Estes* dissent. The first is that a majority of the Court believed that television in the courtroom was "an extremely unwise policy." The second is that a majority of the Court also believed that the demands of TV and other photographers to set up their equipment in a courtroom and portray or broadcast a trial "are not protected by any valid First Amendment claim."

In his *Estes* dissent, not only did Justice Stewart delete this rejection of the First Amendment claim, but he also included an intimation that the First Amendment did support the right of the press to be in the courtroom. The Stewart dissent declares, "The idea of imposing upon any medium of communications the burden of justifying its presence is contrary to where I had always thought the presumption must lie in the area of First Amendment freedoms."[4] This First Amendment presumption was rejected in the *Estes* opinion of the Court ultimately delivered by Justice Clark.[5] It was, however, the basis for the more recent landmark decision in *Richmond Newspapers* v. *Virginia*.[6] One may wonder what effect the original rejection of the First Amendment claim in the Stewart *Estes* draft would have had on the recent law, culminating in *Richmond Newspapers*, if the Stewart draft had been issued as the final *Estes* opinion of the Court.

Soon after the Stewart *Estes* draft opinion of the Court was circulated, draft dissents were sent around by Justice Harlan (May 19), the Chief Justice (May 21), and Justice Goldberg (May 22). The Harlan and Warren drafts were essentially similar to the *Estes* concurring opinions that they ultimately issued. The Goldberg draft was withdrawn when its author joined the eventual Warren concurrence.

If nothing more had occurred in the Court's deliberative process, the Stewart draft would have become the *Estes* opinion of the Court. That would have drastically changed the law on the subject. The Court's imprimatur might well have led to the widespread televising of trials during the past two decades. That was not to happen, however, as once again the bare majority for affirmance in *Estes* did not hold. This time, too, Justice Clark made the crucial switch. In terms of the changed *Estes* decision, the catalysts were a memorandum by Justice Clark and his draft opinion, reprinted on page 206. The draft's role in the decision process and its important points (with emphasis on how they differed from Justice Clark's final opinion of the Court in *Estes*) will be discussed after the Stewart and Clark drafts, which follow.

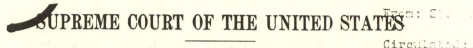

SUPREME COURT OF THE UNITED STATES

No. 256.—October Term, 1964.

Circulated:

Recirculated

Billie Sol Estes, Petitioner,	On Writ of Certiorari to the
v.	Court of Criminal Appeals
State of Texas.	of Texas.

[May —, 1965.]

Mr. Justice Stewart delivered the opinion of the Court.

In this case we deal with the claim that the introduction of newspaper photographers and television cameras into a state criminal trial, over the defendant's objection, is a violation of the Fourteenth Amendment. Limiting our decision to the specific record in this case, we reject that claim.

On October 22, 1962, the petitioner went to trial in the Seventh Judicial District Court of Smith County, Texas, upon an indictment charging him with the offenses of (1) swindling, (2) theft by false pretenses, and (3) theft by a bailee. After a week spent in selecting a jury, the trial itself lasted some three and a half days. At its conclusion the jury found the petitioner guilty of the offense of swindling under the first count of the indictment. Overruling motions by defense counsel based, among other grounds, upon the Fourteenth Amendment, the trial judge permitted portions of the trial proceedings to be televised, under the limitations described below. He also gave news photographers permission to take still pictures in the courtroom under specified conditions.

The Texas Court of Criminal Appeals affirmed the petitioner's conviction, and we granted certiorari, limited to a single question. The question, as phrased by the petitioner, is this:

"Whether the action of the trial court, over petitioner's continued objection, denied him due process

* JMHP.

ESTES *v.* TEXAS.

of law and equal protection of the laws under the
Fourteenth Amendment to the Constitution of the
United States, in requiring petitioner to submit to
live television of his trial, and in refusing to adopt
in this all out publicity case, as a rule of trial procedure, Canon 35 of the Canons of Judicial Ethics
of the American Bar Association, and instead adopting and following, over defendant's objection, Canon
28 of the Canons of Judicial Ethics, since approved
by the Judicial Section of the integrated (State
agency) State Bar of Texas."

The two Canons of Judicial Ethics referred to in the
petitioner's statement of the question presented are set
out in the margin.[1]   But the problem before us is not one

---

[1] Canons of Judicial Ethics. American Bar Association: Judicial
Canon 35. Improper publicizing of Court proceedings.
"Proceedings in court should be conducted with fitting dignity and
decorum. The taking of photographs in the court room, during
sessions of the court or recesses between sessions, and the broadcasting or televising of court proceedings detract from the essential
dignity of the proceedings, distract participants and witnesses in giving testimony, and create misconceptions with respect thereto in the
mind of the public and should not be permitted.
"Provided that this restriction shall not apply to the broadcasting
or televising, under the supervision of the court, of such portions of
naturalization proceedings (other than the interrogation of applicants) as are designed and carried out exclusively as a ceremony for
the purpose of publicly demonstrating in an impressive manner the
essential dignity and the serious nature of naturalization."
Canons of Judicial Ethics, Integrated State Bar of Texas: Judicial
Canon 28. Improper publicizing of Court proceedings.
"Proceedings in court should be conducted with fitting dignity and
decorum. The taking of photographs in the court room, during
sessions of the court or recesses between sessions, and the broadcasting or televising of court proceedings unless properly supervised and
controlled, may detract from the essential dignity of the proceedings,
distract participants and witnesses in giving testimony, and create
misconceptions with respect thereto in the mind of the public. The
supervision and control of such trial coverage shall be left to the

ESTES *v.* TEXAS.

of choosing between the conflicting guidelines reflected in these Canons of Judicial Ethics. It is a constitutional question which must be decided upon the concrete facts of this case. We turn, then, to those facts.

I.

The indictment was originally returned by a grand jury in Reeves County, Texas, and it engendered widespread publicity. After some preliminary proceedings there, the case was transferred for trial to Smith County, more than 500 miles away. The trial was set for September 24, 1962, but it did not commence on that date. Instead, that day and the next were spent in hearings on two motions filed by defense counsel, a motion to bar television and news cameras from the trial, and a motion to continue the trial to a later date. Those proceedings were themselves telecast "live," and news photographers were permitted to take pictures in the courtroom. The activities of the television crews and news photographers led

---

trial judge who has the inherent power to exclude or control coverage in the proper case in the interest of justice.

"In connection with the control of such coverage the following declaration of principles is adopted:

"(1) There should be no use of flash bulbs or other artificial lighting.

"(2) No witness, over his expressed objection, should be photographed, his voice broadcast or be televised.

"(3) The representatives of news media must obtain permission of the trial judge to cover by photograph, broadcasting or televising, and shall comply with the rules prescribed by the judge for the exercise of the privilege.

"(4) Any violation of the Courts' Rules shall be punished as a contempt.

"(5) Where a judge has refused to allow coverage, or has regulated it, any attempt, other than argument by representatives of the news media directly with the Court, to bring pressure of any kind on the judge, pending final disposition of the cause in trial, shall be punished as a contempt."

ESTES *v.* TEXAS.

to considerable disruption of the hearings.[2]   At the conclusion of the hearings the motion for a continuance was
granted, and the case reset for trial on October 22.   The
motion to bar television and news photographers from
the trial was denied.[3]

---

[2] A contemporary newspaper account described the scene as follows:

"A television motor van, big as an intercontinental bus, was parked
outside the courthouse and the second floor courtroom was a forest
of equipment.   Two television cameras had been set up inside the
bar and four marked cameras were aligned just outside the gates.

"A microphone stuck its 12 inch snout inside the jury box, now
occupied by an overflow of reporters from the press table, and three
microphones confronted Judge Dunagan on his bench.   Cables and
wires snaked over the floor."   The New York Times, September 25,
1962, p. —.

[3] In ruling on the motion, the trial judge stated:

"In the past, it has been the policy of this Court to permit televising in the court room under the rules and supervision of the Court.
Heretofore, I have not encountered any difficulty with it.   I was
unable to observe any detraction from the witnesses or the attorneys
in those cases.   We have watched television, of course, grow up from
its infancy and now into its maturity; and it is a news media.   So
I really do not see any justified reason why it should not be permitted
to take its proper seat in the family circle.   However, it will be under
strict supervision of the Court.   I know there has been pro and con
about televising in the court room.   I have heard some say that it
makes a circus out of the Court.   I had the privilege yesterday
morning of sitting in my home and viewing a sermon by the First
Baptist Church over in Dallas and certainly it wasn't any circus in
that church; and I feel that if it is a proper instrument in the house
of the Lord, it is not out of place in the court room, if properly
supervised.

"Now, television is going to be televising whatever the scene is here.
If you want to watch a ball game and that is what they televise, you
are going to see a ball game.   If you want to see a preacher and hear
a sermon, you tune in on that and that is what you are going to get.
If the Court permits a circus in this court room, it will be televised,
that is true, but they will not be creating a circus.

"Now, the most important point is whether or not it would interfere with a fair and impartial trial of this Defendant.   That is the

ESTES *v.* TEXAS.

On October 1, the trial judge issued an order delineating what coverage he would permit during the trial.[4] As a result of that order and ensuing conferences between the

most important point, and that is the purpose, or will be the primary purpose of the Court, to insure that he gets that fair trial.

> .   .   .   .   .

"There is not anything the Court can do about the interest in this case, but I can control your activities and your conduct here; and I can assure you now that this Court is not going to be turned into a circus with TV or without it. Whatever action is necessary for the Court to take to insure that, the Court will take it.

> .   .   .   .   .

"There has been one consideration that the Court has given and it is that this is a small court room and there will be hundreds of people trying to get into this court room to witness this trial. I believe we would have less confusion if they would stay at home and stay out of the court room and look in on the trial. With all those people trying to crowd in and push into this court room, that is another consideration I have given to it."

[4] "In my statement of Sept. 24, 1962, admitting television and other cameras in the courtroom during the trial of Billie Sol Estes, I said cameras would be allowed under the control and direction of the court so long as they did not violate the legal rights of the defendant or the State of Texas.

> .   .   .   .   .

"In line with my statement of Sept. 24, 1962, I am at this time informing both television and radio that live broadcasting or telecasting by either news media cannot and will not be permitted during the interrogation of jurors in testing their qualifications or of the testimony given by the witnesses as to do so would be in violation of Article 644 of the Code of Criminal Procedure of Texas, which provides as follows: 'At the request of either party, the witnesses on both sides may be sworn and placed in the custody of an officer and removed out of the courtroom to some place where they cannot hear the testimony as delivered by any other witness in the case. This is termed placing witnesses under rule.'

> .   .   .   .   .

"[E]ach television network and local television station will be allowed one film camera without sound in the courtroom and the film will be made available to other television stations on a pooled basis.

"Marshall Pengra, Manager of Television Station KLTV, Tyler, will be in charge of the independent pool and individual stations may

ESTES *v.* TEXAS.

judge and representatives of the news media, the environment for the trial, which began on October 22, was in sharp contrast to that of the September hearings. The actual extent of television and news photography in the courtroom was described by the judge, after the trial had ended, in certifying on the petitioner's bill of exceptions. This description is confirmed by our understanding of the entire record and was agreed to and accepted by defense counsel:

> "Prior to the trial of October 22, 1962, there was a booth constructed and placed in the rear of the courtroom painted the same or near the same color as the courtroom with a small opening across the top for the use of cameras, . . .
>
> "Live telecasting and radio broadcasting were not permitted and the only telecasting was on film without sound, and there was not any broadcasting of the trial by radio permitted. Each network, ABC, NBC, CBS and KRLD Television in Tyler was allowed a camera in the courtroom. . . . The telecasting on film of this case was not a continuous camera operation and only pictures being taken at intervals during the day to be used on their regular news casts later in the day. There were some days during the trial that the cameras of only one or two stations were in operation, the others not being in attendance upon the Court each and every day. The Court did

---

contact him. The same will be true of cameras for the press, which will be limited to the local press, Associated Press and United Press.

> .   .   .   .   .

"I am making this statement at this time in order that the two news media affected may have sufficient notice before the case is called on Oct. 22.

"The rules I have set forth above concerning the use of cameras are subject to change if I find that they are too restrictive or not workable, for any reason."

ESTES *v.* TEXAS.

not permit any cameras other than those that were noiseless nor were flood lights and flash bulbs allowed to be used in the courtroom. The Court permitted one news photographer with Associated Press, United Press International and Tyler Morning Telegraph and Courier Times. However, they were not permitted inside the Bar; and the Court did not permit any telecasting or photographing in the hallways leading into the courtroom or on the second floor of the courthouse where the courtroom is situated, in order that the Defendant and his attorneys would not be hindered, molested or harassed in approaching or leaving the courtroom. The Court did permit live telecasting of the arguments of State's counsel and the returning of the verdict by the Jury and its acceptance by the Court. The opening argument of the District Attorney of Smith County was carried by sound and because of transmission difficulty, there was not any picture. The closing argument for the State by the District Attorney of Reeves County was carried live by both picture and sound. The arguments of attorneys for Defendant, John D. Cofer and Hume Cofer, were not telecast or broadcast as the Court granted their Motion that same not be permitted.

"There was not any televising at any time during the trial except from the booth in the rear of the courtroom, and during the argument of counsel to the jury, news photography was required to operate from the booth so that they would not interfere or detract from the attention of either the jurors or the attorneys.

"During the trial that began October 22nd, there was never at any time any radio broadcasting equipment in the courtroom. There was some equipment in a room off of the courtroom where there were

ESTES *v.* TEXAS.

periodic news reports given; and throughout the trial
that began October 22nd, not any witness requested
not to be televised or photographed while they were
testifying.   Neither did any juror, while being inter-
rogated on voir dire or at any other time, make any
request of the Court not to be televised."

Thus, except for the closing arguments for the prosecution and the return of the jury's verdict, there was no
"live" telecasting of the trial.   And, even for purposes of
delayed telecasting on later news programs, no words or
other sounds were permitted to be recorded while the
members of the jury were being selected or while any
witness was testifying.   No witnesses and no jurors were
televised or photographed over their objection.[5]   Finally,
the members of the jury saw no telecasts and no pictures
of anything that went on during the trial.   In accord with
Texas law, the jurors were sequestered, day and night,
from the beginning of the trial until it ended.[6]

II.

It is obvious that the introduction of television and
news cameras into a criminal trial invites many serious
constitutional hazards.   The very presence of photographers and television cameramen plying their trade in a
courtroom would often be so inherently disruptive and

---

[5] There were eight witnesses for the prosecution and no witnesses
for the defense.

[6] Art. 668. 745, 725. Tex. Code Crim. Proc.   The jurors were
lodged each night in quarters provided for that purpose in the courthouse itself.   On the evening of November 6, by agreement of counsel
and special permission of the court, the members of the jury were
permitted to watch the election returns on television for a short
period.   For this purpose a portable television was brought into the
jury's quarters by a court officer, and operated by him.   Otherwise
the jurors were not permitted to watch television at any time during
the trial.   The only newspapers permitted the jury were ones from
which all coverage of the trial had been physically removed.

ESTES *v.* TEXAS.

distracting as to make a fair trial impossible. Thus, if what went on in the courtroom during this jury trial had borne any resemblance to the scene at the September hearings, it is difficult to conceive how a fair trial in the constitutional sense could have been afforded the defendant.[7] And even if, as was true here, the television cameras are so controlled and concealed as to be hardly perceptible in the courtroom itself, many risks of constitutional dimensions lurk in the very process of televising court proceedings at all.

Some of those risks are catalogued in the *amicus curiae* brief filed in this case by the American Bar Association: "Potential or actual jurors, in the absence of enforceable and effective safeguards, may arrive at certain misconceptions regarding the defendant and his trial by viewing televised pre-trial hearings and motions from which the jury is ordinarily excluded. Evidence otherwise inadmissible may leave an indelible mark. . . . Once the trial begins, exposure to nightly rebroadcasts of selected portions of the day's proceedings will be difficult to guard against, as jurors spend frequent evenings before the television set. The obvious impact of witnessing repeated trial episodes and hearing accompanying commentary, episodes admittedly chosen for their news value and not for evidentiary purposes, can serve only to distort the jurors' perspective. . . . Despite the court's injunction not to discuss the case, it seems undeniable that jurors will be subject to the pressure of television-watching family, friends and, indeed, strangers. . . . It is not too much to imagine a juror being confronted with his wife's television-oriented viewpoint. . . . Additionally, the jurors' daily television appearances may make them recognizable celebrities, likely to be stopped by passing strangers, or perhaps harried by intruding telephone calls. . . ." Cf. *Rideau v. Louisiana,* 373 U. S. 723.

---

[7] See note 2.

ESTES *v.* TEXAS.

Constitutional problems of another kind might arise if a witness or juror were subjected to being televised over his objection. Cf. *Griswold* v. *Connecticut,* —— U. S. ——.

On the record of this case, however, we cannot say that any violation of the Constitution occurred. The jurors themselves were prevented from seeing any telecasts of the trial, and completely insulated from association with any members of the public who did see such telecasts.[8] In the courtroom itself, there is nothing to show that the trial proceeded in any way other than it would have proceeded if cameras and television had not been present. In appearance, the courtroom was practically unaltered. There was no obtrusiveness and no distraction, no noise and no special lighting. There is no indication anywhere in the record of any disturbance whatever of the judicial proceedings. There is no claim that the conduct of the judge, or that any deed or word of counsel, or of any witness, or of any juror, were influenced in any way by the presence of photographers or by television.

We are thus presented with virtually an abstract question. We are asked to pronounce that the United States Constitution prohibits all television cameras and all still cameras from every courtroom in every State whenever a criminal trial is in progress. We are asked to enshrine Canon 35 of the American Bar Association into the Four-

---

[8] To be sure, the jurors were drawn from a community which had been exposed to the telecast of the September hearings. But at those hearings there was no discussion whatever of anything bearing on the petitioner's guilt or innocence. All that a television viewer could have learned was that the petitioner's case had been called for trial and that motions had been made and acted upon for a continuance and to exclude cameras and television. This telecast was only one minor ingredient in the wide publicity which preceded the petitioner's trial. But the Texas Court of Criminal Appeals has determined that the members of the jury were not prejudiced by exposure to this publicity, and, in limiting our grant of certiorari, we have declined to review that determination.

ESTES *v.* TEXAS.

teenth Amendment, denying to the States or to individual trial judges any discretion whatever to conduct trials with cameras present, no matter how unobtrusive the cameras may be. We are asked to hold that it is impossible to have a contitutional trial where any part of the proceedings is televised or recorded on film. We are asked to hold that the Constitution absolutely bars television and cameras from every criminal courtroom, even if they have no impact upon the jury, no effect upon any witness, and no influence upon the conduct of the judge.

However strong our personal views on the subject may be,[9] we cannot find that requirement in the federal Constitution. The judgment is

Affirmed.

---

[9] A majority of the Court believe that the introduction of television or still cameras into a courtroom is, at least in the present state of the art, an extremely unwise policy, not only because of the attendant risks of causing an unfair trial, discussed above, but because of the importance of preserving the inherent dignity of a courtroom. Television, radio, and photographers are not permitted and will not be permitted in any federal court. Rule 53, Fed. Rules Crim. Proc., so provides. In addition, the Judicial Conference of the United States adopted the following resolution during its proceedings of March 8–9, 1962:

"*Resolved*, That the Judicial Conference of the United States condemns the taking of photographs in the courtroom or its environs in connection with any judicial proceedings, and the broadcasting of judicial proceedings by radio, television, or other means, and considers such practices to be inconsistent with fair judicial procedure and that they ought not to be permitted in any federal court."

We are informed that all but two of the States follow a similar practice.

A majority of the Court believe that the demands of television, radio, and press photographers to set up their equipment in a courtroom and portray or broadcast all or part of a trial are not supported by any valid First Amendment claim.

SUPREME COURT OF THE UNITED STATES ~~Pro.: Clark, J.~~

MAY

No. 256.—OCTOBER TERM, 1964.   Circulated:_____

Recirculated:_____

Billie Sol Estes, Petitioner, *v.* State of Texas.	On Writ of Certiorari to the Court of Criminal Appeals of Texas.

[June —, 1965.]

MR. JUSTICE CLARK, reversing.

The question presented in this case is whether the petitioner, who stands convicted in the District Court for the Seventh Judicial District of Texas at Tyler for swindling, was deprived of a fair trial through the televising over his objection of the proceedings against him. The petitioner contends that his rights under the Fourteenth Amendment to due process and equal protection of the laws were denied him by the televising and broadcasting of his trial. Both the trial court and the Texas Court of Criminal Appeals found to the contrary.

I.

While petitioner recites his claim in the framework of Canon 35 of the American Bar Association he does not ask that "we enshrine Canon 35 in the Fourteenth Amendment," but only that we recognize that the time-honored principles of fair trial were not followed and that he was thus convicted without due process of law. Canon 35, of course, has of itself no binding effect on the courts but merely expresses the view of the Association in opposition to the broadcasting, televising and photographing of court proceedings. Likewise, Canon 28 of the Integrated State Bar of Texas, 7 S. Tex. L. J. 212, which leaves to the trial judge's sound discretion the use of television and pictures in court proceedings, is of itself not law. In short, the question here is not the advisability or inadvisability of

ESTES *v.* TEXAS.

either Canon 35 of the American Bar Association or Canon 28 of the State Bar of Texas, but whether petitioner was tried in a manner which comports with the due process requirement of the Fourteenth Amendment.

Petitioner's case was originally called for trial on September 24, 1962, in Smith County after a change of venue. However, at that time a defense motion to prevent telecasting, broadcasting by radio and news photography was presented. The remainder of the September proceedings were consumed by arguments on this motion and on a second defense motion for a continuance.

These initial hearings were carried live by both radio and television and news photography was permitted throughout. The videotapes of these hearings clearly illustrate that the picture presented was not one of judicial serenity and calm. However, at this time no evidence or testimony on the merits of the case was presented. A jury was empaneled, but was later released after petitioner's motion for continuance had been granted. The court also had the names of the witnesses called, but when a number of witnesses were found to be absent the trial was continued until October 22, 1962.

When the case was called for trial on October 22 the scene was considerably altered. A booth had been constructed at the back of the courtroom which was painted to blend with the permanent structure of the room. It had an aperture to allow the lens of the camera an unrestricted view of the courtroom. All television cameras and newsreel photographers were restricted to the area of the booth when shooting film.

Live telecasting and radio broadcasting were prohibited during a great portion of the actual trial, except during the opening and closing arguments of the State, the return of the jury's verdict and its receipt by the trial judge which were all carried live with sound. Although

ESTES *v.* TEXAS.

the order allowed videotapes of the entire proceeding
without sound, the cameras operated only intermittently
recording various portions for broadcast on regularly
scheduled newscasts later in the day. At the request
of the defendant, the trial judge prohibited pictures of
any kind, still or television, of the defense counsel during
their summations to the jury.

Because of the restrictions placed on sound and live
telecasting the television showings of the trial were confined largely to film clips shown on the stations' regularly
scheduled news programs. The commentator would use
the film of a particular part of the proceeding as a backdrop for his commentary on the day's activities including
excerpts from testimony, editorializing and the usual
reportorial privileges that commentators exercise. The
result was an image of the trial by fits and snatches, which
was almost certainly confusing to the layman and furnished him at most with only one side of the case. Necessarily this showing of certain portions involved selection by station personnel. Selection, in turn, of necessity injects all of the vagaries of human choice and
commercial marketability into what was shown to the
home viewer.

From a study of the entire record it must be said in all
fairness to the trial judge that he sought to limit the possibly damaging effects of television and to protect against
disruption of the trial process. However, this but illustrates the dangers inherent in allowance of television at
trial since even the best effort could not adequately safeguard the defendant's rights. This is pointed up by the
amount of time expended in the establishment and enforcement of ground rules for the television personnel.
Besides the two-day pretrial hearing which was devoted
exclusively to the question of televising the trial and the
renewed motion made at the time the trial actually began,

ESTES *v.* TEXAS.

the record shows that the court proceedings were interrupted again and again because of the presence of the television cameras and the still photographers.

II.

In *Rideau* v. *Louisiana,* 373 U. S. 723 (1963), this Court constructed a rule that the televising of a defendant in the act of confessing to a crime was *per se* invalid under the Due Process Clause of the Fourteenth Amendment even without a showing of prejudice or a demonstration of the nexus between the televised confession and the trial. See *id.,* at 729 (dissenting opinion of CLARK, J.). Here, although there was nothing so dramatic as a home-viewed confession, there had been a bombardment of the community with the sights and sounds of a two-day hearing during which the original jury panel, the lawyers and the judge were highly publicized. The defendant was subjected to characterization and minute electronic scrutiny. The two-day hearing and the order permitting television at the actual trial were widely known throughout the community. This emphasized the notorious character that the trial would take and, therefore, set it apart in the public mind as an extrardinary case, or as Shaw would say, something "not conventionally unconventional." When the new jury was empaneled at the trial three of the jurors selected had seen and heard the broadcasts of the earlier proceedings.

The introduction of television into petitioner's trial constituted a violation of due process regardless of whether there was a showing of isolatable prejudice. See *Rideau* v. *Louisiana, supra.*

III.

We start with the proposition that it is a "public trial" that the Sixth Amendment guarantees to the "accused." The Constitution says nothing of any comparable right

ESTES *v.* TEXAS.

to the public or to the news media. The purpose of the
requirement of a public trial was to guarantee that the
accused would be fairly dealt with and not unjustly condemned. History had proven that secret tribunals were
effective instruments of oppression. As my Brother
BLACK so well said in *In re Oliver,* 333 U. S. 257 (1948):

> "The traditional Anglo-American distrust for secret
> trials has been variously ascribed to the notorious
> use of this practice by the Spanish Inquisition, to the
> excesses of the English Court of Star Chamber, and
> to the French Monarchy's abuse of the *lettre de
> cachet* . . . . Whatever other benefits the guaran-
> tee to an accused that his trial be conducted in pub-
> lic may confer upon our society, the guarantee has
> always been recognized as a safeguard against any
> attempt to employ our courts as instruments of
> persecution. . . ." At 268–270.

It is said, however, that the freedoms granted in the First
Amendment extend a right to the news media to televise
from the courtroom, and that to refuse to honor this privilege is to discriminate between the newspapers and television. This is a misconception of the rights of the press.
While the state and federal courts have differed over what
spectators may be excluded from a criminal trial, 6 Wig-
more, Evidence § 1834 (3d ed. 1940), it is clear beyond
question that no language in the First Amendment grants
any of the news media such a privilege. The *amici curiae*
brief of the National Association of Broadcasters and the
Radio Television News Directors Association says, as
indeed it must, that "neither of these two amendments
[First and Sixth] speaks of an unlimited right of access
to the courtroom on the part of the broadcasting media."
At p. 7. Moreover, they recognize that the "primary
concern of all must be the proper administration of justice . . the life or liberty of any individual in this land

ESTES *v.* TEXAS.

should not be put in jeopardy because of the action of the news media . . . the due process requirements in both the Fifth and Fourteenth Amendments and the Sixth Amendment require a procedure that will assure a fair trial . . . ."

Nor can the courts be said to discriminate where they permit the newspaper reporter access to the courtroom. The television and radio reporter has the same privilege but he cannot bring his cumbrous camera, heavy wires and other equipment with him. The news reporter is not permitted to bring his typewriter or printing press. When the advances in these arts permits reporting by printing press or by television without their present equippage we will have another case.

IV.

Trials are held for the solemn purpose of endeavoring to ascertain the truth which is the *sine qua non* of a fair trial. Over the centuries Anglo-American courts have devised careful safeguards by rule to protect and facilitate the performance of this high function. Up until today those rules have not permitted the televising and photographing of a criminal trial, save in two States and there only under restrictions. In England no such activity is permitted. This is weighty evidence that our concepts of a fair trial do not tolerate such an indulgence. On the contrary we have always held that the atmosphere essential to the preservation of a fair trial—the most fundamental of all freedoms—must be maintained at all costs. Our approach has been through rules, contempt proceedings and reversal of convictions obtained under such conditions. Here, however, the remedy is clear and certain of application and unless the State clearly carries the burden of showing that the televising and picturing of criminal trials casts no element of unfairness upon them, it is

ESTES *v.* TEXAS.

our duty to continue to enforce the rules that from time immemorial have proven efficacious and necessary to a fair trial.

V.

The State contends that the televising of portions of a criminal trial does not constitute *per se* a denial of due process. Its position is that no prejudice was shown by the petitioner as resulting from the televising; that the "distraction" argument is entirely unfounded; that psychological considerations are for psychologists, not courts, because they are purely hypothetical. It argues further that the public has a right to know what goes on in the courts; that the latter have no power to "suppress, edit or censor events which transpire in proceedings before it." citing *Craig* v. *Harney,* 331 U. S. 367, 374 (1947); and that the televising of criminal trials would be enlightening to the public and promote greater respect for the courts.

At the outset the notion should be dispelled that telecasting is dangerous because it is new. It is true that our empirical knowledge of its full effect on the public is limited. However, the nub of the question is not its newness but, as MR. JUSTICE DOUGLAS says, "the insidious influences which it puts to work in the administration of justice." Douglas, The Public Trial and the Free Press, 33 Rocky Mt. L. Rev. 1 (1960). These influences will be detailed below, but before turning to them the States' argument that the public has a right to know what goes on in the courtroom should be dealt with.

While it is true that the public has the right to be informed as to what occurs in its courts, it is open to serious doubt whether the use of television in trials would promote either enlightenment or respect. The bits and snatches of this trial's coverage were so one-sided and spasmodic as to convey less than a true and representative

ESTES *v.* TEXAS.

image of the judicial process. Moreover, the practice of barring television and picturing from the courtroom in no way suppresses or censors trial events. Reporters are always present if they wish to be and are plainly free to report whatever occurs in open court. These reportorial privileges of the press were stated years ago:

> "The law favors publicity in legal proceedings, so far as that object can be attained without injustice to the persons immediately concerned. The public are permitted to attend nearly all judicial inquiries, and there appears to be no sufficient reason why they should not also be allowed to see in print the reports of trials, if they can thus have them presented as fully as they are exhibited in court, or at least all the material portion of the proceedings impartially stated, so that one shall not, by means of them, derive erroneous impressions, which he would not have been likely to receive from hearing the trial itself."
> 2 Cooley's Constitutional Limitations 931–932 (Carrington ed. 1927).

The State, however, says that the use of television in the instant case was "without injustice to the person immediately concerned," basing its position on the fact that the petitioner has established no isolatable prejudice and that this must be shown in order to invalidate a conviction in these circumstances. The State paints too broadly in this contention, for this Court itself has found instances in which a showing of actual prejudice is not a prerequisite to reversal. This is such a case. It is true that in most cases involving claims of due process deprivations we require a showing of identifiable prejudice to the accused. Nevertheless, at times the procedure or device employed by the State has rendered the likelihood of prejudice so great as to render it inherently lacking in due process. Such a case was *In re Murchison,* 349 U. S. 133

ESTES *v.* TEXAS.

(1955). where MR. JUSTICE BLACK for the Court pointed this up with his usual clarity and force:

> "A fair trial in a fair tribunal is a basic element of due process. Fairness of course requires an absence of actual bias in the trial of cases. But our system of law has always endeavored to prevent even the *probability* of unfairness. . . . To perform its high function in the best way 'justice must satisfy the appearance of justice.' *Offutt* v. *United States,* 348 U. S. 11, 14." At 136.

And. as Chief Justice Taft said in *Tumey* v. *Ohio,* 273 U. S. 510. almost 30 years before:

> "the requirement of due process of law in judicial procedure is not satisfied by the argument that men of the highest honor and the greatest self-sacrifice could carry it on without danger of injustice. Every procedure which would offer a *possible* temptation to the average man . . . to forget the burden of proof required to convict the defendant, or might lead him not to hold the balance nice, clear and true between the State and the accused. denies the latter due process of law." At 532. (Emphasis supplied.)

This rule was followed in *Rideau, supra,* and in *Turner* v. *Louisiana,* 379 U. S. 466 (1964). In each of these cases the Court departed from the approach it charted in *Stroble* v. *California,* 343 U. S. 181 (1952), and in *Irvin* v. *Dowd,* 366 U. S. 717 (1961), where we made a careful examination of the facts in order to determine whether prejudice resulted. But in *Rideau* and *Turner* the Court did not stop to consider the effect of the publicity but struck down the conviction on the ground that prejudice was inherent in it. Likewise in *Gideon* v. *Wainwright,* 372 U. S. 335 (1963), and *White* v. *Maryland,* 373 U. S. 59 (1963), we applied the same rule, although in different contexts.

ESTES *v.* TEXAS.

In this case it is even clearer that such a rule must be applied. In *Rideau, Irvin* and *Stroble,* the pretrial publicity occurred outside the courtroom and could not be effectively curtailed. The only recourse other than reversal was by contempt proceedings. In *Turner* the probability of prejudice was present through the use of a deputy sheriff, who was also a witness in the case, as a shepherd for the jury. No prejudice was shown but the circumstances were held to be inherently bad and, therefore, such a showing was not a requisite to reversal. Likewise in this case the application of this *per se* principle is especially appropriate. Television, by its very nature, reaches into a variety of areas in which it may cause prejudice to an accused. Still one cannot put his finger on it just as was true in *In re Murchison, Tumey, Rideau* and *Turner.* Such untoward circumstances are inherently bad and prejudice to the accused must be presumed. Forty-eight of our States, and the English as well, have deemed the use of television improper, a fact which is most telling in considering any change in procedure that would permit its use in the courtroom. This is of itself weighty testimony in determining our concepts of due process in this field.

VI.

As has been said, the chief function of our judicial machinery is to ascertain the truth. But considered opinion offers not a single benefit that the use of television contributes to this objective. Rather its use amounts to the injection of an entirely irrelevant factor into court proceedings. In addition experience teaches that there are numerous situations in which it might cause actual unfairness—some so subtle as to defy detection by the accused or control by the judge.

1. The potential impact of television on the jurors is perhaps of greatest significance. They are the nerve center of the fact-finding process. It is true that in States

ESTES *v.* TEXAS.

like Texas where they are required to be sequestered in
trials of this nature the jurors will probably not see any
of the proceedings as televised from the courtroom. But
the inquiry cannot end there. From the moment the
trial judge announces that a case will be televised it becomes a *cause celebre*. The whole community, including
prospective jurors, becomes interested in all the morbid
details surrounding it. The approaching trial immediately assumes an important status in the public press and
the accused is highly publicized along with the offense
with which he is charged. Every juror carries with him
into the jury box these solemn facts and thus increases
the chance of prejudice that is present in every notorious
criminal case. And this type of trial, because of the necessity for sponsorship, will be the only kind televised.
The conscious or unconscious effect that this may have
on the juror's judgment cannot be evaluated, but experience indicates that it is not only possible but highly
probable that it will have a direct bearing on his vote as
to guilt or innocence. Where pretrial publicity of all
kinds has created intense public feeling which is aggra-
vated by the telecasting or picturing of the trial the televised jurors cannot help but feel the pressures of knowing
that friends and neighbors have their eyes upon them.
If the community be hostile to an accused a televised
juror, realizing that he must return to neighbors who saw
the trial themselves, may well be led "not to hold the
balance nice, clear and true between the State and the
accused . . . ."

Moreover, while it is practically impossible to assess
the effect of television on jury attentiveness, those of us
who know juries realize the weight of jury "distraction."
The State argues this is *de minimus* since the physical
disturbances have been done away with. But we know
that distractions are not caused solely by the physical
presence of the camera and its telltale red lights. It is

ESTES *v.* TEXAS.

the awareness of the fact of telecasting that is felt by the juror throughout the trial. Human nature being what it is, not only his eyes but his mind will often be on that fact rather than on the witness stand.

Furthermore, in many States the jurors serving in the trial may see the broadcasts of the trial proceedings. Admittedly, the Texas sequestration law would prevent this occurring there. In other States following no such practice jurors would return home and turn on the TV if only to see how they appeared upon it. They would also be subjected to re-enactment and emphasis of the selected parts of the proceedings which the whims of the broadcasters determined would be telecast. Moreover, they would be subjected to broadcaster commentary and the well-meant advice of inquiring strangers who recognized them on the streets, as well as friends and relatives.

Finally, new trials plainly would be jeopardized in that potential jurors will often have seen and heard the original trial when it was telecast. In addition they will rarely have seen an objective presentation. Broadcaster "color," the selection of particular portions for broadcasting and presentation of unfavorable shots of the accused could all contribute to the receipt by the viewer of a slanted and distorted version of what has gone on in the courtroom. Yet he may later be called upon to sit in the jury box during the new trial. The very dangers mentioned here are emphasized in this case where the court, due to the defendant's objections, permitted only the State's opening and closing arguments to be broadcast with sound to the public. A distorted image of the case resulted.

2. The quality of the testimony in criminal trials will often be impaired. The impact upon a witness of the knowledge that he is being viewed by a vast audience is simply incalculable. Some may be demoralized and frightened, some cocky and given to overstatement;

ESTES *v.* TEXAS.

memories may falter, as with anyone speaking publicly, and accuracy of statement may be severely undermined. Embarrassment may impede the search for the truth, as may a natural tendency toward over-dramatization. Furthermore, inquisitive strangers might well approach them on the street with jibes or advice. There is little wonder that the defendant cannot "prove" the existence of such factors. Yet we all know from experience that they exist.

In addition the invocation of the rule against witnesses is frustrated. In most instances witnesses would be able to go to their homes and view broadcasts of the day's trial proceedings, notwithstanding the fact that they had been admonished not to do so. They could view and hear the testimony of preceding witnesses, and so shape their own testimony as to make its impact crucial. And even in the absence of sound, the influences of such viewing on the attitude of the witness toward testifying, his frame of mind upon taking the stand or his apprehension of withering cross-examination defy objective assessment. Indeed, the mere fact that the trial is to be televised might render witness' reluctant to appear and thereby impede the discovery of the truth.

3. A major aspect of the problem is the additional responsibilities the presence of television places on the trial judge. He is a person devoted to the judicial process as a means to the ascertainment of truth. His job is to make certain that the accused receives a fair trial. This most difficult task requires his undivided attention. Still when television comes into the courtroom he must also watch it. In this trial, for example, the judge on at least 10 different occasions—aside from the two days of pretrial—was obliged to have a hearing or enter an order made necessary solely because of the presence of television. Thus, where telecasting is limited as it was here, and as even the State concedes it must be, his task is made much

ESTES *v.* TEXAS.

more difficult and exacting. And, as happened here, such rulings may unfortunately aggravate the unfairness of the trial. In addition, laying physical interruptions aside, there is the ever-present distraction that the mere awareness of television's presence prompts. All such distractions, of course, divert his attention from the task at hand—the fair trial of the accused.

But this is not all. There is the initial decision that must be made as to whether the use of television will be permitted. This is perhaps an even more crucial consideration. Our judges are high-minded men and women. But it is difficult to remain oblivious to the pressures that the news media can bring to bear on them directly and also through the shaping of public opinion as well. Moreover, where one judge in an area permits telecasting, the requirement that the others do the same is almost mandatory. Especially is this true where the judge is selected at the ballot box, as is true in all of our States save six.

4. Finally, we cannot ignore the impact of courtroom television on the defendant. Its presence is a form of mental—if not physical—harassment, resembling a police line-up or the third degree. Freedom of the press grants no license for one to project the telescopic lens of the camera on an accused for the purpose of selling his image to the world at large. The inevitable close-ups of his gestures and expressions during the ordeal of his trial might well transgress his personal sensibilities, his dignity, and his ability to concentrate on the proceedings before him— sometimes the difference between life and death—dispassionately, freely and without the distraction of wide public surveillance. A defendant on trial for a specific offense is entitled to his day in court, not in a stadium, or a city or nationwide arena. Trial by television is foreign to our system. Furthermore, telecasting also deprives an accused of effective counsel. The distractions, intrusions into confidential attorney-client relationships and the

ESTES *v.* TEXAS.

temptation offered by television to play to the public
might often have a direct effect upon effective representation. See Pye, The Lessons of Dallas—Threats to Fair
Trial and Free Press, National Civil Liberties Clearing
House, 16th Annual Conference.

The television camera is a powerful weapon. Intentionally or inadvertently it can destroy an accused and
his case in the eyes of the public. While our telecasters
are honorable men, they too are human. The necessity
for sponsorship weighs heavily in favor of the selection
of infamous cases and invariably focuses the beam of the
lens upon the unpopular or notorious accused. We have
already examined the ways in which public sentiment can
affect the trial participants. To the extent that television
shapes that sentiment, it can strip the accused of a fair
trial.

The State would dispose of all these observations with
the simple statement that they are for psychologists
because they are purely hypothetical. But we cannot
afford the luxury of saying that because these factors are
difficult of ascertainment in particular cases, they must
be ignored. Nor are they "purely hypothetical." They
are no more hypothetical than were the considerations
deemed controlling in *Tumey, Murchison, Rideau* and
Turner. They are real enough to have persuaded all but
two of our States and the English-speaking world besides
to bar television from the courtroom. They are effects
that may, and in some combination almost certainly will,
exist in any case in which television is injected into the
trial process.

VII.

The facts in this case demonstrate clearly the necessity
for the adoption of a *per se* rule. The sole issue before
the court for two days of pretrial hearing was the question
now before us. The hearing was televised live and repeated on tape in the same evening, reaching approxi-

ESTES *v.* TEXAS

mately 100,000 viewers. In addition, the courtroom was a mass of wires, television cameras, microphones and photographers. The petitioner, the panel of prospective jurors, who were sworn the second day, the witnesses and the lawyers were all exposed to this untoward situation. The judge decided that the trial proceedings would be telecast. He announced no restrictions at the time. This emphasized the importance of the coming trial, increased the intensity of the publicity on the petitioner and together with the subsequent televising of the trial beginning 30 days later inherently prevented a sober search for the truth.

Moreover, the good trial judge was harassed himself. After the initial decision to permit telecasting he apparently decided that a booth should be built to confine its operations; he then decided to limit the parts of the trial that might be televised live; then he decided to film the testimony of the witnesses without sound in an attempt to protect those under the rule; and finally he ordered that defense counsel and their argument not be televised, in the light of their objection. Plagued by the insoluble problem—recurring each day of the trial—he did his best to prevent prejudice to the petitioner. But in so doing his orders made the trial more confusing to the jury, the participants and to the viewers. Indeed, it resulted in a public presentation of only the State's side of the case.

As Mr. Justice Holmes said in *Patterson* v. *Colorado*, 205 U. S. 454, 462 (1907):

> "The theory of our system is that the conclusions to be reached in a case will be induced only by evidence and argument in open court, and not by any outside influence, whether of private talk or public print."

In the light of the inherent hazards to a fair trial that are presented by television in the courtroom I would hold that its use violated petitioner's right to due process. I would therefore reverse.

As already indicated, the Stewart draft opinion of the Court in *Estes* was never delivered because Justice Clark changed his vote. That converted the bare majority for affirmance to one for reversal and meant a decision striking down the *Estes* televised trial instead of one the other way.

The changed Clark posture was indicated in a *Memorandum to the Conference* that the Justice sent around on May 25, 1965. After he had considered the drafts that had been circulated, wrote Justice Clark, he had become disturbed "at what could result from this emasculation by TV of the trial of a case." He had now concluded, the memo stated, "that the perils to a fair trial far outweigh the benefits that might accrue in the televising of the proceedings." Justice Clark wrote that he was preparing an opinion embodying his new view, which he would shortly circulate.

Two days later, on May 27, Justice Clark sent around the promised opinion, which is reprinted on page 206. The draft is headed "MR. JUSTICE CLARK, reversing"; but it was plainly intended as a potential opinion of the Court and, with important changes, was used as the ultimate *Estes* opinion. The Clark draft contains strong language rejecting the claim that the First Amendment gives the press any right to attend trials. The Sixth Amendment, the draft notes, guarantees the accused a public trial. "The Constitution says nothing of any comparable right to the public or to the news media." The draft then refers specifically to the assertion that the First Amendment gives the press, including television, a right of access to the courtroom. According to Justice Clark, "This is a misconception of the right of the press. . . . it is clear beyond question that no language in the First Amendment grants any of the news media such a privilege."

Had this categoric language not been deleted from the final *Estes* opinion of the Court (which stated only that the press was "entitled to the same rights as the general public"[8]), the subsequent law on the press and the First Amendment might have been different—particularly if Justice Stewart had left in the rejection of the press's First Amendment right contained in his original *Estes* draft opinion of the Court. Instead, Justice Stewart inserted a paragraph on the First Amendment right of the press toward the end of his *Estes* dissent. This was put in to answer the refusal in Justice Clark's draft to recognize a constitutional right of the press to be present in the courtroom.

The major difference between the Clark draft reprinted on page 206 and the Clark opinion of the Court in *Estes* was the draft's specific rejection of the state's contention "that the televising of portions of a criminal trial does not constitute *per se* a denial of due process." Toward the end of the draft, there is the flat statement "The facts in this case demonstrate clearly the necessity for the adoption of a *per se* rule"—a statement substantially watered down (with the per se language eliminated) in the final opinion. The draft contains other passages that support the statement of a per se rule, such as the following: "The introduction of television into petitioner's trial constituted a violation of due process regardless of whether there was a showing of isolatable prejudice" (omitted from the *Estes* opinion); "Such untoward circumstances are inherently bad and prejudice to the accused must be presumed" (changed in the final opinion to, "Such untoward circumstances as were found in those cases [four cited Supreme Court decisions] are inherently bad and prejudice to the accused must be presumed")[9]; "In light of the inherent hazards to a fair trial that are presented by television in the courtroom I would hold that its use violated petitioner's right to due process" (the draft's concluding sentence, absent in the published opinion).

After Justice Clark's switch, the Chief Justice assigned him the *Estes* opinion. The Justice circulated a revision of his draft as the opinion of the Court. It was issued as the *Estes* opinion on June 7.

One interested in what "might have been" in Supreme Court jurisprudence has ample cause for speculation in *Estes* v. *Texas*. If Justice Stewart's original draft opinion of the Court had been the final *Estes* opinion, the law on television in the courtroom would have evolved differently than it has in the last twenty years. Instead of the relatively slow development of televised court proceedings that has occurred, *Estes* might have opened the broadcast floodgates. By now, the TV camera might be as common in the courtroom as it is in other areas of American life.

On the other hand, had Justice Clark's draft come down as the *Estes* opinion of the Court, television in the courtroom might have been constitutionally doomed. The Clark draft announced a per se rule, under which TV by its very nature became constitutionally incompatible with the proper conduct of criminal trials. This would have meant that, regardless of the circumstances of the particular case and any future improvements that might be made in television coverage, any televised trial would automatically violate due process. Broadcasting in the courtroom would have become constitutionally impermissible and the opening under the more recent *Chandler* case[10] for televising of trials might never have been given.

After Justice Clark sent around his *Estes* draft on May 27, Justice Stewart revised his draft opinion of the Court and circulated it as a dissent. The Stewart draft dissent was intended as an answer to the Clark draft opinion. As such, it began, "If, as I apprehend, the Court today holds that any television of a state criminal trial constitutes a *per se* violation of the Fourteenth Amendment, I cannot agree."[11]

The Stewart animadversion led Justice Clark to delete the per se references from his final *Estes* opinion, and Justice Stewart in turn removed the sentence just quoted from his *Estes* dissent. The *Estes* opinion of the Court, as it was finally issued, could be characterized in the Stewart dissent as a "decision that the circumstances of this trial led to a denial of the petitioner's Fourteenth Amendment rights."[12]

On May 24, Justice White, joined by Justice Brennan, had circulated a draft concurrence, which stated that Stewart's opinion of the Court then did not preclude a future decision that television could prove such a hazard to defendant's rights that it would be violative of due process without any showing of prejudice. On June 1, after Justice Clark's switch, they circulated a modified version as a short dissent, stressing that the new opinion of the Court prevented a flexible approach to use of cameras in the courtroom. It should, however, be stressed that this White draft, which asserted that the new majority was "erecting a flat ban on the use of cameras in the courtroom,"[13] was written while Justice Clark's draft contained the per se references already noted. Justice White did not change his draft's assertion after the Clark opinion of the Court had deleted the references to a per se rule.

Justice Brennan also issued a separate short *Estes* opinion emphasizing that, because of Justice Harlan's concurrence, only four members of the majority held that televised trials would be invalid, regardless of the circumstances. In effect, Brennan was having it both ways, joining with White to condemn the majority's inflexible approach and then denying that a majority had really voted for it. Yet it was the Brennan approach that the Court followed in *Chandler* v. *Florida*,[14] the 1981 case holding that a state rule allowing television coverage of a criminal trial does not violate the Constitution. The *Chandler* opinion is based upon a laborious effort to distinguish *Estes*, rather than overrule that case. Chief Justice Burger refers to "the per se rule embodied in the plurality opinion of Justice Clark"[15] in *Estes*. He then stresses that Justice Harlan's *Estes* concurrence meant that a majority in *Estes* did not vote for a per se rule barring broadcast coverage under all circumstances.

Justice Stewart, who concurred in the *Chandler* judgment, agreed "that *Estes* announced a *per se* rule"[16] and said that, as thus interpreted, he would overrule *Estes*. Justice White, in a separate concurrence, said that he agreed with this Stewart approach.[17]

Our analysis of *Estes* shows, however, that all three *Chandler* opinions are mistaken in their assumption that *Estes* laid down a per se rule. The draft opinion of Justice Clark, supra p. 206, had done so; but largely in response to Justice Stewart's attack in his draft dissent, Justice Clark had removed the per se language from his final *Estes* opinion of the Court. Instead he stated that the "facts of this case demonstrate clearly the necessity"[18] for the decision that Estes was deprived of due process even though he could not establish "isolatable prejudice"[19] from the televising of his trial.

Chief Justice Burger's *Chandler* opinion relies on Justice Harlan's concurrence in *Estes* to show that Justice Clark's statement of a per se rule in his *Estes* opinion of the Court received the support of only a plurality of four Justices. Yet, as just shown, the Clark *Estes* opinion did not announce a per se rule. And Justice Harlan, in his *Estes* concurrence, did no more than stress what should have been obvious once Justice Clark deleted the per se references from his draft—namely, that the *Estes* decision held that the televised trial deprived defendant of due process under the "facts in this case."[20] Despite the contrary assumption in the *Chandler* opinions, the Harlan *Estes* concurrence was not issued to demonstrate Justice Harlan's refusal to subscribe to a per se rule, since the *Estes* opinion of the Court stated no such rule. Instead, Harlan was only stressing that, in an area of such rapid technological change, the decision was based upon "television as we find it in this trial."[21]

In addition, it should be borne in mind that the Harlan *Estes* concurrence was originally drafted as a dissent to the Stewart draft opinion of the Court then upholding the *Estes* televised trial. In dissenting, Justice Harlan was not the type of judge to go to the opposite extreme from a majority decision. Rather than urge the unconstitutionality of all television in the courtroom in all circumstances, the Harlan draft dissent, circulated May 19, 1965, before any of the other dissents to Stewart's draft opinion of the Court had been sent around, focused on the instant fact pattern. After the Court vote had changed and Justice Clark had written the new *Estes* opinion of the Court, Justice Harlan changed his draft dissent to a concurrence. It is unfortunate that the only change he made in its language was a statement of concurrence at the beginning and end, replacing the statement at the end of the draft dissent, "I would reverse this conviction."[22]

The confusion caused by the Harlan *Estes* concurrence—at least to the *Chandler* Court—would have been avoided if the original Stewart draft had come down as the final *Estes* opinion of the Court. In that case, there would have been no need for the *Chandler* decision, since *Estes* would have upheld televised trials over a decade and a half earlier. The question of how far *Estes* went would not have come up. Under the Stewart draft *Estes* opinion of the Court, the state rule permitting television in the courtroom would clearly have been constitutional.

Notes

1. 381 U.S. 532 (1965).
2. Id. at 604.
3. *Estes* v. *Texas*, Mr. Chief Justice Warren, dissenting. Circulated May 21, 1965, p. 1. JMHP.
4. 381 U.S. at 614–615.
5. Id. at 539–540.
6. 448 U.S. 555 (1980).
7. TCCT.
8. 381 U.S. at 540.
9. Id. at 544.
10. Infra note 14.
11. *Estes* v. *Texas*, Mr. Justice Stewart, dissenting. Circulated June 1, 1965, p. 1. JMHP.
12. 381 U.S. at 601.
13. Id. at 615.
14. 449 U.S. 560 (1981).

15. Id. at 572.
16. Id. at 583.
17. Id. at 587.
18. 381 U.S. at 550.
19. Id. at 542.
20. Id. at 550.
21. Id. at 588.
22. *Estes* v. *Texas*, Mr. Justice Harlan, dissenting. Circulated May 19, 1965, p. 10. JMHP.

7

Griswold v. *Connecticut* (*1965*):
Penumbras and Privacy

Though it never received the public attention accorded to *Brown* v. *Board of Education*,[1] *Baker* v. *Carr*,[2] and *Miranda* v. *Arizona*,[3] *Griswold* v. *Connecticut*[4] was as important a case as any decided by the Warren Court, for it established the seminal right of privacy, which has proved as consequential as any constitutional right recognized by the Supreme Court.

Before *Griswold* the right of privacy was essentially a right only between private individuals, with a tort action available to those aggrieved by violations of that right. When Samuel D. Warren and Louis D. Brandeis published their landmark 1890 article first advocating recognition of a legal right of privacy,[5] they were thinking only of the private right of individuals whose privacy was being invaded by other individuals. The Warren–Brandeis article was published less than a decade after the acquisition of *The New York World* by Joseph Pulitzer in 1883, from which the rise of sensationalist journalism in this country is usually dated. The Warren–Brandeis article itself was probably a direct result of the invasion of the private life of one of the coauthors by the "yellow journalism" of the day.[6]

Years later, Justice Brandeis indicated that his 1890 conception of a right of privacy, as one that protected only against infringement by other individuals, was too narrow. In a famous 1928 dissent, the Justice asserted that the Framers

> conferred, as against the Government, the right to be let alone—the most comprehensive of rights and the right most valued by civilized men. To protect that right, every unjustifiable intrusion by the Government upon the privacy of the individual, whatever the means employed, 'must be deemed a violation of the [Constitution].[7]

In this Brandeis conception, the Constitution has erected a wall against unjustifiable governmental intrusions upon individual privacy; the

227

right of the individual to be let alone is included among the personal rights safeguarded in the Constitution.

It is, all the same, most unlikely that the Framers intended to confer, as against government, a right of privacy anything like the sense in which that term is used in the law today. If they did recognize a right of privacy, it was only in the limited sense provided by the Fourth Amendment, guaranteeing against physical intrusions upon the person and the home—what Justice Harlan once termed the privacy of the person and the home in its most basic sense.[8]

Aside from the Fourth Amendment immunity against physical invasion of one's person and private possessions, the right of privacy remained beyond the constitutional pale before *Griswold* v. *Connecticut.* The law had come to recognize the need to protect the right of privacy vis-à-vis other private individuals, but only as a right recognized by the law of torts, not one guaranteed by the Constitution. There was no recognition of any general right to be let alone as a right secured by the Bill of Rights.

Griswold v. *Connecticut* changed all this. It was the first case confirming the existence of a broad right of privacy against government. And the right is a constitutional one, unlike that advocated in the Warren–Brandeis article and since accepted by the law as a right enforced by the private law of torts. Under *Griswold*, for the first time, a general right to privacy was ruled part of the area of personal rights protected by the Constitution. As Justice Black put it, *Griswold* elevated "a phrase which Warren and Brandeis used in discussing grounds for tort relief, to the level of a constitutional rule which prevents state legislatures from passing any law deemed by this Court to interfere with 'privacy.' "[9]

But the *Griswold* decision did not start out that way. The opinion of the Court first drafted by Justice Douglas did not rely upon the right of privacy at all. Had it come down as the *Griswold* opinion, the law on the matter might have been entirely different, the right of privacy might never have been recognized as a constitutional right by the Warren Court and the broad expansion of that right in the Burger Court's jurisprudence might never have taken place.

At issue in *Griswold* was a Connecticut law that prohibited use of contraceptive devices and the giving of medical advice in their use. Though there were other laws, state and federal, prohibiting the transportation or sale of contraceptive devices, the Connecticut statute was unique in making the *use* of them criminal. Griswold was the director of the Planned Parenthood League and Dr. Buxton was the medical director of the League's New Haven center. They gave advice to married persons on preventing conception and prescribed contraceptive devices for the wives. They were convicted of violating the birth control law and their conviction was affirmed by the state's highest court.

The constitutionality of the Connecticut birth-control law had previously been before the Warren Court in the 1961 case of *Poe* v. *Ullman*, where plaintiffs sought a declaratory judgment against the Connecticut law.[10] The Justices had then avoided the constitutional issue by deciding that the case was not ripe for adjudication since no criminal prosecution had been brought. Justices Douglas and Harlan had, however, dissented from the *Poe* decision, urging that the birth-control law violated the right of privacy. To Justice Harlan, the law was contrary to due process as "an intolerable and unjustifiable invasion of privacy in the conduct of the most intimate concerns of an individual's personal life."[11] To Justice Douglas, the law was an invalid "invasion of the privacy that is implicit in a free society." The Bill of Rights, Douglas said, which bars soldiers from being quartered in a home, also "bar[s] the police from investigating the intimacies of the marriage relation."[12]

In *Griswold*, the Justices could not avoid the constitutional merits, since the defendants had been convicted of violating the Connecticut statute, which plainly made the case ripe for constitutional adjudication. So clear was this that all of the Justices voted to hear the appeal from the state judgment affirming the convictions.

The April 2, 1965, conference found a seven-to-two majority in favor of striking down the Connecticut law. But the majority Justices did not articulate a clear theory on which to base the decision. Justice Douglas stated the simplest rationale on which the law could be invalidated, saying that it violated the defendant's First Amendment right of association. The right of association, according to Douglas, was more than a right of assembly. Thus, he reasoned, the right to send a child to a religious school was "on the periphery" of the right of association. He cited the *Pierce* case[13] as such a case. He used the analogy of the right to travel, which the Court had said "is in radiation of First Amendment and so is this right." There was nothing more personal than this right and it too was "on the periphery" and within First Amendment protection.

The *Griswold* opinion was assigned to Justice Douglas, who had, as noted, expressed a simple theory on which the Connecticut law might be stricken down. Douglas quickly prepared the draft opinion of the Court reprinted on page 231. It follows the approach the Justice had urged at the conference. The draft bases the decision that the birth-control law is unconstitutional on the First Amendment, likening the husband-wife relationship to the other forms of association given First Amendment protection.

The draft concedes, "The association of husband and wife is not mentioned in the Constitution nor in the Bill of Rights." But that is also true of "any other kind of association." Yet the First Amendment is "construed to include certain of these peripheral rights." The draft refers to different cases involving rights of association. It then declares that marriage "is a form of association as vital in the life of a man or woman as any other, and perhaps more so." Indeed, it is "a right of association older than the Bill of Rights—older than our political parties, older than our school system."

The Connecticut law, the Douglas draft concludes, invalidly intrudes on the right of marital association. "The prospects of police with warrants searching the sacred precincts of marital bedrooms for telltale signs of the use of contraceptives is repulsive to the idea of privacy and association that make up a goodly part of the penumbra of the Constitution and Bill of Rights."

Had the Douglas draft been issued as the *Griswold* opinion of the Court, the case would stand as a precedent on the freedom of association rather than the right of privacy. Though "privacy" is mentioned in the last sentence of the Douglas draft, that is scarcely enough to make it the foundation for any constitutional right of privacy, particularly for the broadside right established by the final *Griswold* opinion. As a decision based on the right of association, *Griswold* would have been just another constitutional footnote instead of the constitutional landmark it has become.

496—OPINION

No. 496.—OCTOBER TERM, 1964.

Estelle T. Griswold et al.,
Appellants,
v.
State of Connecticut.

On Appeal From the Supreme Court of Errors of Connecticut

[April —, 1965.]

MR. JUSTICE DOUGLAS delivered the opinion of the Court.

Appellant Griswold is Executive Director of the Planned Parenthood League of Connecticut. Appellant Buxton is a licensed physician and a professor at the Yale Medical School who served as Medical Director for the League at its Center in New Haven—a center open and operating from November 1 to November 10, 1961, when appellants were arrested.

They gave information, instruction, and medical advice to *married persons* as to the means of preventing conception. They examined the wife and prescribed the best contraceptive device or material for her use. Fees were usually charged, although some couples were serviced free.

The statutes whose constitutionality are involved in this appeal are §§ 53–32 and 54–196 of the General Statutes of Connecticut (1938). The former provides:

> "Any person who uses any drug, medicinal articles or instruments for the purpose of preventing conception shall be fined not less than fifty dollars or imprisoned not less than sixty days nor more than one year or be both fined and imprisoned."

---

* This opinion has been reset; a copy of the original is in the possession of the author.

OPINION

Section 54–196 provides:

> "Any person who assists, abets, counsels, causes, hires, or commands another to commit any offence may be prosecuted and punished as if he were the principal offender."

The appellants were found guilty as accessories and fined $100 each, against the claim that the accessory statute as so applied violated the Fourteenth Amendment. The Appellate Division of the Circuit Court affirmed. 3 Conn. Cir. 6. The Court of Errors affirmed that judgment. 151 Conn. 544. 200 A. 2d 479. We noted probable jurisdiction. 378 U. S. —.

We think that appellants have standing to raise the constitutional rights of the married people with whom they had a professional relationship. *Tileston* v. *Ullman*, 318 U. S. 44, is different, for there the plaintiff seeking to represent others asked for a declaratory judgment. In that situation we thought that the requirements of standing should be strict lest the standards of "case or controversy" in Article III of the Constitution become blurred. Here those doubts are removed by reason of a criminal conviction for serving married couples in violation of a statute which if invalid makes the conviction unconstitutional. This case is more akin to *Truax* v. *Raich*, 239 U. S. 33, where an employer was permitted to assert the rights of his employees; to *Pierce* v. *Society of Sisters*, 268 U. S. 510, where the owners of a private school were entitled to assert the rights of potential pupils and their parents; and to *Barrows* v. *Jackson*, 346 U. S. 249, where a white defendant, party to a racially restrictive covenant, who was being sued for damages by the covenantor because the defendant had conveyed the property to a Negro, was allowed to raise the issue that enforcement of the covenant violated the rights of Negroes to equal protection, although no Negro was a party to the

OPINION

suit. And see *Meyer* v. *Nebraska,* 262 U. S. 390; *Adler* v. *Board of Education,* 342 U. S. 485; *NAACP* v. *Alabama,* 357 U. S. 449; *NAACP* v. *Button,* 371 U. S. 415.

The rights of husband and wife, pressed here, are likely to be diluted or adversely affected unless those rights are considered in a suit involving those who have this kind of confidential relation to them.

Coming to the merits, we are met with a wide range of questions that implicate the Due Process Clause of the Fourteenth Amendment. Overtones of some arguments suggest that *Lochner* v. *New York,* 198 U. S. 45, should be our guide. But we decline that invitation as we did in *West Coast Hotel Co.* v. *Parrish,* 300 U. S. 379; *Lincoln Union* v. *Northwestern Co.,* 335 U. S. 525; *Williamson* v. *Lee Optical Co.,* 348 U. S. 483; *Olsen* v. *Nebraska,* 313 U. S. 236; *Giboney* v. *Empire Storage Co.,* 336 U. S. 490. We do not sit as a super-legislature to determine the wisdom, need, and propriety of laws that touch economic problems, business affairs, or social conditions. Were this law one that dealt with the manufacturing, sale or marketing of contraceptives we would think no substantial federal question would be presented by this appeal. This case, however, has no commercial aspect nor any marketing aspect. Instead it involves an intimate relation of husband and wife and their physician's role in one aspect of that relation.

The association of husband and wife is not mentioned in the Constitution nor in the Bill of Rights. Neither is any other kind of association. The right to educate a child in a school of the parents' choice—whether public or parochial—is also not mentioned. Nor is the right to study any particular subject or any foreign language. Yet the First Amendment has been construed to include certain of those peripheral rights. By *Pierce* v. *Society of Sisters, supra,* the right to educate one's children as one choses [sic] is made applicable to the States by the

OPINION

force of the First and Fourteenth Amendments. By *Meyer* v. *Nebraska, supra,* the same dignity is given the right to study the German language in a public school. In other words, the State may not, consistently with the spirit of the First Amendment, contract the spectrum of available knowledge. The right to learn, the right to read, the right to know have overtones in freedom of speech and of the press. Without those peripheral rights the specific rights would be less secure. And so we reaffirm the principle of the *Pierce* and the *Meyer* cases.

The family is an instruction unit as much as the school; and husband and wife are both teachers and pupils. And the family, together with its physician, is an instruction unit as much as a school is. To narrow, as does the Connecticut statute, discussion and advice on a problem as important as population and procreation is to introduce a dangerous state influence over the First Amendment right to disseminate knowledge.

Other First Amendment analogies also involve rights of association. In *NAACP* v. *Alabama,* 357 U. S. 449, 462, we protected the "freedom to associate and privacy in one's association," noting that freedom of association was a First Amendment right. Disclosure of membership lists in a constitutionally valid association, we held, was invalid "as entailing the likelihood of a substantial restraint upon the exercise by petitioner's members of their right to freedom of association." *Id.,* at 462. In like context, we have protected forms of "association" that are not political in the customary sense but pertain to the social, legal, and economic benefit of the members. *NAACP* v. *Button,* 371 U. S. 415. 430–431. In *Schware* v. *Board of Bar Examiners,* 353 *U.* S. 232, we held it not permissible to bar a lawyer from practice, because he had once been a member of the Communist Party. The man's "association with that Party" was not shown to be "anything more than a political faith in a political party" (*id.,*

OPINION

at 244) and not action of a kind proving bad moral character. *Id.*, at 245–246.

None of those cases involved the "right of assembly"— a right that extends to all irrespective of their race or oideology. *DeJonge* v. *Oregon,* 299 U. S. 353. The right of "association" like the right of belief (*Board of Education* v. *Barnette,* 319 U. S. 624) is more than the right to attend a meeting; it includes the right to express one's attitudes or philosophies by membership in a group or by affiliation with it or by other lawful means. Association in that context is a form of expression of opinion; and while it is not expressly included in the First Amendment its existence is necessary and useful in making the express guarantees fully meaningful.

The foregoing cases do not decide this case. But they place it in the proper frame of reference. Marriage does not fit precisely any of the categories of First Amendment rights. But it is a form of association as vital in the life of a man or woman as any other, and perhaps more so. We would, indeed, have difficulty protecting the intimacies of one's relations to NAACP and not the intimacies of one's marriage relation. Marriage is the essence of one form of the expression of love, admiration, and loyalty. To protect other forms of such expression and not this, the central one, would seem to us to be a travesty. We deal with a right of association older than the Bill of Rights—older than our political parties, older than our school system. It is a coming together for better or for worse, hopefully enduring, and intimate to the degree of being sacred. This association promotes a way of life, not causes; a harmony in living, not political faiths; a bilateral loyalty, not commercial or social projects. Yet it flourishes on the interchange of ideas. It is the main font of the population problem; and education of each spouse in the ramification of that problem, the health of the wife, and the well-being of the family, is central to family functioning. Those objects are the end products of free expression and these Acts intrude on them.

If the accessory statute can be enforced as it has been here, so can § 53–32 which also has criminal sanctions. The prospects of police with warrants searching the sacred precincts of marital bedrooms for telltale signs of the use of contraceptives is repulsive to the idea of privacy and of association that make up a goodly part of the penumbra of the Constitution and Bill of Rights. Cf. *Rochin* v. *California,* 342 U. S. 165.

Reversed.

At the April 2, 1965, conference on *Griswold* v. *Connecticut*, Justice Black had referred sarcastically to the claim that the challenged Connecticut law violated the defendants' First Amendment right of association. As summarized in the conference notes of one Justice, Black stated, "Right of association is for me right of assembly & rt of husband & wife to assemble in bed is new right of assembly to me."

It must be conceded that the Douglas draft *Griswold* opinion is not legally convincing. This was not unusual for the Justice. "Among legal scholars," asserts a recent biography, "his reputation was not so sturdy. Douglas was guilty, some scholars suggested, of inattention to legal detail and indifference to precedent. . . . His opinions seemed written more for a general audience. It was as if he got bored with the lawyer's craft."[14]

The Douglas draft's reasoning supports such criticism. The right of association under the First Amendment was not meant to protect grouping or coming together as such, but only to protect such activities where essential to fruitful advocacy. When the Supreme Court held in 1958 that the right of association was protected by the First Amendment, it spoke of "freedom to engage in association for the advancement of beliefs and ideas."[15]

That Justice Douglas himself did not originally think of the *Griswold* case as the vehicle by which a broad right of privacy might be imported into the Constitution is surprising. After all, it was Justice Douglas who had been advocating a constitutional right of privacy for some years. In a 1952 dissent, he had asserted that liberty under the Constitution "must include privacy. . . . The right to be let alone is indeed the beginning of all freedom."[16] And, in *Poe* v. *Ullman*, where, as we have seen, Justice Douglas had dissented from the Court's refusal to rule on the constitutionality of the Connecticut law at issue in *Griswold*, his dissent argued that the law invalidly infringed the right of privacy. That right, Justice Douglas asserted, was protected by the Constitution. In language anticipating his final *Griswold* opinion, the Douglas *Poe* dissent declared, "This notion of privacy is not drawn from the blue. It emanates from the totality of the constitutional scheme under which we live."[17]

Despite this, the Douglas draft opinion of the Court in *Griswold* v. *Connecticut* did not use the privacy approach and relied upon the not wholly apposite First Amendment right of association. It took the suggestion of another Justice for *Griswold* to be transformed into the leading case establishing the existence of a far-ranging constitutional right of privacy.

As soon as Justice Douglas received copies of his *Griswold* draft opinion from the Court's print shop, he sent one headed "Desk Copy not cir[culated] 4-23-65" to Justice Brennan. The latter sent Justice Douglas a letter the next morning urging him to abandon his First Amendment right of association approach. Justice Brennan wrote that the "association" of married couples had little to do with the advocacy protected by the First Amendment freedom of association. The Douglas draft's broad-gauged approach, Justice Brennan warned, might lead to First Amendment protection for the Communist Party simply because it was a group, an approach that Justice Douglas himself had rejected in the discussions on the original Communist Party registration case almost a decade earlier.[18]

In his letter Justice Brennan suggested that the expansion of the First Amendment to include freedom of association, upon which the Douglas *Griswold* draft had been based, be used as an analogy to justify a similar approach in the area of privacy. Justice Douglas followed the Brennan suggestion and circulated a *Griswold* draft opinion of the Court on April 28, which stated the "specific guarantees in the Bill of Rights have penumbras, formed by emanations from those guarantees that help give them life and substance."[19] A constitutional right of privacy was included in these penumbras. The right of marital privacy—"older than the Bill of Rights—older than our political parties, older than our school system"[20]— was violated by the Connecticut law.

The circulated Douglas draft was essentially similar to the final *Griswold* opinion. It did, however, contain two sentences omitted from the final opinion that touched upon the newly established right of privacy. After referring to the "notions of privacy surrounding the marriage relationship" toward the end of the opinion, the circulated draft stated, "We think that the enforcement of the aider-and-abettor statute in this marital setting likewise dilutes the right of privacy by demeaning it." And the draft's last sentence declared that marriage "flourishes only in the regime of privacy which we think the Bill of Rights creates."

Even with the last-quoted sentence deleted, the *Griswold* opinion of the Court holds squarely that the Bill of Rights does establish a constitutionally protected zone of privacy. This *Griswold*-created right has served as the foundation for some of the most controversial Supreme Court decisions in the past two decades. By 1977, the Court could state, "*Griswold* may no longer be read as holding only that a State may not prohibit a married couple's use of contraceptives."[21] The right of privacy recognized in *Griswold* is not one that inheres only in the marital relationship. Instead, "If the right of privacy means anything, it is the right of the *individual*, married or single, to be free from unwarranted governmental intrusion into matters so fundamentally affecting a person."[22]

The *Griswold*-created right has evolved into a virtual right of personal autonomy, which protects individual independence in making decisions affecting personal life. Thus, freedom of personal choice in matters of family life is now treated by the Court as one of the liberties protected by the Constitution.[23] Among the decisions that an individual may make without unjustified governmental interference are personal decisions relating to marriage, procreation, contraception, family relationships, and child rearing.[24]

Perhaps the most controversial application of the *Griswold*-created right was in *Roe* v. *Wade*,[25] where the Court decided that a state law proscribing most abortions was violative of the right of privacy. That right was held to include the right to terminate pregnancies. The right of privacy was ruled broad enough to encompass the abortion decision. (By contrast, it should be noted, at the *Griswold* conference Chief Justice Warren had stated that he could not say that the state had no legitimate interest, noting that that could apply to abortion laws—implying that he thought such laws were valid.)

The present law on the matter might be entirely different if the original Douglas draft had come down as the *Griswold* opinion of the Court. If the broadside right of privacy established by the final Douglas opinion had not been recognized by the Warren Court, it is unlikely that its successor would have made its decisions building on that right. From this point of view, the change in the Douglas opinion, from the uncirculated draft relying on freedom of association to the circulated draft and final *Griswold* opinion establishing a Bill of Rights–created "regime of privacy," was of fundamental significance. If the change had not occurred, it may be doubted that *Roe* v. *Wade* and the other decisions based on the *Griswold*-created right would have been made.

Notes

1. 347 U.S. 483 (1954).
2. 369 U.S. 186 (1962).
3. 384 U.S. 436 (1966).
4. 381 U.S. 479 (1965).
5. Warren and Brandeis, "The Right to Privacy," 4 *Harv. L. Rev.* 193 (1890).
6. See Prosser, "Privacy," 48 *Cal. L. Rev.* 383 (1960).
7. *Olmstead* v. *United States*, 277 U.S. 438, 478 (1928).
8. Dissenting, in *Poe* v. *Ullman*, 367 U.S. 497, 548–549 (1961).
9. Dissenting, in *Griswold* v. *Connecticut*, 381 U.S. at 510, n. 1.
10. 367 U.S. 497 (1961). The statute had also been challenged in *Tileston* v. *Ullman*, 318 U.S. 44 (1943), but the action there had been dismissed on the ground that plaintiff lacked standing to bring the suit.
11. 367 U.S. at 539.
12. Id. at 522.
13. *Pierce* v. *Society of Sisters*, 281 U.S. 370 (1925).
14. Simon, *Independent Journey: The Life of William O. Douglas*, 252–253 (1980).
15. *NAACP* v. *Alabama*, 357 U.S. 449, 460 (1958).
16. Dissenting, in *Public Utilities Commission* v. *Pollak*, 343 U.S. 451, 467 (1952).
17. 367 U.S. at 521.
18. *Communist Party* v. *Control Board*, 351 U.S. 115 (1956).
19. 381 U.S. at 484.
20. Id. at 486.
21. *Carey* v. *Population Services International*, 431 U.S. 678, 687 (1977).
22. *Eisenstadt* v. *Baird*, 405 U.S. 438, 453 (1972) (emphasis in original).
23. *Quilloin* v. *Walcott*, 434 U.S. 246, 255 (1978).
24. *Carey* v. *Population Services International*, 431 U.S. 678, 685 (1977).
25. 410 U.S. 113 (1973).

8

Time, Inc. v. *Hill* (*1967*): *Privacy Suits and the First Amendment*

In the 1965 case of *Griswold* v. *Connecticut*,[1] the Warren Court had rec-
ognized a constitutional right of privacy. A year later, in *Time, Inc.* v.
Hill,[2] the Court came close to expanding that right to the point where
Justice Black could claim that the Justices had "by their own fiat created
a right of privacy equal to or superior to the right of a free press that the
Constitution created."[3]

Time, Inc. v. *Hill* arose out of a story in *Life* magazine about a
Broadway play, *The Desperate Hours*, which had been inspired by the
experience of James J. Hill and his family, who had been held hostage in
their home by escaped convicts. The play was fictionalized and had
added scenes of violence for dramatic effect. The *Life* article portrayed
the play as a reenactment of the Hills's experience and it contained photographs of scenes acted in the home where the Hills had been held. Hill
sued *Life*'s publisher under a New York statute prohibiting invasions of
privacy and making it an actionable tort to use the name, portrait, or picture of any person "for advertising purposes or for the purposes of trade"
without written consent. Hill alleged that the *Life* article falsely represented that the play mirrored the Hill family's experience. The New
York courts awarded Hill $30,000. The Supreme Court was closely di-
vided on whether to hear the publisher's appeal, with the Chief Justice
and Justices Clark, Stewart, and Fortas voting to dismiss.

Time, Inc. v. *Hill* came to the Warren Court against a background
of prior decisions by that tribunal which had substantially changed the
law on damage suits against the press. The leading Warren Court decision in that area was *New York Times Co.* v. *Sullivan*.[4] The too-freely-
used hyperbolic term *landmark decision* may truthfully be employed to
describe the action of the Supreme Court in that case. For, in its *New
York Times* decision, the Court ruled for the first time that the governmental power to fix the bounds of libelous speech is confined by the
First Amendment.

According to one of the most celebrated of Justice Holmes's aphorisms, "Great cases like hard cases make bad law."[5] From this point of view, the facts in *New York Times Co.* v. *Sullivan* certainly presented a hard case, as well as a great case. The immediate fact pattern there exercised a kind of hydraulic pressure that made what was previously clear seem doubtful and before which even seemingly settled principles of law had to bend.[6]

The case arose out of a libel action brought by the elected police commissioner of Montgomery, Alabama, against four individual defendants and the *New York Times*. The complaint alleged that plaintiff had been libeled by statements in a full-page advertisement in the *Times*. The advertisement was flamboyant in character and described alleged violations of Negro rights by the police in Montgomery. The text appeared over the names of sixty-four persons, many of whom were widely known, and then there appeared the names of the four defendants, as individual Southern clergymen. The advertisement was inserted and paid for by the Committee to Defend Martin Luther King and the Struggle for Freedom in the South, a militant civil-rights organization. Because the advertisement was placed by a responsible person, was signed by so many well-known persons, and seemed accurate on its face, the *Times* published it without seeking to confirm its accuracy.

The state courts had ruled that the apparently impersonal statements contained in the advertisement were libelous per se so far as plaintiff was concerned and had upheld a verdict in his favor of half a million dollars. According to a federal judge, "The Supreme Court of the United States was confronted by a somewhat baffling problem insofar as the facts of the case were concerned. The jury had rendered a grotesquely huge verdict for $500,000, although there was no contention that the plaintiff had suffered any pecuniary loss. . . . If the verdict had stood, it does not seem unreasonable to suggest that there would have been a miscarriage of justice."[7]

That result could have been avoided by a reversal on narrow grounds related to libel law, such as the lack of evidence to show that the general statements made about "the police" really defamed plaintiff police commissioner.[8] But the Supreme Court chose to reverse instead on broad constitutional grounds. The starting point of the *New York Times* decision is the "general proposition that freedom of expression upon public questions is secured by the First Amendment."[9] The *Times* case must consequently be considered "against the background of a profound national commitment to the principle that debate on public issues should be uninhibited, robust, and wide-open, and that it may well include vehement, caustic, and sometimes unpleasantly sharp attacks on government and public officials."[10]

The Court then went on to bring the advertisement at issue, "as an expression of grievance and protest on one of the major public issues of our time,"[11] within the bounds of constitutional protection. However,

"The question is whether it forfeits that protection by the falsity of some of its factual statements and by its alleged defamation of respondent."[12]

The Court answered the question thus posed by asserting first that "the First Amendment guarantees have consistently refused to recognize an exception for any test of truth."[13] Erroneous statement, too, must be protected if debate on public issues is to be truly free, for "factual error affords no warrant for repressing speech that would otherwise be free."[14]

Under the *New York Times* decision then, neither factual error nor defamatory content suffices to remove the constitutional shield from criticism of official conduct, and the combination of the two elements is no less inadequate. The First Amendment is held to require a "rule that prohibits a public official from recovering damages for a defamatory falsehood relating to his official conduct unless he proves that the statement was made with 'actual malice'—that is, with knowledge that it was false or with reckless disregard of whether it was false or not."[15]

The result is to limit the power to award damages for libel in actions brought by public officials against critics of their official conduct.[16] The role of "the citizen-critic of government" is deemed so important in the society—"It is as much his duty to criticize as it is the official's duty to administer"[17]—that it is necessary to immunize him from the deterrent of libel suits unless malice on his part can actually be proved. Honest error on the critic's part is thus protected as much as wholly truthful criticism.

Under *New York Times Co.* v. *Sullivan*, the First Amendment requires the law of libel to recognize a "privilege for criticism of official conduct"[18] that extends to honest misstatements of fact.[19] In a later case, *New York Times* v. *Sullivan* was extended to public figures.[20] Under it, neither a public official nor a public figure could maintain an action for damages for defamation unless actual malice was shown.

Is the same true of damage suits against the press under a statute prohibiting violations of an individual's right of privacy?

At the first conference on *Time, Inc.* v. *Hill*, on April 29, 1966, the majority answered this question in the negative, agreeing with the position stated by the Chief Justice that there was no First Amendment problem here because the *Life* story was "a fictionalization of these people's experience and false."[21] The Justices voted six to three to affirm the New York judgment, with Justices Black, Douglas, and White voting for reversal. The Chief Justice assigned the case to Justice Fortas, who circulated a sixteen-page draft opinion of the Court on June 8, 1966. This opinion, in a recirculated version sent around on June 14, is reprinted on page 245.

The Fortas draft is far-reaching both in its language and its conclusions. Justice Black is said to have told the other Justices that it was the worst First Amendment opinion he had seen in a dozen years.[22] Had the Fortas draft come down as the *Time, Inc.* v. *Hill* opinion of the Court, it would have restricted the Warren Court decisions expanding First Amendment rights in favor of the individual right of privacy. If there is an inevitable tension between the press and privacy, the Fortas draft comes down unmistakably on the side of the latter.

There are two themes worthy of note in Justice Fortas's draft opinion of the Court. In the first place, there is what one of the Justices termed an "invective" against the press. After summarizing the case, Justice Fortas declares,

> The facts of this case are unavoidably distressing. Needless, heedless, wanton and deliberate injury of the sort inflicted by *Life*'s picture story is not an essential instrument of responsible journalism. Magazine writers and editors are not, by reason of their high office, relieved of the common obligation to avoid inflicting wanton and unnecessary injury. The prerogatives of the press—essential to our liberty—do not preclude reasonable care and avoidance of casual infliction of injury. . . . They do not confer a license for pointless assault.

The Fortas draft condemns the *Life* article as "a fictionalized version of the Hill incident, deliberately or heedlessly distorted beyond semblance of reality." Far from being a legitimate news story, it was a

> deliberate, callous invasion of the Hills' right to be let alone—this appropriation of a family's right not to be molested or to have its name exploited and its quiet existence invaded. . . . This is exploitation, undertaken to titillate and excite, for commercial purposes. It was not a retelling of a newsworthy incident or of an event relating to a public figure. It was not such an account. It was not so designed. It was fiction: an invention, distorted and put to the uses of the promotion of Life magazine and of a play.

The second theme in the Fortas draft worth comment is its panegyric of privacy—as broad a statement of that right as any ever made by a member of the highest court.

> There is . . . no doubt that a fundamental right of privacy exists, and that it is of constitutional stature. It is not just the right of a remedy against false accusation, provided, within limits, by the law of defamation; it is not only the right to be secure in one's person, house, papers and effects, except as permitted by law; it embraces the right to be free from coercion, however subtle, to incriminate oneself; it is different from, but akin to the right to select and freely to practice one's religion and the right to freedom of speech; it is more than the specific right to be secure against the Peeping Tom or the intrusion of electronic espionage devices and wiretapping. All of these are aspects of the right to privacy; but the right of privacy reaches beyond any of its specifics. It is, simply stated, the right to be let alone; to live one's life as one chooses, free from assault, intrusion or invasion except as they can be justified by the clear needs of community living under a government of law.

Building upon its two basic themes, the Fortas draft concludes that the New York statute, as applied to this case, was not contrary to the First Amendment. Freedom of the press is not violated by imposition of liability on publications responsible for "misappropriation of [plaintiff's] identity for purposes which . . . are nothing more than the knowingly false attribution of events to a named person for the purpose of accentuating the dramatic or entertainment value of a publication."

On June 9, 1966, the day after the Fortas draft opinion of the Court was circulated, Justice Douglas sent around the short draft dissent reprinted on page 265. The Douglas draft is similar to the draft concurrence that the Justice ultimately issued in the case. There are some minor differences—particularly the draft's emphasis on the irrelevancy of the fact that *Life* was published for profit: "I can think of few papers or magazines that can be said to be charities."

Justice Harlan, on the other hand, circulated a concurrence, reprinted on page 267, which, as summarized in the memorandum by Justice Black reprinted on page 272, reached the majority result "on the basis of what he calls a 'weighing process' under which he found that Hill's 'right to privacy,' under the particular circumstances here, outweighed the public's interest in being informed of the particular subject dealt with in *Life*'s news story."

As already noted, the Fortas draft opinion of the Court reprinted on page 245 is a recirculated version. Justice Fortas revised his original June 8 draft in order to answer the draft dissent reprinted on page 288, which had been circulated July 9 by Justice White. The White draft asserts that the state court, in affirming the award to Hill, had indicated that the New York right-to-privacy statute could be applied even to true news accounts if they were commercially exploited. This indication "that an otherwise newsworthy item, truthfully reported, loses its privileged character if the jury finds it was published for purposes of trade is an obvious license to impose liability whenever the jury wishes to do so." Because of the New York interpretation, Justice White asserted, "I think the Court should make it unmistakably clear that the First Amendment will not permit the imposition of liability for publishing a truthful account of the news of general public interest."

SUPREME COURT OF THE UNITED STATES

No. 562.—October Term, 1965.

Time, Inc., Appellant,
v.
James J. Hill.

On Appeal to the Court of Appeals of the State of New York.

[June —, 1966.]

Mr. Justice Fortas delivered the opinion of the Court.

This case presents for decision appellant's challenge to the constitutionality of the New York "right of privacy" statute (Civil Rights Law §§ 50–51). Since this case involves a claimed conflict between the statute and the fundamental guarantees of the First Amendment, a clear understanding of the facts is essential.

I.

On September 9, 1952, three convicts escaped from the federal prison at Lewisburg. They stole an automobile, shotguns and ammunition, and money. Police and federal agents were in hot pursuit of the dangerous fugitives. On September 11, they entered the home of James J. Hill, in the quiet, prosperous Whitemarsh suburb of Philadelphia. They remained there for 19 hours, resting and eating. Hill, his wife, their three daughters aged 11, 15 and 17, and twin sons aged 4, were, in effect, captives. They were treated courteously by the fugitives, but were warned not to call the police until after the men had left. Except for the general restraint of the family, the convicts were "gentlemanly" towards the family.

After the bandits departed, Hill advised the police of the incident. The family lived in fear of the fugitives and in the discomfort and embarrassment of public attention. Not the least of their discomfort was caused by

TIME, INC. *v.* HILL.

inquiry as to whether the teen-age daughters and Mrs. Hill "had been violated."

Shortly after Hill telephoned the police, the press, radio and television arrived in large numbers. Upon advice of the FBI and police, Hill went to the front of the house and made a statement of the event, emphasizing the courteous behavior of the fugitives. Apart from this, he refused comment. He declined urgent requests for press, magazine, radio and television interviews, some of them lucrative.[1]

Ten days after the incident the police apprehended the fugitives. In the ensuing gun battle, two of the convicts and a detective were killed. The third fugitive was arrested.

In November 1952, the Hills accelerated previously made plans to move to Connecticut. They obviously did this to protect the family, so far as possible, from public curiosity and comment, and to shield them from reminders of the traumatic episode. Gradually, the publicity died away.

In April and May 1953, Joseph Hayes wrote a novel entitled "The Desperate Hours." He thereafter adapted it as a play and a motion picture. "The Desperate Hours" was a dramatic narration of a fugitive-hostage incident. This theme had interested Hayes for some years. In 1946 he had written and published a short story involving the hostage theme. In 1947 he began collecting newspaper accounts of such incidents. In 1952 and 1953 Hayes read newspaper reports of fugitive-hostage incidents, similar to the Hill occurrence, in Cali-

---

[1] For example, the record contains a copy of a letter that Hill wrote to a writer who offered him half of the proceeds of a planned magazine article. Mr. Hill replied that he and Mrs. Hill had decided "For the best interests of our children . . . to avoid any course of action that might remind them of our experience in September 1952." The article was not written.

TIME, INC. *v.* HILL.

fornia, New York, and Detroit. He was aware of the Hill incident. He steadfastly denied, however, that the Hill incident inspired his novel.

In various interviews, published in widely circulated media, Hayes stated that his work was a product of his "imagination," based upon "various news stories of incidents from many places including California, New York State, Detroit and Philadelphia." Until publication of the Life picture story which is the cause of this lawsuit, the Hill family was not mentioned in any of the publicity occasioned by Mr. Hayes' novel or drama. In his testimony at trial, Hayes reiterated that it was not his intention to tell the story of the Hill incident. He did not have it consciously in mind. He asserted that he never had said that his work was inspired by the Hill incident, and it is not claimed that he made any such statement.[2]

In the autumn of 1954, Hayes' play went into production. Pre-Broadway tryouts were scheduled in New Haven and Philadelphia. The director of the play suggested to Life that the production be covered by it. Life's Entertainment Editor, Prideaux, was interested, particularly because of a novel stage setting which was to be used. Shortly thereafter, a free-lance photographer sometimes employed by Life told Prideaux that he was a neighbor of Hayes and that the play had a "substantial connection" with a true-life incident in Philadelphia. Prideaux telephoned the press agents for the play and

---

[2] The dramatic coincidence which chance sometimes creates is illustrated by Hayes' use of "Hilliard" as the name of his hostage family. He testified that it was not suggested to him by the name of the Hill family. On the contrary, he explained that he and his children used to go to a drive-in movie in Florida which exhibited excessively frequent commercials of a local automobile dealer named Hilliard. As Hayes searched for names to use for his novel, this grain of sand produced the pearl.

TIME, INC. *v.* HILL.

asked them about an "incident in Philadelphia and they said they knew nothing about it." They suggested he call the author. He did so, but he did not ask Hayes whether his play "was related to this specific Philadelphia incident." He never made such inquiry, nor did anyone else on the magazine's staff.

Prideaux and other members of Life's staff then began to create the picture story about the play which gave rise to this lawsuit. Prideaux located the former Hill home outside of Philadelphia. He arranged for actors in the cast of the play to stage scenes in the house. These were photographed. One of Life's crew testified that Prideaux told her that there was "a similarity" between the play and the incident that occurred in the house, and that it would be a "good gimmick." The theatrical costs of the photographic work incident to the Life story, including the costs of stage hands and actors, were paid by the producers of the play.

Prideaux drafted the text of the Life article in mid-February 1955. He had before him news clippings of the 1952 Hill incident. The file included Hayes' article, published in the New York Times on February 20, 1955, stating that his work was a product of his imagination based on a number of actual incidents.

Prideaux's first draft reflected recognition that the play was not an account of the Hill family's experience. This draft did not use the Hill name. It recited that the play was "a somewhat fictionalized" account of a real life incident.

But writers write and editors revise. Prideaux's research assistant, charged with carefully checking copy, placed a check mark over the word "somewhat," to raise a question as to whether the play "was fictionalized or *somewhat* fictionalized." But a senior editor thought the draft of the article was not "newsy enough." So he rewrote it in critical respects. Caution and restraint

TIME, INC. *v.* HILL.

were discarded. In his hands, the play became a re-enactment of the "desperate ordeal" of the "James Hill family." The "somewhat fictionalized" phrase was abandoned.[3] The article, as published in Life, accompanied photographs of scenes from the play taken at the Hills' former home. Two of the photographs were headlined "Brutish Convict" and "Daring Daughter." The "Brutish Convict" is shown violently shaking the young son. A picture of a revolver in the hand of another convict is in the foreground. The "Daring Daughter" is shown biting the hand of a convict to make him drop his gun. The total effect is of violence in which the son and daughter were involved.

The effect on the Hill family was serious. For two and a half years, they "had done everything humanly possible to put the Whitemarsh incident behind us. We wanted to forget it, individually and as a family." Mr. Hill felt that the publication had "wiped out in just one minute" everything we had done, that "we were going to be subjected from that time on to continued, added insinuations, insults and so on." He testified that "we certainly couldn't understand how Life Magazine could publish an article such as this without . . . at least picking up a telephone to find out whether this was the truth or how we felt about it. It was just like we didn't exist, like we were dirt, like they didn't care." Mrs. Hill became seriously ill. The record contains the testimony of psy-

---

[3] The first part of the article as published reads as follows:

"True Crime Inspires Tense Play

"The ordeal of a family trapped by convicts gives Broadway a new thriller, 'The Desperate Hours.'

"Three years ago Americans all over the country read about the desperate ordeal of the James Hill family, who were held prisoners in their home outside Philadelphia by three escaped convicts. Later they read about it in Joseph Hayes' Broadway play based on the book, and next year will see it in his movie, which has been filmed but is being held up until the play has a chance to pay off."

TIME, INC. *v.* HILL.

chiatrists to the effect that the Life article was "the direct precipitating cause of her condition."

Mr. Hill resisted his impulse to resort to the direct remedy of a simpler age—physical violence upon those whom he considered had perpetrated an outrage on his family. He consulted an attorney and this lawsuit resulted. It was brought under the New York right-of-privacy statute. §§ 50–51, of the New York Civil Rights Law.[4] Ultimately, a judgment in favor of Mr. Hill for $30,000 as compensatory damages was entered against appellant in the New York Supreme Court. Punitive or exemplary damages were not included.[5] The appellate

---

[4] In relevant part, these read as follows:

"§ 50. *Right of privacy*

"A person, firm or corporation that uses for advertising purposes, or for the purposes of trade, the name, portrait or picture of any living person without having first obtained the written consent of such person, or if a minor of his or her parent or guardian, is guilty of a misdemeanor.

"§ 51. *Action for injunction and for damages*

"Any person whose name, portrait or picture is used within this state for advertising purposes or for the purposes of trade without the written consent first obtained as above provided may maintain an equitable action in the supreme court of this state against the person, firm or corporation so using his name, portrait or picture, to prevent and restrain the use thereof; and may also sue and recover damages for any injuries sustained by reason of such use and if the defendant shall have knowingly used such person's name, portrait or picture in such manner as is forbidden or declared to be unlawful by the last section, the jury, in its discretion, may award exemplary damages . . . ."

[5] Initially, Hill and his wife were plaintiffs. The jury returned a verdict of $75,000 compensatory damages for Mrs. Hill, $50,000 compensatory damages for Mr. Hill, and $25,000 each as punitive damages. The Appellate Division affirmed the judgment but directed a new trial on the amount of damages. By stipulation, the background of which does not appear in the record, Mrs. Hill's action was dismissed, and the present suit proceeded with only Mr. Hill as plaintiff. The Court of Appeals affirmed the decision of the Appellate Division and the subsequent judgment in favor of appellee.

TIME, INC. *v.* HILL.

division (18 App. Div. 2d 485, 240 N. Y. S. 2d 286)
and Court of Appeals affirmed (15 N. Y. 2d 986, 207
N. E. 2d 604). On appeal, we noted probable jurisdiction. 382 U. S. 936.

II.

The facts of this case are unavoidably distressing.
Needless, heedless, wanton and deliberate injury of the
sort inflicted by Life's picture story is not an essential
instrument of responsible journalism. Magazine writers
and editors are not, by reason of their high office, relieved
of the common obligation to avoid deliberately inflicting
wanton and unnecessary injury. The prerogatives of the
press—essential to our liberty—do not preclude reasonable care and avoidance of casual infliction of injury to
others totally unexplainable by any purpose or circumstances related to its function of reporting or discussing
the news or publishing matters of interest to its readers.
They do not confer a license for pointless assault.[6]

But this does not resolve the problem. We are dealing with a problem of law, and not merely a question
of civilized standards. Our problem is whether the picture story here involved, regardless of its offensiveness,
is entitled to immunity because of the First Amendment.
This Nation and this Court are committed to the immunity which that Amendment extends to the press. We
are committed to its broad and generous application.
This Nation is prepared to pay a heavy price for the
immunity of the press in terms of national discomfort
and danger and in the tolerance of a measure of indi-

---

[6] On oral argument before us, counsel for Hill, the appellee, paid
tribute to the care evidenced by Life's procedures in checking copy.
But here, meticulous editing resulted not in correction of error, but
in magnifying a false and destructive identification. Appellee's brief
is closer to the fact in saying that "the injury to the Hill family
illustrates the consequences of recklessness and irresponsibility in
the use of mass media."

TIME, INC. *v.* HILL.

vidual assault. See *New York Times Co.* v. *Sullivan,* 376 U. S. 254.

The New York right-of-privacy statute was enacted in 1903, following a decision of the New York Court of Appeals which held that New York's common law did not vindicate the right of privacy. The case involved use of a private person's portrait, without her consent, to advertise a commercial product. *Roberson* v. *Rochester Folding Box Co.,* 171 N. Y. 538, 64 N. E. 442 (1902). The statute, designed to overrule *Roberson,* forbids use "of the name or likeness of any living person without that person's consent for advertising purposes, or for the purposes of trade" (§ 50). Such use is a misdemeanor, and the aggrieved person may obtain injunctive relief and may also recover compensatory and exemplary damages (§§ 50–51).

We have before us only the application of the statute for recovery of compensatory damages,[7] but we must, of course—since this is essentially a First Amendment problem—take into account the possible applications of the statute as well as the specific employment that is before us. *NAACP* v. *Button,* 371 U. S. 428, 432–433; *Dombrowski* v. *Pfister,* 380 U. S. 479, 487.

The substance of the New York statute is narrow and particularized. It is not subject to attack on the grounds that the public and private tort which it defines is so broad as to constitute a chilling threat to freedom. Contrast *Ashton* v. *Kentucky,* —— U. S. ——, and cases collected in footnote 2 of *Ashton.* The New York statute relates to only a segment of the basic right—the right of privacy. Judge Cooley long ago referred to it as

---

[7] The statute has rarely been used as a basis for criminal prosecution. Appellant urges that the criminal penalty invalidates the statute. That issue is not before us. Appellant has not been prosecuted nor is there any realistic threat of prosecution. Cf. *United States* v. *Raines,* 362 U. S. 17, 20–24 (1960).

TIME, INC. *v.* HILL.

"the right to be let alone."[8] In 1890, Warren and Brandeis published their famous article "The Right to Privacy," in which they eloquently argued that the "excesses" of the press in "overstepping in every direction the obvious bounds of propriety and decency" made it essential that the law recognize a right of privacy, distinct from traditional remedies for defamation, to protect private individuals against the unjustifiable infliction of mental pain and distress.[9] A distinct right of privacy is now recognized, either as a "common-law" right or by statute, in at least 35 States.[10] Its exact scope varies in the respective jurisdictions.

There is, however, no doubt that a fundamental right of privacy exists, and that it is of constitutional stature. It is not just the right to a remedy against false accusation, provided, within limits, by the law of defamation; it is not only the right to be secure in one's person, house, papers and effects, except as permitted by law;[11] it embraces the right to be free from coercion to incriminate oneself, however subtle;[12] it is different from, but akin to the right to select and freely to practice one's religion and the right to freedom of speech;[13] it is more than the specific right to be secure against the Peeping Tom or the intrusion of electronic espionage devices and wiretapping. All of these are aspects of the right to privacy; but the right of privacy reaches beyond any of its specifics. It is, simply stated, the right to be let alone; to live one's life as one chooses, free from assault, intrusion or invasion except as they can be justified by the

---

[8] Cooley, Torts, 29 (2d ed. 1888).

[9] 4 Harv. L. Rev. 1931 (1890). See Prosser, Law of Torts, pp. 829 ff. (3d ed. 1964).

[10] Prosser, *op. cit. supra.* pp. 831, 832.

[11] U. S. Const., Amendment IV.

[12] U. S. Const., Amendment V.

[13] U. S. Const., Amendment I.

TIME, INC. *v.* HILL.

clear needs of community living under a government of
law.   As Brandeis said in his famous dissent in *Olmsted
v. United States,* 277 U. S. 438, 478, the right of privacy
is "the most comprehensive of rights and the right most
valued by civilized men."

This Court has repeatedly recognized this principle.
As early as 1886, in *Boyd v. United States,* 116 U. S. 616,
630, this Court held that the doctrines of the Fourth and
Fifth Amendments "apply to all invasions on the part
of the government and its employees of the sanctity of
a man's home and the privacies of life.   It is not the
breaking of his doors, and the rummaging of his drawers,
that constitutes the essence of the offence; but it is the
invasion of his indefeasible right of personal security,
personal liberty and private property."

In 1949, the Court, in *Wolf v. People of the State of
Colorado,* 338 U. S. 25, 28–29, described the immunity
from unreasonable search and seizure in terms of "the
right of privacy." [14]

Then, in the landmark case of *Mapp v. Ohio,* 367
U. S. 645 (1961), this Court referred to "the right to
privacy" as "basic to a free society."   367 U. S., at 656.
MR. JUSTICE CLARK, speaking for the Court, referred to
"the freedom from unconscionable invasions of privacy"
as intimately related to the freedom from convictions
based upon coerced confessions.   He said that both
served the cause of perpetuating "principles of humanity
and civil liberty [secured] only after years of struggle."
367 U. S., at 657.   He said that they express "supple-
menting phases of the same constitutional purpose—to
maintain inviolate large areas of personal privacy."   *Ibid.*

---

[14] *Wolf* held that the basic values of the Fourth Amendment apply
to the States via the Fourteenth, but declined to require the States
to exclude illegally seized evidence in criminal trials.   In this latter
respect it was overruled by *Mapp v. Ohio, infra.*

TIME, INC. *v.* HILL.

In *Griswold* v. *Connecticut*, 381 U. S. 479, decided at the last Term of Court, the Court held unconstitutional a state law under which petitioners were prosecuted for giving married persons information and medical advice on the use of contraceptives. The holding was squarely based upon the right of privacy which the Court derived by implication from the specific guarantees of the Bill of Rights. Citing a number of prior cases, the Court (per DOUGLAS, J.) held that "These cases bear witness that the right of privacy which presses for recognition here is a legitimate one." 381 U. S., at 485. As stated in the concurring opinion of Mr. Justice Goldberg, with whom THE CHIEF JUSTICE and MR. JUSTICE BRENNAN joined: "the right of privacy is a fundamental personal right, emanating 'from the totality of the constitutional scheme under which we live.'" 381 U. S., at 494.[15]

If, then, privacy is a basic right, whether one considers it derived from the First, Fourth, Fifth or Ninth Amendments,[16] or otherwise, it follows that the States may, by appropriate legislation and within proper bounds, enact laws to vindicate that right. Cf. *Kovacs* v. *Cooper*, 336 U. S. 77 (1949), sustaining a local ordinance regulating the use of sound trucks; and *Breard* v. *Alexandria*, 341 U. S. 622 (1951), sustaining a state law restricting solici-

---

[15] Recently, in *Rosenblatt* v. *Baer*, 383 U. S. 75, 92, MR. JUSTICE STEWART, concurring, referred to the "right of man to the protection of his own reputation from unjustified invasion and wrongful hurt" as reflecting "our basic concept of the essential dignity and worth of every human being—a concept at the root of any decent system of ordered liberty." He referred to the "protection of private personality, like the protection of life itself," as entitled to "recognition by this Court as a basic of our constitutional system." See also MR. JUSTICE DOUGLAS, dissenting, in *Poe* v. *Ullman*, 367 U. S. 497, 521.

[16] See Goldberg, J., concurring, in *Griswold* v. *Connecticut*, 381 U. S. 479, 486 ff.

TIME, INC. *v.* HILL.

tation in private homes of magazine subscriptions.   Difficulty presents itself because the application of such state
legislation may impinge upon conflicting rights of those
accused of invading the privacy of others.   But this is
not automatically a fatal objection.[17]   In the present
case, the claimed conflict is with the First Amendment.
To appraise this, we must first evaluate the sweep of the
statute as construed by the New York courts.

Prior to the decision in the present case, the New
York courts, although they usually did not discuss the
problem by specific reference to the First Amendment,
have demonstrated an awareness that careful limits must
be set to the operation of the privacy statute lest it come
into fatal collision with the pervasive protection accorded
to the freedom of the press and to public's right freely
to communicate.   They have excluded from the ambit
of the statute, news, newsworthy events and informa-
tional communications and material of whatever nature
relating to "public figures."   These, the New York courts
have held, are not publications "for purposes of trade"
within the meaning of the New York statute.[18]   Although
they may promote circulation and increase profits or
yield direct profits, they are not the type of unauthorized use of a living person's name contemplated by the

---

[17] Cf. *Breard, supra*, at 625–626:

". . . There is equal unanimity that opportunists, for private
gain, cannot be permitted to arm themselves with an acceptable privilege, such as that of a right to work, a privilege to engage in interstate commerce, or a free press, and proceed to use it as an iron
standard to smooth their path by crushing the living rights of others
to privacy and repose."

[18] See, *e. g., Gautier* v. *Pro-Football, Inc.*, 304 N. Y. 354, 358–359,
aff'n, 278 App. Div. 431, 435 (1952); *Binns* v. *Vitagraph Co.*, 210
N. Y. 51, 56–58, 103 N. E. 1108 (1913); *Koussevitsky* v. *Allen,
Towne & Heath, Inc.*, 188 Misc. 479, 482–484, 68 N. Y. S. 2d 779
(Sup. Ct.), aff'd mem., 272 App. Div. 759, 69 N. Y. S. 2d 432 (1st
Dept. 1947); *Lahiri* v. *Daily Mirror, Inc.*, 162 Misc. 776 (1937).

TIME, INC. *v.* HILL.

law.   There is an "almost absolute privilege" for the use of names in news.   *Gautier* v. *Pro-Football, Inc.*, 278 App. Div. 431, 435, aff'd, 304 N. Y. 354 (1952).[19]

On the other hand, the New York courts have evolved a concept of "fictionalization," which may be described as the deliberate, intentional creation of a fictional narrative which is knowingly and falsely presented as a representation of events involving a named, living person whose consent has not been obtained.[20]   If a publication which might be outside of the ambit of the statute as a narrative relating to actual events in a person's life, is "fictionalized" in the described sense, it does not enjoy exemption from the statute.[21]

---

[19] As the Court of Appeals said in *Gautier, supra:* "It has long been recognized that the use of name or picture in a newspaper, magazine, or newsreel, in connection with an item of news or one that is newsworthy, is not a use for purposes of trade within the meaning of the Civil Rights Law [citing cases]."

[20] The earliest case is *Binns* v. *Vitagraph Co.,* 210 N. Y. 51, at 56 (1913), where the New York Court of Appeals described the concept as follows: "In the case before us the series of pictures [*i. e.*, a movie] were not true pictures of a current event but mainly a product of the imagination, based, however, largely upon such information relating to an actual occurrence as could readily be obtained." 210 N. Y., at 55–56. See also *Spahn* v. *Julian Messner, Inc.,* 43 Misc. 2d 219, aff'd, 23 App. Div. 2d 216, motion for leave to appeal denied, 16 N. Y. 2d 485 (1965); *Koussevitsky* v. *Allen, Towne & Heath, Inc.,* 188 Misc. 479, aff'd, 272 App. Div. 759 (1947); *Youssoupoff* v. *Columbia Broadcasting System, Inc.,* 41 Misc. 2d 42, aff'd, 19 App. Div. 2d 865 (1965); *Molony* v. *Boys Comics Publishers, Inc.,* 277 App. Div. 166 (1950); *Gautier* v. *Pro-Football, Inc.,* 278 App. Div. 431, aff'd, 304 N. Y. 354 (1952).

[22] The most important recent case is *Spahn, supra,* note 20. There, the Supreme Court of New York observed: "While untrue statements do not necessarily transform a book into the category of fiction, the *all-pervasive* distortions, inaccuracies, invented dialogue, and the narration of happenings out of context, clearly indicate, at the very best, a careless disregard for the responsibility of the press and within the context of this action, an abuse of the press' limited

TIME, INC. *v.* HILL.

The distinction sought to be effected by the concept
of "fictionalization" is obviously intended to confine
liability under the statute to situations where the publication is not designed to convey information or comment,
but solely and exclusively to present a consciously fabricated account for commercial purposes and for these purposes knowingly to appropriate the identity of a living
person without his consent. In other words, the New
York courts construe the statute as applicable to situations where the publication, for profit, deliberately and
knowingly identifies a person, by name or likeness, with
a story or account with which that person was not connected. This, the courts held, is an inexcusable invasion
of the person's right to privacy.

The New York cases illustrate that the distinction
which they draw is not without difficulty in application
to the facts of life. The cases are not altogether consistent. The lines are not always drawn with precision.
In part, this seems to be due to the plethora of opinions
written by different judges at the trial and Appellate
Division level, and the paucity of opinions of the Court
of Appeals. The trend of the cases, however, has been
generously to construe the area of immunity. For example, the immunity includes publication in any of its
forms: newspapers, books, magazines, radio, television,

---

privilege to inquire into an individual's life." 43 Misc. 2d, at 230.
Affirming, the Appellate Division, Breitel, J., observed that the book
in question had been "fictionalized, concededly, in order to make it
suitable for a juvenile readership" and the publishers "made no
effort and had no intention to follow the facts concerning plaintiff's
life, except in broad outline." 23 App. Div. 2d, at 219. The Appellate Division stated that *Koussevitsky, Youssoupoff* and the present
Hill case (which came down before *Spahn*) were all based on the
"distinction between *an intentionally fictionalized treatment* and a
straight factual treatment (subject to inadvertent or superficial
inaccuracies). . . ." *Id.,* at 220. (Italics added.)

TIME, INC. *v.* HILL.

comic books, and motion pictures.[22] It is not confined
to news accounts. It includes biographies, dramatiza-
tions, comic strips and "Believe-It-or-Not Ripley, gossip
and social columns."[23] In the case of public figures,
there is a broad immunity which embraces an unauthorized biography replete with apocrypha and incidents
of dubious reliability, however offensive. *Koussevitsky
v. Allen, Towne & Heath,* 188 Misc. 479, aff'd, 272 App.
Div. 759 (1947). The category of public figure is broadly
defined. In any case, negligent misstatements, and devi-
ations from fact, do not destroy the exemption with respect to news or public figures. The publication must
be an "all-pervasive" distortion—a deliberate work of
fiction—in order to trigger the statutory requirement
that the person's consent must be obtained.

We cannot say that the First Amendment prohibits
a State from enacting a statute so confined. We cannot
say that the First Amendment forbids a State from enacting a statute which in effect merely prohibits the deliberate appropriation of a person's identity—not as an
incident of news or comment, but for the purposes of
intensifying the appeal of a work of fiction (whether
represented as fiction or not)—which merely requires
that a person's consent be obtained before his name or
portrait may be deliberately used so as to identify him
with a knowingly false and fictionalized narration. Cf.
Spahn v. *Julian Messner, Inc.,* 23 App. Div. 2d 216, 219–

---

[22] See *Gautier* v. *Pro-Football, Inc.,* 278 App. Div. 431, 435, and
304 N. Y. 354, 359 (1952).

[23] *Molony* v. *Boys Comics Publishers, Inc.,* 277 App. Div. 166,
171 (1950). See also *Youssoupoff* v. *Columbia Broadcasting System,
Inc.,* 41 Misc. 2d 42, aff'd, 19 App. Div. 2d 865 (1965). Compare
Koussevitsky v. *Allen, Towne & Heath,* 188 Misc. 479, aff'd, 272
App. Div. 759 (1947), with *Spahn* v. *Julian Messner, Inc.,* 43 Misc.
2d 219, aff'd, 23 App. Div. 2d 216, motion for leave to appeal denied,
16 N. Y. 2d 485 (1965).

TIME, INC. *v.* HILL.

222 (1965) (Breitel, J.). Freedom of the press does not require that the State withhold its aid from persons threatened with misappropriation of their identity for purposes which have no relation to public information and which are nothing more than the knowingly false attribution of events to a named person for the purpose of accentuating the dramatic or entertainment value of a publication.

We do not believe that such a statute, so construed and applied, can or will inhibit the freedom of the press. It does not penalize mere error. It places no restraint upon comment and discussion. It is not an overhanging danger. It cannot ensnare the unwary or even the negligent. It reaches only those who deliberately circulate an account which is pervasively fictionalized and is falsely and deliberately attributed to a living person.

In the present case, this narrow standard was properly applied by the trial judge's charge to the jury. The jury was required to determine whether in publishing the article in question, the defendant "altered or changed the true facts concerning plaintiff's relationship to The Desperate Hours, so that the article, as published, constituted substantially fiction or a fictionalized version for trade purposes; that is, to amuse, thrill, astonish or move the reading public so as to increase the circulation of the magazine or for some other material benefit"; whether the defendant published "the article, not to disseminate the news, but was using the plaintiff's name, in connection with a fictionalized episode." The trial judge charged that plaintiff could not recover unless the statements "constituted fiction, as compared with news, or matters which were newsworthy"; and unless it published "a fictionalized article for its own purposes or . . . as an advertising medium to increase patronage for the play." The court expressly admonished the jury that an "incidental mistake" of fact would not be enough to

TIME, INC. *v.* HILL.

support a verdict for the plaintiff. It must find that the defendant "altered or changed" the facts so as to create a fictionalized version. It is entirely clear from this that the jury was required, as an element of a verdict for the plaintiff, to find that the defendant had engaged in deliberate, willful and knowing fabrication.[24]

Appellant argues that the article was a report on a newsworthy item—the exhibition of the play. So it was, and if the account published in Life had been essentially a report concerning the play, we do not understand that the New York courts would regard it as within the scope of the statute, even if plaintiff's name had been used. Compare *Dallesandro* v. *Henry Holt & Co.,* 4 App. Div. 2d 470 (1st Dept. 1957), app. dism., 7 N. Y. 2d 735 (1959); *Siegel* v. *Esquire, Inc.,* 4 App. Div. 2d 477 (1st Dept. 1957). But the jury was amply justified in evaluating the account not as a news report of the play, but as essentially, a fictionalized version of the Hill incident, deliberately distorted beyond semblance of reality by its explicit, insistent and knowingly false identification with the play.[25]

The Appellate Division affirmed the judgment for the plaintiff in a majority opinion in which three of the judges joined. A concurring opinion was written by one judge. Presiding Judge Botein dissented in part. The

---

[24] The defendant requested a charge which incidentally included a phrase to the effect that the jury must find that the "statements concerning plaintiffs in the Life article were fiction, and known by Time, Inc., at the time to be fiction. . . ." The trial judge was justified in not giving the charge. The element of "knowledge" had been adequately covered as had the other parts of the requested charge which correctly stated the law, and the requested charge as a whole was not a correct statement of the law.

[25] Contemporaneous reviewers of the play characterized it—in sharp contrast with the real events—by phrases such as "ruthless invasion," "melodrama," "will pulverize your nerves," "glowering figure behind every door and a nervous finger on every trigger."

TIME, INC. *v.* HILL.

New York Court of Appeals affirmed, two judges dissenting. Unfortunately, the Court of Appeals did not write an opinion. Its memorandum decision merely recited "Judgment affirmed, with costs, on the majority and concurring opinions at the Appellate Division." The majority opinion of the Appellate Division is principally devoted to an analysis of the particular case with only brief references to the legal standards. The concurring opinion correctly emphasizes that defendant "fictionalized" the Hill incident by portraying the play as a true representation of the actual events, "which it was not." The opinion states, as New York law makes clear, that the Hill incident could have been "referred to" in the article without subjecting defendant to liability because the "right of privacy must give way to the public interest in having newsworthy material disseminated." But the concurring opinion then proceeds to announce in dictum that if "the newsworthy item is presented, not for the purpose of disseminating news, but rather for the sole purpose of increasing circulation, then the rationale for the exemption from Section 51 no longer exists. . . . In such circumstances the privilege to use one's name should not be granted even though a true account be given. . . ."

If we were to construe the decision of the New York Court of Appeals as endorsing this principle as a statement of New York law which it had applied in the present case, we should be constrained to reverse. Reports of news or newsworthy events and comments upon public figures are not deprived of immunity merely because of the purpose of the publication. They cannot be subjected to the sanctions of the law if a true account is given. This is not a correct statement of New York law, as we read it. If it were, we should be presented with an acute First Amendment problem. As we understand New York law, there must be deliberate, intentional, pervasive fictionalization, in the sense that we have dis-

TIME, INC. *v.* HILL.

cussed. It was on this theory that the case was submitted to the jury, and we assume that the Court of Appeals did not intend by its cryptic reference to a concurring opinion by a single judge of the Appellate Division to indicate its endorsement of any other standard.

On this basis, we affirm the decision below. Our conclusion follows from *New York Times* v. *Sullivan*, 376 U. S. 254. *New York Times* did not provide blanket immunity to publications relating to "public figures." Consistently with this Court's solicitude for broadly protecting the freedom of the press and public debate, it held that a public official could not maintain an action for an allegedly libelous criticism unless he showed that the statements were made with " 'actual malice,' that is, with knowledge it was false or with reckless disregard of whether it was false or not." 376 U. S., at 272. See also *Rosenblatt* v. *Baer*, 380 U. S. 941; *Garrison* v. *Louisiana*, 379 U. S. 64. The requirements for liability under the New York right-of-privacy statute as applied in this case are well within this test.[26]

The deliberate, callous invasion of the Hills' right to be let alone—this appropriation of a family's right not to be molested or to have its name exploited and its quiet existence invaded—cannot be defended on the ground that it is within the purview of a constitutional guarantee designed to protect the free exchange of ideas and

---

[26] Since, as Dean Prosser has noted, a "false light" privacy case such as this, although labeled a "privacy" action, shares the salient characteristics of a defamation claim (see Prosser, Torts, 838–839 (3d ed. 1964); Prosser, Privacy, 48 Calif. L. Rev. 383, 398–401 (1960)), we regard the First Amendment analysis of *New York Times* as dispositive of this case. It should be noted that the New York statute, as interpreted and applied, does not raise the serious problems of infringing freedom of the press which Dean Prosser has pointed out in connection with the category of "false light" privacy cases generally.

TIME, INC. *v.* HILL.

opinions. This is exploitation, undertaken to titillate and excite, for commercial purposes. It was not a retelling of a newsworthy incident or of an event relating to a public figure. It was not such an account. It was not so designed. It was fiction: an invention, distorted and put to the uses of the promotion of Life magazine and of a play. Many difficult problems may arise under the right-to-privacy statute, but we conclude that the present case, on its facts and on the New York law as construed by the courts of that State, does not permit the appellant to claim immunity from liability because of the First Amendment.

Accordingly, the judgment is

Affirmed.

SUPREME COURT OF THE UNITED STATES

Frcm: Douglas,

Circulated: 6

Recirculated:__

No. 562.—October Term, 1965.

Time, Inc., Appellant, *v.* James J. Hill.

On Appeal to the Court of Appeals of the State of New York.

[June —, 1966.]

Mr. Justice Douglas, dissenting.

As intimated in my separate opinion in *Rosenblatt* v. *Baer*, 383 U. S. 75, 88, and in the opinion of my Brother Black in the same case, *id.*, at 94, state action to abridge freedom of the press is barred by the First and Fourteenth Amendments where the discussion concerns matters in the public domain. The episode around which this book was written had been news of the day for some time; the novel did not make it such. A fictionalized treatment of the event is, in my view, as much in the public domain as would be a watercolor of the assassination of a public official. It would be one thing if the press were battering down barricades to the sanctuary of our homes (cf. *Griswold* v. *Connecticut*, 381 U. S. 479). But here a private person is catapulted into the news by events over which he had no control. He and his activities are then in the public domain as fully as the matters at issue in *New York Times Co.* v. *Sullivan*, 376 U. S. 254. Such privacy as one normally has, ceases when a person's life has ceased to be private.

Some might well want to let a sad public event be lost in memory. But I see no qualification of the First Amendment that permits it. Once we narrow its ambit, creative writing is imperiled and the "chilling effect" on free expression which we feared in *Dombrowski* v. *Pfister*, 380 U. S. 479, 487, is almost sure to take place.

* JMHP.

TIME, INC. *v.* HILL.

The fact that the publication is for profit would seem quite irrelevant. For I can think of few papers or magazines that can be said to be charities. "It should be remembered that the pamphlets of Thomas Paine were not distributed free of charge." *Murdock* v. *Pennsylvania,* 319 U. S. 105, 111.

SUPREME COURT OF THE UNITED STATES

No. 562.—October Term, 1965.

Time, Inc., Appellant,	On Appeal to the Court of Appeals of the State of New York.
v.	
James J. Hill.	

[June 20, 1966.]

Mr. Justice Harlan, concurring in the result.

I would affirm the judgment because in my view the New York privacy law is constitutional as applied to the present facts and because it seems inappropriate in this instance to consider other possible applications of the statute which might prove constitutionally unacceptable.

In defining the constitutional scope of free speech and press the decisions of this Court reflect a weighing process whereby relevant interests are taken into account in framing a solution for the case at hand, *e. g., Mills* v. *Alabama,* —— U. S. ——, or more rarely a guiding principle for the future, *e. g., New York Times Co.* v. *Sullivan,* 376 U. S. 254. The conflict between free press and privacy is so new to this Court, the possible fact situations so varied, and the interests so elastic that I doubt whether it is now feasible to frame general rules that provide much guidance in hard cases. However, the present facts, to which I now turn, persuade me that the Life article is not privileged under the Constitution.[1]

---

[1] As is clear from the discussion and citations in *New York Times Co., supra,* 376 U. S., at 285, the ultimate judgment whether particular facts bring the constitutional guarantees of free speech and press into play is for this Court to make. So far as underlying facts are seriously disputed, I take them in favor of the appellant save on the few points where the jury verdict together with the instructions shows the contrary.

TIME, INC. *v.* HILL.

A foremost consideration must always be the public interest in learning about the subject dealt with, and on this score Life's involvement of the Hill family in its story seems to me to rank quite low. Without quarreling about whether the discussion was "news," which seems to me a matter of degree and not of fixed category, plainly the item is comparatively unimportant to the public. The Hill incident had never involved someone of public interest; it was no longer any part of current affairs, and its reappearance was largely window dressing for a review of the play. At best, this is poles apart from the interests so scrupulously guarded in *New York Times Co., supra.*

The article was also materially false in imparting an aura of violence and brutality to the Hill incident through the combined effect of headings, pictures, and story.[2] Importantly, the falsity is due in good part to what was at best undeniable carelessness in the writing and editing process, whatever legal adjective be applied.[3] Both these points work against constitutional protection, the falsity because it drastically reduces or eliminates all

---

[2] The atmosphere of violence was conveyed chiefly through the photographs and captions, see *ante,* p. 5, and it was identified with the Hills' experience by language in the text and by the article heading and running heads.

[3] Contemporaneous news accounts evidenced the lack of violence and misbehavior by the actual convicts; the original draft of the Life article indicated that the play was not a literal recounting of the event but these qualifications were removed summarily; apparently no effort was made to verify the facts with the Hills themselves.

The jury's award of punitive damages indicates that it too thought Life culpable; a dissenting statement that this "part of the verdict was set aside upon review and is no longer in the case," *post,* p. 4, n. 5, fails to note that the appeals court expressed no doubt about culpability but set aside the entire verdict as excessive, and the trial judge on remand then reduced the actual damages and omitted the punitive damages without further explanation.

TIME, INC. *v.* HILL.

legitimate public interest in seeing the item and the culpability because it shows the falsity to have been avoidable.

There are several other considerations in this case. The article was hardly of such overtly offensive character to induce Life to the greatest caution, though one might expect the risk to be known to an enterprise of such experience. On the other hand, there is unusually firm evidence that real harm was done, see *ante,* pp. 5–6, and the sanction involves no punitive damages and certainly no criminal penalties. Limiting the award to compensation fulfills a need for private redress while minimizing any deterrent effect on free speech and press.

Taking these elements together, I cannot say that the New York judgment represents an impermissible limitation on freedom of speech and press. In a normal case, this conclusion would suffice to uphold the judgment, but I recognize that where speech and press are concerned, this Court on occasion has struck down judgments because the statute imposing them also extended to protected conduct. See cases cited, *post,* p. 13. Without seeking to appraise this policy in general, I think there are good reasons for not applying it here.

The first reason is that the reach of the New York privacy law itself is highly uncertain, and to evaluate it fully is to engage in a series of guesses about what the Constitution might require in a variety of wholly abstract situations. Apart from the charge given the jury in this case itself, which I find very hard to understand,[4] the quite contrary readings of the New York cases by my Brothers FORTAS and WHITE seem to illustrate the difficulty of pinning down the statute sufficiently to judge it "on its face." Relevant on this score is the comprehensive discussion of Mr. Justice Rutledge

---

[4] The appellant has raised no constitutional objection on this score.

TIME, INC. *v.* HILL.

in *Rescue Army* v. *Municipal Court,* 331 U. S. 549, in which the Court dismissed an appeal involving First and Fourteenth Amendment claims assertedly because the complexity of the statutory scheme unrefined by state court interpretation did not furnish a sound basis for constitutional adjudication.[5]

The uncertainty of New York law in other applications, though perhaps less significant than conceded overbreadth would be, does itself contain seeds for mischief. Fears on this score should be assuaged, however, by two considerations. Principal is the knowledge that the New York statute is not being misused to infringe upon freedom of speech and press. On the contrary, the courts in New York have shown a careful and continuing regard for "news," see *ante,* pp. 12–13, and there is no reason to think that in practice publishers feel themselves restrained by the statute in selecting legitimate material. Cf. *Mills* v. *Alabama,* —— U. S. —— (separate opinion of DOUGLAS, J.). Since the prime purpose in judging a statute on its face in this area is to secure against its deterrent impact in other cases, the relative absence of that danger here sharply reduces the unwelcome need for striking down a judgment itself permissible.

In the same vein, I think it important that no criminal penalty is here involved and there is no indication

---

[5] "To the more usual considerations of timeliness and maturity, of concreteness, definiteness, certainty, and of adversity of interests affected, are to be added in cases coming from state courts involving state legislation those arising when questions of construction, essentially matters of state law, remain unresolved or highly ambiguous." 331 U. S., at 573–574. See also, *id.,* at 565–575. Though the appeal in *Rescue Army* was taken from a final judgment, the procedural situation made it possible that the issues might be tendered to the Court at a later stage. But the Court conceded the costs of delay for the appellant, *id.,* at 584, while the appellant here does not even have a valid constitutional claim on its own facts in my view.

TIME, INC. *v.* HILL.

that New York in practice employs that penalty in aid of its right of privacy. Notwithstanding that the criminal sanction appears in a different section of the law than does that here involved, there might at least be more warrant for taking this occasion to guard against its use if that use were likely. But as matters stand, the criminal penalty seems to be a chimera rather than a sound reason for attacking this judgment. See *ante,* p. 8, n. 7. It is, I think, highly relevant that the cases cited by my Brother WHITE to support judging a statute on its face all involved criminal prosecutions or equity suits to restrain such prosecutions or to restrain state regulatory schemes backed by criminal penalties.

In short, I see nothing in the circumstances of this case which affords any solid constitutional basis for denying vindication of this individual right within the limits here accorded by New York.

SUPREME COURT OF THE UNITED STATES

No. 22.—October Term, 1966.

Time, Inc., Appellant,	On Appeal to the Court of Appeals of the State of New York.
v.	
James J. Hill.	

[October —, 1966.]

Memorandum of Mr. Justice Black.

This case was argued orally last Term, a majority voted to affirm, Mr. Justice Fortas wrote an opinion for the Court. Mr. Justice Harlan concurred being of the view that it is permissible to abridge free speech and press if it is concluded by a "weighing process" that, under the circumstances, it is more important to abridge than to permit the exercise of free speech. Mr. Justice Douglas wrote a dissent in which I concurred based squarely on our opinions in *New York Times Co.* v. *Sullivan,* 376 U. S. 254, 293, and *Rosenblatt* v. *Baer,* 383 U. S. 75, 88, 94. Mr. Justice White wrote a dissent, obviously resting on the premise that it is permissible to curtail speech and press by the "weighing process." On weighing here, however, he found the New York privacy statute invalid as applied, because under the trial court's charge and the appellate courts' opinions Time was penalized for a mere negligent error in reporting the news. He also apparently wanted to hold the state law unconstitutional for such overbreadth and ambiguity as to constitute an overhanging threat to free expression.

Mr. Justice Harlan, while viewing the reach of the statute as so "highly uncertain" that it contains "seeds of mischief" in the field of free expression and while finding the trial judge's charge as to the coverage of the statute "hard to understand," nevertheless voted to uphold the New York statute and the jury's verdict for Hill. He reached this, to me surprising, result on the basis of

* JMHP.

TIME, INC. *v.* HILL.

what he calls a "weighing process" under which he found
that Hill's "right to privacy," under the particular cir-
custances here, outweighed the public's interest in being
informed of the particular subject dealt with in Life's
news story about a forthcoming Broadway play. Although recognizing that the New York law as applied
did place limitations on Life's exercise of freedom of
speech and press, MR. JUSTICE HARLAN's "weighing
process" thus enabled him to hold that this limitation,
which of course is an abridgment of the press, is not an
"impermissible" one. Thus, the First and Fourteenth
Amendments' command that Congress and the States
"shall make no law . . . abridging the freedom of speech,
or of the press . . ." now, in effect, has added to it, under
Brother HARLAN's "weighing process," the language "unless a majority of the United States Supreme Court in its
sole, unreviewable wisdom decides that it would or might
serve the public interest to curtail or penalize publication of certain matters."

Were MR. JUSTICE HARLAN's weighing suggestions
limited to him, they would not be so disturbing, but unfortunately this is not the case. For while not expressly
adopting the weighing formula so clearly as my Brother
HARLAN does, the Court's opinion plainly reaches its
conclusion by its own weighing of its own values. And
even MR. JUSTICE WHITE, while dissenting from the
Court's holding, nevertheless implicitly, if not expressly,
writes on the premise that First Amendment freedom of
the press is subject to dilution by this Court through a
process of weighing the value of press freedom against
other societal values. And indeed my Brother WHITE
seems to be perfectly willing to subordinate constitutional press freedom to "a new right of privacy" fashioned not by the people in their Constitution and not
even by legislators under their power to make laws, but
fashioned by judges based upon their "strong judicial

TIME, INC. *v.* HILL.

sentiment that some segments of the press and mass
media have abused their privilege and must in some
respects be curbed."

I.

The use of the weighing process, which has here produced such divergent results, means simply to me that
by legal legerdemain the First Amendment's promise of
unequivocal press freedom, the freedom constitutionally
promised, has been transmuted into a debased alloy—
transmuted into a freedom which will vacillate and grow
weaker or stronger as the Court personnel is shifted from
time to time. This means that the scope of press freedom is not to be decided by what the Founders wrote,
but by what a Court majority thinks they should have
written had they been writing now. I prefer to have
the people's liberty measured by the constitutional
language the Founders wrote rather than by new views [1]
of new judges as to what liberty it is safe for the people
to have. The weighing process makes it infinitely easier
for judges to exercise their newly proclaimed power to
curb the press. For under its aegis judges are no
longer to be limited to their recognized power to make
binding *interpretations* of the Constitution. That power,
won after bitter constitutional struggles, has apparently
become too prosaic and unexciting. So the judiciary
now confers upon the judiciary the more "elastic" and
exciting power to decide, under its value-weighing process,
just how much freedom the courts will permit the press
to have. And in making this decision the Court is to
have important leeway, it seems, in order to make the
Constitution the people adopted more adaptable to what
the Court deems to be modern needs. We, the judiciary,
are no longer to be crippled and hobbled by the old

---

[1] Mr. Justice Harlan frankly recognizes that "the conflict between free press and privacy is so new to this Court . . . ."

TIME, INC. *v.* HILL.

admonition that "We must always remember it is a Constitution we are *expounding*," but we are to work under the exhilirating new slogan that "We must always remember that it is a Constitution we are *rewriting* to fit the times." I cannot join nor can I even acquiesce in this doctrine which I firmly believe to be a violation of the Constitution itself. While the Court's opinion does not so forthrightly and clearly embrace the doctrine as does Brother HARLAN, I think it does so implicitly. Indeed a substantial part of the Court's opinion is devoted to rhapsodical descriptions of the great value of "right to privacy," said to be an individual's "right to be let alone." Describing it as a right "which the Court derived by implication from the specific guarantees of the Bill of Rights" yet proclaiming that it "reaches beyond any of its specifics," the Court holds that this right is so "basic to a free society" that its invasion can only be "justified by the clear needs of community living" and that its value here outweighs the constitutional right of Time and the public in general to a free press.

No one can deny that it is an exquisite thing to be let alone when one wants to be. But few people want all other people to let them alone forever. In past centuries there were crusading zealots who spent a large part of their lives sitting astride tall poles where they could meditate and commune only with themselves, "far from the madding crowd." Their few imitators today indicate that their experiences in being let alone are not dreamed of as a goal worthy of striving for. But regardless of their value, neither the "right to be let alone" nor "the right to privacy," while appealing phrases, were enshrined in our Constitution as was the right to free speech, press and religion. Government can coexist with unfettered freedom of speech, press and religion, and the First Amendment stands as a monument to the Founders' belief that these freedoms are essential

TIME, INC. *v.* HILL.

to the existence of a democratic society like ours. But
the very existence of Government negatives any claim
that citizens have a general, unconditional, unequivocal
"right to privacy" or "to be let alone." If every person
carries with him an unconditional right to privacy or
to be let alone, the burglars, rapists, robbers, murderers
and other law violators would be completely immune
from all governmental investigations, arrests, trials and
punishments. It is true that individuals are to be let
alone by government except where it moves against them
under valid laws and in a way that is not expressly or
impliedly prohibited by the law of the Constitution or
valid laws passed pursuant to it. Some examples of an
individual's constitutional right to be let alone except
when proceeded against in certain ways are the Third
Amendment's mandate that no soldier shall in time of
peace be quartered in any house without the owner's
consent, the Fourth Amendment's prohibition of unreasonable searches and seizures, the Fifth Amendment's
command that no person shall be compelled to be a witness against himself. Each of these can be loosely said to
result in protecting a man's right to privacy or right to be
let alone unless proceeded against in accord with these
explicit Bill of Rights safeguards. But I think it approaches the fantastic for judges to attempt to create
from these a general, all-embracing constitutional provision guaranteeing a general right to privacy. And I
think it equally fantastic for judges to use these specific
constitutional guarantees as an excuse to arrogate to
themselves authority to create new and different alleged
constitutional rights to be free from governmental control in all areas where judges believe modern conditions
call for new constitutional rights. More particularly, in
my judgment, judges do not have power to create new
individual rights, or to approve the creation of such
rights by States, where to do so will neutralize or destroy

TIME, INC. *v.* HILL.

a right or privilege the Constitution has expressly granted to a group or class, such as the unequivocal right to freedom of the press. For judges to have such power would amount to authority on their part to override the people's Constitution.

II.

In this case, Time has been held liable in damages for the publication by Life of an article about an approaching Broadway play. That this is news no one I think will deny who has ever turned the pages of a newspaper or news magazine to find out what theatre or play he might enjoy. Life, which published this review, had no financial or other interest in the play or the theatre. Life did not publish the review as an advertisement. It was not paid to publish the article. It was simply published, as were other articles, as a part of the routine news coverage of this news magazine. Certainly Life is a part of the kind of "press" which the First Amendment was designed to make free from Federal censorship, and it is now established by numerous holdings of this Court that the Fourteenth Amendment forbids state abridgment of the press to the same extent as the First forbids federal abridgment. The money judgment against Time rests on a suit for damages for publication of this article brought under a New York statute which makes it a criminal offense and authorizes suits for damages, compensatory and punitive, by "any person whose name, portrait or picture is used within this state for advertising purposes, or for the purpose of trade without . . . written consent . . . ." I may assume that the stark naked language of this New York statute (which I think is too broad and too vague to be constitutional) would not of itself, if literally construed, violate the First Amendment. For the statute, as drawn and as its history indicates, was enacted merely to prohibit the unauthorized use of a person's name or picture to advertise something for commercial

TIME, INC. *v.* HILL.

purposes. It is true that the article did republish an
old news item about the Hill incident and that the old
news article as well as the Life review contained Hill's
name. But there is not in this record a shred of evidence from which any reasonable inference could be
drawn that the Life article was an advertisement. In
truth and in fact it simply was not an advertisement.
The trial court charged the jury however that it could
find the article was for trade purposes if its purpose was
"to amuse, thrill, astonish or move the reading public
so as to increase the circulation of the magazine or for
some other material benefit." As thus construed the
New York statute deprives all units of the press of their
constitutional freedom to print a person's name if a purpose of the publication is to increase circulation by writing and publishing articles the public enjoys. This
perhaps is the first time in American history that a law
penalizing or punishing the press for printing has been
upheld where a principal prerequisite to penalize is that
the printer have a desire to increase the circulation of his
news publication. This is also the first time I suspect
in which freedom of the press has been denied to news
publications based in substantial part on a showing that
the publication was for profit or some other material
benefit. But passing over the foregoing and many other
reasons that I believe should bring about a reversal of
this judgment, I would reverse on the ground that the
New York statute as applied is a gross, flagrant refusal
to give Time the benefit of the First Amendment.

III.

After mature reflection I am unable to recall any prior
case in this Court that offers a greater threat to freedom
of speech and press than this one does, either in the
tone and temper of the Court's opinion or in its resulting
holding and judgment. For even if I were to agree,

TIME, INC. *v.* HILL.

which I do not, that First Amendment freedoms can be weighed by judges against a judge-made right of privacy, or some other judge-made right, at the very least this weighing should be done with a clear and complete understanding of what is being weighed against freedom of the press. Of course, it is understandable that the more despicable Life's conduct, the easier to balance away freedom of the press in favor of Hill's right to privacy.

Thus, the Court's choice of inferences supposedly drawn from the evidence in the record and their stacatto-like repetition could hardly be pointed to as models of understatement even in an advocate's brief. Some of them are: "caution and restraint were discarded"; "heedless, wanton and deliberate injury"; "deliberately inflicting wanton and unnecessary injury"; "recklessness and irresponsibility in the use of mass media"; "pointless assault"; "deliberate, callous invasion"; "consciously fabricated account"; "all-pervasive distortion—a deliberate work of fiction"; "deliberate, wilful and knowing fabrication"; "deliberately distorted beyond semblance of reality"; "explicit, insistent and knowingly false identification"; Hill's conclusory testimony that Life treated his family "just like they were dirt." It can be noted that the state court opinions found it possible to decide the legal questions involved without having to resort to so many graphic and biting characterizations. This Court's repeated use of such sharp criticisms and invectives against Time's writers, researchers, and editors I think is completely unsupported by the record.

In summary the record shows these facts. Hayes, the author of the novel and play, did not as the Court says, "steadfastly" deny that the Hill incident "inspired" his novel and play. Immediately after the novel "The Desperate Hours" was published, Hayes wrote several articles explaining how he came to write it. One, entitled "Fic-

TIME, INC. *v.* HILL.

tion Out of Fact" with the running head "Transforming
Fact into Fiction," advertised the fact that "the novel
and the play version of it—was based on various news
stories" of hostage incidents occurring in California, New
York State, Detroit and Philadelphia. In another, Hayes
mentioned only the New York and Philadelphia incidents
as triggering his writings.[2]   At the trial, when confronted
with these prior acknowledgments, Hayes admitted that
the Hill incident "did inspire the book," but sought to
draw a distinction between a novel's being "inspired by"
a real event and being "based on" such an event. All he
insisted was that the Hill incident was not the sole inspi-
ration. Yet he concluded that "the Hill incident—
unconsciously—triggered the book *in a very direct way.*"
(Emphasis added.)[3]   And Hayes further testified that
he told the free-lance photographer, Life's source of information, that one of the incidents to which his novel
was connected occurred in Philadelphia. Of course, this
was reported to Prideaux, Life's writer, as a "substantial
connection," but there were many circumstances to lead
Prideaux and his research assistant to believe this was
the case. First, contrary to the Court's statement that
"until publication of the Life picture story . . . the Hill
family was not mentioned in any of the publicity occasioned by Mr. Hayes' novel or drama," there were several
book reviews on "The Desperate Hours" which con-

---

[2] Although this article did not expressly refer to the Hill incident
as such, Hayes' description of the Philadelphia incident and its date
leaves no doubt that it was the Hill incident to which he was
explicitly referring.

[3] This becomes clear upon comparing the novel to the only four
actual incidents ever mentioned by Hayes. As to the setting, the
characters, and the sequence of action, only the Hill incident has
any similarity to the novel. Only the general hostage theme and
the element of violence give the novel any resemblance to the other
three incidents.

TIME, INC. *v.* HILL.

nected the novel to the Hill incident.[4] Though Hayes
had read these reviews, many of which were also in Life's
files, he never made any effort to protest the identification of his novel with the Hill incident or to call
its inaccuracy to Prideaux's attention.   Second, with this
identification "staring us in the face," Prideaux called
Hayes to enlist his assistance in obtaining access to the
old Hill residence and in supervising the photographic
work. The Court asserts that Prideaux "did not ask
Hayes whether his play 'was related to this specific Philadelphia incident,'" but the record belies this assertion.
On direct examination by Hill's counsel, Hayes was asked,
"Did he [Prideaux] ask you whether there had been an
incident in Philadelphia?" and replied, "Yes, he did."
And when asked whether he told Prideaux that there had
been an incident, Hayes replied, "I told him there had
been."   Third, the very purpose of Prideaux's phone
call was to secure Hayes' agreement to locate the Hill
home for the purpose of there photographing scenes of
the play for the Life story. And Hayes the author did
agree. Indeed it was he, the author, and not Prideaux, Life's writer, who located the Hill home and arranged with its present occupants for Life to take the
photographs. Hayes met Prideaux on his arrival in
Philadelphia, discussed with him the play and Prideaux's
idea for the Life story, and accompanied Prideaux to the
Hill residence. He again was with Prideaux at the
former Hill home when the photographs were actually

---

[4] One reviewer wrote: "In this tense, compactly built tale of terror,
Philadelphia readers will recognize a slice of real life out of the
fairly recent past. Joseph Hayes has simply drawn to its logical
conclusion, in a single time sequence, what might have happened
when three escaped convicts took over the home of a well-known
Whitemarsh physician as a hideout and held members of the family
hostages for a considerable length of time before moving on."

TIME, INC. *v.* HILL.

made.   Although the Court's opinion completely omits
any inference to these salient facts, as Prideaux later
testified, Hayes' very presence throughout the creation
of Life's picture story was "tacit proof" of the relationship between the Hill incident and the play.

Of course, Hayes' trial assertions that his novel and
play were not based on the Hill incident are somewhat
understandable in light of the common-sense recognition
that few novelists worth their salt would be eager to
confess that their artistic creations are mechanical like-
nesses of real events rather than products of the imagination.   And even more so is this true where as here,
though the Court neglects to indicate it, the author
himself is a defendant in the lawsuit.   Hayes was a
defendant in this suit to the very end—until the jury
exonerated him, the producer of the play and the company which made the play into a movie apparently on
the theory that the Life story was not an advertisement
for which they had paid.   In fact in his original complaint Hill proceeded against Hayes, and every publisher who had printed the novel, on the theory, later
abandoned, that the novel itself invaded his right to
privacy.   And in order to make out such a cause of
action—neither Hill's name or picture being used in
the novel—it was necessary for Hill to swear to the
assertion in the original complaint that the "novel was
based upon the actual occurrences of September, 1952
in which plaintiffs Hill were involved," the precise assertion which Life has so unsuccessfully made in its defense.   And aside from Hayes' defensive trial assertions,
Hill, as well as Life, had good reason to believe that
the novel was based on his experience.   For the novel
itself, prior to the Life story, did not go unnoticed by
Hill and his friends.   Mr. Hill testified that upon the
publication of the novel many of his friends informed

TIME, INC. *v.* HILL.

him of the similarity of the novel—which he did not read until long after this litigation commenced—to his experience. Mrs. Hill deposed that from conversations among her friends—one of whom even sent her a copy of "The Desperate Hours"—at social affairs, where the subject almost invariably came up, she felt that the novel was "very similar" to the real event and "could have been basically the story of the incident." The Court, in what seems to me to be an obvious and unjustified effort to characterize Life's reaction as a reckless and heedless journalistic effort at deliberate fabrication, has stepped lightly over all references to the reaction of the Hills, their friends, and other reviewers of "The Desperate Hours."

And to heighten its invidious characterizations of Life, the Court has emphasized the role played by Prideaux's senior editor who allegedly, without restraint or caution, transformed his first draft "recognition that the play was not an account of the Hill family's experience" into a complete fabrication. It is true that Prideaux's editor omitted the phrase "somewhat fictionalized" and repeated Hill's name in the body of the text. But Prideaux's first draft clearly reflected the fact that the "true story" of a suburban Philadelphia family "sparked off Hayes to write" the novel, and the photo layout accompanying this first draft captioned the republished news account of the Hill incident "Actual event in 1952, as reported in newspaper above, took place in isolated house 10 miles outside Philadelphia, where three convicts from KOMING [a term used by Life writers for information to be supplied by researchers] penitentiary held family of James Hill as prisoners . . . ." This caption was virtually unchanged by the senior editor. In short, Prideaux merely drew the same natural conclusions that Hill, his friends, and other reviewers had previously drawn—supported in

TIME, INC. *v.* HILL.

Prideaux's case by the author's acquiescence while participating in the preparation of the photographs—and his
senior editor merely drew the same natural inferences
from Prideaux's first draft.

Thus, this record convinces me that the Court's statement of the facts in such a way as to buttress its determination to deprive Life of its First Amendment rights,
needlessly, and I think unjustifiably, reflects upon the
honesty, ability, and integrity of Life's researchers, writers, and editors. As MR. JUSTICE WHITE's opinion indicates, neither the trial court's charge nor the appellate
courts' opinions remotely suggest that the jury, as a prerequisite to imposing damages—either compensatory or
punitive—had to find Life's conduct as reprehensible as
does the Court here. Indeed, this illustrates a further
danger in balancing away First Amendment freedoms, for
before the judges perform the judicial weighing, it is the
judges who must judicially determine what is involved to
be weighed. If freedom of the press is to be weighed and
if in this process, as the Court so laudably asserts, it
is to receive a "broad and generous application." then
I regret that this admonition, for whatever solace it
might give to the press. has been transformed into lip-
service by a reading of the record which draws every
possible inference adverse to what the press has done.

IV.

But even if I am mistaken, even if harsher statements
were justified to describe Life's action, it would still not,
in my judgment, justify New York in limiting the protections of the First Amendment as it here has unless
it can be done by use of the weighing and balancing process. Some of us have pointed out from time to time
that the First Amendment freedoms could not possibly
live with the adoption of that Constitution ignoring and

TIME, INC. *v.* HILL.

destroying technique.[5] The prohibitions of the Constitution were written to prohibit certain specific things,
and one of the specific things prohibited is a law which
abridges freedom of the press. That freedom was written into the Constitution and that Constitution is or
should be binding on judges as well as other officers. The
"weighing" doctrine plainly encourages and actually invites judges to choose for themselves between conflicting
values, even where, as in the First Amendment, the
Founders made a choice of values, one of which is a free
press. Though the Constitution requires that judges
swear to obey and enforce it, it is not altogether strange
that all judges are not always dead set against constitutional interpretations that expand their powers, and
that when power is once claimed by some, others are
loath to give it up. As stated before, I recognize that
there is a strong appeal in the concept that we the modern generation should not be bound down by eighteenth
century governmental doctrines. There is also a certain
surface appeal to the professorial concept that the courts
should keep our eighteenth century Constitution in tune
with the times, adapt it to present-day needs. But that
doctrine, interpreted out of its legal jargon context, simply means that the best way to amend the Constitution
is to let the judges do it. The Founders emphatically
did not think so, see, *e. g., Griswold* v. *Connecticut*, 381
U. S. 479, 513, n. 6 (dissenting opinion), and I am
wholly unwilling for judges to change the Founders'
handiwork now. If it be said, as some do, that the
amending process is too cumbersome and difficult, who
is wise enough to *know* that this difficult way of amend-

---

[5] See, *e. g., In re Anastaplo*, 366 U. S. 82, 97 (dissenting opinion);
Braden v. *United States*, 365 U. S. 431, 438 (dissenting opinion);
Barenblatt v. *United States*, 360 U. S. 109, 140–145 (dissenting
opinion).

TIME, INC. *v.* HILL.

ment would not be best in the long run, as the Founders believed. Moreover, the people have not heretofore failed to amend in the constitutional fashion, when conditions made amendments necessary. Only recently in looking over a list of suggested amendments that had failed to be adopted, I saw none which I thought the failure of the people to adopt had worked any hardship on the Nation. I did find quite a number of suggested amendments, triggered by temporary excitements, whose adoption I am confident the Nation was fortunate to have escaped.

Finally, if the judicial balancing choice of constitutional changes is to be adopted by this Court, I could wish it had not started on the First Amendment. The freedoms guaranted by that Amendment are essential freedoms in a government like ours. That Amendment was deliberately written in language designed to put its freedoms beyond the reach of government to change while it remained unrepealed.[6] If judges have, however, by their own fiat today created a right of privacy equal to or superior to the right of a free press that the Constitution created, then tomorrow and the next day and the next the judges can create more rights that balance away other cherished Bill of Rights freedoms. If there is any one thing that could strongly indicate that the Founders were wrong in reposing so much trust in a free press, I would suggest that it would be for the press itself not to wake up to the grave danger to its freedom, inherent and certain in this "weighing process" which is today

---

[6] Jefferson wrote that the purpose of the First Amendment is ". . . guarding in the same sentence, and under the same words, the freedom of religion, of speech, and of the press: insomuch, that whatever violates either, throws down the sanctuary which covers the others, and that libels, falsehood and defamation, equally with heresy and false religion, are withheld from the cognizance of federal tribunals." 8 Jefferson, Works 464–465 (Ford ed. 1904).

TIME, INC. *v.* HILL.

the means used to penalize Life for what I think was at most a mere understandable and incidental error of fact in reporting a newsworthy event. One does not have to be a prophet, I think, to foresee that judgments like the one in this case can frighten and punish the press so much that publishers will cease trying to report news in a lively and readable fashion as long as there is—and there always will be—doubt as to the complete accuracy of the newsworthy facts.[7] Such a consummation hardly seems consistent with the clearly expressed purpose of the Founders to guarantee the press a favored spot in our free society. I would reverse this judgment and order the case dismissed under the record as it now stands.

[7] See for example, *Butts* v. *Curtis Publishing Co.*, 351 F. 2d 702 ($3,000,000 libel judgment, cut to $460,000 on appeal); *The Associated Press* v. *Walker*, 393 S. W. 2d 671 (Tex. Civ. App.) ($500,000 libel judgment); *New York Times* v. *Sullivan*, 376 U. S. 254 ($500,000 libel judgment, reversed).

SUPREME COURT OF THE UNITED STATES

m: White

Circulated:

Recirculate

No. 562.—OCTOBER TERM, 1965.

Time, Inc., Appellant,
    v.
James J. Hill.

On Appeal to the Court of Appeals of the State of New York.

[June —, 1966.]

MR. JUSTICE WHITE, dissenting.

With all due respect, I dissent. As construed and applied in this case, the New York privacy law has the following characteristics:

First, the Court of Appeals, by a divided vote and in a brief *per curiam* opinion, affirmed the decision of the Appellate Division on both the majority and concurring opinions in that court. The concurring opinion in the Appellate Division conceded that the right of privacy "must give way to the public interest in having newsworthy material disseminated albeit the presentation of such newsworthy material increases the publisher's circulation and trade benefit flows therefrom." 18 App. Div. 2d 485, ——, 240 N. Y. S. 2d 286, 293. The opinion nevertheless went on to hold: "If it can be clearly demonstrated that the newsworthy item is presented not for the purpose of disseminating news, but rather for the sole purpose of increasing circulation, then the rationale for exemption . . . no longer exists and the exemption should not apply. In such circumstances the privilege to use one's name should not be granted even though a true account of the event be given—let alone when the account is sensationalized and fictionalized." *Id.*, at ——, 240 N. Y. S. 2d, at 294. As thus construed in this case the New York law would permit civil and criminal liability[1] for publishing a truthful account of the newsworthy

---

[1] New York Civil Rights Law §§ 50–51.

TIME, INC. *v.* HILL.

event, whether current or past, as long as the jury finds that the publication was solely for the purposes of trade.[2]

Second, the trial court did not go nearly so far, but it did instruct the jury that if the defendant published the article, "not to disseminate news, but was using plaintiffs' names, in connection with a fictionalized episode as to plaintiffs' relationship to the 'Desperate Hours' its verdict must be for the plaintiffs." While an "incidental mistake" of fact would not be enough,[3] the plaintiff was entitled to a verdict if the article "constituted fiction, as compared with news, or matters which were newsworthy, and were published for purposes of trade." Under these instructions, if the jury found the article substantially misrepresented plaintiffs' actual experiences, Time, Inc., was to be liable, whether the misrepresentations were deliberate, negligent or without any fault at all. There was no room for exonerating Time if it believed the story to be true and was not negligent in so believing. While the trial judge, in initially reviewing the issues for the jury, observed that Time claimed it published only the facts known to it and which its writer believed to be true, the issue of negligence or non-negligence was not presented to the jury in connection with compensatory damages.[4] Indeed, the trial judge

---

[2] This interpretation is reinforced by previous decisions by the New York courts. Occasionally recovery has been allowed although the publication was true, *Blumenthal* v. *Picture Classics*, 235 App. Div. 570, 257 N. Y. S. 800, and when "fictionalization" is discussed, it is frequently contrasted with truth and no mention is made of a requirement of deliberate or negligent falsification, *Lahiri* v. *Daily Mirror, Inc.*, 162 Misc. 776, 295 N. Y. S. 382.

[3] The fact that the judge felt it necessary to qualify the word "mistake" with the word "incidental" may have persuaded the jury that a substantial, although innocent, mistake could lead to liability.

[4] In fact, the necessity of showing negligence, gross negligence, or willfulness in order to award compensatory damages is negated by

TIME, INC. *v.* HILL.

specifically rejected a request for an instruction directing the jury to bring in a verdict for the defendant Time
if it found that Time "published its statements in the
belief that they were true" or unless Time "knew it was
fiction at the time the article was published." The
appellate courts found no fault with the instructions as
given. Substantial falsity in the report of a current or
past news event, whatever its origin or explanation, subjects the publisher to criminal and civil action under
the New York law as long as the jury finds the requisite
purpose to be present.

Third, there was not a word in the instructions to the
jury to indicate that the New York law reaches only
that published material which the publisher "should
have realized . . . would be offensive to persons of ordinary sensitivities" and which go "beyond the limits of
decency." Restatement of Torts § 867, comment d.[5]
Compare *Melvin* v. *Reed*, 112 Cal. App. 285, 297 P. 91.
Substantial fictionalization with respect to a past or current newsworthy event, whether negligent or wholly
blameless, satisfies the statute as long as the jury finds

the fact the jury was instructed that if it found any of these elements
present it could award punitive damages in addition to compensatory
damages. Punitive damages were authorized if "such defendant or
defendants knowingly referred to the plaintiffs without first obtaining their consent, and falsely connected plaintiffs with The Desperate
Hours, and that this was done knowingly or through failure to make
a reasonable investigation." Although the jury did return punitive damages, that part of the verdict was set aside upon review and
is no longer in this case, as is recognized by the majority opinion.

[5] "[L]iability exists only if the defendant's conduct was such
that he should have realized that it would be offensive to persons
of ordinary sensibilities. It is only where the intrusion has gone
beyond the limits of decency that liability accrues." Restatement
of Torts § 867. See *Garner* v. *Triangle Publications*, 97 F. Supp. 546.

TIME, INC. *v.* HILL.

the requisite commercial purpose, and whether or not there is provable damage to the plaintiff.

Given these characteristics, the New York privacy law cannot be squared with the First Amendment.

I.

The dramatic development of the tort of privacy in this century, in State after State and usually by court decision,[6] reflects a strong judicial sentiment that some segments of the press and mass media have abused their privilege and must in some respects be curbed.[7] This cumulative judgment over the past 60 years cannot easily be ignored. But these same judges and writers have been aware of the danger of impinging on fundamental rights of speech and press.[8] *Jenkins* v. *Dell Publishing Co.,* 251 F. 2d 447. Accordingly, in the process of fashioning the outlines of the new right of privacy, almost all judges have been careful to protect what they have deemed to be the rightful function of the press. *Donahue* v. *Warner Bros. Pictures,* 194 F. 2d 6, 15 (Phillips, J., dissenting); *Berg* v. *Minneapolis Star & Tribune Co.,* 79 F. Supp. 957. In case after case, both federal and state courts have enunciated the rule that claims of privacy must give way to the right to publish news,[9] whether the

---

[6] See Prosser, Law of Torts, pp. 831–832, for a listing of the state cases that have recognized a right to privacy.

[7] It was this feeling that prompted the Warren and Brandeis article, "The Right to Privacy," 4 Harv. L. Rev. 1931 (1890).

[8] See, *e. g.,* Note, 28 Ind. L. Rev. 179.

[9] There is no necessity in this case to propose a definitive definition of news. However, it may be that news does not encompass advertising, certain trivial or commonplace events, or events that are neither current nor reasonably related to current events. For a general discussion of the newsworthiness of past events, see *Burnstein* v. *National Broadcasting Co.,* 232 F. 2d 369; *Samuel* v. *Curtis Publishing Co.,* 122 F. Supp. 327. See *Donohue* v. *Warner Bros. Pictures,* 194 F. 2d 6; *Gill* v. *Curtis Publishing Co.,* 38 Cal. 2d 273.

TIME, INC. *v.* HILL.

event which involves the plaintiff was his own doing or
that of another. Names and pictures, however unwelcome, may be published in this context. Likewise, where
the plaintiff is shown to have a sufficient connection
with the subject matter, he cannot complain in the name
of privacy when informative or educational materials
appearing in the press refer to him without his consent.
Rozhon v. *Triangle Publications,* 230 F. 2d 359. And
when an otherwise obscure person becomes involved in
the news, whether voluntarily or not, that event is in
the public domain and the usual rule would permit it
to be again reported. *Jenkins* v. *Dell Publishing Co.,*
251 F. 2d 447. *A fortiori,* the public figure who has provoked public interest or concern by the course of his own
activities may everywhere find his privacy severely limited. *Sidis* v. *F–R Publications Corp.,* 113 F. 2d 806;
Estill v. *Hearst Publishing Co.,* 186 F. 2d 1017.

In speaking against this background of development
in an important area of tort law, I think the Court should
make it unmistakably clear that the First Amendment
will not permit the imposition of liability for publishing
a truthful account of the news of general public interest.
The statement of the Apellate Division, affirmed by the
Court of Appeals, that an otherwise newsworthy item,
truthfully reported, loses its privileged character if the
jury finds it was published for purposes of trade is an
obvious license to impose liability whenever the jury
wishes to do so.[10]

---

[10] A newspaper or magazine generally publishes to make money,
and to that end it tries to make the articles interesting. *Kousse-
vitzky* v. *Allen, Towne & Heath,* 188 Misc. 479, 68 N. Y. S. 2d 779,
aff'd mem. 272 App. Div. 759, 69 N. Y. S. 2d 432. Practically
speaking, a tolerance for certain news styles is required by necessity
quite as much as is a tolerance for a certain amount of "puffing" in
a commercial situation.

TIME, INC. *v.* HILL.

II.

Even if the aspect of the New York law making actionable the truthful publication of a newsworthy event is somehow ignored, one must still deal with the fact that the statute exposes to criminal and civil liability the innocent mistake in reporting the news. Assuming arguendo that the deliberate fictionalization of a news story about an identified person is always actionable, a proposition on which there is far from unanimity, *Donahue* v. *Warner Bros. Pictures*, 194 F. 2d 6, 15 (Phillips, J., dissenting), there remains the question of innocent mistake, the good faith reporting of a story believed to be wholly true. Whatever finding the evidence in this case might have justified with respect to the awareness of Life Magazine of the divergence between its story and the actual events, the instructions in this case, and the opinions on appeal, require the imposition of liability for innocent as well as conscious misrepresentation—for any "substantial fictionalization" whether deliberate, negligent or without fault of any kind. It is on this basis that we must assess the New York law.

Neither the instructions in the trial court nor the opinions in the appellate court drew any distinction between reporting current and past news. If Life is to be liable here for an invasion of privacy, I don't see how a newspaper could escape a like liability for a report of current news containing a misrepresentation of fact about a living person. I cannot hold that the First Amendment permits criminal penalties and civil damages to be imposed upon a publisher of a news story who makes an unintended mistake, at least where there is no negligence involved.

There are inherent difficulties in ascertaining the "truth" in many, many cases, difficulties which cannot be

TIME, INC. *v.* HILL.

surmounted in the context of the work of the ordinary
newspaper attempting, as it does, to report an endless
stream of varied events, some simple, some very complex.
The press of time and concepts of current newsworthiness
make it wholly impractical, if not impossible, to produce
news which is factually accurate in every detail. Dead-
lines and certitudes will never be a perfect mix. The
unimpeachable source may prove to be poorly informed
or as subject to human frailty as the average person.
One alert person who has seen or heard the event reported may differ completely with the version reported
by another equally competent observer. Lawsuits, as
we all know, very often arise from honest differences
about what was said or done; witnesses swear to squarely
contradictory stories and, for the most part, neither commits perjury in the process. The reporters' sources are
these same "witnesses," and if the news is to be reported at all, there will inevitably be discrepancies, and
often very important ones between the news and the
actual fact, if indeed the "fact" can be reliably ascertained at all in the seriously disputed cases.

This is not to say that falsehood, intended or otherwise, has any inherent value entitled to constitutional
protection. But the unintended misrepresentation in
reporting the news cannot be subjected to criminal or
civil penalties without a serious impact on honest attempt to report the truth. In *New York Times* v. *Sullivan*, the Court extended constitutional protection to
the negligent falsehood in order not to stifle public discussion of public business in the hands of public officers.
Likewise, the law of privacy should not be permitted to
stifle the reporting of the news or educational or entertainment materials by extending a cause of action for
invasion of privacy without requiring the allegation and
proof of deliberate or negligent falsehood. Cf. *Smith* v.
California, 361 U. S. 147.

TIME, INC. *v.* HILL.

It is true that in the law of defamation, where the interest protected is that of reputation, the law ordinarily exposes to liability any falsehood sufficiently damaging to reputation, whether negligent or otherwise unintended. Restatement of Torts, §§ 579, 580, but if such a rule is constitutional in the area of defamation, the same constitutional immunity should not be extended to the tort of privacy. In the first place, the very nature of most libels—usually on their face very damaging to reputation—is a sufficient warning to the publisher and ample justification for placing the risk of falsehood on the enterprise that spawns the report. This is borne out by the rule in the *per quod* cases, where evidence is necessary to prove the defamatory character of the publication and where the plaintiff must prove actual pecuniary loss before he can recover any damages at all for injury to his reputation. See Prosser, Law of Torts, p. 782.

Moreover, this aspect of the law of defamation, which treats the printed word like a dangerous animal or an inherently dangerous substance which one unleashes at his peril, has been seriously questioned in responsible quarters for a long time. See Prosser, Law of Torts, p. 792–793 (1964), and cases cited in nn. 36–38. However inherently perilous defamation may be, the doctrine has no place in the law of privacy where the law has not carved out categories of utterances which are recognizable invasions of privacy and where the injury is personal to the plaintiff, not in the minds of others. There may be many situations in which a publisher will suspect or know that what he is publishing will annoy the person named, but certainly there are many others where he can only speculate and where one person would be outraged and another not bothered at all.

One who publishes the news and facts behind it has a constitutional right to do so, even if those he writes about would rather he had not written at all. The same

TIME, INC. *v.* HILL.

result should obtain when he uses ordinary care to report the news but falls short of the truth in some respects. Clearly this should be so if he uses ordinary care to report only the truth if he has no thought or warning that what is being written would offend the taste of ordinary persons and if what he writes does not exceed the bounds of ordinary decency. Under the New York law as it was interpreted and applied in this case, there is no necessity for Mr. Hill to show that Time was at least negligent, that the defendant had any idea the story would offend anyone or that what was written exceeded ordinary decency. Under the New York law substantial, though unknowing, fictionalization apparently demonstrates that the publication is for commercial purposes and automatically dispenses with the First Amendment.

III.

Although the instructions on compensatory damages which the trial court gave made no allowance for the innocent mistake, they did require knowing or negligent fictionalization for an award of punitive damages. Since the jury awarded punitive damages, it might be said that Time, Inc., has no standing to complain of the shortcomings of the New York law since the jury in any event found either knowledge or negligence and the New York law was thus constitutionally applied in this case.

There are at least two answers to this view. First, the judgment for punitive damages was set aside by the appellate courts, and as the case comes to us only compensatory damages, ~~and~~ an award requiring neither knowledge nor negligence on Time's part. ~~are involved~~. Second, this is a First Amendment case in which a statute, on its face and as construed, reaches a wide variety of conduct extending well into the area entitled

TIME, INC. *v.* HILL.

to First Amendment protection. In such cases we have not denied standing to a litigant to challenge the overbreadth of the statute solely because his conduct might well be punishable under a more narrowly drawn law. We have instead permitted him to attack the statute on its face, primarily because of its deterrent effect on the exercise of First Amendment rights. *Dombrowski* v. *Pfister*, 380 U. S. 479; *Baggett* v. *Bullitt*, 377 U. S. 360; *NAACP* v. *Button*, 371 U. S. 415, 432–433; *Winters* v. *New York*, 333 U. S. 507; *Thornhill* v. *Alabama*, 310 U. S. 88, 97–98, and *Lanzetta* v. *New Jersey*, 306 U. S. 451.

Had the Fortas draft come down as the opinion of the Court in *Time, Inc.* v. *Hill*, it would, in effect, have applied the pre–*New York Times Co.* v. *Sullivan* libel rule (under which truth alone was a valid defense even in suits brought by government officials and public figures) to privacy suits. This would have made for a substantial difference between libel actions for defamation and actions for invasion of privacy, so far as the press was concerned. More important, it might have made it possible for plaintiffs to avoid the *New York Times* limitations by framing their actions against the press in privacy, rather than defamation, terms. The result might have been a chilling effect that would have discouraged press ardor in vindicating First Amendment rights. As Justice Black put it in his memorandum criticizing the Fortas draft, reprinted on page 272, "One does not have to be a prophet, I think, to foresee that judgments like the one in this case can frighten and punish the press so much that publishers will cease trying to report news in a lively and readable fashion as long as there is—and there always will be—doubt as to the complete accuracy of the newsworthy facts."

As already seen, the draft dissent by Justice White asserted that the New York court had interpreted the state's privacy statute to apply to true news accounts if they were commercially exploited. Justice Fortas then revised his draft opinion of the Court to meet the White assertion. His answer to Justice White, contained in the recirculated draft reprinted on page 245, declares that the White version "is not a correct statement of New York law as we read it. If it were, we should be presented with an acute First Amendment problem. As we understand New York law, there must be deliberate, intentional pervasive fictionalization." As Justice Fortas saw it, under New York law the press "cannot be subjected to the sanctions of the law if a true account is given."

The Fortas view of the New York case law was correct, and this was confirmed by the highest New York court in a case decided October 27, 1966, after the reargument in *Time, Inc.* v. *Hill*.[23] Had the New York court handed down its decision before the Fortas–White dispute in the matter, it would have settled the matter in favor of the Fortas view. If that had happened, the Fortas draft would have come down as the opinion of the Court, since it was the doubt among some of the Justices over whether Justice Fortas or Justice White was correct in the interpretation of New York law that led to the scheduling of reargument in *Time, Inc.* v. *Hill*.

The doubt among the Justices on the matter was great enough to lead Justice Fortas himself, on June 16, to propose an order, which was issued June 20, setting the case for reargument in the coming 1966 term.[24] The order requested that counsel argue the meaning of the "fictionalization" standard applied by the New York courts.

At this point, the key role in the case was played by Justice Black. With his absolutist view of the First Amendment, Justice Black, of course, had no difficulty with a case such as *Time, Inc.* v. *Hill*. In a noted 1962 interview, the Justice was asked whether he would make an exception in

the First Amendment for the law of defamation. He answered that he had
no doubt that the amendment "as written and adopted, intended that
there should be no libel or defamation law in the United States . . . ,
just absolutely none so far as I am concerned."[25]

Holding this view, Justice Black speedily agreed to join Justice Douglas' draft dissent, reprinted supra page 265, with its assertion that "state action to abridge freedom of the press is barred by the First and Fourteenth
Amendments where the discussion concerns matters in the public domain." But Justice Black was not satisfied with only joining the Douglas
draft. Instead he sought to ensure that the Fortas draft would not come
down as the *Time, Inc.* v. *Hill* opinion of the Court. He accomplished
that result by circulating the memorandum reprinted on page 272 on October 17, 1966—the day before the reargument in the case.

The Black memorandum contains a much fuller discussion than the
concurrence that Justice Black ultimately issued in the case. Its tone is
unusually sharp, but that reflects the strong feelings of the Justice on
First Amendment issues as well as his personal antipathy toward Justice
Fortas, the author of the previous term's draft opinion of the Court. The
Black memo contains one of the most eloquent statements of its author's
views. It is reprinted both for that reason and because it played a key role
in changing the Court's *Time, Inc.* v. *Hill* decision.

Soon after Justice Fortas was appointed to the Court, he was met by
Justice Black's continuing hostility.[26] It is not clear why the Alabaman
displayed such distaste for his new colleague. In part, at least, it was
caused by Justice Black's fear that Justice Fortas was reviving the constitutional approach of balancing competing interests that had been urged
by Justice Frankfurter, for so many years Justice Black's principal an-
tagonist on the Court.[27]

The Black memorandum begins with an acerbic attack on the "weighing process," under which "it is concluded . . . that, under the circumstances, it is more important to abridge than to permit the exercise of free
speech." (The memorandum is more scathing in its condemnation of the
"weighing process" than anything else ever published by Justice Black.
What the Justice wrote on the matter in his ultimate *Time, Inc.* v. *Hill*
concurrence was but a pale reflection of the polemic contained here.)
Diplomatically perhaps, the main Black animadversion here is aimed at
Justice Harlan's draft concurrence. But there is no doubt that the Black
attack applied equally to the Fortas draft, since, as the Black memorandum notes, "the Court's opinion plainly reaches its conclusion by its own
weighing of its own values."

Justice Black's language rejecting the "weighing" approach is so
striking that it deserves quotation (even though the pertinent passages
were used by the author in a recent book).[28] "The use of the weighing
process . . . ," the Black memorandum asserts,

> means simply to me that by legal legerdemain the First Amendment's
> promise of unequivocal press freedom, the freedom constitutionally prom-

ised, has been transmuted into a debased alloy—transmuted into a freedom which will vacillate and grow weaker or stronger as the Court personnel is shifted from time to time. This means that the scope of press freedom is not to be decided by what the Founders wrote, but by what a Court majority thinks they should have written had they been writing now. I prefer to have the people's liberty measured by the constitutional language the Founders wrote rather than by new views of new judges as to what liberty it is safe for the people to have.

To Justice Black, the weighing approach masked a blatant usurpation of power by the judiciary:

For under its aegis judges are no longer to be limited to their recognized power to make binding *interpretations* of the Constitution. That power, won after bitter constitutional struggles, has apparently become too prosaic and unexciting. So the judiciary now confers upon the judiciary the more "elastic" and exciting power to decide, under its value-weighing process, just how much freedom the courts will permit the press to have. And in making this decision the Court is to have important leeway, it seems, in order to make the Constitution the people adopted more adaptable to what the Court deems to be modern needs. We, the judiciary, are no longer to be crippled and hobbled by the old admonition that "We must always remember it is a Constitution we are *expounding*," but we are to work under the exhilirating [sic] new slogan that "We must always remember that it is a Constitution we are *rewriting* to fit the times." I cannot join nor can I even acquiesce in this doctrine which I firmly believe to be a violation of the Constitution itself.

The Black memorandum is sarcastic on what it terms the "rhapsodical descriptions of the great value of" privacy contained in the Fortas draft opinion of the Court. "No one can deny," writes Justice Black, "that it is an exquisite thing to be let alone. . . . But regardless of their value, neither the 'right to be let alone' nor the 'right to privacy,' while appealing phrases, were enshrined in our Constitution." In the Black view, "the very existence of Government negatives any claim that citizens have a general, unconditional, unequivocal 'right to privacy' or 'to be let alone.' . . . I think it approaches the fantastic for judges to attempt to create . . . a general, all-embracing constitutional provision guaranteeing a general right to privacy."

Above all, the Black memorandum stresses the baneful effect that, it asserts, the tentative majority decision would have on First Amendment rights. Under the Fortas and Harlan draft opinions, the First Amendment prohibition against abridging freedom of speech and the press "has added to it . . . the language 'unless a majority of the United States Supreme Court in its sole, unreviewable wisdom decides that it would or might serve the public interest to curtail or penalize publication of certain matters.' "

The Fortas draft, according to Justice Black, had stated "the facts in such a way as to buttress its determination to deprive Life of its First

Amendment rights." Justice Black was particularly biting in his comments on the language in Fortas's proposed *Time* v. *Hill* opinion. The result would be that stated in a passage of the Black memorandum already quoted—a chilling effect that would frighten the press so much that publishers would hesitate to report news as long as there was "doubt as to the complete accuracy of the newsworthy facts."

That result, Justice Black concluded, would hardly be consistent with the intent of the Framers "to guarantee the press a favored spot in our free society." Indeed, the Black memorandum goes so far as to assert, "After mature reflection I am unable to recall any prior case in this Court that offers a greater threat to freedom of speech and press than this one does, either in the tone and temper of the Court's opinion or in its resulting holding and judgment."

The scathing Black memorandum had the effect its author intended. At the October 21, 1966, postreargument conference, the Court changed its decision and voted seven to two for reversal. Only Chief Justice Warren and Justice Fortas still voted for affirmance. Justice Black, as senior majority Justice, assigned the case to Justice Brennan.

The new Brennan opinion of the Court held that the *New York Times* v. *Sullivan* standard must be applied to actions under the New York privacy statute. In a case like *Time, Inc.* v. *Hill*, plaintiff must show not only "fictionalization," but also "knowledge of the falsity or that the article was prepared with reckless disregard of the truth."[29] The case was remanded to give the New York courts an opportunity to apply the statute in the constitutionally prescribed manner.

The new opinion of the Court was joined by Justices White and Stewart, as well as by Justices Black and Douglas, who agreed to concur in Justice Brennan's opinion in order to preclude any retreat from the step toward their First Amendment position taken in *New York Times*. But they also issued concurrences that reaffirmed their absolutist views.

When Justice Brennan delivered his opinion of the Court setting aside the New York judgment, he spoke for only a bare majority. Justice Fortas issued a dissent that was more moderate in its language than his proposed opinion of the previous term. The Chief Justice joined Justice Fortas; Justice Clark changed his October 21 conference vote and also joined. Justice Harlan dissented as well, taking the view that negligent, rather than knowing or reckless, "fictionalization" was all that should be required.

The new *Time, Inc.* v. *Hill* decision did, of course, settle the case before the Supreme Court. But the decision was not the last word on the legal issue presented to the Justices. Cases decided by the Court since the retirement of Chief Justice Warren have narrowed the scope of both *Time, Inc.* v. *Hill* and the *New York Times* v. *Sullivan* doctrine upon which it is based.

As already seen, *Time, Inc.* v. *Hill*, as finally decided, held that Hill's action under the New York privacy statute was governed by the *New*

York Times doctrine—i.e., Hill had to prove not only that the *Life* account was fictionalized, but also that it was written "with 'actual malice'—that is, with knowledge that it was false or with reckless disregard of whether it was false or not."[30] Hill himself was treated by the Court as a "public figure" to whose suit the *New York Times* standard was applicable. Under the 1974 decision in *Gertz* v. *Robert Welch, Inc.*,[31] however, someone like Hill would no longer be treated as a "public figure" for purposes of the *New York Times* doctrine. *Gertz* holds that, absent clear evidence of general fame or notoriety in the community and pervasive involvement in the affairs of society, an individual should not be deemed a public figure unless he voluntarily injects himself into a particular public controversy, thereby becoming a public figure for a limited range of issues relating to the controversy.[32]

Under *Gertz*, someone in Hill's position would not be a "public figure" to whose libel suit the *New York Times* limitation would apply. The same should now logically be true of Hill's privacy action. This view is borne out by a more recent statement by Justice Powell, who delivered the *Gertz* opinion. According to him, "The Court's abandonment [in *Gertz*] of the 'matter of general or public interest' standard as the determining factor for deciding whether to apply the *New York Times* malice standard to defamation litigation brought by private individuals . . . calls into question the conceptual basis of *Time, Inc.* v. *Hill*."[33]

Since *Time, Inc.* v. *Hill* applies the *New York Times* standard to privacy suits, the *Gertz* modification of *New York Times* should also apply to such suits. Though the Supreme Court itself has stated that the question is still open,[34] this means that an action such as that brought by Hill, "under a false-light theory of invasion of privacy"[35] (which alleges publication of false and misleading information as well as invasion of privacy), would now be governed by a more relaxed standard of liability for the publisher than that laid down in both *New York Times* and *Time, Inc.* v. *Hill*. This appears to bring the law on the matter back to where it would have been if *Time, Inc.* v. *Hill* had been decided in accordance with the original opinion of the Court drafted by Justice Fortas.

Notes

1. 381 U.S. 479 (1965), supra Chapter 7.
2. 385 U.S. 374 (1967).
3. In the memorandum, reprinted supra p. 272.
4. 376 U.S. 254 (1964).
5. Dissenting, in *Northern Securities Co.* v. *United States*, 193 U.S. 197, 400 (1904).
6. Compare ibid.
7. *Clark* v. *Pearson*, 248 F. Supp. 188, 194 (D.C. 1965).
8. This type of failure was held to violate the Fourteenth Amendment in *Thompson* v. *Louisville*, 362 U.S. 199 (1960).

9. 376 U.S. at 269.
10. Id. at 270.
11. Id. at 271.
12. Ibid.
13. Ibid.
14. 84 Sup. Ct. at 722. The version in 376 U.S. at 272 is slightly different.
15. 376 U.S. at 279–280.
16. See id. at 283.
17. Id. at 282.
18. Ibid.
19. See *Pauling* v. *News Syndicate Co.*, 335 F.2d 659, 671 (2d Cir. 1964).
20. *Curtis Publishing Co.* v. *Butts*, 388 U.S. 130 (1967).
21. See Schwartz, *Super Chief: Earl Warren and His Supreme Court—A Judicial Biography* 643 (1983).
22. Shogan, *A Question of Judgment: The Fortas Case and the Struggle for the Supreme Court* 134 (1972).
23. *Spahn* v. *Julian Messner, Inc.*, 18 N.Y.2d 324 (1966).
24. 384 U.S. 995 (1966).
25. "Justice Black and First Amendment 'Absolutes,' " 37 *N.Y.U.L. Rev.* 549, 557 (1962).
26. Shogan, op. cit. supra note 22 at 132–134.
27. See Schwartz, op. cit. supra note 21, at 33–35, 41–48.
28. Id. at 645.
29. 385 U.S. at 386–387.
30. 376 U.S. at 279–280.
31. 418 U.S. 323 (1974).
32. See id. at 352.
33. Concurring, in *Cox Broadcasting Co.* v. *Cohn*, 420 U.S. 469, 498, n.2 (1975).
34. Id. at 490, n.19.
35. Ibid.

9

Shapiro v. Thompson (1969): Rational Basis, Compelling Interest, and Fundamental Rights

In terms of legal impact, no decision rendered by the Warren Court was more far-reaching than that in *Shapiro* v. *Thompson*.[1] The "fundamental right-compelling interest" doctrine articulated in the opinion there has transformed the scope of judicial review on constitutional issues. But the Court at first agreed to decide the case differently and to do so on the basis of the traditional rational-basis test that had governed judicial scrutiny in prior cases. Under the rational-basis test, a law must be upheld if it is supported by a rational basis—that is, if the law is reasonably related to a legitimate governmental objective. The compelling-interest test requires stricter scrutiny; under it, a law will be invalidated unless it is justified by a governmental interest that is so important that it can be considered "compelling."

Shapiro v. *Thompson* arose out of an application by Thompson, a pregnant unwed mother of one child, to the Connecticut Welfare Department for assistance under the Program for Aid to Families with Dependent Children. Her application was denied because she had not lived in the state for a year as required by a Connecticut law. The Social Security Act required the Secretary of Health, Education and Welfare to approve state AFDC plans. It provided that he was not to approve any plan that contained a residence requirement of more than one year. The lower court held the state residence requirement unconstitutional. Justices Black, Stewart, White, and Fortas voted to hear the state's appeal.

For Chief Justice Warren, the case was an easy one. The case originally came before the Court during the 1967 term and was first argued on May 1, 1968. Though the lower court and the briefs virtually ignored the Social Security Act provision on the residence requirements, the Chief Justice indicated during the argument that, for him at least, that provision was the key to the case. When one of the attorneys arguing against the residence requirement conceded that it did not violate the Social Security Act, Warren asked, "Is it in conformity with the Act?"[2]

At the May 3, 1968, conference, Chief Justice Warren focused on the Social Security Act in urging reversal. "Congress," he said, "allowed the one-year requirement," since it permitted state statutes that "limited this particular kind of relief to residents of a year or more." To the Chief Justice, the Social Security Act was plainly within Congressional power. "I can't see," he declared, "how I can say that the federal statute is unconstitutional."[3]

The conference agreed with the Chief Justice, voting six to three to reverse the lower-court decision and uphold the residence requirement. Chief Justice Warren and Justices Black, Harlan, Brennan, Stewart, and White made up the majority.

The Chief Justice took the opinion for himself and circulated the draft opinion of the Court reprinted on page 308 on June 3, 1968. This draft is far more elaborate than the dissent that the Chief Justice ultimately issued in the case. It contains a detailed summary of the legislative history of the Social Security Act and the problems with which it was intended to deal that is absent from the later Warren *Shapiro* dissent. There is also a strong affirmative statement of the Congressional power to enact the Social Security Act and the limited review available over such a statute. The Chief Justice's draft opinion of the Court relies entirely on the Social Security Act provision which, according to the draft, authorized the states to impose the one-year requirement.

The Warren draft categorically rejects the claim on which the ultimate opinion of the Court by Justice Brennan was to be based—that the residence requirement invalidly restricted the constitutional right to travel. Congress, asserts the Chief Justice, had the power under the Commerce Clause to authorize the states to impose the requirement. He goes on to declare that Congress

> has not acted to prohibit interstate movement by welfare recipients. Such individuals are still free to move from State to State and to establish residence wherever they please. . . . At most, Congress has authorized the States to act in a manner which imposes a burden of uncertain degree on the welfare recipient who chooses to travel interstate to establish a new residence.

Most important, in view of the way the case was ultimately decided, is the Warren draft's treatment of the equal protection issue. The Chief Justice refuses to accept the contention that equal protection had been denied because residence requirements "discriminate between two classes of residents in a State—those who have resided in the State for more than one year and those who have resided in the State for less than a year."

In dealing with the equal protection claim, the Warren draft specifically declines to subject the challenged law to stricter scrutiny than that permitted under the traditional rational-basis test, under which "a legislative classification will pass constitutional muster if it is reasonably related to a legitimate legislative purpose." The Chief Justice recognizes that there are cases which "represent an exception to the rational basis test" in which stricter scrutiny may be required. That is true, however, only "when the statutory classification is drawn along lines which are constitutionally impermissible or 'suspect,' . . . or when the classification is invidious or wholly arbitrary." In the instant case, "there is nothing inherently suspect, arbitrary or invidious about the durational residence requirements challenged in these cases to warrant the application of the stricter equal protection test advocated by appellees."

Thus, according to the Warren draft, "The question, stated quite simply, is whether the congressional authorization for durational residence requirements is rationally related to a legitimate legislative purpose. To state the question is to answer it." The legislative history showed that "Congress viewed the authorization for durational residence requirements as essential to securing state participation in that comprehensive scheme. We cannot say that the congressional judgment was unreasonable, and we hold, therefore, that the congressional authorization of durational residence requirements has the necessary rational basis to overcome an equal protection attack."

On June 5, 1968, Justice Douglas circulated the short dissent reprinted on page 342. It stresses the right to move to another state as "a privilege or immunity of citizenship" which has been abridged by the residence requirement. "There can be no doubt that for some indigent citizens, this one-year residency restriction will deter, handicap, chill, and stand as obstacles to the constitutional right to change state residence."

On June 10, Justice Harlan sent around the concurrence reprinted on page 347. This opinion is utterly unlike the dissent that Justice Harlan ultimately delivered in *Shapiro* v. *Thompson*. The Harlan draft emphasizes the strong presumption in favor of the constitutionality of acts of Congress. It also finds power in the states to enact residence restrictions and states that their validity "turns on familiar questions of reasonableness and degree." Justice Harlan finds the residence requirement rationally related to legitimate state purposes. He rejects the notion that the states must adopt less restrictive alternatives: "at most . . . these are questions of policy and degree about which reasonable men may readily differ."

Those who had voted to affirm at the May 3 conference had decided that the principal dissenting opinion would be prepared by Justice Fortas. On June 13, he circulated the draft dissent reprinted on page 357. The Fortas draft starts with a detailed analysis of the reasoning in the Chief Justice's draft opinion of the Court. The majority reasoning, Justice Fortas asserts, is based "upon a total rejection of reality and a resort to debating devices to obscure the palpable and obvious truths . . . reflected by the legislative record." The real purpose of the residence requirement was to discourage poor people from coming into the state. "This is the fact; and the necessity of the majority to rely upon fiction merely underscores the untenable nature of its conclusion."

It is thus clear, says the Fortas draft, that the residence requirement had as its "purpose to keep needy people out. . . . [I]t is designed to protect the jurisdiction from an influx of persons seeking more general public assistance than might be available elsewhere." Such a purpose "cannot be sustained because it is a material interference with the constitutional right to travel—an interference that is not justified by any measurable or substantial reason which is constitutionally admissible." Here, the legislative restriction "serves no substantial purpose other than to burden, deter, and chill the right to travel of the persons at whom it is aimed."

The Fortas draft also finds that the residence requirement violated equal protection because "Congress and the States have discriminated 'between "rich" and "poor" as such.'" Referring to the lower court, Justice Fortas notes that it "was unable to find a reasonable basis or purpose for the distinction between the two groups except the constitutionally impermissible purpose of deterring poor people from moving to the jurisdiction. This, they held, offends the Constitution. I agree."

The Fortas draft dissent, like the Warren draft opinion of the Court, employs the rational-basis test in its equal protection review. In the passage just quoted, Justice Fortas agrees that there is "no reasonable basis" for the discrimination between rich and poor. The constitutional guaranty, says the Justice, "insists upon reasonable defensible classifications and denies governmental power otherwise to distinguish between the treatment accorded citizens."

SUPREME COURT OF THE UNITED STATES

Nos. 813. 1134, and 1138.—October Term, 1967.

Bernard Shapiro, Commissioner of Welfare of Connecticut, Appellant, 813 *v.* Vivian Thompson.	On Appeal From the United States District Court for the District of Connecticut.
Walter E. Washington, Commissioner of the District of Columbia, et al., Appellants, 1134 *v.* Clay Mae Legrant et al.	On Appeal From the United States District Court for the District of Columbia.
Roger A. Reynolds et al., Appellants, 1138 *v.* Juanita Smith et al.	On Appeal From the United States District Court for the Eastern District of Pennsylvania.

[June —, 1968.]

Mr. Chief Justice Warren delivered the opinion of the Court.

These appeals bring before this Court for the first time the question of the constitutionality of durational residence requirements as a condition of eligibility for public welfare benefits. In each case, the appellees were denied public assistance on the sole ground that they had not satisfied the minimum one-year residence requirement imposed by statute. And in each case, the three-judge District Court that had been convened declared the challenged durational residence requirement unconstitutional. One judge dissented in each case. For reasons we shall explain at length, we cannot agree with the conclusions

---

* JMHP.

SHAPIRO *v.* THOMPSON.

of the District Courts on the constitutional questions presented, and we reverse their judgments.

The factual setting for each of the three appeals before us can be briefly summarized.

No. 813: Appellee was 19 years old, the unwed mother of one child and pregnant with her second child when, in June 1966, she decided to move from Dorchester, Massachusetts, to Hartford, Connecticut. Her purpose in moving was to be near her mother, who had lived in Hartford for eight years and who promised to support appellee as best she could. Appellee and her child lived with and received support from the mother until late August, when the mother found she could no longer carry the burden of support. Appellee and her child moved into their own apartment and, on September 7, 1966, appellee applied to the Connecticut Welfare Department for benefits under that form of public assistance known as Aid to Families with Dependent Children (AFDC).[1] Appellee's application was denied on November 1 on the sole ground that she had failed to meet the one-year durational residence requirement prescribed by § 17–2d of the Connecticut General Statutes for AFDC assistance.[2] Subsequently, appellee filed her complaint in the

---

[1] On the same day, appellee applied to the Hartford Department of Public Welfare for assistance, and she received a check the following day. However, that local agency informed appellee that it could assist her only temporarily, for a period not exceeding 60 days. On the advice of Hartford welfare officials, appellee submitted her application to the Connecticut Welfare Department for the more permanent AFDC aid.

[2] Section 17–2d provides:

"See. 17–2d. Eligibility for temporary aid pending return of non-residents. When any person comes into this state without visible means of support for the immediate future and applies for aid to dependent children under chapter 301 or general assistance under part I of chapter 308 within one *year* from his arrival, . . . such person shall be eligible only for temporary aid or care until arrangements are made for his return, *provided ineligibility for aid to de-*

SHAPIRO *v.* THOMPSON.

United States District Court for the District of Connecticut, seeking a declaration that § 17–2d is unconstitutional and an injunction against its enforcement. A three-judge court was convened and it ruled, with one dissent, that § 17–2d unconstitutionally abridged appellee's right to travel freely from State to State and denied her the equal protection of the laws. 270 F. Supp. 331 (1967). Appellant, who is Commissioner of Welfare for Connecticut appealed to this Court, and we noted probable jurisdiction. 389 U. S. 1032 (1968).

No. 1134: This appeal arises from a complaint filed in the United States District Court for the District of Columbia on June 12, 1967. The plaintiff was Minnie Harrell, who has since died. Her complaint stated that she had moved with her three children from New York to Washington, D. C., in September 1966. She alleged that her move was prompted by the fact that she had contracted cancer and that she wanted to be near members of her family in the event she was hospitalized. Her formal application for AFDC assistance was denied in May 1967 on the ground that she had not resided in Washington for the one year immediately preceding her application, as required by § 3–203 of the District of Columbia Code.³ Her complaint sought a declaration

---

pendent children shall not continue beyond the maximum federal residence requirement."

³ Section 3–203 provides in relevant part:

"§ 3–203. Eligibility for public assistance.

"Public assistance shall be awarded to or on behalf of any needy individual who either (a) has resided in the District for one year immediately preceding the date of filing his application for such assistance; or (b) who was born within one year immediately preceding the application for such aid, if the parent or other relative with whom the child is living has resided in the District for one year immediately preceding the birth; or (c) is otherwise within one of the categories of public assistance established by this chapter. . . . ."

SHAPIRO *v.* THOMPSON.

that § 3–203 is unconstitutional and an injunction against
its enforcement.   Shortly thereafter, appellees Barley and
Brown filed complaints in the District Court, making a
similar attack on § 3–203 and requesting similar relief.[4]
The three cases were consolidated and a three-judge court
was convened as requested.   Subsequently, appellee Legrant was permitted to intervene in the Harrell and
Brown cases.[5]   The District Court ruled, with one dissent, that the durational residence requirement of § 3–203
denied appellees the equal protection of the laws guaranteed them by the Due Process Clause of the Fifth Amend-

[4] Appellee Barley, a former resident of the District of Columbia,
returned to the District in March 1941 and she was committed
a month later to St. Elizabeth's Hospital as mentally ill. She has
remained in the hospital ever since. Mrs. Barley has been deemed
competent since 1965, and her doctors have approved a plan to
place her in a foster home. Such a plan, however, depended upon
Mrs. Barley obtaining welfare assistance to provide for her support.
Her application for Aid to the Permanently and Totally Disabled
was denied under § 3–203 on the ground that she had not resided
in the District for one year immediately preceding her hospitalization.
    Appellee Brown moved to the District of Columbia in February
1966. She had resided in the District as a child and, immediately
prior to returning there, she had lived with her mother and two of
her three children in Fort Smith, Arkansas. Her third child was
living with her father in the District. Appellee Brown made the
decision to move to the District when her mother moved to Oklahoma. Her application for AFDC aid was approved to the extent
that it sought assistance for the child who had been living in the
District with appellee's father. However, the two children who had
moved from Arkansas to the District with appellee were disqualified for failure to meet the durational residence requirement of
§ 3–203.
    [5] Appellee Legrant moved to the District of Columbia with her
two children in March 1967 after the death of her mother. She
planned to live in the District with her sister. Because she was
pregnant and in poor health she was unable to obtain employment,
and she applied for AFDC assistance in July 1967. Her application
was rejected because she and her children had not satisfied the
residence requirement of § 3–203.

SHAPIRO *v.* THOMPSON.

ment.[6]   279 F. Supp. 22 (1967).   We noted probable jurisdiction.   390 U. S. 940 (1968).

No. 1138: Appellee Smith and her five minor children moved from Delaware to Philadelphia, Pennsylvania, in December 1966.   Appellee and her children were initially supported by her father, but that source of support ended in February 1967 when the father lost his job.   Mrs. Smith applied for public assistance, and she received two checks for AFDC assistance before aid was terminated[7] because she and her children had failed to meet the one-year residence requirement prescribed by § 432 (6) of the Pennsylvania Public Welfare Code.   Pa. Stat. Ann., Tit. 62, § 432 (6) (Supp. 1967).[8]   Appellee Smith filed a com-

---

[6] Although the Fifth Amendment contains no explicit guarantee of equal protection comparable to that found in the Fourteenth Amendment, the District Court properly ruled that the Due Process Clause of the Fifth Amendment embraces the concept of equal protection of the laws.   See *Bolling* v. *Sharpe*, 347 U. S. 497 (1954); *Schneider* v. *Rusk*, 377 U. S. 163, 168 (1964).

[7] AFDC assistance was initially given to Mrs. Smith without reference to Pennsylvania's durational residence requirement because the County Board of Assistance was under the mistaken impression that a reciprocal agreement with Delaware was still in effect.

[8] Section 432 (6) provides:

"(6) Assistance may be granted only to or in behalf of a person residing in Pennsylvania who (i) has resided therein for at least one year immediately preceding the date of application; (ii) last resided in a state which, by law, regulation or reciprocal agreement with Pennsylvania, grants public assistance to or in behalf of a person who has resided in such state for less than one year; (iii) is a married woman residing with a husband who meets the requirement prescribed in subclause (i) or (ii) of this clause; or (iv) is a child less than one year of age whose parent, or relative with whom he is residing, meets the requirement prescribed in subclause (i), (ii) or (iii) of this clause or resided in Pennsylvania for at least one year immediately preceding the child's birth.   Needy persons who do not meet any of the requirements stated in this clause and who are transients or without residence in any state, may be granted assistance in accordance with rules, regulations, and standards established by the department."

SHAPIRO *v.* THOMPSON.

plaint in the United States District Court for the Eastern District of Pennsylvania on March 31, 1967, asking for a declaration that § 432 (6) is unconstitutional and for an injunction against its enforcement. Subsequently, appellee Foster, whose application for public assistance was denied for failure to satisfy the durational residence requirement of § 432 (6),[9] was permitted to intervene. The three-judge court, with one dissent, ruled that § 432 (6) violated the Equal Protection Clause of the Fourteenth Amendment. 277 F. Supp. 65 (1967).[10] We noted probable jurisdiction. 390 U. S. 940 (1968).

With one exception, each of the appellees sought and was denied AFDC assistance, which is a welfare program funded jointly by the States and the Federal Government under the Social Security Act. 42 U. S. C. §§ 602–608 (Supp. II, 1966). The one exception was appellee Barley in No. 1134, who applied for and was denied the form of public assistance known as Aid to the Permanently and Totally Disabled, which is also funded jointly by the States and the Federal Government under the Social Security Act. 42 U. S. C. §§ 1351–1355 (Supp. II, 1966). With respect to each of the two public assistance programs, the Social Security Act requires the Secretary of Health, Education, and Welfare to approve any participation plan by a State which is otherwise valid and which

---

[9] Appellee Foster had resided in Pennsylvania from 1953 to 1965 and had received public assistance during the last four years of that period. In the summer of 1965, appellee and her four children traveled to South Carolina to care for her grandfather and invalid grandmother. Two years later she and her children returned to Pennsylvania, and her application for AFDC assistance was denied on the basis of § 432 (6).

[10] Subsequently, a three-judge federal court in the Middle District of Pennsylvania ruled that § 432 (6) was constitutional. *Waggoner v. Rosen*, — F. Supp. — (January 29, 1968). The conflicting decision threw the administration of the State's public assistance laws into considerable confusion.

SHAPIRO *v.* THOMPSON.

contains a permissible durational residence requirement.
42 U. S. C. §§ 602 (b).[11] 1352 (b).[12]   The District Courts
in these cases found little or no significance in the congressional authorization of durational residence requirements imposed by States as a condition of eligibility for
public assistance benefits under the Social Security Act.[13]

---

[11] Section 602 (b) provides:

"(b) The Secretary shall approve any plan which fulfills the
conditions specified specified in subsection (a) of this section, except
that he shall not approve any plan which imposes as a condition
of eligibility for aid to families with dependent children, a residence
requirement which denies aid with respect to any child residing in
the State (1) who has resided in the State for one year immediately
preceding the application for such aid, or (2) who was born within
one year immediately preceding the application, if the parent or
other relative with whom the child is living has resided in the State
for one year immediately preceding the birth."

[12] Section 1352 (b) provides:

"(b) The Secretary shall approve any plan which fulfills the conditions specified in subsection (a) of this section, except that he shall
not approve any plan which imposes, as a condition of eligibility
for aid to the permanently and totally disabled under the plan—

"(1) Any residence requirement which excludes any resident of
the State who has resided therein five years during the nine years
immediately preceding the application for aid to the permanently
and totally disabled and has resided therein continuously for one
year immediately preceding the application;

"(2) Any citizenship requirement which excludes any citizen of
the United States."

Although the statutory authorization is for a durational residence
requirement of five years out of the nine immediately preceding the
application for Aid to the Permanently and Totally Disabled, the
District of Columbia has chosen to impose a lesser requirement of
one year.   Thus, although appellee Barley applied for a form of
categorical assistance different than that sought by the other appellees, we deal in these cases only with the validity of one-year durational residence requirements as conditions of eligibility for categorical
assistance benefits.

[13] The District Courts in Nos. 813 and 1134 made only passing
reference to 42 U. S. C. § 602 (b).   See *Thompson* v. *Shapiro*, 270 F.

SHAPIRO *v.* THOMPSON.

In our view, however, the relevant provisions of the Social Security Act place the appellees' constitutional challenges to durational residence requirements in a wholly different light and require a reversal of the judgments below.

I.

The Social Security Act of 1935 represented the first massive and systematic venture by the Federal Government into the realm of public welfare assistance. Prior to that enactment, public welfare assistance had been viewed in this country as the exclusive responsibility of local and state governments.[14] The state and local public welfare programs were generally patterned after the English poor laws. They reflected a grudging acceptance of government's responsibility for the poor and destitute in society, and the assistance provided under the state and local poor laws seldom rose above the level of bare subsistence. See generally J. Brown, Public Relief 1929–1939, at 3–59 (1940). The Great Depression of the 1930's exposed the inadequacies of state and local welfare programs and dramatized the need for federal participation. The Social Security Act adopted a selective approach to the problems of welfare assistance. The public assistance titles of the Act selected certain categories of needy people who would be the beneficiaries of federal

---

Supp. 331, 333 (1967); *Harrell* v. *Tobriner*, 279 F. Supp. 22, 30 (1967). The majority of the District Court in No. 1138 did not mention or discuss § 602 (b). The indifference of the courts below to the federal statutory provisions is reflected in the briefs and the arguments of the parties in this Court.

[14] The most notable exception to the general rule was the Federal Emergency Relief Act of 1933. 48 Stat. 55. That statute created the Federal Emergency Relief Administration (FERA) and established a program of federal grants to states for attacking the problems of widespread unemployment and poverty spawned by the depression of the 1930's. The story of the FERA is recounted at length in J. Brown, Public Relief 1929–1939, at 145–298 (1940).

SHAPIRO *v.* THOMPSON.

aid.[15]   The result was a major new form of public welfare aid—known as categorical assistance [16]—in which federal funds were made available on a matching basis to enable and to encourage States to increase the amount of aid given to the various categories of needy people.   However, those individuals who are needy and destitute and who are unable to meet the eligibility requirements for categorical assistance remain the primary responsibility of the States. All States today have wholly state-financed welfare programs, known as general assistance or general relief, to provide for the residual class of needy people.[17]   Because all of the appellees in the three cases before us applied for and were denied categorical assistance, we decide only the question of the validity of dura-tonal residence requirements as applied to eligibility for categorical assistance.

When Congress met in 1935 to consider the Social Security Act, the Nation was in the midst of one of the severest and most widespread economic crises in its history.   More than 18,000,000 people were wholly dependent upon public assistance for the necessities of life;

---

[15] The categories of public assistance provided for in the Social Security Act are Old-Age Assistance, 42 U. S. C. § 301 *et seq.*, Aid to Families with Dependent Children, 42 U. S. C. § 601 *et seq.*, Aid to the Blind, 42 U. S. C. § 1201 *et seq.*, and Aid to the Permanently and Totally Disabled, 42 U. S. C. § 1351 *et seq.*

[16] Prior to the enactment of the Social Security Act, a number of States had passed legislation authorizing welfare assistance for the categories of needy people singled out by the federal statute. However, the benefits provided under state categorical assistance programs were so meager that such programs were only ineffective supplements to state and local poor laws. See J. Brown, *supra,* n. 14, at 26–32. But the state programs did provide the administrative framework for implementing the categorical assistance programs funded by the Federal Government under the Social Security Act.

[17] See Wedemeyer & Moore, The American Welfare System, 54 Calif. L. Rev. 326–334 (1966).

SHAPIRO *v.* THOMPSON.

10,000,000 workers were wholly dependent upon work relief programs for their income. Report of the Committee on Economic Security 1 (1935). The Federal Emergency Relief Act of 1933, 48 Stat. 55, had been enacted as a stopgap measure to assist the States in dealing with the problem of widespread unemployment. However, there was general agreement in Congress that a permanent and long-term federal program was necessary to attack the problems of unemployment and economic insecurity. See H. R. Rep. No. 615, 74th Cong., 1st Sess., 3 (1935); S. Rep. No. 628, 74th Cong., 1st Sess., 2 (1935). The Social Security Act, which was drafted initially by the President's Committee on Economic Security, was the congressional response to that national need.

The Act made a two-pronged attack on the problems of economic insecurity. Its major innovative feature was a system of unemployment and old-age insurance "to reduce destitution and dependency in the future." H. R. Rep. No. 615, 74th Cong., 1st Sess., 3 (1935). The public assistance titles of the Act, which authorized federal grants for categorical assistance, were designed to provide for the needy until the social insurance programs could become fully operative and, thereafter, to provide for those who would not or could not qualify for benefits under the insurance programs. We are concerned in these cases only with the public assistance titles of the Act.

The prolonged depression of the 1930's had demonstrated quite starkly the inability of the States alone to deal effectively with the public welfare problems generated by widespread unemployment. The plight of the States was most dramatically illustrated in their inability to provide needed assistance through mother's pensions, the pre-1935 equivalent of AFDC, and pensions for the

SHAPIRO *v.* THOMPSON.

elderly. For example, Dr. E. E. Witte, Executive Director of the President's Committee on Economic Security, gave Congress this picture of mother's pension laws in the various States:

"There are 45 States that have such laws. These laws, however, are not operative in all States over the entire area of these States. Of 2,714 counties authorized to grant aid, only 1,490 were actually doing so in 1931. Since 1931 there has been a decrease in this number due to the financial exhaustion of counties and States. At least 162 counties that were giving aid in 1931 had abandoned the giving of aid to dependent children by 1934.

.   .   .   .   .

"The States expended $37,000,000; that is, States and local governments combined. The States themselves put up $6,000,000. The local governments put up $31,000,000. [The aid was being distributed to 109,000 families with 280,000 children.] The largest number of these families are in the larger cities . . . . [I]t is the urban communities that have given most of the aid. The rural communities, because of financial difficulties have given far less extensive aid.

"During the depression the need for this form of assistance has very greatly increased, as has the need for all other forms of assistance, but the actual assistance given has increased but slightly, if at all.

.   .   .   .   .

"Federal aid is the only possibility for making the mother's pension laws operative throughout the country. They exist on the statute books of all but three States, but they are inoperative in a large portion of the States which have such laws, due to the financial embarrassment of these States." Hearings

SHAPIRO *v.* THOMPSON.

on H. R. 4120 before the House Committee on Ways and Means, 74th Cong., 1st Sess., 158–159 (1935).[18]

The President's Committee found similar problems in the operation of state old-age pension plans. Report of the Committee on Economic Security 26–27 (1935). The public assistance titles of the Social Security Act were adopted against that background of national need and were designed to promote several legislative goals. The central purpose of the federal grants for categorical assistance was to encourage the States to provide greatly increased welfare benefits for the needy who could meet the eligibility requirements. See, *e. g.,* S. Rep. No. 628, 74th Cong., 1st Sess., 5–6, 18–19 (1935); H. R. Rep. No. 615, 74th Cong., 1st Sess., 4 (1935). The federal aid would mean an immediate increase in the amount of benefits paid under the categorical assistance programs. In addition, however, federal aid was conditioned upon the financial participation of States in such programs. 42 U. S. C. § 602 (a)(2). That provision was specifically designed to prevent state governments from shifting the financial burden of categorical assistance to local governmental units with inadequate financial resources. At the same time, Congress clearly wanted public welfare assistance to remain principally a responsibility of state and local governments. The Federal Government would provide financial aid for categorical assistance on a matching fund basis and would prescribe certain requirements that state participation plans would have to meet to qualify for federal grants. However, the States were to remain the basic administrative units in the categorical assistance programs and were required to make significant financial contributions. See Advisory Com-

---

[18] The Committee heard similar testimony from Katharine Lenroot, Chief of the Children's Bureau of the Department of Labor. *Id.,* at 262–274.

SHAPIRO *v.* THOMPSON.

mission on Intergovernmental Relations, Statutory and Administrative Controls in Federal Grants for Public Assistance 9–26 (1964). Significantly, the categories of assistance programs prescribed by the public assistance titles corresponded to those already in existence in a number of States. See J. Brown, Public Relief 1929–1939, at 26–32. In a very real sense, the categorical assistance programs of the Social Security Act were a significant experiment in "cooperative federalism," *King* v. *Smith, post,* at —, as a means of solving the problems of economic insecurity generated by the depression of the 1930's.

Each of the categorical assistance programs contained in the 1935 Act authorized participating States to impose durational residence requirements as a condition of eligibility for benefits. Section 602 (b), n. 11, *supra,* permits a residence requirement of up to one year for AFDC benefits. The other forms of categorical assistance permit the States to require that an applicant reside in the State five of the nine preceding years and continuously for the year immediately preceding the application. 42 U. S. C. §§ 302 (b) (Old-Age Assistance), 1202 (b) (Aid to the Blind).[19] Congress was aware that States which had mothers' pension and old-age pension programs imposed durational residence requirements far more restrictive than those authorized by the federal statute. The

---

[19] Aid to the Permanently and Totally Disabled, which was the form of categorical assistance sought by appellee Barley in No. 1134, was added to the Social Security Act in 1950. 64 Stat. 555. Congress authorized the States to impose for that program the same five-of-nine residence requirement that was incorporated in Old-Age Assistance and Aid to the Blind in 1935. 42 U. S. C. § 1302 (b). That authorization was made despite proposals made to the same Congress to reduce drastically or eliminate the permissible durational residence requirements already in the Act. H. R. 2892, 81st Cong., 1st Sess. (1949); Hearings on H. R. 6000 before Senate Committee on Finance, 81st Cong., 2d Sess., 16 (1950).

SHAPIRO *v.* THOMPSON.

residence requirements in the 45 States having mothers' pension plans ranged from one to five years, and 30 States imposed a residence requirement in excess of one year. Hearings on H. R. 4120 before the House Committee on Ways and Means, 74th Cong., 1st Sess., 298 (1935). The residence requirements for old-age pensions ranged generally from 10 to 35 years. Only one State, Delaware, imposed a residence requirement of less than 10 years. *Id.,* at 78 (Table 17). The congressional hearings on the Social Security Act produced statements of support for [20] and opposition to [21] durational residence requirements as conditions to eligibility for categorical assistance. The opponents of residence requirements stressed the unfairness of such requirements to transient workers and to those in the country who were forced by the economic dislocation of the depression to seek work far from their homes. Those who spoke in favor of the residence requirements emphasized the fears of the States that the adoption of liberal categorical assistance benefits would encourage an influx of persons seeking higher welfare payments and thereby place an intolerable strain on depleted state treasuries.

Faced with these competing arguments, Congress chose a middle course. It required States seeking federal grants for categorical assistance to reduce their existing durational residence requirements to what Congress viewed as an acceptable maximum. However, Congress accommodated state fears by authorizing the maximum residence requirements specified in the public assistance titles of the Act. This middle course comported with the broader congressional purpose in enacting the categorical assistance programs. By alleviating state fears and au-

---

[20] See, *e. g.,* Hearings on H. R. 4120 before the House Committee on Ways and Means, 74th Cong., 1st Sess., 831–832, 861–871 (1935).

[21] See, *e. g.,* Hearings on S. 1130 before the Senate Committee on Finance, 74th Cong., 1st Sess., 522–540, 643, 656 (1935).

SHAPIRO *v.* THOMPSON.

thorizing only the lower residence requirements, Congress could reasonably hope that the various States would respond to the stimulus of federal matching funds and greatly liberalize benefits under the categorical assistance programs. And States would not be deterred from responding to that stimulus by the prospect of a sudden influx of persons from States having less generous benefit programs.[22] As Mr. Justice Cardozo, speaking for the Court, observed in *Helvering* v. *Davis,* 301 U. S. 619, 644 (1937):

> "A system of old age pensions has special dangers of its own, if put in force in one state and rejected in another. The existence of such a system is bait to the needy and dependent elsewhere, encouraging them to migrate and seek a haven of repose."

Congress quickly saw evidence that the public assistance titles of the Social Security Act had in fact encouraged the States to expand and improve their categorical assistance programs. For example, the Senate was told in 1939:

> "The rapid expansion of the program for aid to dependent children in the country as a whole since 1935 stands in marked contrast to the relatively stable picture of mothers' aid in the preceding 4-year period from 1932 to 1935. The extension of the program in the last 3 years is due to Federal contri-

---

[22] There is no disputing that categorical assistance benefits vary greatly in amount from State to State. As we noted in *King* v. *Smith, ante,* at ——, n. 15, the average family payment for AFDC ranged from $233 in New York to $38 in Mississippi in 1966. And, as District Judge Holtzoff pointed out in his dissent in the District Court in No. 1134, a family receiving AFDC benefits could increase its monthly check by $45 by simply moving from Virginia to the District of Columbia and by $15 by moving from Maryland to the District of Columbia. *Harrell* v. *Tobriner,* 279 F. Supp. 22, 37 (1967).

SHAPIRO *v.* THOMPSON.

butions which encouraged the matching of State and local funds." S. Rep. No. 734, 76th Cong., 1st Sess., 29 (1939).

The Social Security Act has been amended many times since 1935, and the trend of the legislation has been toward increasing the federal financial contribution to categorical assistance programs and adding to the Act a wider variety of programs and services. There has been a corresponding improvement in the amount of benefits provided by the States under categorical assistance. See, *e. g.,* Wedemeyer & Moore, The American Welfare System, 54 Calif. L. Rev. 326, 347–356 (1966).

The amending process has been accompanied by repeated efforts to modify or eliminate the Act's authorization for ~~minimum~~ durational residence requirements. One of the earliest attempts to abolish residence requirements in federally funded public assistance programs was in 1943. H. R. 2861, 78th Cong., 1st Sess., Tit. XII (1943). More than 60 bills have been introduced in Congress to modify or eliminate the Act's authorization for ~~minimum~~ durational residence requirements. None has been reported out of committee.[23] At the same time,

---

[23] Major efforts were made to amend the statutory authorizations for durational residence requirements in 1950 and 1962. In 1950, the bill that was introduced and considered by the House Ways and Means Committee would have reduced to a one-year maximum the permissible residence requirement for all forms of categorical assistance. H. R. 6000, 81st Cong., 2d Sess. (1950). The proposal was killed in committee. Congress did, however, approve a minor amendment to the statutory authorization for duration residence requirements for AFDC assistance. In addition, Congress authorized durational residence requirements for the newly enacted Aid to the Permanently and Totally Disabled ~~durational residence requirements~~ comparable to those contained in Old-Age Assistance and Aid to the Blind, n. 19, *supra,* and refused to lower the permissible

SHAPIRO *v.* THOMPSON.

the opponents and proponents of residence requirements
have repeatedly expressed their views to congressional
committees, frequently making arguments which parallel
those of the parties in these cases.[24] Yet the durational
residence requirements authorized by Congress in 1935
remain unaltered 28 years later.

---

residence requirement in Aid to the Blind to a maximum of one
year. See H. R. Rep. No. 2771, 81st Cong., 2d Sess., 116–117 (1950).

In 1962, the Social Security Act amendments sponsored by the
Kennedy Administration would have provided bonus payments to
those States which eliminated their durational residence requirements
for categorical assistance. Hearings on H. R. 10032 before the
House Committee on Ways and Means, 87th Cong., 2d Sess., 32
(1962). That proposal did not survive the Committee's consideration of the proposed amendments. The Administration also proposed
lowering all durational residence requirements to a permissible
maximum of one year. Hearings on H. R. 10606 before the Senate
Committee on Finance, 87th Cong., 2d Sess., 181 (1962). That
proposal also was not reported out of the House Committee. The
Conference Report on the 1962 amendments contains no mention of
the deleted proposals.

The other bills which have proposed modification of the statutory
authorization for durational residence requirements fall generally into
three categories. The first group would abolish all durational residence requirements. *E. g.,* H. R. 1884, 86th Cong., 1st Sess. (1959);
S. 3164, 85th Cong., 2d Sess. (1958); H. R. 5686, 79th Cong., 2d
Sess. (1946). The second group would reduce to one year the
permissible residence requirement in all or in selective categorical
assistance programs. *E. g.,* S. 1358, 88th Cong., 1st Sess. (1963);
H. R. 2775, 86th Cong., 1st Sess. (1959). The third group would
provide direct federal payments to those individuals who are disqualified from categorical assistance by durational residence requirements. *E. g.,* S. 1511, 87th Cong., 1st Sess. (1961); H. R. 186,
86th Cong., 1st Sess. (1959); S. 1793, 85th Cong., 1st Sess. (1957).

[24] The arguments made before congressional committees by those
favoring elimination of durational residence requirements echo the
legal and policy arguments made by appellees in these cases. Thus,
the Report of the Ad Hoc Committee on Public Welfare to the
Secretary of Health, Education, and Welfare recommended elim-

SHAPIRO *v.* THOMPSON.

II.

It is against the legislative background outlined above that the constitutional arguments of the appellees in these cases must be assessed. We are not unmindful that their arguments have found acceptance in several federal district courts which have been asked to pass upon the constitutionality of durational residence requirements.[25] Neither are we unmindful that the burden

inating all residence requirements and relied principally on this Court's decision in *Edwards* v. *California*, 316 U. S. 160 (1941), which is cited extensively by appellees. Hearings on H. R. 10032 before the House Committee on Ways and Means, 87th Cong., 2d Sess., 104–105 (1962). Witnesses before the committees stressed that the economy of the Nation depended upon a mobile working force, that indigents do not travel from State to State in search of higher welfare payments and that durational residence requirements operate in a discriminatory manner against the poor who move from one State to another for wholly legitimate reasons. See, *e. g.*, Hearings on H. R. 10032 before the House Committee on Ways and Means, 87th Cong., 2d Sess., 355, 385–405, 437 (1962); Hearings on H. R. 6000 before the Senate Committee on Finance, 81st Cong., 2d Sess., 142–143 (1950).

Those who spoke in favor of continuing the authorization for durational residence requirements without change were principally representatives of state and local welfare agencies. They stressed the fears of the States that an elimination of residence requirements would result in a heavy influx of individuals into those States providing the most generous benefits. See, *e. g.*, Hearings on H. R. 10032 before the House Committee on Ways and Means, 87th Cong., 2d Sess., 309–310, 327, 621, 644 (1962); Hearings on H. R. 6000 before the Senate Committee on Finance, 81st Cong., 2d Sess, 324–327 (1950).

[25] In addition to the cases before the Court, three other federal disrict courts have held durational residence requirements unconstitutional. *Green* v. *Department of Public Welfare*, 270 F. Supp. 173 (D. C. D. Del. 1967); *Robinson* v. *Johnson*, — F. Supp. — (N. D. Ill., February 20, 1968); *Robertson* v. *Ott*, — F. Supp. — (D. C. D. Mass., May 21, 1968). Two other three-judge federal courts have issued preliminary injunctions in suits challenging durational

SHAPIRO *v.* THOMPSON.

of residence requirements falls upon the Nation's poor,
who are in search of a more meaningful share of the
bounty of the country's growing economy.   The plight
of the poor has pricked the Nation's conscience in recent
years,[26] and concerned citizens and legislators have been
moving with a sense of increased urgency to alleviate
that plight.[27]   To the extent that the appellees have attempted to show that durational residence requirements
impose hardships upon the poor of the Nation, they
appeal to the right instincts of all men.

However, instinct cannot be our guide when we are
asked to declare unconstitutional part of a statutory
scheme enacted by Congress [28] against the backdrop of

residence requirements in Wisconsin and California. *Ramos* v.
Health & Social Services Board, 276 F. Supp. 474 (D. C. E. D. Wis.
1967); *Burns* v. *Montgomery*, —— F. Supp. —— (D. C. N. D. Cal.,
April 19, 1968).   Only the Middle District of Pennsylvania has
concluded that durational residence requirements are constitutional.
Waggoner v. *Rosen*, —— F. Supp. —— (January 29, 1968).   We
are informed by *amicus curiae* that more than 20 other suits challenging various durational residence requirements are pending in
federal courts in 13 other States.

[26] See generally Report of the National Advisory Commission on
Civil Disorders (1968); Harrington, The Other America (1963);
Stern, The Shame of a Nation (1965).

[27] Among the many federal programs enacted in the past several
years to attack the problems of poverty are the Economic Opportunity Act, 78 Stat. 508, as amended, 42 U. S. C. §§ 2921–2925;
the Housing and Urban Development Act of 1965, 79 Stat. 451,
as amended, 42 U. S. C. § 1401 *et seq.;* the Food Stamp Act of
1964, 78 Stat. 703, as amended, 7 U. S. C. §§ 2011–2025; Title I
of the Elementary and Secondary Education Act of 1965, 79 Stat.
27, 42 U. S. C. § 241a *et seq.*

[28] Although appellees' constitutional arguments are directed almost
exclusively at the validity of state durational residence requirements
without considering the impact of the congressional authorization,
the inevitable effect of holding for appellees would be to rule that
Congress acted unconstitutionally in authorizing durational residence
requirements.

SHAPIRO *v.* THOMPSON.

the depression of the 1930's and preserved unchanged despite repeated and vigorous efforts to alter it. We deal here with a major piece of social welfare legislation which required close and difficult policy judgments by those who enacted it. When such legislation is at stake, we must proceed cautiously to avoid basing our conclusions on our assessment of the wisdom of the legislative approach adopted by Congress. "[C]ourts are concerned only with the power to enact statutes, not with their wisdom." *United States* v. *Butler*, 297 U. S. 1, 78 (1936) (dissenting opinion of Mr. Justice Stone). In a similar vein, Mr. Justice Holmes observed observed that "[t]he criterion of constitutionality is not whether we believe the law to be for the public good." *Adkins* v. *Children's Hospital*, 261 U. S. 525, 570 (1923) (dissenting opinion). The day is long past when those views must be relegated to dissenting opinions. Those views are now our guideposts as we approach the question of the constitutionality of legislation touching upon economic and social problems. See *Ferguson* v. *Skrupa*, 372 U. S. 726 (1963); *Williamson* v. *Lee Optical Co.*, 348 U. S. 483 (1955).

Congressional enactments brought to this Court for review carry strong presumptions of validity. "Every presumption is to be indulged in favor of faithful compliance by Congress with the mandate of the fundamental law." *United States* v. *Butler, supra,* at 67. That salutary principle is particularly apt in this case. Congress viewed a legislative solution based on cooperative federalism as the most effective long-range approach to the economic and social problems caused by the depression. The public assistance titles of the Social Security Act sought deliberately to encourage the States to adopt more generous categorical assistance benefits for their impoverished residents. The interest of the States in durational residence requirements was demonstrated to Congress by the prevalence of such requirements in state welfare legislation. The opponents of those require-

SHAPIRO *v.* THOMPSON.

ments argued that they were undesirable, and Congress responded by requiring the States to reduce their residence requirements to a minimum which Congress viewed as compatible with its general legislative goals. However, Congress quite clearly believed that total elimination of durational residence requirements would be self-defeating because the prospect of a sudden influx of new residents might deter the States from significantly increasing categorical assistance benefits. We cannot ignore these legislative realities in assessing the validity of the congressional decision to authorize the ~~minimum~~ durational residence requirements challenged in these cases.

The Social Security Act was enacted by Congress pursuant to the specific grant of power in Art. I, § 8, to spend for the general welfare. *Helvering* v. *Davis, supra,* at 640–645. That grant of power, standing alone, is broad and sweeping. See, *e. g., United States* v. *Gerlach Live Stock Co.,* 339 U. S. 725, 739 (1950). And, in exercising that power, Congress is specifically authorized to "make all Laws which shall be necessary and proper" to effectuate its purposes. *M'Culloch* v. *Maryland,* 4 Wheat. 316, 421 (1819). The authorization to the States to impose durational residence requirements is an important part of the total statutory scheme of the public assistance titles of the Social Security Act. Congress made the judgment that such a statutory authorization was "necessary and proper" to achieve its stated goal of encouraging the States to increase the amount of benefits paid for categorical assistance, and we cannot upset that judgment unless we find it to be clearly unreasonable, cf. *Katzenbach* v. *Morgan,* 384 U. S. 641 (1966), or unless we find that Congress has legislated in a manner which is prohibited by other constitutional provisions. For legislation will be deemed "necessary and proper" only if the means chosen by Congress "are not prohibited, but

SHAPIRO *v.* THOMPSON.

consist with the letter and spirit of the constitution."
M'Culloch v. *Maryland, supra,* at 421. Consequently,
we turn to the arguments made by appellees in their
efforts to show that durational residence requirements
are prohibited by the Constitution. Appellees find such
prohibitions in the constitutional guarantees of the right
to travel from State to State and of the equal protection
of the laws.[29]

III.

As we understand their arguments, appellees claim that
durational residence requirements interfere with the right
to travel in two related but somewhat different ways.
First, appellees tell us that the existence of such requirements operates to discourage interstate movement by
indigents and that the exercise of a protected constitutional right is thereby chilled. Secondly, appellees assert
that, for those indigents who are not deterred from interstate movement, the residence requirements operate to
deny them categorical assistance benefits because they
have recently exercised their right to travel. We note
that the appellees in these cases allege the second form
of interference with their right to travel, since none
claims that her decision to move interstate was in any
way influenced by the existence of durational residence
requirements. For purposes of this decision, however,
we may assume that the two burdens isolated by appellees
are coextensive.

---

[29] The appellees in Nos. 813 and 1138 have framed the issue in
terms of whether durational residence requirements violated the
Equal Protection Clause of the Fourteenth Amendment. However,
because we deal only with the question whether Congress could
validly authorize the States to impose durational residence requirements, the issue before us is whether Congress has acted to deny
the equal protection of the laws guaranteed by the Due Process
Clause of the Fifth Amendment. See n. 6, *supra.*

SHAPIRO *v.* THOMPSON.

We agree with appellees that the right to travel from
State to State is a constitutional right. "Although there
have been recurring differences in emphasis within the
Court as to the source of the constitutional right of interstate travel, . . . [a]ll have agreed that the right exists."
United States v. *Guest,* 383 U. S. 745, 759 (1966). We
also agree with appellees that decisions of this Court
support the view that the right of interstate movement
is a "fundamental" or "basic" right. *E. g., United States*
v. *Guest, supra,* at 757; *Kent* v. *Dulles,* 357 U. S.
116, 126 (1958). However, these two settled proposi-
tions do not lead us, as they seem to lead appellees, in-
exorably to the conclusion that durational residence requirements are an impermissible burden on the right to
travel. For that right, even when the label "fundamental" or "basic" is appended to it, is susceptible to
reasonable regulation by the Federal Government. This
is particularly true when an important and legitimate
governmental interest is served by the regulation. See
Zemel v. *Rusk,* 381 U. S. 1 (1965); cf. *United States* v.
O'Brien, ante.

A principal focus in appellees' right to travel argument
is this Court's decision in *Edwards* v. *California,* 314 U. S.
160 (1941). That case involved a challenge to a California statute which made it a misdemeanor to bring into
the State a nonresident indigent. The Court held that
the statute was an unconstitutional regulation of interstate movement. Five members of the Court adopted
the view that the movement of persons from State to
State constituted interstate commerce and that the
California statute was "an unconstitutional barrier to
interstate commerce." *Id.,* at 173. Four Justices in
concurring opinions took the position that interstate
travel was a privilege and immunity of national citizenship and, as such, was protected from state regulation

SHAPIRO *v.* THOMPSON.

by the Privileges and Immunities Clause of the Fourteenth Amendment. There is no need in these cases to choose between those competing theories. We decide here the validity of a federal statute touching upon the right to travel, and the *Edwards* decision was addressed only to a state regulation of interstate movement imposed without the congressional authorization involved in these cases. It is quite clear that Congress has been given plenary powers by Art. I, § 8, to regulate commerce among the several States and that Congress can regulate what the States cannot. Thus, in *Crandall* v. *Nevada*, 6 Wall. 35 (1867), a case cited by appellees to support their right-to-travel argument, the Court struck down a Nevada tax assessed against all persons leaving the State by common carrier. There is no doubt, however, that Congress has the power under the Commerce Clause to impose a tax on travel by common carrier. It is equally clear that the Fourteenth Amendment limitation discussed by the concurring Justices in *Edwards* is directed only at state regulation of the privileges and immunities of national citizenship; that limitation in no sense restricts the power of the Federal Government to regulate the same privileges and immunities.

It might be argued in these cases that it is the States which are imposing the durational residence requirements and that the principles enunciated in *Edwards* remain applicable despite the congressional authorization for such requirements in the Social Security Act. Our decisions suggest quite the contrary. For example, the Court has recognized that Congress can specifically authorize the States to regulate what the Commerce Clause, by the force of its negative implications, would otherwise prohibit the States from regulating. *Prudential Insurance Co.* v. *Benjamin*, 328 U. S. 408 (1946); see *In re Rahrer*, 140 U. S. 545 (1891). Thus, our inquiry in these cases is limited to the power of Congress to burden the right

SHAPIRO *v.* THOMPSON.

to travel by authorizing the imposition of durational residence requirements.

Congress clearly has the power to regulate and burden interstate movement. That power is exercised whenever Congress imposes a tax on air and rail fare or on the gasoline needed to power cars and trucks which move interstate. Any of the many regulations imposed by federal agencies on common carriers which cross state lines burdens the right to travel. And Congress has prohibited by criminal statute interstate travel for certain purposes. *E. g.,* 18 U. S. C. § 1952. This is not to say that Congress' power to regulate and to burden interstate movement is without limits. In *Aptheker* v. *Secretary of State,* 378 U. S. 500 (1964), the Court ruled that the right to travel is an aspect of liberty protected by the Due Process Clause of the Fifth Amendment. However, ~~the~~ the Court observed in *Zemel* v. *Rusk, supra,* at 14, "the fact that a liberty cannot be inhibited without due process of law does not mean that it can under no circumstances be inhibited." Our task is to determine whether Congress has exceeded permissible bounds in these cases.

It is important to recognize what Congress has *not* done in authorizing durational residence requirements. It has not acted to prohibit interstate movement by welfare recipients. Such individuals are still free to move from State to State and to establish residence wherever they please. Thus, the decisions in *Aptheker* v. *Secretary of State, supra,* and *Kent* v. *Dulles, supra,* which struck down flat prohibitions on travel, are not controlling here. At most, Congress has authorized the States to act in a manner which imposes a burden of uncertain degree [30] on the welfare recipient who chooses

---

[30] The burden is uncertain in degree because indigents who are disqualified from categorical assistance by durational residence requirements are not left wholly without assistance. Each of the

SHAPIRO *v.* THOMPSON.

to travel interstate to establish a new residence.[31]   The question, then, is whether that burden is impermissible. We think not.   Since congressional burdens on interstate travel are not *per se* prohibited, our inquiry is limited to whether Congress has acted reasonably under the circumstances.   The existence of the burden on travel is not the sole measure of the reasonableness of the statutes we review.   We must also take account of the congressional purpose in authorizing the burden and the importance of that purpose in the total legislative scheme. The statutory authorization for durational residence requirements was an important part of the incentive scheme devised by Congress to encourage the States to join the Federal Government in a cooperative effort to improve and liberalize the benefits available under categorical assistance programs.   Although Congress was legislating under a broad grant of power to spend for the general welfare, it was also acting in an area traditionally

---

appellees in these cases found alternative sources of assistance after their disqualification, although the alternative assistance was concededly not as generous as the categorical assistance they sought. In addition, the disqualification is only temporary in nature, and there is nothing in the federal statute which requires that States impose durational residence requirements.   In fact, 10 States impose no durational residence requirement for AFDC assistance.   Department of Health, Education, and Welfare, Characteristics of State Public Assistance Plans: General Provisions (P. A. Rep. No. 50, 1965).

[31] Appellees have told us that durational residence requirements limit the economic horizons of the needy by restricting their ability to travel interstate in search of jobs.   That assertion is not at all accurate, since a welfare recipient can leave his place of residence for temporary interstate trips without being affected by durational residence requirements.   Such temporary trips do not terminate the recipient's legal residence, and he will remain eligible for welfare benefits at his place of residence while he is traveling.   See Department of Health, Education, and Welfare, Handbook of Public Assistance Administration, Pt. IV, § 3620 (1967).

SHAPIRO *v*. THOMPSON.

thought to be the responsibility of state and local governments. Congress might have chosen the course of occupying the entire field of public welfare legislation if it had viewed such a course as being in the national interest. However, Congress deliberately adopted the alternative course of an incentive program founded upon cooperative federalism which would encourage the States to assume greater responsibilities and would give the States the necessary financial support for such an undertaking. There is no doubt that Congress acted within its constitutional powers, and we should be quite reluctant to upset the delicate balance struck by Congress in this area of federal-state relations. Given the urgency of the economic and social crisis facing the Nation in 1935 and the continuing urgency of the problems of the poor in the country, we cannot say that Congress acted unreasonably in authorizing the burdens on travel which appellees claim that durational residence requirements impose.

We, of course, do not mean to imply that Congress, under the guise of securing state cooperation in grant-in-aid programs, can permit the States to attach unconstitutional conditions to public welfare assistance programs. We hold only that, where the regulation of the claimed constitutional right could have been imposed by Congress in the first instance and where Congress has acted reasonably in authorizing the right to be burdened, no such unconstitutional condition exists.

IV.

Appellees also contend that durational residence requirements deny them equal protection of the laws. To the extent that appellees' claim is based on the assertion that durational residence requirements unlawfully discriminate against those indigents who have recently exercised their right to travel, appellees add nothing to their right to travel arguments which we have found to be

SHAPIRO *v.* THOMPSON.

without merit. Appellees also argue, however, that durational residence requirements are invalid because they discriminate between two classes of residents in a State—those who have resided in the State for more than one year and those who have resided in ~~a~~ State for less than one year. We address ourselves to that argument.

It is well settled that a legislative classification will pass constitutional muster if it is reasonably related to a legitimate legislative purpose. A classification need not be drawn "with mathematical nicety" and it will not be held invalid "because in practice it results in some inequality." *Lindsley* v. *Natural Carbonic Gas Co.,* 220 U. S. 61, 78 (1911). The rule recognizes that legislative "reform may take one step at a time, addressing itself to the phrase of the problem which seems most acute to the legislative mind," *Williamson* v. *Lee Optical Co.,* 348 U. S. 483, 489 (1955), and that the legislature is not to be faulted because it did not "strike at all evils at the same time." *Semler* v. *Dental Examiners,* 294 U. S. 608, 610 (1935). Consequently, the guarantee of equal protection of the laws "avoids what is done only when it is without any reasonable basis and therefore is purely arbitrary." *Lindsley* v. *Natural Carbonic Gas Co., supra,* at 78.

Appellees do not dispute the general applicability of the rational basis test to equal protection claims. However, they point to a line of cases in which the Court has ruled that the mere showing of a rational basis will not save a challenged classification, see, *e. g., Harper* v. *Board of Elections,* 383 U. S. 663 (1966); *McLaughlin* v. *Florida,* 379 U. S. 184 (1964), and they urge that the principles of those cases be applied here. The cases relied on by appellees require that certain legislative classifications "must be closely scrutinized," *Harper* v. *Board of Elections, supra,* at 670, and they impose upon the Government a "heavy burden of justification" for

SHAPIRO *v.* THOMPSON.

such classifications to be sustained. *McLaughlin* v. *Florida, supra,* at 196. However, the cases cited by appellees represent an exception to the rational basis test, and special circumstances must be shown to make the principles of those cases applicable. Thus, the stricter equal protection test urged by appellees will apply when the statutory classification is drawn along lines which are constitutionally impermissible or "suspect," see, *e. g., Loving* v. *Virginia,* 387 U. S. 1 (1967); *Harper* v. *Board of Elections, supra,* or when the classification is invidious or wholly arbitrary, see, *e. g., Levy* v. *Louisiana, ante; Skinner* v. *Oklahoma,* 316 U. S. 535 (1942). Neither circumstance is present in these cases. States make statutory distinctions based on length of residence for a variety of purposes, including eligibility for certain professions, for licenses and for voting,[32] and this Court has never suggested that such distinctions are in any sense suspect. In fact, the Court has repeatedly stated that reasonable residence requirements may be imposed as a condition to voting. *E. g., Harper* v. *Board of Elections, supra,* at 666; *Carrington* v. *Rush,* 380 U. S. 89, 91 (1965); *Pope* v. *Williams,* 193 U. S. 621 (1904). The approval of reasonable residence requirements simply recognizes that, in our federal system, States are under no obligation to legislate for the benefit of nonresidents and that States can properly make reasonable distinctions based upon length of residence to assure that only bona fide residents will benefit from state programs and expenditures. Thus, there is nothing inherently suspect, arbitrary or invidious about the durational residence requirements challenged in these cases to warrant the application of the stricter equal protection test advocated by appellees.

---

[32] In his dissenting opinion in the District Court in No. 813, District Judge Clarie itemized the many Connecticut statutes which contain durational residence requirements. *Thompson* v. *Shapiro,* 270 F. Supp. 331, 340 (1967).

SHAPIRO *v.* THOMPSON.

Applying the rational basis test does not mean that the challenged classification will slip past without careful scrutiny by this Court. We must still satisfy ourselves that the challenged classification rests upon a rational basis. The less restrictive rational basis test means only that the burden of justification placed upon the Government is not as great and that the "[o]ne who assails the classification . . . must carry the burden of showing that it does not rest upon any reasonable basis, but is essentially arbitrary." *Lindsley* v. *Natural Carbonic Gas Co., supra,* at 78–79. Consequently, our task is limited to determining whether appellees have carried their burden of showing that the challenged classification is lacking in a rational basis.

The question, stated quite simply, is whether the congressional authorization for durational residence requirements is rationally related to a legitimate legislative purpose. To state the question is to answer it. There can be no doubt concerning the legitimacy of the congressional purpose in enacting the Social Security Act. That question was laid to rest in *Steward Machine Co.* v. *Davis,* 301 U. S. 548 (1937), and *Helvering* v. *Davis,* 301 U. S. 619 (1937). Although those cases dealt only with the social insurance titles of the Act, the public assistance titles involved in these cases were an important part of the comprehensive scheme devised by Congress to attack the problems of social and economic insecurity which plagued the Nation. And, as we have noted, Congress viewed the authorization for durational residence requirements as essential to securing state participation in that comprehensive scheme. We cannot say that the congressional judgment was unreasonable, and we hold, therefore, that the congressional authorization of durational residence requirements has the necessary rational basis to overcome an equal protection attack.

SHAPIRO *v.* THOMPSON.

Appellees' arguments are addressed principally to the
question whether there is any rational basis for the insistence by the States that they be permitted to impose
durational residence requirements as conditions of eligibility for categorical assistance. Appellees examine at
length the justifications advanced by the States for such
residence requirements, and appellees attempts to marshall statistics and other data to refute the asserted
justifications. Because the congressional authorization
for the residence requirements makes the rationality of
Congress' action the determinative factor, we need not
decide in these cases the validity of appellees' position.
However, we do note that, whatever logical appeal appellees' arguments may have to the judicial mind, they do
not undermine the rationality of Congress' action. The
plain fact is Congress recognized that the absence of all
residence requirements would jeopardize meaningful participation by the States in the cooperative effort to improve categorical assistance benefits. The realities of the
legislative process required that Congress act with the
fears of the States in mind, and those legislative realities
must necessarily be taken into account when we are asked
to pass up the reasonableness of congressional action.

What we have said disposes of the equal protection
arguments raised by the appellees in Nos. 813 and 1138.
However, No. 1134 presents a somewhat different problem. For, although the District of Columbia participates
like a State in the matching fund provisions of the public
assistance titles of the Social Security Act, it was Congress which enacted the durational residence requirements contained in § 3–203 of the District of Columbia
Code. In deciding whether to permit such residence
requirements for the District, Congress faced none of
the difficult problems of federalism involved in deciding
whether the States should be permitted to retain min-

SHAPIRO *v.* THOMPSON.

imum residence requirements. Consequently, we turn to the question whether Congress acted contrary to the guarantee of equal protection of the laws in enacting durational residence requirements for the District of Columbia.

It is quite clear that Congress, in legislating for the District of Columbia, need not legislate for the benefit of nonresidents of the District or impose upon the District an obligation to provide for the support of nonresidents. Further, it is settled law that an individual's residence depends upon his presence in a particular place and his subjective intent to remain there on a permanent basis. The question, therefore, is whether durational residence requirements are a reasonable means of testing objectively the subjective intent of an individual who is newly arrived in the District and who claims welfare benefits as a resident. We conclude that they are such a reasonable means. The argument to the contrary generally takes two forms. First, it is said that there are alternative means of determining the subjective intent which are not so broadly disqualifying. However, our task is limited to determining whether there is *a* rational basis for the means adopted and not whether the means adopted is the *most* rational of available alternatives. See, *e. g., Williamson* v. *Lee Optical Co., supra,* at 489; *Lindsley* v. *Natural Carbonic Gas Co., supra,* at 78–79. Congress could well have concluded that a detailed examination of each welfare recipient's subjective intent to establish residence would have involved unnecessary administrative costs that would drain public funds otherwise available for bona fide residents who need public welfare assistance.[33] Congress could also have concluded

---

[33] New York, which has no durational residence requirements, makes as a basis for disqualification from public assistance the fact that an individual has entered the State for the sole purpose of collecting welfare benefits. N. Y. Social Welfare Law § 139–a. That

SHAPIRO *v.* THOMPSON.

that such inquiries into subjective intent pose a special danger of abuse in the administration of welfare laws.[34] Consequently, there is a wholly rational basis for the means adopted by Congress, and appellees' alternative means argument is unavailing. Secondly, it is suggested that, although some waiting period for benefits might be consistent with equal protection of the laws, one year is simply too long. This argument does no more than invite us to re-examine the legislative wisdom in setting the permissible residence period at one year rather than at some lesser period of time. This we decline to do. While a durational residence requirement might, at some point, exceed the bounds of reasonableness in the length of the waiting period imposed, we cannot say that a one-year period is unreasonable.

Appellees also take the position that, even if durational residence requirements are deemed a reasonable means to test the intent to establish residence, they are impermissible because they are imposed for an illegitimate governmental purpose. The illegitimate purpose, according to appellees, is to keep poor people out of the District of Columbia. Appellees point to nothing in the legislative history of the District's residence requirements to show that Congress acted with such a purpose in mind, and we will not attribute such a purpose to it if the result would be to strike down an otherwise valid statute. See *United States* v. *O'Brien, ante,* at ——. As we have noted, Congress in legislating for the District of Columbia need only legislate on behalf of bona fide

---

statute, however, requires a detailed administrative inquiry into the applicant's motives, and Congress could not quite reasonably have viewed the objective durational residence requirement as a more sensible alternative to the New York procedure.

[34] In fact, the potential for abuse in such subjective inquiries has been urged in this Court as a basis for invalidating Alabama's "substitute father" regulation, which operated to disqualify AFDC recipients. See Brief for Appellee, pp. 53–60, *King* v. *Smith, ante.*

SHAPIRO *v.* THOMPSON.

residents of the District, and durational residence requirements impart predictability to the process of allocating limited tax funds to public assistance programs in an annual budget. Thus, in furthering budgetary predictability and in providing an objective test of residence, the durational residence requirements promote the legitimate legislative goal of providing the maximum benefits possible for the bona fide residents who are the objects of legislative concern.

V.

We conclude that Congress has the power to authorize the ~~State~~ to impose reasonable durational residence requirements as a condition of eligibility for categorical assistance benefits and that the one-year requirements challenged in these cases are not unreasonable. Whether residence requirements of any longer duration would meet the test of reasonableness we need not decide on the facts of the cases before us. Nothing that we have said, however, requires that such residence tests remain a permanent part of categorical assistance programs. In authorizing the residence requirements challenged in these cases, Congress also required the States to reduce those requirements to the permissible maximums now prescribed in the Social Security Act. There is nothing to prevent Congress in the future from requiring the elimination of all residence requirements in categorical assistance programs or from adopting alternative programs for individuals who are disqualified from categorical assistance by such requirements. Our decision recognizes only that, where such questions are within the power of Congress to resolve, appeals for change should be made to Congress rather than to the courts.

Reversed.

SUPREME COURT OF THE UNITED STATES

Nos. 813, 1134, AND 1138.—OCTOBER TERM, 1967

Bernard Shapiro, Commissioner of Welfare of Connecticut, Appellant, 813 v. Vivian Thompson.	On Appeal From the United States District Court for the District of Connecticut.
Walter E. Washington, Commissioner of the District of Columbia, et al., Appellants, 1134 v. Clay Mae Legrant et al.	On Appeal From the United States District Court for the District of Columbia.
Roger A. Reynolds et al., Appellants, 1138 v. Juanita Smith et al.	On Appeal From the United States District Court for the Eastern District of Pennsylvania.

[June —, 1968.]

MR. JUSTICE DOUGLAS, dissenting.

If the power to provide this residence requirement for welfare rested on the Commerce Clause, I would join the opinion of the Court. But as I stated in my concurring opinion in *Edwards* v. *California*, 314 U. S. 160, ——, the right of citizens to move from State to State is a "privilege" or "immunity" protected by § 1 of the Fourteenth Amendment. That section states that "No State shall make or enforce any law which shall abridge the privileges or immunities of citizens of the United States." If this residence requirement is not "made" by Connecticut but imposed or sanctioned by Congress, it is nonetheless "enforced" by Connecticut and in my view abridges a privilege or immunity of citizenship.

---

* JMHP.

SHAPIRO *v.* THOMPSON.

The federal social security program, approved by the Court in *Helvering* v. *Davis,* 301 U. S. 619, is mostly administered by the States. While old-age benefits are provided in uniform amounts at the national level, the other benefits vary from State to State.

State plans for aid to dependent children, for maternal and child health services, for crippled children, and for child welfare services must be submitted to the federal agency for approval. While the States receive federal financial support, the amounts of benefits vary from State to State. Some States provide minimal amounts; others are generous. Mr. Justice Cardozo in speaking of the decision of Congress to provide a uniform old-age benefit system said:

> "The problem is plainly nation in area and dimensions. . . . A system of old age pensions has special dangers of its own, if put in force in one state and rejected in another. The existence of such a system is a bait to the needy and dependent elsewhere, encouraging them to migrate and seek a haven of repose. Only a power that is national can serve the interests of all." 301 U. S., at 644.

The other benefits available as a result of the federal plan now in force has created great variation in benefits available from State to State.

The welfare benefits vary from State to State.* A family with dependent children that might receive $38.85

---

*In May 1967 the average monthly payments under old-age assistance programs was $68.20 nationwide. In California it was $101.70, in New Hampshire $98.95, in Mississippi $39.30, and in South Carolina $41.40. The average monthly payments to families under aid to families with dependent children programs showed even greater variations. The national average in May 1967 was $152.25 per month per eligible family. In New Jersey it was $224.50, in New York $221.25, in Alabama $52.75, and in Mississippi $38.85. Hearings on H. R. 12080 before the Senate Committee on Finance, 90th Cong., 1st Sess., pt. 1, at 293, 296–297 (1967).

SHAPIRO *v.* THOMPSON.

a month in Mississippi, would receive $221.25 a month in New York. The latter State might therefore become an attractive haven for the indigents.

Climate is a factor in the migration of people. The prospect of a warm winter sun on one's back may be a magnet to people in States where snow and ice persist for months on end. Even the prospect of not having to buy overshoes and overcoats for the children may be enough to cause a migration. Weather that will reduce the risk of asthma to one will promise a lower family budget to another. Job opportunities, like weather, may produce a migration. Technological disemployment may generate a movement from a rural to an urban environment or from one urban center to another. Travel State to State is the prerogative of the poor as well as the rich. The indigent, more than any other, may indeed have an imperative need to move to another community.

The early law classed indigents with pestilence and gave them a second-class citizenship. That day is gone by reason of the Privileges and Immunities Clause of the Fourteenth Amendment. Poverty is not a source of right; nor is it a status around which the law can create disabilities.

A State should be as powerless to deny a migrant, indigent family the benefits of its welfare program as it is to deny that family the pleasures of its sunshine or its wide-open places.

A state welfare program, like a state school system or a state policy on racial integration or a state program of outdoor recreation, may be the magnet that draws the indigents to that area. They have the constitutional right to move there; and that constitutional right may not be burdened or conditioned in any way.

I assume that no one would dispute that if a State denied all state services and protections to newly arrived residents, the right to move freely from State to State

SHAPIRO *v.* THOMPSON.

would be abridged.   It is inconceivable that a man would voluntarily enter a State knowing that he would be, for his first year of residence, without police and fire protection, hospital and health services, schools for his children, state-provided utilities such as water, etc.   Existence under these conditions would be intolerable.   But to the destitute. the State's welfare assistance is probably as critical as other services are to the rich.

The term "abridge" is used in five provisions of the Constitution.   The First Amendment prohibits laws "abridging" freedom of speech and press and the right of assembly and of petition for redress.   The cases which give a very broad meaning to the term "abridging" in this amendment are many and are well known.   To "deter" (*NAACP* v. *Button,* 371 U. S. 415, 433), "stifle" (*Keyishian* v. *Board of Regents,* 385 U. S. 589, 601, 602), or "impair" (*Shelton* v. *Tucker,* 364 U. S. 479, 485) First Amendment freedoms is to abridge them.   So is creating a "chilling effect on free expression." *Dombrowski* v. *Pfister,* 380 U. S. 479, 487.

The Fifteenth, Nineteenth, and Twenty-fourth Amendments provide that the right to vote shall not be "abridged" by reason of race, sex, and nonpayment of poll taxes.   In *Harmon* v. *Forssenius,* 380 U. S. 528, we indicated that abridgment occurred when the States made voting more onerous, handicapped the right, or imposed obstacles to its exercise.   380 U. S., at 540–541.

There can be no doubt that for some indigent citizens, this one-year residency restriction will deter, handicap, chill, and stand as obstacles to the exercise of the constitutional right to travel.

The imposition of a year's residence before welfare starts does partial service for the policy struck down in *Edwards* v. *California.*   The rich and prosperous people no longer stop the migrants at the border.   But they impose conditions that make it difficult if not impossible for

SHAPIRO *v.* THOMPSON.

the indigent to reach the community where a new life may be possible.

While the Connecticut and Pennsylvania statutes are invalid under the Fourteenth Amendment, the District of Columbia Code provision must fall under the Due Process Clause of the Fifth Amendment. The teaching of our cases is that " 'The right to travel is a part of the "liberty" of which the citizen cannot be deprived without due process of law.' " *United States* v. *Laub,* 385 U. S. 475, 481. The District of Columbia has presented no different justifications for the interference with the right to travel caused by § 3–203 of its Code than those argued by the States. As indicated, the purported justifications are not substantial. The citizens' right to move freely into the District of Columbia must accordingly prevail.

I would affirm the judgments of the District Courts in these cases.

SUPREME COURT OF THE UNITED STATES

From: Har

Nos. 813, 1134, AND 1138.—OCTOBER TERM, 1967.

Circulate

Recircula

Bernard Shapiro, Commissioner of Welfare of Connecticut, Appellant, 813 *v.* Vivian Thompson.	On Appeal From the United States District Court for the District of Connecticut.
Walter E. Washington, Commissioner of the District of Columbia, et al., Appellants, 1134 *v.* Clay Mae Legrant et al.	On Appeal From the United States District Court for the District of Columbia.
Roger A. Reynolds et al., Appellants, 1138 *v.* Juanita Smith et al.	On Appeal From the United States District Court for the Eastern District of Pennsylvania.

[June —, 1968.]

MR. JUSTICE HARLAN, concurring in the result.

Although I concur in the results ultimately reached by the Court. I believe that its opinion has omitted or obscured certain of the principles and circumstances that. in my view, compel the reversal of the judgments below. I shall therefore describe the rather different path by which I have reached these results.

The pertinent facts may be briefly summarized. Congress has expressly authorized the States to impose durational residence requirements upon welfare assistance jointly provided from state and federal funds. There is, as the Court demonstrates, evidence that such an authorization was thought by Congress to be an essen-

SHAPIRO *v.* THOMPSON.

tial prerequisite to any program of national welfare
assistance. Some 46 States have since adopted residence
requirements, although these vary widely in duration
and scope of application. Further, Congress has, pursuant to its general legislative authority within the
District of Columbia, imposed a durational residence
requirement upon welfare assistance provided by the
District. Appellees urge, and the courts below held,
that these residence requirements are invalid under the
Constitution for either or both of two reasons. *First,*
it is said that they create an impermissible burden upon
a constitutional right to change residences from one to
another of the several States.[1] *Second,* it is contended
that these requirements deny the equal protection of the
laws by arbitrarily discriminating between those who
have, and those who have not, recently changed their
States of residence.[2]

I.

I turn first to the argument that these requirements
place an impermissible burden upon a right to make
interstate changes of residence. It is important at the
outset to emphasize that, unlike *Kent* v. *Dulles,* 357
U. S. 116, and *Aptheker* v. *Secretary of State,* 378 U. S.
500, these cases do not involve any absolute prohibition
upon any form of travel or interstate movement; it can

---

[1] The right in question in these cases has been generally described
by the parties and by the courts below as the right to travel. Although this may be the ultimate premise of the argument, I think
it important to emphasize that appellees and others similarly situated have not in any fashion been forbidden to travel. As I shall
show, it can at most be said that their right to change residences
among the several States has been rendered economically more
difficult.

[2] I have frequently described the governmental bodies involved
in these cases simply as the States. I do not, of course, overlook
the presence of the District of Columbia; I have employed this
terminology as a convenient simplification.

SHAPIRO *v.* THOMPSON.

at most be said that durational residence requirements for welfare assistance may serve to discourage changes of residence by, in some few cases, rendering such changes economically more hazardous. The burden, if any, upon travel is oblique and consequential. It can scarcely be disputed that not all legislative measures that may in this fashion discourage interstate changes of residence are forbidden by the Constitution. Congress plainly has wide authority to impose restrictions upon the interstate movement of goods and passengers, including those movements that ultimately terminate in changes of residence. Congress may, as this Court has previously observed, adopt whatever measures it deems necessary for the regulation of interstate movement, so long as those measures are reasonably related to purposes otherwise within Congress' authority, and so long as they do not, when examined in light of the purposes Congress has sought to achieve, "sweep unnecessarily broadly and thereby invade the area of protected freedoms." *NAACP* v. *Alabama*, 377 U. S. 288, 307; *Aptheker* v. *Secretary of State, supra,* at 508. Moreover, where Congress has formulated its judgment as to these questions into a statute, this Court must accord that statute the customarily heavy presumption of constitutional validity. See, *e. g., Brown* v. *Maryland*, 12 Wheat. 419, 436; *Insurance Co.* v. *Glidden Co., United States* v. *National Dairy Corp.*, 372 U. S. 29, 32.

A similar presumption of constitutional validity attaches to the judgments of the several state legislatures, particularly where, as here, the States have acted upon the specific authorization of Congress. See, *e. g., Powell* v. *Pennsylvania*, 127 U. S. 678, 684–685. Compare *United States* v. *Des Moines & Co.*, 142 U. S. 510, 544–545. The cases now before the Court do not, it must be emphasized, involve circumstances in which individual States have, contrary to the wishes of the National Legis-

SHAPIRO *v.* THOMPSON.

lature, sought to close their borders to any class of interstate traffic.

Moreover, it is clear that state legislatures are not forbidden to adopt measures that may incidentally lessen the desirability of interstate changes of residence, so long as the measures are otherwise within the State's competence and do not excessively or unnecessarily hinder free movement among the several States. In particular, the States may, for this purpose, distinguish between those who have, and those who have not, recently changed their States of residence. States have, to select common illustrations, imposed durational residence requirements upon the practice of various professions and occupations, the right to vote, the right to become a candidate for public office, and the availability in local courts of matrimonial relief. Compare *Pope* v. *Williams,* 193 U. S. 621; *Carrington* v. *Rash,* 380 U. S. 89; *Drueding* v. *Devlin,* 380 U. S. 125. This does not mean that every such restriction is necessarily valid; but neither may it be said that they are uniformly, or even characteristically, invalid. The validity of each restriction instead turns on familiar questions of reasonableness and degree.

The purposes intended to be served by these residence requirements are evidently three.[3] First, it was expected that the specifications of a fixed period of physical presence within a State would ameliorate the difficult administrative problems of determining whether a prospective welfare recipient intends in good faith to remain per-

---

[3] I do not mean that each of these purposes was sought by each of the legislatures that have adopted durational residence requirements. In Connecticut, for example, the budget for welfare is evidently open-ended, which perhaps suggests that at least that State is not seriously concerned with the need for more accurate budgetary estimates of prospective welfare costs. I have sought simply to illustrate the varieties of problems with which Congress and the state legislatures have been concerned.

SHAPIRO *v.* THOMPSON.

manently within that State.   In turn, it was anticipated that if these difficulties were in fact ameliorated, two general policies would be served: it would facilitate the allocation of welfare funds exclusively among those with durable interests in the State; and it would prevent the expenditure of a disproportionate part of severely limited funds upon costs of administration.   Second, it was expected that fixed residence requirements would permit more accurate budgetary estimates of the prospective need for welfare funds.   Third, it was supposed that, without residence requirements, a substantial number of persons would enter States temporarily, solely for the purpose of obtaining assistance payments.   Congress and the state legislatures evidently hoped that durational residence requirements would guarantee both that assistance would be given only to those persons with deeper and more nearly permanent interests in the State, and that the rising and already substantial costs of welfare programs would be held to acceptable levels.[4]

I am aware that certain of those familiar with these issues have concluded that these problems are less severe than Congress and the several state legislatures have supposed, and that many such persons believe that any difficulties might be effectively overcome by the adoption of other, and more flexible, administrative devices. It has been suggested that such testimony permits this

---

[4] The discussion in Connecticut prior to its adoption in 1965 of a welfare residence requirement may be taken as an illustration.   Representative Cohen, the principal spokesman for the bill, emphasized that the costs of welfare had "probably doubled since 1961," and urged that "there is sufficient emergency in this acceleration in welfare costs that we should look for all possible solutions to this problem."   He stated his belief that there "are some people who come to Connecticut simply to get benefits of public assistance," although "the proportion of these is small."   Connecticut General Assembly, 1965 Feb. Spec. Sess., 2 House of Representatives Proceedings 3505.

SHAPIRO *v.* THOMPSON.

Court to invalidate these legislative judgments. I cannot agree. None of the evidence before us establishes that the problems by which Congress and 46 state legislatures were troubled are, or might become, illusory; the evidence indicates at most that these are questions of policy and degree, about which reasonable men may readily differ. We can at least be certain that these conflicting assessments of the situation were presented to Congress and the state legislatures,[5] and we must assume that, after consideration of the pertinent materials, these differences in emphasis and viewpoint were resolved by them in favor of residence requirements.

Other administrative methods might certainly have been selected, but no evidence has been presented that durational residence requirements are irrational or unsuitable for the purposes the legislatures sought to achieve. It is true that these other methods might not deny assistance to persons who, although they have only recently entered a State, have genuine interests within that State; such methods arguably might, therefore, less frequently discourage interstate changes of residence. But the adoption of an alternative method would also compel Congress and the States to surrender the advantages of administrative simplicity and relative certainty that characterize durational residence requirements. Perhaps any such method would, in addition, ultimately increase the proportion of the available welfare funds consumed by costs of administration. I cannot, in these circumstances, say that some slight incremental hazard of discouraging changes of residence obliges Congress and

---

[5] For Congress, see, *e. g.*, Problems of Hungary Children in the District of Columbia, Hearings before the Subcommittee on Public Health, Education, Welfare, and Safety of the Senate Committee on the District of Columbia, 85th Cong., 1st Sess. For Pennsylvania, see Appendix in No. 1138, at 96a–98a.

SHAPIRO *v.* THOMPSON.

the States to abandon an otherwise permissible and convenient administrative device.   It is proper to recall that the selection of administrative methods involves questions particularly inappropriate for judicial determination, and that, in any event, this Court is not empowered to compel either Congress or the States to adopt those methods of administration that may seem to it most prudent or desirable.

Nonetheless, it is necessary to examine one ancillary contention.   It has been urged that these requirements are impermissible because their principal purpose is beyond the constitutional authority both of Congress and of the States.   It is said that this purpose is to restrict the ingress from other States of the poor or indigent. To the extent that this argument would require the Court to attribute to legislators improper motives for an apparently permissible statute, it suffices to reiterate that we will not, upon such a basis, invalidate an otherwise valid legislative act.   See, *e. g., Fletcher* v. *Peck,* 6 Cranch 87; *Barenblatt* v. *United States,* 360 U. S. 109; *United States* v. *O'Brien,* —— U. S. ——.

To the extent that appellees instead suggest that welfare payments may not be limited to those persons who are bona fide permanent residents of a given State or community, I find the argument untenable.   I perceive no reason why Congress may not endeavor to restrict its largesse to those who are permanently established in the District of Columbia, or why it may not prescribe administrative limitations reasonably calculated to achieve that purpose.   And if such regulations are within the competence of Congress, surely the several States may, upon the authorization of Congress, adopt substantially identical measures.   The question is thus simply one of the reasonableness of the methods selected by Congress and by the States, and, for reasons described above, I

SHAPIRO *v.* THOMPSON.

have concluded that durational residence requirements
do not "sweep unnecessarily broadly," and thus do not
"invade the area of protected freedoms." *NAACP* v.
Alabama, supra, at 307.

II.

I turn next to the argument that these residence requirements are invalid because they deny to those who
have recently changed their States of residence equal protection of the laws.[6] The standard applicable here is
familiar and well-established: a legislative measure is
invalid as a denial of equal protection of the laws only
if "it is without any reasonable basis and therefore is
purely arbitrary." *Lindsley* v. *Natural Carbolic Gas Co.,*
220 U. S. 61, 78. It is not enough that the measure
results incidentally "in some inequality," or that it is not
drawn "with mathematical nicety," *id.*; the statutory
classification must instead cause "different treatments . . .
so disparate, relative to the difference in classification,
as to be wholly arbitrary. *Walters* v. *City of St. Louis,*
347 U. S. 231, 237. Such a determination again demands
consideration both of the purposes of residence requirements and of their reasonableness as a device to achieve
those purposes.

Durational residence requirements have, as I have
sought to demonstrate, purposes rooted in not implau-
sible fears that the administrative costs of welfare pro-

---

[6] I have consistently characterized this argument as one based
upon an alleged denial of the equal protection of the laws. I do
not mean by this to disregard the fact that this argument is
applicable in *Washington* v. *Legrant,* involving the District of
Columbia, only through the terms of the Due Process Clause of the
Fifth Amendment. Neither do I mean to suggest that these two
constitutional phrases "are always interchangeable." *Bolling* v.
Sharpe, 347 U. S. 497, 499. In the circumstances of this case, I do
not believe myself obliged to decide what differences, if any, there
may be in the scope of protection given by the two constitutional
provisions.

SHAPIRO *v.* THOMPSON.

grams would become onerous, and that those programs would be abused by those without durable interests within the donor State. The severity and importance of these problems have been variously estimated, but there is no evidence now before the Court that suggests that they are, or might become, illusory. The question is therefore again whether the administrative classification adopted by Congress and the several state legislatures is, in any other sense, arbitrary or unreasonable.

Although the prescription of a fixed period of physical presence within a State as a condition of assistance concededly means that some persons otherwise within the class sought to be benefited are excluded, this alone need not render the classification "wholly arbitrary." This Court cannot so easily disregard the judgments of Congress and 46 States that such a requirement is imperative if welfare funds are to be allocated with reasonable administrative costs among those persons with permanent interests within the donor community. It must, after all, be recalled that these are questions which legislators, and not judges, are better prepared to resolve. Moreover, the attractiveness of durational residence requirements as a method of administration can scarcely be surprising; they offer simplicity and relative certainty in an area of law in which those qualities are properly prized. Finally, there is no reason now to suppose that the periods of residence involved in these cases so exceed the requirements of the purposes for which they were imposed as to render them "without any reasonable basis." This does not mean that any residence requirement, of whatever duration, is necessarily permissible; but in the circumstances of these cases, I can find no objection under the Due Process Clause of the Fifth Amendment to the residence requirement imposed by Congress in the District of Columbia, or, under the Equal Protection Clause of the Fourteenth Amendment, to the similar-

SHAPIRO *v.* THOMPSON.

measures adopted by the States of Connecticut and Pennsylvania.

The principle which, in my view, is decisive in these cases may be briefly stated. Questions of the prudence and necessity of durational residence requirements involve difficult issues of policy, about which differing views may readily be entertained. But the resolution of those differences in emphasis and viewpoint is entrusted to Congress and the legislatures of the several States, and not to this Court. Our responsibilities are more limited, and our authority more constricted. We are empowered to declare acts of the national and state legislatures impermissible, not on "slight implication and vague conjecture," but only on a "clear and strong conviction" of their inconsistency with the commands of the Constitution. *Fletcher* v. *Peck, supra,* at 128. I can reach no such conviction here, and would therefore reverse the judgments below.

Mr. Justi

From: Fortas,

Circulated:__

Recirculated:

SUPREME COURT OF THE UNITED STATES

Nos. 813, 1134, AND 1138.—OCTOBER TERM, 1967.

Bernard Shapiro, Commissioner of Welfare of Connecticut, Appellant,

813   *v.*

Vivian Thompson.

On Appeal From the United States District Court for the District of Connecticut.

Walter E. Washington, Commissioner of the District of Columbia, et al., Appellants,

1134   *v.*

Clay Mae Legrant et al.

On Appeal From the United States District Court for the District of Columbia.

Roger A. Reynolds et al., Appellants,

1138   *v.*

Juanita Smith et al.

On Appeal From the United States District Court for the Eastern District of Pennsylvania.

[June —, 1968.]

MR. JUSTICE FORTAS, dissenting.

I.

The path by which the majority of the Court reaches its result in these cases may be summarized as follows:

1. The majority does not dispute the obvious fact that requiring an applicant for welfare benefits to have resided one year or longer in a State before he becomes eligible for welfare benefits interferes with the right to travel.

2. The majority does not dispute the established principle that the right to travel is guaranteed by the Constitution and that it is a "fundamental" or "basic" right.

---

* JMHP.

SHAPIRO *v.* THOMPSON.

3. The majority does not attempt to defend the constitutionality of state statutory provisions imposing the
durational residence requirement as a condition for welfare benefits as purely state legislation: that is, as if the
requirement were imposed by the State without congressional authorization. It does not dispute that *Edwards*
v. *California,* 314 U. S. 160 (1941), has settled the point
that the States may not impose such a burden on the
right to travel. See also *Crandall* v. *Nevada,* 6 Wall.
35 (1867). The majority does not dispute this; but it
relies upon the fact that *Edwards* "was addressed only
to a *state* regulation of interstate movement imposed
without congressional authorization involved in these
cases." *Ante,* p. 24. (The Court overlooks the fact that
one phase of No. 1138, the Pennsylvania case, involves
a purely state-financed and authorized public assistance
program.[1] As to this phase of the appeal in No. 1138,
it is clear error to fail to hold that the durational residence requirement is invalid and unconstitutional as a
state-imposed burden on the right to travel.)
4. The majority argues that since Congress "author
ized" the durational residence requirements, the constitutional question turns upon whether the Congress—not
the States—has power to "regulate" or interfere with the
right to travel in the manner involved here. It reasons

---

[1] The Pennsylvania statute at issue here, Pa. Stat. Ann., Tit.
62, § 432 (6), applies to public "assistance" programs which, under
Pennsylvania law, include categorical assistance programs and the
state-financed general assistance program. See Pa. Stat. Ann., Tit.
62, §§ 402, 432 (1), 432 (2). The complaint in the Pennsylvania
case alleges that the appellees applied for public "assistance" and
were denied that "assistance" solely because they did not satisfy
the durational residency requirement embodied in Pa. Stat. Ann.,
Tit. 62, § 432 (6). The State admitted these allegations. The District Court declared the statute unconstitutional without differentiat-
ing among the kinds of programs encompassed in the complaint and
covered by the statute.

SHAPIRO *v.* THOMPSON.

that Congress has undoubted power to regulate commerce among the several States (Art. I, § 8). It argues that if we treat the right to travel, not as derived from the Commerce Clause, but as a right of national citizenship protected by the Privileges and Immunities Clause of the Constitution, it is nevertheless not immune from the regulatory power of the Federal Government because "that limitation [the Privileges and Immunities Clause of the Fourteenth Amendment] in no sense restricts the power of the Federal Government to regulate the same privileges and immunities." *Ante,* p. 24.

5. It concedes that the federal power over the right to travel while "plenary" is not without limits, and it says that the question therefore is "whether Congress has acted reasonably under the circumstances." *Ante,* p. 26. The majority then concludes that Congres was justified in authorizing the State to interfere with the right to travel because it did so *in order to induce the States to cooperate in the program to provide improved welfare benefits to the needy.*

This is the *only* reason advanced to justify the state legislation. The majority states it as follows: "The statutory authorization for durational residence requirements was an important part of the incentive scheme devised by Congress to encourage the States to join the Federal Government in a cooperative effort to improve and liberalize the benefits under categorical assistance programs." *Ante,* p. 26.

6. Having thus disposed of the interference with the right to travel, the majority is faced with an obvious difficulty: If we assume that Congress could burden the right to travel to this substantial extent, can it do so in a measure which affects only the poor? This is the equal protection argument.

The Court first takes comfort in pointing out "what Congress has *not* done in authorizing durational residence

SHAPIRO *v.* THOMPSON.

requirements. It has not acted to prohibit interstate movement by welfare recipients. Such individuals are still free to move from state to state and to establish residence wherever they please." (This statement disregards the spirit of *Griffin* v. *Illinois,* 351 U. S. 12 (1956); *Gideon* v. *Wainwright,* 372 U. S. 335 (1963); *Douglas* v. *California,* 372 U. S. 353 (1963); and *Harper* v. *Board of Elections,* 383 U. S. 663 (1966).

The majority then seems to recognize, but only in passing, that this interference with the "basic" or "fundamental" right to travel operates only on the poor, and only those of the poor who have lived in the jurisdiction for less than a year. It repeats vaguely that the test, presumably of the equal protection standard, is whether the contested provision is "rationally related to a legitimate legislative purpose." The majority says "To state the question is to answer it" because "Congress viewed the durational residence requirements as essential to securing state participation in [the] comprehensive scheme." *Ante,* p. 30. It is the "realities of the legislative process"; it is the fact that "the absence of all residence requirements would jeopardize meaningful participation by the states in the cooperative effort," *ante,* p. 31—it is these which justify the undisputed discrimination "between two classes of residents in a state— those who have resided in the state for more than one year and those who have resided in the state for less than one year." *Ante,* p. 28.

7. Turning to the District of Columbia case (No. 1134), the majority recognizes that this *quid pro quo* justification is not applicable because Congress is the legislature for the District. Congress itself enacted the durational residence requirement of the District of Columbia, and the majority cannot very well argue that Congress authorized the contested restriction as a neces-

SHAPIRO *v.* THOMPSON.

sary inducement to itself. To sustain its constitutionality for the District, the majority then adopts all of the arguments advanced by the States in support of their legislation, and which it does not rely upon in its effort to justify that legislation. It asserts that Congress in legislating for the District may confine the benefits of such legislation to "residents" of the District, and it might adopt the one-year residence requirement as a convenient method of identifying "residents." The majority does not and could not contend that this was in reality the purpose of the provision because, as I shall show and as the District Court pointed out, the durational residence requirement was not in fact imposed for this purpose. The majority then asks the reader to reject the idea that the restriction was imposed to keep poor people out of the District because, it says, there is nothing which expressly shows that Congress imposed the durational residence requirement for "an illegitimate governmental purpose"—namely, "to keep poor people out of the District of Columbia." *Ante,* p. 33. The majority also, for good measure, tosses in the thought that durational requirements impart "budgetary predictability."

II.

With the utmost respect, I am compelled to state my disagreement. In the District of Columbia case, the majority surprisingly relies upon a total rejection of reality and a resort to debating devices to obscure the palpable and obvious truths found by the District Court and reflected by the legislative record: As I shall show, *infra,* the one-year residence requirement obviously and palpably was not adopted for, is not reasonably related to, and does not in fact serve as "objective" proof of residence or domicile; the residence requirement and the durational requirement are distinct and independent. The one-year residence requirement obviously and pal-

SHAPIRO *v.* THOMPSON.

pably was designed to discourage poor people from coming to the District; or having come, to leave; and to
protect the public treasury by denying relief to *residents*
who have been residents for less than a year. This is the
fact; and the necessity of the majority to rely upon fiction
merely underscores the untenable nature of its conclusion.

In the *State Cases,* the principle announced by the
majority—that Congress may constitutionally burden or
authorize the States to burden a "fundamental" constitutional right in order to enlist state cooperation—is
utterly devoid of support in law or reason. It is startling
to learn from the majority that Congress may barter the
constitutional rights of citizens for the political acquies-
cense of the States. The need, real or apparent, to enlist
state cooperation in a joint federal-state program cannot
provide a "rational basis" for congressional authorization
of interference with a constitutional right. There is not
a single instance in this Court's history where such a
basis has been accepted as providing a "reason" for burdening commerce or travel between the States, or for discriminating between two classes of citizens. The majority cites none. I know of none. And, indeed, until the
majority opinion in these cases, the possibility has never,
to my knowledge, been suggested. The parties did not
so contend in these cases.

It is obviously of no constitutional relevance that Congress, as the majority says had to authorize durational
residence requirements in order to secure state cooperation. I am confident, for example, that Congress could
obtain enthusiastic cooperation of many States in a
school-building program if it authorized the construction,
with joint funds, of segregated schools. But could it be
seriously contended that Congress would be constitutionally justified in such authorization by the "need" "to
secure state cooperation?" The fact that here we deal
with the right to travel makes no difference. The as-

SHAPIRO *v.* THOMPSON.

serted principle—the *only* one advanced to support the challenged authorization in the case of the States—is utterly foreign to our law. Its implications are pernicious, and its progeny are likely to be evil.

III.

I come, then, to a consideration of the issues presented by these cases, on their merits. At the outset, it is well to recognize that there are three different types of situations presented: The "categorical assistance" program,[2] which are joint federal-state projects, in which the federal legislation directs approval of state plans imposing a durational residence requirement within state limits (42 U. S. C. §§ 302 (b)(2)(A), 602 (b), 1201 (b)(1), 1352 (b)(1);[3] the public assistance program in the District of Columbia, which is, of course, entirely authorized by Congress; and the Pennsylvania general assistance program which is entirely state authorized.[4] Each of these involves somewhat separate constitutional considerations. All present the problem of the power of government, State or Federal, under our Constitution to deny welfare payments to persons who have not resided in the jurisdiction for one year or more.

---

[2] The so-called categorical assistance programs provide for old-age assistance (42 U. S. C. § 301 *et seq.*), aid to families with dependent children (42 U. S. C. § 601 *et seq.*), aid to the blind (42 U. S. C. § 1201 *et seq.*), and aid to the permanently and totally disabled (42 U. S. C. § 1351 *et seq.*).

[3] A one-year requirement is allowed for AFDC programs. 42 U. S. C. § 602 (b). For the other categorical assistance programs the States are permitted to impose a durational requirement as long as the requirement does not exclude "any resident of the State who has resided therein five years during the nine years immediately preceding the application . . . and has resided therein continuously for one year immediately preceding the application." The jurisdictions involved here have imposed a one-year requirement for the programs relevant to these cases.

[4] See n. 1, *supra.*

SHAPIRO *v.* THOMPSON.

It must be emphasized that the analysis which follows
and the conclusions which I present do not apply to a
domiciliary requirment—that is, a requirement that recipients be bona fide "residents" or domiciliaries of the
jurisdiction. Nor does the conclusion herein apply to
provisions requiring a limited waiting-period necessary
for investigation and processing of applications, and uniformly applicable to all. My analysis and conclusions
apply only to the durational residence requirements
involved here.

IV.

The durational residence requirements in American
welfare legislation has its roots in the settlement laws
of England. In the Middle Ages, the poor law as ex-
pounded by the cannonists and administered by the
church did not include a residence requirement.[5] Presumably this stemmed from the biblical admonition with
respect to the duty owed to strangers.[6] The only test
was need.

In 1348–1349, however, the Black Death reduced England's population by about 25%, and further declines
occurred in the following years. The resulting social up-
heaval and labor shortage were accompanied by large-
scale mobility of the lower classes, some to better
themselves by finding superior jobs, and some to plunder
and loot.[7]

Gradually, because of the danger and the economic
pressure upon the employer groups which were attendant
upon the restless movement of the lower classes, poverty

[5] B. Coll, Perspectives in Public Welfare: The English Heritage
(HEW, Welfare in Review, March 1966), at 3. See generally
B. Tierney, Medieval Poor Law, pp. 24–35, 57, 60–71, 91–109.

[6] "Love they neighbor as thyself"; "Do unto others as you would
have them do to you."

[7] Jordan, Philanthropy in England: 1480–1660 (Russel Sage
Foundation, 1959), pp. 78–80, 83.

SHAPIRO *v.* THOMPSON.

came to be linked and identified with vagrancy—with the wanderer, the worthless and the dangerous vagabond. In 1388, the first Law of Settlement ^was promulgated. Able-bodied beggars were subject to punishment. Those unable to work were permitted to beg only at their place of residence or their birthplace.[8]

In subsequent years, phenomenal increases in England's population, the beginnings of the factory system and vast migration from rural areas into London began to place a heavy burden on the church and on private facilities for coping with the destitute. In 1597–1601 the Elizabethan Poor Law was enacted placing the basic responsibility for the poor in the secular agencies.[9] The mass of the poor, however, were still regarded as victims of misfortune.[10] This attitude changed in the 17th century following the advent of Calvanism. Poverty "came to be regarded as a question of individual character."[11]

Workhouse schemes were devised as an attempted answer to the problem. The Law of Settlement and Removal of 1662 was enacted. This law made it possible to eject individuals and families from parishes if local authorities thought they might become dependent. The preamble to the Act recited a now-familiar theme: that large numbers of the poor were moving to parishes where more liberal welfare policies were in effect. In actual practice, the Settlement and Removal Law did not result in many removals, but it operated as harassment and as an expression of disapproval which undoubtedly comforted the more affluent and settled parishoners.[12]

---

[8] B. Coll, *supra*, at 4.

[9] Jordan, *supra*, at 77, 85; Tierney, *supra*, at 128–132.

[10] Webb, English Local Government: English Poor Law History, pp. 81–92.

[11] B. Coll, *supra*, at 6.

[12] B. Coll, *supra*, at 6.

SHAPIRO *v.* THOMPSON.

The Elizabethan Poor Law and the Settlement and Removal Law of 1662 were the models adopted by the American colonies. Residence in the city, town, or county was required as a condition of aid, although minimum periods of residence were not included in the laws. Most early laws also required some property qualification. Removal laws were common.[13] Newcomers who might become public charges were "warned out" or "passed on" to the next locality. It has been ruefully suggested that through the years a grossly disproportionate amount of money has been spent in contesting which locality has the responsibility for the case of indigents.[14] Initially, the funds for welfare payments were raised by local tax rates, and the controversy as to responsibility for particular indigents raged between localities in the same State. As States—first alone and then with federal grants—assumed the major responsibility, the contest of nonresponsibility became interstate. The present cases are part of this human and fiscal history.

Migration among the States is a characteristic of American demography. Without doubt, it is a vital contributory factor in the Nation's economic growth and stability. It is fair to say that it is a cardinal principle of our federal union now, as on a much smaller scale, it was in the days of the founding of the republic. Population in this

---

[13] In the earlier reports of the decisions of this Court appear two quaint cases involving removal orders. In *Fallowfield Township* v. *Marlborough Township*, 1 U. S. 32, 1 Dall. 32 (1776), an order for removal of a pauper was upheld despite the objection that the order of sessions did not show that an examination of the pauper had been made. In *Upper Dublin Overseers of the Poor* v. *Germantown Overseers of the Poor*, 2 U. S. 213, 2 Dall. 213 (1793), an order removing paupers from one town to another was quashed because the justices who issued the removal order were taxpayers in the former and therefore interested in the result.

[14] See B. Coll, Perspectives in Welfare: Colonial Times to 1860 (HEW, Welfare in Review, November-December 1967), at 3.

SHAPIRO *v.* THOMPSON.

country tends to follow employment opportunity and economic requirements. This is a nation of travelers. Our flexible responses to changes in technology and in world and domestic conditions depend upon population mobility. Migratory workers are considered essential to our agriculture. In huge numbers they follow the seasons and the crops, and they are excluded from the protection of such national and state statutes to protect labor as the Labor-Management Relations Act, the Fair Labor Standards Act and unemployment insurance. Interstate migration of industrial workers is also a familiar part of our national life and an important aspect of our industrial strength and flexibility. In the year ending March 1967, more than 6,500,000 of our people moved their residence from one State to another—almost 3.4% of our population. The character of the migration, so far as the present problem is concerned, can be gauged by the income level of the persons concerned. In the March 1966–1967 year, about 28.7% of the males in the age group of 18 years and older had incomes less than $3,000, and about 45.6% had incomes of less than $5,000.[15]

This is the background of the constitutional problem that we face in these cases. It is a problem that stems from the indisputable purpose of our Constitution to safeguard the mobility of people of this Nation among the States, and to guarantee their freedom of movement without encountering discrimination or being burdened because of their interstate migration.

V.

Despite this history and the special value ascribed by our constitutional scheme to free interstate migration,

---

[15] See U. S. Dept. of Commerce, Bureau of the Census, Current Population Reports, Population Characteristics, Mobility of the Population of the United States, March 1966 to March 1967, April 30, 1968.

SHAPIRO *v.* THOMPSON.

some of the States have long endeavored to encourage the entry of the affluent and "desirable" in-migrants and of only those poor who were needed for labor and could be counted on to leave after the need for their services has been met. They have endeavored to discourage the entry of the poor except on this basis. It was an effort of this sort that led to the landmark case of *Edwards* v. *California,* 314 U. S. 160 (1941) which is fundamental to the problems presented by the cases before us.

The case arose as a result of California's effort to stem the flow of indigent migrants. Blessed with benign climate, resources, and economic opportunity, that State has attracted large numbers of migrants. As early as 1860, it adopted a law making it a crime to bring into the State any person known to be indigent. A subsequent version of this statute was at issue in *Edwards* v. *California, supra.* In that case, Mr. Justice Byrnes, writing for the Court, acknowledged the "staggering" problems of "health, morals, and especially finance" which the huge influx of migrants into California had caused. 341 U. S., at 173. But he concluded for the Court that the legislation exceeded permissible bounds.

Mr. Justice Byrnes said that none of the boundaries to permissible state legislative activity "is more certain than the prohibition against attempts on the part of any single State to isolate itself from difficulties common to all of them by restraining the transportation of persons and property across its borders." (314 U. S., at 173.) He observed that the "express purpose and inevitable effect [of the law] is to prohibit the transportation of indigent persons across the California border." (314 U. S., at 174.) He noted the argument that the concept underlying the California statute had a firm basis in English and American history. (See *supra.*) But he firmly rejected this as a guide to current constitutional decision because, he said, it "no longer fits the facts." (314 U. S.,

SHAPIRO *v.* THOMPSON.

at 174.) He said that "the task of providing assistance to the needy has ceased to be local in character." (314 U. S., at 174–175.) In support of this, he pointed to the growth of industrialization and of the federal programs which, as he put it, "illustrate that in not inconsiderable means the relief of the needy has become the common responsibility and concern of the whole nation." (314 U. S., at 175.)

In a memorable sentence Mr. Justice Byrnes said, "Poverty and immorality are not synonymous." (314 U. S., at 177.) He repudiated the venerable but obsolete words of Justice Barbour in *City of New York* v. *Miln*, 11 Pet. 102, 142–143 (1836), that "it is as competent and as necessary for a state to provide precautionary measures against the moral pestilence of paupers, vagabonds, and possibly convicts; as it is to guard against the physical pestilence, which may arise from unsound and infectious articles imported, or from a ship, the crew of which may be labouring under an infectious disease."

In *Edwards*, five members of the Court, including Justice Byrnes, rested the unanimous decision invalidating California's law, upon the Commerce Clause. Four, Justices BLACK, DOUGLAS, Jackson, and Murphy, based their conclusion on the Privileges and Immunities Clause, holding that California's interference with the right to travel, a privilege of national citizenship, was a violation of that clause.[16]

In a series of cases subsequent to *Edwards*, this Court has firmly established that the right to travel from one

---

[16] In *Edwards*, MR. JUSTICE DOUGLAS, joined by Justices BLACK and Murphy, concurred on the ground that the California statute, by invading the right to move freely from State to State, violated the right of national citizenship protected by the Privileges and Immunities Clause of the Fourteenth Amendment. (314 U. S., at 177). Mr. Justice Jackson's concurring opinion also rested on this clause. (314 U. S., at 181.)

SHAPIRO *v.* THOMPSON.

State to another is "fundamental" and "basic." *Kent v. Dulles*, 357 U. S. 116, 125–127 (1958); *Aptheker* v. *Secretary*, 378 U. S. 500, 505–506 (1964); *Zemel* v. *Rusk*, 381 U. S. 1, 14 (1965); *United States* v. *Guest*, 383 U. S. 745, 759 (1966).

In the present cases, the lower courts and this Court, therefore, must consider the issues in light of this constitutional guaranty of the right to travel interstate; in light of the guaranty against state interference with the privileges and immmunities of citizens which, as this Court has held, extends to rights of national citizenship (cf. *Twining* v. *New Jersey*, 211 U. S. 78 (1908); *Slaughter House Cases*, 16 Wall. 36 (1872); *Crandall* v. *Nevada*, 6 Wall. 35 (1867)), and in light of the Equal Protection Clause, which binds the States under the Fourteenth Amendment and which is a restriction upon congressional power by reason of the Due Process Clause of the Fourteenth Amendment. (*Bolling* v. *Sharpe*, 347 U. S. 497 (1954); *Schneider* v. *Rusk*, 377 U. S. 163, 168 (1964). In my opinion, these fundamental principles compel the conclusion that the challenged durational residence requirement is unconstitutional.

VI.

All of the district courts from which these cases come to us have declared the durational residence requirement unconstitutional. Other three-judge district courts have reached the same result. *Robertson* v. *Ott*, —— F. Supp. —— (D. C. D. Mass., May 21, 1968); *Robinson* v. *Johnson*, —— F. Supp. —— (N. D. Ill., Feb. 20, 1968); *Ramos* v. *Health and Social Services Bd. of Wisc.*, 276 F. Supp. 474 (D. C. E. D. Wis. 1967); *Green* v. *Department of Public Welfare*, 270 F. Supp. 173 (D. C. D. Del. 1967). There is one district court decision to the contrary, *Waggoner* v. *Rosen*, —— F. Supp. —— (D. C. M. D. Pa.,

SHAPIRO *v.* THOMPSON.

Jan. 29, 1968). See also *People ex rel. Heydenreich* v. *Lyons,* 374 Ill. 557 (1940).

In No. 813, the three-judge federal district court in Connecticut held (per Smith, CJ.)[17] that the Connecticut durational residence requirement is unconstitutional because it "has a chilling effect on the right to travel." Cf. *Dombrowski v. Pfister,* 380 U. S. 479, 487 (1965). The Court also held that the provision was a violation of the Equal Protection Clause of the Fourteenth Amendment because the denial of relief to those resident in the State for less than a year is not based on any permissible purpose, but is solely designed, as 'Connecticut states quite frankly," "to protect its fisc by discouraging entry of those who come needing relief." 270 F. Supp., at 336–337.

In No. 1138, the three-judge federal district court in the Eastern District of Pennsylvania similarly held that Pennsylvania's durational residence requirement of one year is unconstitutional. It held (per Lord, DJ.)[18] that the classification is "without rational basis and without legitimate purpose or function" and therefore a violation of the Equal Protection Clause. 277 F. Supp., at 67. The court did not rely on the right to travel although it noted that if the purpose of the statute was "to erect a barrier against the movement of indigent persons into the state or to effect their prompt departure after they have gotten there" it would be "patently improper and its implementation plainly impermissible." 277 F. Supp., at 67–68.

In No. 1134, the District of Columbia case, the three-judge federal district court (per Fahy, CJ.)[19] also placed its decision that the one-year residence requirement was unconstitutional upon the Equal Protection Clause.

---

[17] Clarie, DJ., dissenting.

[18] Kalodner, CJ., dissenting.

[19] Holtzoff, DJ., dissenting.

SHAPIRO *v.* THOMPSON.

The District of Columbia provision is, of course, congressional legislation, but the Fifth Amendment's Due Process Clause embraces equal protection requirements.[20] The court held that the distinction between one-year residents and those needing welfare payments who were residents for less than one year was not reasonably related to the welfare purposes of the statute.

In the first section of this opinion, I outlined the arguments by which the majority reached a result contrary to each of the courts below. In the state cases, it considered only the question of federal power on the ground that Congress "authorized" the States to adopt the durational residence restriction. In fact, Congress did no more than direct the Secretary of HEW to accept state plans which might include a durational requirement of not more than a specified period.[21] I believe that the courts below, in the state cases, did not err in considering the constitutionality of the restrictions from the viewpoint of the constitutional limitations upon the States. But since the restrictions is unconstitutional viewed as an exercise of either federal or state power, or of both, I shall not pursue the point.

From either viewpoint, the constitutional result depends, at bottom, upon the intended purpose and effect of the restriction, and it is first necessary that this be properly analyzed. I shall not elaborate upon the majority's holding in the state cases that Congress was justified in burdening the right of interstate travel and apparently in breaching equal protection requirements because the restriction was necessary to induce the States to cooperate in a welfare program. As I have discussed, this is obviously and clearly not a permissible purpose. I

---

[20] *Bolling* v. *Sharpe, supra; Schneider* v. *Rusk, supra.*
[21] See n. 3, *supra.*

SHAPIRO *v.* THOMPSON.

shall therefore address myself to the arguments which the majority discusses only in the District of Columbia case, but which are also essential to proper disposition of the position in the state cases.

VII.

It is first necessary to repeat that we are not here concerned with the requirement that the applicant be a resident of the jurisdiction. The issue is not raised in any of the cases. The question is whether a period of residence of one year may be specified as a condition to obtaining the welfare payments.

As I have said, it is clear that the intended effect of this provision is to deter certain types of persons from exercising their right to travel to the State and to settle there. There is no finding in any of the courts below that this provision serves any other purpose. On the contrary, the contention that such requirement permits more effective or economical administration of the residence requirement was rejected below, as was the argument that it serves an important function by permitting prediction of needs and orderly budgeting.

These arguments are palpably straws, grasped in the hope that they will keep the restrictive provision afloat. Under the applicable statutes and regulations, it is clear that the durational requirement is not an "objective" test for residence. The fact that the applicant is a resident and the length of his residence are distinct criteria. It appears that each is separately inquired into with respect to applicants.[22] For example, the HEW Handbook of Public Assistance Administration clearly distinguishes between the two. It defines residence, as is conventional,

---

[22] See Pa. Stat. Ann., Tit. 62, § 432 (6), and Pa. Welfare Manual,. §§ 3151.11 and 3152.21a. See D. C. Code, § 3–203.

SHAPIRO *v.* THOMPSON.

in terms of intent to remain in the jurisdiction,[23] and it instructs interviewers that residence and length of residence "are two distinct aspects . . . to which it is necessary to give consideration in interviews with applicants for assistance." (§ 3650.)[24]

Similarly, the argument as to budget predictability is not only trivial but largely unfounded. Prediction of the number of persons who are likely to require relief is not an exact science nor does the state fisc depend upon its exactness. The State must in any event take into account the prospective in-migration of persons present in the jurisdiction for less than a year, in order to budget sums for temporary welfare payments. It must consider the burden of reciprocal welfare payments under arrangements with other States.[25] In these circumstances, it is impossible to argue that durational residency requirements were enacted to serve the purpose of making the welfare budget more predictable.

There is no escaping the plain fact that the purpose— and the only true or substantial purpose—of the durational residence requirement is to exclude people who need relief, or who may need it, from the jurisdiction. That is the hope; that is the intended purpose. As the

---

[23] "[An applicant] shall be considered to have his residence at the place where he is living, if he is found to be living there voluntarily and not for a temporary purpose, that is with no intention of presently removing therefrom." Part IV, § 3620.

[24] See also §§ 3651 and 3652 which detail standards for these "distinct aspects."

[25] The statutes of the three jurisdictions involved here provide the welfare officials with authority to enter into such agreements. Pa. Stat. Ann., Tit. 62, § 208; D. C. Code § 3–202 (b)(4); Gen. Stat. Conn. § 17–10. In addition Connecticut has entered into an open-ended interstate compact in which it has agreed to eliminate durational residence requirement for anyone who comes from another State which has also entered into the compact. Gen. Stat. Conn. §§ 17–21a—17–21d.

SHAPIRO *v.* THOMPSON.

majority opinion states, Congress was asked to include in the Social Security Act of 1935, provisions assuring that the States would be allowed to include durational residence requirments because of "the fears of the States that the adoption of liberal categorical assistance benefits would encourage an influx of persons seeking higher welfare payments and thereby place an intolerable strain on depleted state treasuries." *Ante,* p. 14. This continues to be the argument made by States opposing repeal of the authorization See *ante,* pp. 17–18, n. 24.[26]

The jurisdictions involved here make it plain, by the words of their welfare statutes as well as by their administration, that, it is indeed the purpose to keep needy people out. The sponsor of the Connecticut durational requirement said this in support of the requirement: "I doubt that Connecticut can and should continue to allow unlimited migration into the State on the basis of offering instant money and permanent income to all who can make their way to the State regardless of their ability to contribute to the economy." HB 82 Connecticut General Assembly House Proceedings, February Special Session, 1965, Vol. II, Pt. 7, p. 3504.[27]

In Pennsylvania, shortly after the enactment of the 1937 law, the Attorney General issued an opinion construing the durational requirement strictly because "any other conclusion would tend to attract the dependents of

---

[26] The very reason which the majority invokes to support congressional authorization of the restriction—to induce state cooperation—certainly implies something weightier than administrative convenience or budgetary predictability as the reason for state insistance.

[27] The Connecticut Legislature made its desire to exclude needy newcomers apparent when it provided that temporary aid should be available only "until arrangements are made for [the] return" of the newly arrived applicant to his prior home.

SHAPIRO *v.* THOMPSON.

other states to our Commonwealth." 1937–1938 Official Opinions of the Attorney General, No. 240, 109, 110.[28]

In the District of Columbia case, the constitutionality of the statute was frankly defended in the court below and in this Court on the ground that it is designed to protect the jurisdiction from an influx of persons seeking more generous public assistance than might be available elsewhere.

This, then, is the impelling reason for these arbitrary restriction, turning as they do not on residence but on the duration of residence—one year in the cases before us. Our problem is whether these limits, in light of the purpose they serve, are constitutionally permissible. We do not consider their merits or lack thereof.

It is interesting to note that, as of 1964, 11 jurisdictions, including the migratory focus of New York State, imposed no durational residence requirement whatever for AFDC assistance.[29] New York merely denies categorical assistance to persons who come there for the purpose of obtaining it.[30]

---

[28] Although Pennsylvania will not provide welfare benefits to new residents, a welfare official testified below that the State does provide money to assist these new residents to return to their prior homes. Section 3154.12 of the Pennsylvania Welfare Manual specifically so provides.

[29] The 11 jurisdictions include eight States (Alaska, Georgia, Hawaii, Kentucky, New Jersey, New York, Rhode Island, and Vermont), and Guam, Puerto Rico, and the Virgin Islands. See Dept. of HEW, Characteristics of State Public Assistance Plans Under the Social Security Act: General Provisions (P. A. Rep. No. 50, 1964 ed.)

[30] In 1963, the Moreland Commission on Public Welfare in New York, after a lengthy study stated that "welfare aid is not a lure for people on the move." State of New York, Moreland Commission on Welfare, Public Welfare in the State of New York, 28 (1963). It expressed its opposition to durational residence requirements on the ground that "the present laws [designed to prevent abuse] are sufficient to protect the taxpayer without penalizing the unfor-

SHAPIRO *v.* THOMPSON.

The purpose and effect, then, of the restriction are clearly to exclude indigent or potentially indigent migrants or to discourage their migration into the jurisdiction. This purpose is chargeable to both the District of Columbia statute and the statutes of the States. The "inevitable effect" of these statutes is to penalize someone because he exercised his right to travel and thereby to deter his migration into the jurisdiction. See *United States* v. *O'Brien*, Slip Opinion, at 16–17. Given this purpose, and given the absence of any other substantial, constitutionally admissible reason, there is no basis as I shall discuss, for disagreement with the courts below that the durational residence requirement is unconstitutional.

VIII.

Fundamentally, the deterrent to poor people's migration from State to State that is the reason and the effect of the durational residence requirement cannot be sustained because it is a material interference with the constitutional right to travel—an interference that is not justified by any measurable or substantial reason which is constitutionally admissible.

There is no doubt that the Constitution guarantees to citizens of this Nation the right of interstate mobility. In *Guest*, this Court (per Mr. Justice Stewart) said: "The constitutional right to travel from one State to another . . . occupies a position fundamental to the con-

---

tunate." *Id.*, at 28. See also Hyde, The Trouble With Residence Laws, 16 Public Welfare 103, 105 (1958). Kasius, What Happens in a State Without Residence Requirements, in Residence Laws: Road Block to Human Welfare 19–20 (1956). A student of the New York system concluded in 1956, that "to assume that people are influenced to move according to the availability of help on a relief basis is to misunderstand the dynamics of human behavior." Kasius, at 20.

SHAPIRO *v.* THOMPSON.

cept of our Federal Union. It is a right that has been firmly established and repeatedly recognized." 383 U. S., at 757. It "has long been recognized as a basic right under the Constitution." *Id., at* 758. "Although there have been recurring differences in emphasis within the Court as to the source of the constitutional right of interstate travel . . . all have agreed that the right exists." *Id.,* at 759.

In *Zemel* v. *Rusk, supra,* at 15, this Court (per THE CHIEF JUSTICE) said: "The right to travel within the United States is of course . . . constitutionally protected." In *Kent* v. *Dulles, supra,* at 125–126, MR. JUSTICE DOUGLAS, speaking for the Court, said: It "is a part of the 'liberty' of which the citizen cannot be deprived without due process of law . . . . Freedom of movement is basic to our scheme of values." See also *United States* v. *Laub,* 385 U. S. 475, 481 (1967); *Slaughterhouse Cases,* 16 Wall. 36, 80 (1873); *Crandall* v. *Nevada,* 6 Wall. 35 (1867). Cf. *Truax* v. *Raich,* 239 U. S. 33, 42 (1915); *Takahashi* v. *Fish Commission,* 334 U. S. 410 (1948).

In his concurring opinion in *Edwards,* Mr. Justice Jackson in language which has become part of our national heritage described the right of citizens to travel, free from "state abridgment" and in particular, free from distinctions based upon poverty or affluence. He said:

"[The right to travel] is a privilege of citizenship of the United States, protected from state abridgment, to enter any state of the Union, either for temporary sojourn or for the establishment of permanent residence therein and for gaining resultant citizenship thereof. If a national citizenship means less than this, it means nothing.

"State citizenship is ephemeral. It results only from residence and is gained or lost therewith. That choice of residence was subject to local approval is

SHAPIRO *v.* THOMPSON.

contrary to the inescapable implications of the west-
ward movement of our civilization." 314 U. S., at
183.

~~Where divisions~~ are conclusive in the present case. It
is no answer to say that the durational residence requirement does not absolutely prohibit travel. As I have
discussed, the requirement of one-year residence, which
effectively penalizes the exercise of the constitutional
right to travel by depriving benefits to applicants simply
on the basis that they have recently exercise the right,
serves no substantial purpose other than to burden, deter,
and chill the right to travel of the persons at whom it
is aimed. In these circumstances, the requirement that
any burden on the right to travel must conform with due
process requirements is not met. *Kent* v. *Dulles, supra.*
And it is settled that, as we recently stated in *United
States* v. *Jackson,* —— U. S. ——, if a law has "no other
purpose or effect than to chill the assertion of constitutional rights by penalizing those who choose to exercise them, then it would be patently unconstitutional."
Id., at ——. See also *Dombrowski* v. *Pfister,* 380 U. S.
479, 487 (1965); *Speiser* v. *Randall,* 357 U. S. 513 (1958);
Gardner v. *Broderick, ante,* at ——; *Uniformed Sanitation
Men* v. *Commissioner of Sanitation, ante,* at ——; *Griffin*
v. *California,* 380 U. S. 609 (1965).

It is impossible to read this Court's opinions relating
to the right to travel and to settle in States of one's
choice without concluding that it is established as a
right of "fundamental" or "basic" importance in our
constitutional scheme. This being so, this Court's decision in *Sherbert* v. *Verner,* 374 U. S. 398 (1963), is
in point for the present cases. There, the State of South
Carolina denied appellant unemployment compensation
because she failed to accept "available suitable work"
within the meaning of the state unemployment compensation statute. The reason appellant refused this em-

SHAPIRO *v.* THOMPSON.

ployment was because it required her to work on Saturdays in violation of her religious principles. As in the present cases, the State denied appellant's statutory right to a social security payment because she had exercised a constitutional right. We said:

> "Not only is it apparent that appellant's declared ineligibility for benefits derives solely from the practice of her religion, but the pressure upon her to forego that practice is unmistakable. The ruling forces her to choose between following the precepts of her religion and forfeiting benefits, on the one hand, and abandoning one of the precepts of her religion in order to accept work, on the other hand. Governmental imposition of such a choice puts the same kind of burden upon the free exercise of religion as would a fine imposed against appellant for her Saturday worship.
>
> "Nor may the South Carolina court's construction of the statute be saved from constitutional infirmity on the ground that unemployment compensation benefits are not appellant's 'right' but merely a 'privilege.' It is too late in the day to doubt that the liberties of religion and expression may be infringed by the denial of or placing of conditions upon a benefit or privilege. . . . To condition the availability of benefits upon this appellant's willingness to violate a cardinal principle of her religious faith effectively penalizes the free exercise of her constitutional liberties." 374 U. S., at 404, 406.

And in response to South Carolina's claim that its law was justified because it had legitimate purposes other than the infringement of free exercise of religion, this Court said:

> "It is basic that no showing merely of a rational relationship to some colorable state interest would suffice; in this highly sensitive constitutional area,

SHAPIRO *v.* THOMPSON.

'only the gravest abuses, endangering paramount interests, give occasion for permissible limitation . . . .' " *Id.,* at 406.

See also *Speiser* v. *Randall,* 357 U. S. 513 (1958).

Certainly, "in this highly sensitive constitutional area" of interstate mobility, which is basic to ideas of a *federal* union, only the gravest and weightiest purpose would justify the imposition of the deterrent embraced in the legislation before us. The justifications advanced, other than the mere assertion of the right to deny equal welfare payments to the poor in order to save money, are relatively trivial; nor is it arguable that these purposes—identification of "residents" and "budgetary predictability"—could not be adequately served by other means than a burden upon the right to travel. As to the ascertainment if whether the applicant is a "resident," the techniques are well-known and are commonly and effectively used. They are described in the HEW Handbook [31] which is in general use. Cf. *Carrington* v. *Rash,* 380 U. S. 89, 95 (1965); *Haman* v. *Forenssius,* 380 U. S. 528, 542–43 (1965); *Rinaldi* v. *Yeager,* 384 U. S. 305, 310 (1966). As to the asserted function of "budgetary predictability," it cannot be seriously asserted that reasonably accurate estimates cannot be made whether or not the one-year residence requirement is in effect. The testimony of the Director of the Bureau of Asssitance Policies and Standards in the Pennsylvania Office of Public Assistance in No. 1138 bears witness to this.[32]

It is clear not only that "some remote administrative benefit" will not suffice to support a ~~broader or~~ an im-

---

[31] Part IV, § 3651.

[32] She testified that, based on experience in Pennsylvania and elsewhere, her office had already estimated how much the elimination of the durational requirement would cost and that the estimates of costs of other changes in regulations "have proven exceptionally accurate."

SHAPIRO *v.* THOMPSON.

portant constitutional right, but that even if the permissible purpose were substantial, it would not be
constitutionally adequate if there were "less drastic"
alternative means to secure the same purpose. This
Court so held in a right to travel case. In *Aptheker* v.
Secretary, supra, the Court said, quoting from *Shelton* v.
Tucker, 364 U. S. 479, 488 (1960):

> "Even though the governmental purpose be legiti-
> mate and substantial, that purpose cannot be pur-
> sued by means that broadly stifle personal liberties
> when the end can be more narrowly achieved. The
> breadth of legislative abridgment must be viewed in
> the light of less drastic means for achieving the same
> purpose." 378 U. S., at 508.

The Court struck down the congressional statute involved
in that case because "the section, judged by its plain
import and by the substantive evil which Congress sought
to control sweeps too widely and too indiscriminately
across the liberty guaranteed in the Fifth Amendment."
378 U. S., at 514.

This principle was reiterated in another right-to-travel
case. In *Zemel* v. *Rusk, supra,* after re-emphasizing
that the right to travel was part of the liberty protected
by the Due Process Clause of the Fifth Amendment, we
said, "The requirements of due process are a function
not only of the extent of the governmental restriction
imposed, but also of the extent of the necessity for the
restriction." 381 U. S., at 14.

The same principle was applied in a voting rights case.
In *Carrington* v. *Rash, supra,* this Court struck down a
Texas law which prevented a member of the Armed
Forces who moved to Texas during the course of his
military duty from voting in Texas as long as he remained in the Army. In justification, Texas asserted,
inter alia, that it was reasonable to assume that military
people were transients. Membership in the Armed

SHAPIRO *v.* THOMPSON.

Forces was, in this way, adopted as an "objective" test for bona fide residence. This Court would not accept that justification. "We deal here with matters close to the core of our constitutional system. . . . [The right to vote] means, at least, that States may not casually deprive a class of individuals of the vote because of some remote administrative benefit to the State. *Oyama* v. *California*, 322 U. S. 633." 380 U. S., at 95–96.[33]

Accordingly, the durational residence requirement is unconstitutional as an impermissible and unjustified burden on the right to travel. This is so whether the burden is imposed by state or by federal authority.

IX.

The courts below also invalidated the durational residence requirement because it denies the equal protection of the law. Each of them held that a statutory provision which refuses welfare payments to persons who have

---

[33] It is true that in *Carrington* the Court said Texas had "power to impose reasonable residence restrictions on the availability of the ballot." 380 U. S., at 91. Durational requirements for voting, however, are quite different from the durational requirements before us today. Neither their purpose nor their effect is to discourage exercise of the right to travel. The loss of a vote for a period of time has much less immediate impact on an individual than does the loss of welfare benefits which may be the only means for the welfare applicant's survival. Also, durational requirements for voting have a haphazard impact on individuals who move from one jurisdiction to another. Depending upon the time of the move and the time of the next election, an individual who changes residence may not be affected at all. There are justifications for the voting regulations which do not apply here. See *Pope* v. *Williams*, 193 U. S. 631 (1904); *Dreuding* v. *Devlin*, 234 F. Supp. 721 (D. C. D. Md. 1964), aff'd 380 U. S. 125 (1965). With respect to other durational requirements imposed for various purposes, it is sufficient to say that none has been cited which involves the direct, substantial discouragement to interstate travel and migration that is involved in the present cases.

SHAPIRO *v.* THOMPSON.

been resident in the State for less than one year, and gives such payments to others, is a denial of equal protection of the laws to the former in violation of the Fourteenth Amendment. Each of the courts was unable to find a reasonable basis or purpose for the distinction between the two groups except the constitutionally impermissible purpose of deterring poor people from moving to the jurisdiction. This, they held, offends the Constitution. I agree.

In a line of cases from *Griffin* v. *Illinois*, 351 U. S. 12 (1956), to *Harper* v. *Board of Elections*, 383 U. S. 663 (1966), this Court has repudiated statutes which make distinctions in important rights on the basis of poverty. See also, *e. g., Douglas* v. *California*, 372 U. S. 353 (1963); *Smith* v. *Bennett*, 365 U. S. 708 (1961); *Burns* v. *Ohio*, 360 U. S. 252 (1959). In *Griffin* and *Harper*, the Court struck down laws, neutral on their face, which had the effect of depriving poor people of important, though not constitutional, rights.[34] Here the statutes, by direct specific provision, penalize and burden a constitutional right. Here the statutes are not "neutral" in any sense. Congress and the States have discriminated "between 'rich' and 'poor' *as such.*" *Douglas* v. *California*, 372 U. S., at 361 (emphasis in the original) (dissenting opinion). And whatever is the disagreement concerning the laws involved in *Griffin* and *Harper*, there can be no doubt that "discrimination against 'indigents' by name [is] unconstitutional." *Griffin* v. *Illinois*, 351 U. S., at

---

[34] In *Griffin*, the Court specifically said there was no constitutional right to appellate review. 351 U. S., at 18. Similarly in *Harper*, the Court said that the right to vote in state elections is "nowhere expressly mentioned" in the Federal Constitution. And we did not deal with appellant's argument there that the right to vote was implicit in the Constitution. 383 U. S., at 665.

SHAPIRO *v.* THOMPSON.

35 (dissenting opinion).   Cf. *Griswold* v. *Connecticut,*
381 U. S. 479, 503 (1965) (concurring opinion).

Again, I turn to Justice Jackson's concurring opinion
in *Edwards* v. *California* for an eloquent statement of
the principle.   He said:

> "Any measure which would divide our citizenry on
> the basis of property into one class free to move
> from state to state and another class that is poverty-
> bound to the place where it has suffered misfortune
> is not only at war with the habit and custom by
> which our country has expanded, but is also a short-
> sighted blow at the security of property itself.
> Property can have no more dangerous, even if un-
> witting, enemy than one who would make its posses-
> sion a pretext for unequal or exclusive civil rights.
> Where those rights are derived from national citizen-
> ship no state may impose such a test, and whether
> the Congress could do so we are not called upon to
> inquire." 314 U. S., at 185.

If we consider the problem before us from the viewpoint of federal power, it is equally clear that the durational residence requirement must fall because of the
invidious discriminations against, on the one hand, poor
persons who might desire to travel and settle in the jurisdiction and those resident in the jurisdiction for less
than a year, and, on the other hand, persons of means
who wish to migrate and poor persons resident for more
than a year.   In terms of federal power, these discriminations violate the Due Process Clause of the Fifth Amendment.   That clause, like the express provision of the
Fourteenth Amendment, insists upon reasonable defensible ~~clarifications~~ and denies governmental power otherwise to distinguish between the treatment accorded
citizens.   "[W]hile the Fifth Amendment contains no
equal protection clause, it does forbid discrimination that

SHAPIRO *v.* THOMPSON.

is 'so unjustifiable as to be violative of due process.' "
Schneider v. *Rusk, supra,* at 168; *Bolling* v. *Sharpe, supra.*
Certainly it cannot be doubted that Congress may not
constitutionally deny equal treatment to two groups of
citizens based upon poverty or affluence.

Accordingly, I believe that the decisions below should
be affirmed.

In both the Warren draft opinion of the Court and the Fortas draft dissent, the rational-basis test was used as the governing review criterion for deciding *Shapiro* v. *Thompson*. Had the Warren and Fortas opinions come down as the principal opinions in the case, it would have made a substantial difference in the law. The strict scrutiny that has become so important might never have become widely established in constitutional jurisprudence.

As it turned out, neither the Warren opinion of the Court nor the Fortas dissent was delivered in *Shapiro* v. *Thompson*. After he had read the Fortas dissent (which had been shown to him even before it was circulated), Justice Brennan told Justice Fortas that he was joining his opinion. At the next conference, on June 13, Justice Stewart refused to cast a vote. With Justice Brennan's switch, that made for a four-to-four division. It was now almost the end of the term and it was decided to set the case for reargument in the coming 1968 term. An order to that effect was issued on June 17, the last day of the 1967 term.[4]

At the reargument, on October 23, 1968, Professor Archibald Cox made what one of the Justices has termed "an impressive presentation for the appellees." Justice Stewart, for one, was strongly influenced by the Cox argument. At the October 25 conference after the reargument, Justice Stewart indicated that he was now in favor of affirmance. The new vote was five (Justices Douglas, Brennan, Stewart, Fortas, and Marshall) to three (Chief Justice Warren and Justices Black and Harlan) to strike down the residence requirement, with Justice White passing. Justice Brennan was now assigned the opinion. Despite the closeness of the vote, he wrote a broad opinion expanding the scope of judicial review in equal protection cases. Justice Brennan's draft, circulated early in November, 1968, adopted the compelling-interest test as the governing review criterion. Justice Brennan wrote that, since the classification between new and old residents served to penalize the exercise of the fundamental right to interstate travel, it had to be justified by a *compelling* governmental interest. Chief Justice Warren, in his draft majority opinion of the previous June, had specifically refused to apply the compelling-interest standard, holding instead that the traditional rational-basis test was all that had to be met.

Justice Brennan had begun to think along the lines of his *Shapiro* v. *Thompson* opinion when he had read Justice Fortas's draft dissent the previous June. This is shown by marginal comments he made on his copy of the Fortas draft. In his draft, Justice Fortas notes, "The majority then seems to recognize . . . that this interference with the 'basic' or 'fundamental' right to travel operates only on the poor."[5] Justice Brennan underlined the latter part of this passage and wrote next to it *"compelling."* This indicates that the Justice had begun to think of the compelling-interest test as the governing criterion on review of governmental action restricting "basic" or "fundamental" rights.

This indication is confirmed by Justice Brennan's marginal note on the following statement in the Fortas draft: "It is impossible to read the Court's opinions relating to the right to travel and to settle in States of one's choice without concluding that it is established as a right of 'fundamental' or 'basic' importance in our constitutional scheme."[6] Next to this Justice Brennan wrote, "It is only for 'compelling' reasons."

The Brennan marginal comments show that the Justice had not only concluded that his original conference vote for reversal was wrong, but that he had decided that the residence requirement should be subject to review under the compelling-interest standard. Justice Brennan then changed his vote and joined the Fortas draft dissent. That led to reargument when Justice Stewart indicated, at the June 13 conference, that he was now on the fence. Then, when he was given the opportunity to write the new majority opinion for affirmance, Justice Brennan wrote his draft incorporating the compelling-interest test as a major component of equal protection review.

Justice Brennan had previously asserted the compelling-interest test as the governing criterion in First Amendment cases. In the 1963 case of *National Association for the Advancement of Colored People* v. *Button*,[7] the Brennan opinion of the Court stated that "only a compelling state interest in the regulation of a subject within the State's power to regulate can justify limiting First Amendment freedoms."[8] In the 1968 case of *United States* v. *O'Brien*,[9] Justice Brennan had tried to induce Chief Justice Warren to accept the same test in his opinion of the Court, but the Chief Justice had refused.[10] Now Justice Brennan was able to secure a much more important acceptance of the compelling-interest test in his *Shapiro* v. *Thompson* opinion of the Court.

Despite the fact that that aspect of the case had not been discussed at the conference or in the previous draft opinions in the case, Justice Brennan's broad opinion applying the compelling-interest standard won speedy agreement from Justices Douglas, Marshall, Fortas, and Stewart. It is true that Justice Stewart had second thoughts about the compelling-interest analysis.[11] He told Justice Brennan that the case should be decided on the traditional rational-basis test of equal protection. Within a few days, however, Justice Stewart had reconsidered and said to Justice Brennan that his insistence on the traditional equal protection standard had been mistaken. Justice Stewart now agreed that the compelling-interest analysis was appropriate here because the right of interstate travel was a constitutional right.

After Justice Harlan sent around a draft dissent in early January 1969, substantially similar to his final dissent in the case, Justice White, who had passed at the October 25, 1968, conference and had not been heard from since, joined Justice Brennan's opinion. That made six votes for the Brennan opinion of the Court. Chief Justice Warren, joined by Justice Black, issued a dissent that was an abbreviated version of the draft opinion of the Court he had prepared the previous June. It refused to accept the compelling-interest approach on which Justice Brennan's majority opinion was based. Since Justice Harlan also issued his dissent, the final vote in *Shapiro* v. *Thompson* was six to three.

On June 19, 1968, Chief Justice Warren had circulated a copy of a memorandum which one of his law clerks had "prepared for me in connection with the welfare residence cases."[12] The clerk's memorandum[13] had stressed that the decision in the case "ultimately will turn on what test of validity is applied to durational residence requirements as they affect the right to travel." If a strict test is applied, it "holds the government to a heavy burden of justification and would probably require that durational residence tests be declared invalid if it prevails." Then, referring to the Chief Justice's draft opinion of the Court, the memorandum notes, "Your opinion adopted essentially a balancing approach and concluded that the burden on interstate movement was justified by the importance of the congressional purpose in authorizing such a burden. If your approach prevails, I have no doubt that your conclusion that durational residence tests are valid is correct."

The memorandum's conclusion that "the result in [the] case turns on the test of validity to be applied" is essential to an understanding of the impact of *Shapiro* v. *Thompson*. Justice Holmes once characterized the Equal Protection Clause as "the usual last resort of constitutional arguments."[14] That was true because prior to *Shapiro* v. *Thompson* judicial scrutiny of governmental action challenged on equal protection grounds was normally governed by the traditional rational-basis test. Since it is the rare law that is based upon classification without any rational basis, this meant that very few equal protection challenges could succeed. As Justice Marshall more recently put it, "[T]he mere rationality test . . . , when applied as articulated, leaves little doubt about the outcome: the challenged legislation is always upheld."[15]

Under *Shapiro* v. *Thompson*, the test of mere rationality gives way to one of strict scrutiny under which a challenged law will be held to deny equal protection unless justified by a "compelling" governmental interest.[16] Since *Shapiro* v. *Thompson*, judicial review under the Equal Protection Clause has taken place primarily within a two-tier framework, with two principal modes of analysis: strict scrutiny and mere rationality. The upper tier is narrowly limited,[17] applying only to legislation that invades a fundamental right or discriminates against a suspect class and is subject to strict scrutiny under the compelling-interest test. All remaining legislation drops into the bottom tier and is measured by the rational-basis test.[18]

The two-tier framework is now of fundamental importance in equal protection cases. The tier in which legislation is placed all but determines the outcome of equal protection challenges. As already seen, challenged legislation is virtually always upheld under the mere-rationality test, since a law is almost never based upon classification without any rational basis. The converse is true under the compelling-interest test: If a statute is subject to strict scrutiny, it is nearly always struck down.[19]

The difference in result as between the two tiers is shown by *Massachusetts Retirement Board* v. *Murgia*,[20] where a law requiring the mandatory retirement of state policemen at age fifty was subjected to equal protection challenge. If strict scrutiny was the governing review standard, the Court would have had difficulty in upholding the law. As the dissenting opinion points out, the retirement requirement is so overinclusive that it could not pass the compelling-interest test. But the Court held that strict scrutiny was not appropriate, since the right of governmental employment was not a fundamental right and the elderly did not constitute a suspect class for purposes of equal protection analysis. The appropriate standard was thus that of rational basis, which the law clearly met, since the state's classification rationally furthered the purpose identified by the state: to protect the public by assuring physical preparedness of its uniformed officers.

It is true that *Shapiro* v. *Thompson* was not the first case in which the compelling-interest test was applied. But, in Justice Brennan's opinion there, the " 'compelling interest' doctrine . . . is articulated more explicitly than ever before."[21] Before *Shapiro* v. *Thompson*, there were a few cases which indicated that stricter scrutiny than that provided under the rational-basis test might sometimes be required. The starting point was the statement in *Korematsu* v. *United States*[22] that "all legal restrictions which curtail the civil rights of a single racial group are immediately suspect. . . . courts must subject them to the most rigid scrutiny."[23] Ironically, *Korematsu* was the one case in which a discriminatory racial classification survived Court scrutiny.[24] But the notion of race as a "suspect" classification, subject to strict scrutiny, was implanted in equal protection jurisprudence and has not since been challenged. Even Justice Harlan, who delivered a strong dissent in *Shapiro* v. *Thompson*, conceded "that this branch of the 'compelling interest' doctrine is sound when applied to racial classification."[25]

In *Skinner* v. *Oklahoma*,[26] the Court struck down a state law providing for compulsory sterilization of "habitual criminals." The opinion stated that the law was subject to "strict scrutiny" because "We are dealing here with legislation which involves one of the basic civil rights of man. Marriage and procreation are fundamental [rights]."[27] In the Warren Court, this *Skinner* approach was applied to the "fundamental" right of suffrage.[28] As the Court expressed it in a case in which a poll tax was invalidated, "We have long been mindful that where fundamental rights and liberties are asserted under the Equal Protection Clause, classifications which might invade or restrain them must be closely scrutinized and carefully confined."[29]

Shapiro v. *Thompson* makes specific the tie-in between fundamental rights and the compelling-interest test. The Brennan opinion of the Court expressly rejects the argument that a mere showing of the rational relationship between the residence requirement and permissible governmental objectives will suffice to justify the requirement.[30] Instead, Justice Brennan stresses that the state requirement restricted "the fundamental right of interstate movement. . . . and any classification which serves to penalize the exercise of that right, unless shown to be necessary to promote a *compelling* governmental interest, is unconstitutional."[31]

Shapiro v. *Thompson* lays the doctrinal base for the rule that classifications which burden fundamental rights deny equal protection unless they are supported by a *compelling* governmental interest. This expands the scope of equal protection review far beyond that previously permitted.[32] As Justice Harlan stated in his *Shapiro* v. *Thompson* dissent, the opinion of the Court "creates an exception which threatens to swallow the standard equal protection rule. Virtually every statute affects important rights. . . . to extend the 'compelling interest' rule to all cases in which such rights are affected would go far toward making this Court a 'super-legislature.' "[33]

In the Burger Court, the *Shapiro* v. *Thompson* approach has become established doctrine. It has been applied to a wide range of rights deemed fundamental: the rights guaranteed by the First Amendment,[34] the right to vote,[35] the right to marry,[36] and the right of women to control their own bodies, including the right to terminate pregnancies.[37]

Particularly significant in this respect was the decision in *Roe* v. *Wade*,[38] the last of the cases to which reference has just been made. In striking down state abortion laws as an invalid infringement of the pregnant woman's right to decide whether or not to terminate her pregnancy, the Court applied the compelling-interest test. "Where certain 'fundamental rights' are involved . . . ," states Justice Blackmun's opinion, "regulation limiting these rights may be justified only by a 'compelling state interest.' "[39] The state's determination to recognize prenatal life was held not to constitute a compelling state interest, at least during the first trimester of pregnancy.

What is significant here is that *Roe* v. *Wade* was a due process, not an equal protection, case. What Madison once said of power—that it is of an encroaching nature[40]—has also proved true of the compelling-interest test. As used in *Roe* v. *Wade*, the test makes for an expansion of due process review that has been characterized as a revival of substantive due process doctrine[41] as it had been applied in supposedly discredited cases such as *Lochner* v. *New York*.[42]

> As in *Lochner* and similar cases applying substantive due process standards to economic and social welfare legislation, the adoption of the compelling interest standard will inevitably require this Court to examine the legislative policies and pass on the wisdom of these policies in the very process of deciding whether a particular state interest put forward may or may not be "compelling."[43]

It may be doubted that the expansion of review power under the compelling-interest test—both in equal protection and due process cases—would have occurred in the Burger Court had *Shapiro* v. *Thompson* not

laid the doctrinal foundation. From this point of view, it was of fundamental importance that the draft opinion of the Court by Chief Justice
Warren did not come down as the final opinion in the case. If it had, the
rational-basis test would have been confirmed as the standard of review in
equal protection cases in a case where the fundamental right of interstate
movement was involved. The compelling-interest test would not have
become "an increasingly significant exception to the long-established rule
that a statute does not deny equal protection if it is rationally related to a
legitimate governmental objective."[44] Nor would the test have encroached
upon the due process area as it did in *Roe* v. *Wade*. Some of the most
controversial Court decisions of the past decade and a half might never
have been made.

Notes

1. 394 U.S. 618 (1969).
2. 36 *U.S. Law Week* 3423 (1968).
3. See Schwartz, *Super Chief: Earl Warren and His Supreme Court—A Judi-cial Biography* 25 (1983).
4. 392 U.S. 920 (1968).
5. Supra p. 360.
6. Supra p. 379.
7. 371 U.S. 415 (1963).
8. Id. at 438.
9. 391 U.S. 367 (1968).
10. See Schwartz, op. cit. supra note 3, at 684.
11. See id. at 728–729.
12. EW, *Memorandum for the Conference*, June 19, 1968. JMHP.
13. CHW, *Memorandum to the Chief Justice, Re: Welfare Residence Cases* (Nos. 813, 1134 & 1138, 1967 Term), June 18, 1968. JMHP.
14. *Buck* v. *Bell*, 274 U.S. 200, 208 (1927).
15. Dissenting, in *Massachusetts Board of Retirement* v. *Murgia*, 427 U.S. 307, 319 (1976).
16. See Harlan, J., dissenting, in *Shapiro* v. *Thompson*, 394 U.S. at 658.
17. Powell, J., concurring, in *Craig* v. *Boren*, 429 U.S. 190, 211 (1976).
18. Marshall, J., dissenting, in *Massachusetts Board of Retirement* v. *Murgia*, 427 U.S. 307, 319 (1976). The Court has also developed what may now be a third tier, involving an intermediate level of judicial scrutiny—e.g., in cases involving classifications by gender or legitimacy. See *Craig* v. *Boren*, 429 U.S. 190 (1976); *Trimble* v. *Gordon*, 430 U.S. 762 (1977).
19. Marshall, J., dissenting, in *Massachusetts Board of Retirement* v. *Murgia*, 427 U.S. 307, 319 (1976).
20. 427 U.S. 307 (1976).
21. Harlan, J., dissenting, in *Shapiro* v. *Thompson*, 394 U.S. at 658.
22. 323 U.S. 214 (1944).
23. Id. at 216.
24. Compare Gunther, *Cases and Materials on Constitutional Law* 745 (10th ed. 1980).

25. 394 U.S. at 659.
26. 316 U.S. 535 (1942).
27. Id. at 541.
28. See *Reynolds* v. *Sims*, 377 U.S. 533, 561–562 (1964).
29. *Harper* v. *Virginia Board of Elections*, 383 U.S. 663, 670 (1966).
30. 394 U.S. at 634.
31. Id. at 638, 634 (emphasis in original).
32. See Harlan, J., dissenting, id. at 655.
33. Id. at 661.
34. See *Buckley* v. *Valeo*, 424 U.S. 1, 93–94 (1976).
35. *Bullock* v. *Carter*, 405 U.S. 134 (1972).
36. *Zablocki* v. *Redhail*, 434 U.S. 374 (1978).
37. *Roe* v. *Wade*, 410 U.S. 113 (1973).
38. 410 U.S. 113 (1973).
39. Id. at 155.
40. *The Federalist*, No. 48.
41. Gunther, op. cit. supra note 24, at 570.
42. 198 U.S. 45 (1905).
43. Rehnquist, J., dissenting, in *Roe* v. *Wade*, 410 U.S. at 174.
44. Harlan, J., dissenting, in *Shapiro* v. *Thompson*, 394 U.S. at 658.

10

Maxwell v. *Bishop* *(1969)*: *The Death Penalty in the Warren Court*

A few years ago, *The Brethren*[1] revealed that the Warren Court, in *Maxwell* v. *Bishop*,[2] had come close to striking down the Arkansas death penalty law during the Chief Justice's last term. *The Brethren* account of what happened behind the scenes in that case is, however, incomplete and inaccurate. The true story of *Maxwell* v. *Bishop* is more revealing both in what it tells us about the internal operation of the Supreme Court and how a case becomes a legal landmark manqué.

Maxwell was a black who had been convicted of raping a white woman, a crime that Arkansas made punishable by death. The jury was given the right to return a verdict of life imprisonment in capital cases. Maxwell's jury had imposed the death penalty. The trial was a unitary trial, with the same jury deciding the issues of guilt and punishment and rendering a verdict on each at the same time. In addition, no standards were provided to guide the jury in deciding whether the death penalty should be imposed. The highest state court affirmed the conviction and sentence. The Chief Justice and Justices Brennan, Stewart, White, Fortas, and Marshall voted to grant certiorari.

In the Supreme Court, Maxwell challenged the Arkansas law's provision for a unitary trial, as well as its failure to provide standards. There was no challenge to the constitutionality of the death penalty as such. It was, indeed, not until the 1972 case of *Furman* v. *Georgia*[3] that such a challenge was made. Before then, the death penalty was never considered an index of the constitutional limit on punishment;[4] on virtually every occasion that any opinion touched on the question of the constitutionality of the death penalty, it was asserted affirmatively, or tacitly assumed, that the Constitution does not prohibit the penalty.[5]

In the Warren Court, however, there was an effort by Justice Goldberg to have the death penalty invalidated as cruel and unusual punishment. During the 1963 term, at least six capital cases were presented to the Court.[6] In none of them was the issue of the constitutionality of the death penalty as such raised, neither in the lower courts nor in the Supreme Court. Despite this, Justice Goldberg circulated a printed *Memorandum to the Conference From Mr. Justice Goldberg. Re: Capital Punishment.* In it, the Justice informed his colleagues that in the conference discussion of the cases (involving two convictions for murder, two for felony murder, and two for rape), he would raise the issue "Whether, and under what circumstances, the imposition of the death penalty is proscribed by the Eighth and Fourteenth Amendments to the United States Constitution."

The Goldberg memorandum is virtually the draft of an opinion striking down the death penalty as cruel and unusual punishment nine years before any published opinions were issued on the subject.[7] As such, it deserves inclusion in this volume. It is reprinted on page 401, with the exception of its first section, headed "Background." That section, consisting of a little over eight pages, discusses the previous cases raising the Eighth Amendment issue, both in those involving the death penalty and other cases.

Justice Goldberg draws his theme from the Chief Justice's statement in *Trop* v. *Dulles*[8] that the Eighth Amendment "must draw its meaning from the evolving standards of decency that mark the progress of a maturing society." The Goldberg memorandum asserts that the "evolving standards of decency" in our society "now condemn as barbaric and inhuman the deliberate institutionalized taking of human life by the state." Even if public opinion does not go that far, in cases such as these "this Court traditionally has guided rather than followed public opinion in the process of articulating and establishing progressively civilized standards of decency."

In addition, the Goldberg memorandum contends, the death penalty is cruel and unusual since "a less severe one can as effectively achieve the permissible ends of punishment." The Justice concludes that "since there is no persuasive evidence that capital punishment uniquely deters capital crime, and since doubts should be resolved against the death penalty, this penalty runs afoul of the . . . test which proscribes punishments unnecessarily severe in relation to the permissible goals of punishment."

The Goldberg memorandum concedes, "I recognize that my Brethren may not agree with . . . my view that capital punishment, as such, is unconstitutional." At the conference, Justice Goldberg received no support for his motion that "this Court should now request argument and explicitly consider this constantly recurring issue."[9] In fact, several of the Justices had been shocked at Justice Goldberg's raising of the issue. After the memorandum was circulated (during the long vacation before the beginning of the 1963 term), Justice Harlan came to see Justice Goldberg and complained that if the Goldberg memorandum were acted upon, any Justice could raise an issue on his own motion at any time and set aside established doctrine. At the conference itself, a dominant theme was that no lawyer had ever even raised the issue that Justice Goldberg had posed.

When Justice Goldberg saw that he had no support at the conference, he did not persist in his motion. Though his memorandum could easily have served as a dissenting opinion, he decided not to issue any dissent. He feared that a published eight-to-one decision on the Eighth Amendment issue would only serve to legitimate the death penalty.

Instead, Justice Goldberg fell back to the position stated in the last part of his memorandum, that infliction of the death penalty for sexual crimes such as rape, which do not endanger life, violated the Eighth Amendment. Justices Douglas and Brennan supported Justice Goldberg on this point. When the others refused to go along and declined, in *Rudolph* v. *Alabama*,[10] to grant certiorari to determine whether the death penalty for rape was constitutional, Justice Goldberg, joined by Justices Douglas and Brennan, dissented. The dissent urged that the Court should consider whether the Eighth Amendment "permits the imposition of the death penalty on a convicted rapist who has neither taken nor endangered human life."[11] The questions posed in this short Goldberg dissent are those raised and discussed in the Justice's memorandum, reprinted on page 401.

Justice Goldberg wrote his brief *Rudolph* dissent the way he did to start the process of professional and judicial inquiry into the constitutionality of the death penalty. Above all, the dissent was intended as a "signal to the Bar," to alert the Bar that it was worthwhile to raise the issue. The "signal" approach bore fruit in *Furman* v. *Georgia*[12] and *Gregg* v. *Georgia*.[13] Although the Goldberg view on the broad constitutional issue was ultimately rejected by the Court, the *Furman* and *Gregg* dissents by Justices Brennan and Marshall were only more elaborate versions of Justice Goldberg's 1963 memorandum.

By the time *Maxwell* v. *Bishop* came before the conference, Justice Goldberg had resigned from the Court and no Justice raised the issue of the constitutionality of the death penalty as such. The *Maxwell* conference discussion was confined to the issues raised by Maxwell—namely, the constitutionality of the Arkansas unitary trial and the failure to provide standards to guide the jury.

At the first *Maxwell* conference, the vote was eight to one to reverse, with only Justice Black for affirmance. Various views were expressed by the majority Justices, but it was not clear that there were five votes for any rationale. The next day, Justice Harlan wrote the Chief Justice that he was having second thoughts "on my yesterday's vote to reverse this case on the basis of the 'split-trial' issue." Justice Harlan suggested "relisting the case for further discussion at the next Conference, before the case is assigned."[14] Justice Douglas summarized the conference discussion in an April 4, 1969, *Memorandum to the Conference*: "As I recall, there never were more than four votes to hold that standards for the imposition of the death penalty were constitutionally necessary. There was finally, however, a majority vote holding that a bifurcated trial was constitutionally required. But those who made up the majority include perhaps one who felt that standards were not required."

According to the Douglas memo, "The Conference discussions of the case were not very conclusive or illuminating."[15] By the end of the second conference, however, each Justice's position had become clear. The Chief Justice declared, "The jury cannot be given an absolute right to say death without standards to guide them." As he saw it, that made for arbitrary justice that discriminated against the poor: "Death seems to be allowed usually for the poor and underprivileged—rarely does one who can afford a lawyer suffer the death penalty." The Chief Justice was supported on the standards issue by Justices Douglas and Brennan. The same three, as well as Justices Fortas and Marshall, also thought that a bifurcated trial (with a *separate* hearing on sentencing) was constitutionally required.

Justice Harlan said that, though he had not completely made up his mind, he was certain that he could not "go along on standards." If the Warren view were to be followed, "where do we stop as to standards? Won't we be in the business of second guessing?" On the bifurcation issue Justice Harlan said, "I do have trouble with the split trial in light of the burden on the privilege against self-incrimination. He's got a tough choice to make on whether to take the stand." The Justice concluded that he tended to believe that due process required a bifurcated trial.

Justices White and Stewart wanted to dispose of the case under the rule laid down the previous term in *Witherspoon* v. *Illinois*[16]—that is, that a conviction must be reversed where those opposed to the death penalty are automatically excluded from the jury. Justices White and Stewart urged the *Witherspoon* ground even though the issue had not been raised by petitioner and the grant of certiorari had been limited to the bifurcation and standards questions. Justice Black still voted to affirm.

The *Maxwell* opinion was assigned to Justice Douglas. On April 4, 1969, he circulated the draft opinion of the Court reprinted on page 412. As usual, the Douglas draft was prepared quickly. The April 4 memorandum transmitting the draft to the conference states, "I am now circulating [it] because I did not want to wait any longer, as the hour is already late in the present Term."

As noted, the conference was divided on whether the case should be reversed because of the failure to have a bifurcated trial, the failure to have standards, or both. The Douglas memo indicates that the Justice's draft opinion relies on both failures, saying, "As I got deeper into the two problems they became inseparable to me."

Accordingly, the Douglas draft opinion of the Court reverses on both the bifurcation and standards grounds. The unitary trial, writes Douglas, compelled defendant to forego his privilege against self-incrimination by taking the stand to make his case on punishment. As the draft explains, "This privilege against self-incrimination may be important. Yet if the

defendant is to escape death, his testimony may be essential." The same
was true, Douglas asserts, of defendant's right to testify.

> It may be that only by presenting his mitigating evidence may an ac-
> cused make an impact on the jury's determination of the penalty. Yet he
> may not dare exercise his right of allocution at the unitary trial, lest he
> suffer irreparable harm on the guilt issue. He thus purchases a fair trial
> on the issue of guilt at the cost of sacrificing his right to a fair trial on the
> issue of punishment.

The Douglas draft also rules the Arkansas law invalid for lack of
standards. "Under Arkansas law those who should receive death and
those who should not are undefined." Standards to guide the sentencing
jury are constitutionally required; the state "must provide 'legally fixed
standards' lest the law become capricious." Where that is not done, due
process is violated.

> Where there are no guidelines or relevant evidence one jury may decide
> that one defendant is not "fit to live" . . . because he is a black who
> raped a white woman, while another defendant is "fit to live" because he is
> a white who raped a black. Or whatever the race of the defendant one
> jury may be seized by the spirit of the mob, while another, dealing with
> the same quality of offense, may be more reasoned and compassionate.

On April 9, Justice Stewart circulated the separate opinion reprinted
on page 424. It would vacate the decision below on the *Witherspoon*
ground already mentioned, since "It appears clear from even a cursory
look at the trial record that several prospective jurors were removed from
the panel upon grounds held impermissible in the *Witherspoon* case."
The Stewart draft on this point is similar to the per curiam ultimately
issued in *Maxwell* v. *Bishop*.[17]

The Brethren, in its account of the *Maxwell* case,[18] states that the
conference vote was six to three, with Justices Black, Stewart, and White
dissenting. In actuality, only Justice Black voted to affirm. Justices Stewart and White voted with the majority to reverse, though they did so on
the *Witherspoon* ground only. Thus, Justice Stewart's draft opinion was
prepared as a concurrence, not a dissent.

A draft dissent was, however, circulated on April 16 by Justice
Black. This brief opinion is reprinted on page 427. It points out that the
Court had never suggested that the Constitution requires bifurcated trials
and waspishly notes, "This country has managed to get along without the
constitutional requirement of such trials for around 180 years and it seems
late in the day for this Court to announce such a constitutional rule."

On April 7, Justice Fortas wrote to Justice Douglas that he could
not join the section of the draft opinion of the Court dealing with standards. Justice Douglas replied with a tart April 8 letter: "Perhaps those
who insist that there be standards before costs can be assessed, *Giaccio* v.
Pennsylvania, 382 U.S. 399 [a decision Fortas had joined in 1966], can

explain why standards are necessary for the assessment of costs but not for assessment of the death penalty. But that is a feat which surpasses my limited capacities."[19]

Two weeks later, on April 21, Justice Fortas circulated the short concurrence reprinted on page 429. It restates the view contained in the Fortas April 7 letter: "The basic fact is that it is impossible, as far as I am concerned, to state standards which would justify capital punishment. . . . Further, I think that if standards are legislated, the result will be substantially to increase the number of cases of imposition of death penalty."[20]

Justice Harlan also wrote to Justice Douglas that he disagreed with the Douglas opinion's section on standards. This meant that there was no majority to support the standards requirement. Because of this, Douglas decided to abandon the discussion of standards in his opinion. He circulated a new draft dealing only with the bifurcation requirement. Justice Fortas then withdrew his separate concurrence and joined the Douglas opinion. There were now five votes for the Douglas opinion—the Chief Justice and Justices Douglas, Brennan, Fortas, and Marshall.

However, the Chief Justice and Justice Brennan, who had voted for reversal because of the lack of standards as well as bifurcation, refused to allow the decision to come down without discussion of the standards requirement. On May 14, Justice Brennan circulated the draft concurrence reprinted on page 431. It stresses that "the most elementary requirement of due process is that judicial determinations concerning life or liberty must be based on pre-existing standards of law and cannot be left to the unlimited discretion of a judge or jury." The Brennan draft asserts that standards are as necessary as bifurcation to protect defendant.

> Without such standards, however, the separate penalty trial which the Court now requires could not conceivably afford a full and fair hearing for those faced with the possibility of a sentence of death. The convicted offender would be in the Kafkaesque situation of having his life at stake and not knowing which arguments will hurt him and which might save him.

The latter portions of the Brennan draft seek to show the defects of Justice Fortas's draft concurrence. The Chief Justice and Justice Douglas agreed to join the Brennan concurrence.

There is also a draft opinion by Justice Harlan, concurring in the result, which is reprinted on page 438. As we shall see, after Justice Fortas resigned on May 13, 1969, Justice Harlan's became the crucial vote on the Douglas draft opinion of the Court. On April 9, Justice Harlan had written to Justice Douglas, "[W]hile I continue to think a split trial on the issue of punishment was constitutionally required, I have not yet come to rest on the precise scope of what due process would require in this regard. Pending further research and consideration, I therefore cannot at this time say whether I would be able to join your Part I."[21] Harlan indicated that he was considering writing a separate opinion on the bifurcation issue.

Though the Harlan law clerks indicated to the clerks of other Justices that the Justice had not been able to make up his mind and had not yet begun to write his concurrence, the draft reprinted on page 438 is contained in typewritten form in Justice Harlan's papers.[22] The Harlan draft emphasizes the right of the defendant in a capital case "to present to the jury evidence in mitigation of his punishment." The implication is that vindication of the right requires a bifurcated trial, though the bifurcation requirement is not specifically spelled out. The Harlan draft also takes issue with Justice Brennan's draft concurrence, terming "ephemeral" the Brennan argument that standards are required to enable defendant effectively to exercise his right to present mitigating evidence.

MEMORANDUM TO THE CONFERENCE FROM MR. JUSTICE GOLDBERG.

Re: CAPITAL PUNISHMENT.

INTRODUCTION.

The current Conference list includes at least six capital cases.[1] In the discussion of these cases, I propose to raise the following issue: Whether, and under what circumstances, the imposition of the death penalty is proscribed by the Eighth and Fourteenth Amendments to the United States Constitution.

In none of these cases has the cruel and unusual punishment issue been explicitly presented to this Court; nor does it appear that the issue was raised in the lower courts.[2] But in knowingly sustaining the death penalty in each of these cases, the courts necessarily passed on the legality of its imposition; and considering the nature of the issue, petitioners' failure to urge it should not preclude this Court from considering this matter. Cf. *Weems* v. *United States*, 217 U. S. 349, 362.

I circulate this memorandum—which simply raises some of the relevant considerations and does not purport to be definitive—to afford an opportunity for consideration of the matter prior to our discussion.

. . .

---

[1] *Walker* v. *Nevada* (felony murder) 85 Misc.; *Arnold* v. *North Carolina* (murder) 138 Misc.; *Snider* v. *Cunningham* (rape of a young girl) 169 Misc.; *White* v. *Washington* (murder) 232 Misc.; *Rudolph* v. *Alabama* (rape) 308 Misc.; and *Smith* v. *Bomar* (felony murder) 336 Misc.

[2] The legality of the penalty was alluded to, however, by the Washington Supreme Court in *White* v. *Washington* and the Alabama Supreme Court in *Rudolph* v. *Alabama*.

Is Capital Punishment, as Such, Unconstitutional
Under the Tests Recognized by This Court?

A. *The evolving standards of decency.*

This Court has never explicitly considered whether, and
under what circumstances, the Eighth and Fourteenth
Amendments to the United States Constitution proscribes
the imposition of the death penalty. The Court has, of
course, implicitly decided (in every case affirming a capital
conviction) that the death penalty is constitutional. But
in light of the worldwide trend toward abolition, I think
this Court should now request argument and explicitly
consider this constantly recurring issue.

I am convinced that whatever may be said of times past,
"the evolving standards of decency that mark the progress
of [our] maturing society" now condemn as barbaric and
inhuman the deliberate institutionalized taking of human
life by the state.

Many, if not most, of the civilized nations of the western
world have abolished the death penalty; and few that
have abolished it have ever restored it. The worldwide trend is unmistakenly in the direction of abolition.[9]

---

[9] The United Nations' Report on Capital Punishment (1962) lists
the following jurisdictions as having abolished capital punishment
completely: Argentina (1922), Australia (Queensland), Austria
(1945), Brazil (1889), Columbia (1910), Costa Rica (1882), Den-
mark (1930), Dominican Republic (1924), Ecuador (1897), Federal Republic of Germany (1949), Finland (1949), Greenland (1954),
Iceland (1950), Italy (1944), Mexico (25 states out of 29 and the
federal territory (Constitution, 1931), Norway (1905), Netherlands
(1870), Netherlands Antilles (1957), New Zealand (1961), Portugal
(1867), Republic of San Marino (1865), Sweden (1921), Switzerland
(1937), Uruguay (1907), Venezuela (1863), Belgium (1867), Liecht-
enstein (1798), Luxembourg, Vatican City State. The following jurisdictions are listed as having abolished capital punishment "almost
completely": "Australia; New South Wales, where the death penalty
is abolished for murder but not for treason or piracy; it is not, however,, applied in fact. Nicaragua: the death penalty is applicable
only if the crime is committed with one or more aggravating circumstances."
The following jurisdictions have retained capital punishment:
"Afghanistan, Australia (except two states), Burma, Canada, Cam-

Moreover, in this country (where Wisconsin, Maine, Minnesota, Alabama, Delaware, Michigan, Rhode Island, North Dakota, Hawaii, Virgin Islands and Puerto Rico have abolished the death penalty),[10] it seems that public opinion (at least as measured by public opinion polls, of whose general unreliability we are all aware) does not strongly favor the retention of the death penalty. The most recent Roper survey indicates that only 42% of those polled favored the retention of capital punishment; 50% opposed it; and 8% were undecided. The most recent Gallop survey indicates that 51% of those polled favored the retention of capital punishment; 36% opposed it; and 13% were undecided. (The comparable figures seven years earlier were 68%, 25% and 7%.) [11]

It may be suggested that since the death penalty is a mode of punishment "about which opinion is fairly divided," a State does not violate the Constitution when it "treats [the prisoner] by [such] a mode." *Louisiana ex rel. Francis* v. *Resweber* (Frankfurter, J., concurring). With all deference, this reasoning does not seem persuasive here. In certain matters—especially those relating to fair procedures in criminal trials—this Court traditionally has guided rather than followed public opinion in the

bodia, Central African Republic, Ceylon, Chile, China (Taiwan), Cuba, Czechoslovakia, Dahomey, El Salvador, France, Gambia, Ghana, Gibraltar, Greece, Guatemala, Hong Kong, India, Indonesia, Iran, Iraq, Ireland, Ivory Coast, Japan, Laos, Lebanon, Liberia, Federation of Malaya, Mauritius, Mexico (four states out of 29—i. e., the states of Morelos, Oaxaca, San Luis Potosi and Tabasco), Morocco, Netherlands New Guinea, Nigeria, Northern Rhodesia, Myasaland, Pakistan, Philippines, Poland, Senegal, Seychelles, Somalia (Northern), Somalia (Central and Southern), Spain, Republic of South Africa, Sudan, Surinam, Tanganyika, Thailand, Togo, Turkey, United Arab Republic, Union of Soviet Socialist Republics, United Kingdom, Republic of Viet-Nam, Western Pacific Islands, Yugoslavia, Zanzibar."

[10] Michigan and Rhode Island have retained—but never impose— the death penalty for treason. Cf. *Pennsylvania* v. *Nelson*, 350 U. S. 497. Rhode Island has retained it also for murder committed by a prisoner under sentence of life imprisonment.

[11] The Roper Poll was conducted in 1958, the Gallop Poll in 1960.

process of articulating and establishing progressively civilized standards of decency. If only punishments already overwhelmingly condemned by public opinion came within the cruel and unusual punishment proscription, the Eighth Amendment would be a dead letter; for such punishments would presumably be abolished by the legislature. The Eighth Amendment, like the others in the Bill of Rights, was intended as a countermajoritarian limitation on governmental action; it should be applied to nurture rather than to retard our "evolving standards of decency." Can there be any doubt that if this Court condemns the death penalty as cruel and unusual—whatever the initial effect—before too long that penalty will no longer be "a mode of punishment about which opinion is fairly divided." As the Court recognized in *Weems*: "Our contemplation cannot be only of what has been but of what may be."

There is another consideration which, in all frankness, enters into my thinking on this subject. Whenever capital punishment is considered, concern is expressed about the possibility of mistakenly and irremediably executing an "innocent" man. The concept of innocence has, of course, at least two meanings when used by a court. A person is "innocent" if he is not the one who committed the crime. A person is also innocent, regardless of whether or not he is the one who committed the crime, if his conviction was improperly secured. The thought of innocent men—in the first sense—being executed in any substantial number would certainly be enough to condemn the penalty of death in most people's eyes. This Court is equally concerned with the possibility of innocent men—in the second sense—being executed. Our evolving concepts of due process and fundamental fairness (apart from those relating to punishment) require this Court—not infrequently—to hold that what was considered permissible yesterday is prohibited today; that what was viewed as a limitation solely on the Federal Government yesterday, is a limitation also on the States today; that what this Court felt itself precluded from reviewing yesterday, it may review today. Moreover, these same concepts require us to reverse and vacate today, criminal convictions which were deemed constitutional when secured. But when such convictions resulted in the penalty of death, they cannot be reversed and vacated. Of course in law, as in life generally, a price must be paid for progress. But when this price is in human life, we must surely make every effort to avoid unnecessary sacrifice. Compare, for example, the cases of *Williams* v. *Georgia,* 349 U. S. 375, and *Fay* v. *Noia,* 372 U. S. 391. In each case, the accused was convicted of first degree murder by a process which was not deemed unconstitutional at the time it was conducted; [12] in each case the process was subsequently declared unconstitutional; in each case the accused did not properly raise constitutional objections to the process. The only difference was that Williams was sentenced to death and executed (see Prettyman, Death and the Supreme Court (1961), 211 ff.) while Fay was sentenced to life imprisonment. Fay is now free; so undoubtedly would Williams have been (after the decision in *Fay* v. *Noia* which would have permitted Williams collaterally to attack his conviction) but for the finality of his sentence.

I conclude therefore that under the "evolving standard of decency" test, punishment by death is cruel and unusual.

B. *Unnecessary and Excessive Punishment.*

Even if it could be said that our "evolving standards of decency" do not yet condemn the death penalty, I suggest nevertheless that this penalty is unconstitutional under the following additional test derived from the *Weems* case: Giving full weight to reasonable legislative

---

[12] Williams was indicted by a grand jury whose composition was determined by the drawing of tickets whose color differed with the race of the person named on the ticket; Fay's conviction was secured with the help of a coerced confession.

findings, a punishment is cruel and unusual if a less severe one can as effectively achieve the permissible ends of punishment.

Little discussion need be devoted to rehabilitation and isolation (*i. e.*, removal from the community): capital punishment obviously does not rehabilitate; nor could a State be heard to argue that the death penalty better serves the isolation goal of punishment (because it is cheaper to execute than safely and securely to imprison for life). Moreover, vengeance is no longer considered an acceptable goal of punishment. Cf. *Williams* v. *New York,* 337 U. S. 241, 249.

Thus the crucial question is whether capital punishment has any uniquely *deterrent* effect upon potential criminals. If it does not, then a less severe punishment (*e. g.*, life imprisonment) would as effectively deter; and it would follow that the death penalty is unconstitutional under the above test.[13]

Much research has recently been conducted in an effort to learn whether capital punishment is a unique deterrent to capital crime; and many claims (favoring abolition) have been predicated upon the results of this research.

---

[13] Many thoughtful commentators suggest that if it could be shown that the death penalty really does prevent murders, then capital punishment for murder is justified. For then the State would not be "taking" a life; it would merely be choosing to save one life at the cost of another. As Michael and Wechsler put it:

"We need not pause to reconsider the universal judgment that there is no social interest in preserving the lives of aggressors at the cost of their victims. Given the choice that must be made, the only defensible policy is one that will operate as a sanction against unlawful aggression." A Rationale of the Law of Homicide, 37 Col. L. Rev. 701.

Or as more recently stated:

"the only conceivable moral ground which a state can have that will justify it in taking a citizen's life . . . is simply that one man's life is necessary and indispensable for the protection and preservation of many other citizen's lives." Morris, Thoughts on Capital Punishment, 35 Wash. L. Rev. 335 (1960).

The most that can be said, however, is that "there is no clear evidence in any of the figures . . . that the abolition of capital punishment has led to an increase in the homicide rate, or that its reintroduction has led to a fall." Royal Comm. Report on Capital Punishment (1953) 23.[14]

Thus, the meaningful question—at least at this point in the development of our methods of studying the relationship between punishments and crimes—is not whether capital punishment really deters crime (for we do not know the answer to this question); it is: "where [does] the onus of proof [lie] in this matter of the death penalty." [15] If the State must affirmatively show that capital punishment has a unique deterrent impact, then it has failed. If the advocates of abolition must prove that capital punishment lacks a unique deterrent impact, then they have failed.

Whatever standard is generally applicable in passing on legislative findings based on conflicting evidence, the State must, in my opinion, show an overriding necessity before it can take human life.[16] This principle was recognized as long ago as 1794, when the preamble to the Pennsylvania criminal statutes announced that ". . . the punishment of death ought never to be inflicted, where it is not *absolutely necessary* to the public safety . . . ." (Emphasis added.) The Court has frequently held that

---

[14] As Professor H. L. A. Hart has warned, this conclusion (and the statistics upon which it is based) should be taken to mean only that "there is no evidence from the statistics that the death penalty is a superior deterrent to imprisonment;" it should not be taken to mean (as some have argued) that "there is evidence that the death penalty is not a superior deterrent to imprisonment." Hart, Murder and its Punishment, 12 N. W. L. Rev. 433, 457 (1957). Professor Francis Allen has joined this caveat; Review, 10 Stan. L. Rev. 595 (1958) ("[S]uch inquiries rarely approach any minimum standards of decent scientific rigor." *Id.*, at 600). Professor Richard Donnelly has expressed similar caution. Capital Punishment in Connecticut, 35 Conn. Bar J. 39 (1961).

[15] Hart, *supra*, 460.

[16] Cf. *Schneider* v. *State*, 308 U. S. 147, 161.

doubts should always be resolved against the application of the death sentence.   See, *e. g., Andres* v. *United States,* 333 U. S. 740, 752.

I conclude therefore that since there is no persuasive evidence that capital punishment uniquely deters capital crime, and since doubts should be resolved against the death penalty, this penalty runs afoul of the *Weems* test which proscribes punishments unnecessarily severe in relation to the permissible goals of punishment.[17]

---

[17] The views of the Reporter (Professor Wechsler) and Advisory Committee to the American Law Institute's Model Penal Code are summarized as follows:

"[J]udgment of death is executed in a trivial fraction of the cases in which it might legally be imposed; and that there is no quantitative evidence that either its availability or its execution has noticeable influence upon the frequency of murder.   This conclusion is not surprising when it is remembered that murders are, upon the whole, either crimes of passion, in which a calculus of consequences has small psychological reality, or crimes of such depravity that the actor reveals himself as doubtfully within the reach of influences that might be especially inhibitory in the case of an ordinary man.   There is, there-fore, room for substantial doubt that any solid case can be maintained for the death penalty, as it is employed in the United States, as a deterrent to murder.   The social need for grievous condemnation of the act can be met, as it is met in abolition states, without resorting to capital punishment.

"Apart from the efficacy of the death penalty as a deterrent, its possible imposition has, we believe, a discernible and baneful effect on the administration of criminal justice.   A trial where life is at stake becomes inevitably a morbid and sensational affair, fraught with risk that public sympathy will be aroused for the defendant without refer-ence to guilt or innocence of the crime charged.   In the rare cases where capital sentence is imposed, this unwholesome influence carries through the period preceding execution, reaching a climax when sentence is carried out.

"The special sentiment associated with judgment of death is re-flected also in the courts, lending added weight to claims of error in the trial and multiplying and protracting the appellate processes, including post-conviction remedies developed during recent years.   As astute and realistic an observer as Mr. Justice Jackson, observed to the Reporter shortly prior to his death that he opposed capital punish-

Is Capital Punishment Unconstitutional as Applied to Certain Types of Crimes and Certain Types of Criminals?

I recognize that my Brethren may not agree with the reasoning set forth in the preceeding portion of the memorandum in support of my view that capital punishment, as such, is unconstitutional. I submit for consideration therefore, the proposition that the infliction of death at least for certain types of crimes and on certain types of offenders violates the Eighth and Fourteenth Amendments.

Consider, for example, the constitutionality of death as a penalty for sexual crimes which do not endanger life (*e. g.,* rape). A persuasive argument can be made—much more persuasive than can be made in relation to murder considered as a general category—that the threat of capital punishment is not a unique deterrent to sexual crimes. Again, there is no convincing statistical data. But the psychiatric and psychological observations about the motivation of sexual offenses seem persuasive of the conclusion that if these crimes can be deterred at all, they can be deterred as well by the threat of a long prison sentence as by the threat of death.

---

ment because of its deleterious effects on the judicial process and stated that he would appear and urge the Institute to favor abolition.

"Beyond these considerations, it is obvious that capital punishment is the most difficult of sanctions to administer with even rough equality. A rigid legislative definition of capital murders has proved unworkable in practice, given the infinite variety of homicides and possible mitigating factors. A discretionary system thus becomes inevitable, with equally inevitable differences in judgment depending on the individuals involved and other accidents of time and place. Yet most dramatically when life is at stake, equality is, as it is generally felt to be, a most important element of justice.

"Finally, there is the point that erroneous convictions are inevitable and beyond correction in the light of newly discovered evidence when a capital sentence has been executed."

Moreover, even assuming that sexual crimes not endangering life are uniquely deterred by the threat of
death, there remains the question posed by the third
test derived from the *Weems* case: May human life constitutionally be taken by the State to protect a value other
than human life?   Certainly, if the value sought to be
preserved was economic, the taking of human life would
be unconstitutional regardless of the efficacy of the deterrent.   Here, however, the value sought to be preserved
is undoubtedly considered much more important than
economic values.   I believe, nevertheless, that the general consensus is that the value is less than life.   When
this consensus is coupled with the questionable efficacy
of capital punishment as a unique deterrent to sexual
crimes, they result in a persuasive argument against the
constitutionality of death as a punishment for sexual
crimes not endangering human life.[18]

The Court—consistent with its approach in *Robinson*
v. *California*—should also consider the constitutionality
of death as a penalty for certain types of offenders, such as
those incapable of exercising any volition (or control) over
their conduct (and who are consequently nondeterrable
themselves and not likely to serve as models for each other
potential offenders who might be deterrable).

The cases of *White* v. *Washington*, 374 P. 2d 942 (232
Misc.), and *Snider* v. *Cunningham* (169 Misc.), presently
before this Court on petitions for certiorari, seem to raise
this issue.   In *White,* the highest court of the State
sanctioned the imposition of the death penalty on a mur-
derer, about whom the psychiatric evidence was unanimous that he could not possibly have been deterred by the
threat of any penalty no matter how severe, and about
whom the court concluded that: "There was substantial

---

[18] This would also eliminate the well-recognized disparity in the
imposition of the death penalty for sexual crimes committed by whites
and nonwhites. See, *e. g.*, National Prison Statistics, April 1952,
which indicates that between 1937 and 1951, 233 Negroes and 26
whites were executed for rape in the United States.

evidence from which the jury could have found that appellant could not control his own behavior . . . ." In *Snider,* the District Court, after a hearing on federal habeas, found that the accused "has an irresistible sex urge which he is, at times, unable to control." And the Court of Appeals concluded that "he has little or no control of his sex urges in the presence of a female under his control in a secluded place." Thus, it seems clear that although the accused may have had some control over the situations in which he might find himself, once he was alone with a female, the fear of capital punishment would not uniquely deter an attempt to satisfy his "sex urge."

It seems clear that for this type of offender capital punishment is not a unique deterrent; thus, under the test previously outlined, the imposition of the death penalty on such an offender would violate the constitutional proscription on cruel and unusual punishments.

CONCLUSION.

The foregoing expresses my substantial doubts concerning the constitutionality of the death penalty.

SUPREME COURT OF THE UNITED STATES

No. 622.—October Term, 1968.

William L. Maxwell, Petitioner, *v.* O. E. Bishop, Superintendent, Arkansas State Penitentiary.	On Writ of Certiorari to the United States Court of Appeals for the Eighth Circuit.

[April —, 1969.]

Mr. Justice Douglas delivered the opinion of the Court.

Petitioner, a Negro, was convicted of rape of a white woman, a crime which Arkansas makes punishable by death. Ark. Stat. Ann. § 41–3403. Arkansas, however, gives discretion to the jury to impose life imprisonment instead: "The jury shall have the right in all cases where the punishment is now death by law, to render a verdict of life imprisonment in the State penitentiary at hard labor." [1]

The jury elected punishment by death. The Supreme Court of Arkansas affirmed. 236 Ark. 694, 370 S. W. 2d 113. No review of that decision was sought here. A federal habeas corpus proceeding was then filed; but it

---

[1] This type of statute is kin to the Federal Act adopted in 1897. See *Andres* v. *United States,* 333 U. S. 740. As stated by Mr. Justice Frankfurter "The statute reflects the movement, active during the nineteenth century, against the death sentence. The movement was impelled both by ethical and humanitarian arguments against capital punishment, as well as by the practical consideration that jurors were reluctant to bring in verdicts which inevitably called for its infliction. Almost every State passed mitigating legislation." 333 U. S., at 753 (concurring opinion). And see *Cotton* v. *Utah,* 130 U. S. 83, 86–87.

Arkansas' present law appeared in 1915 in the following form: "That the jury shall have the right in all cases where the punishment is now death by law, to render a verdict of life imprisonment in the State penitentiary at hard labor." Acts 1915, p. 775.

MAXWELL v. BISHOP.

brought no relief. *Maxwell v. Stephens*, 279 F. Supp. 205, aff'd 348 F. 2d 325 (one judge dissenting). We denied certiorari. 382 U. S. 944. The present habeas corpus proceeding was commenced by a second federal petition. The District Court denied petitioner's application for the writ. 257 F. Supp. 710. The Court of Appeals affirmed. 398 F. 2d 138. The case is here on a petition for a writ of certiorari which we granted. 394 U. S. —.

The criminal trial in Arkansas is a unitary trial, the same jury resolving the issues of guilt and punishment and rendering a verdict on each question at the same time.

There are standards to guide the jury in determining the question of guilt. But the legislature has provided no standards for guiding the jury on the penalty of death and no instructions limiting or directing the exercise by the jury of its absolute discretion were given by the judge in the trial of this case.

The initial question in this case is whether a unitary trial, as distinguished from a bifurcated trial, affords an accused in a capital case an effective and practical opportunity to tender evidence relevant to the issue of punishment as distinguished from the issue of guilt; and if so whether the choice between remaining silent to protect ones innocence and speaking out to encourage rational sentencing "needlessly penalizes the assertion of [ones] constitutional right[s]." *United States v. Jackson*, 390 U. S. 570, 583.

The difficulties of the accused in introducing evidence relevant to the issue of punishment are not as difficult in California as in Arkansas. because California has bifurcated trials.[2] In California—once guilt is deter-

---

[2] West's Ann. Calif. Code § 190.1. And see 39 McKinneys Consol. L. N. Y. Ann. § 125.35; 18 Pa. Stat. Ann. § 4701; Conn. Gen. Stat. Ann. § 53–10 (Supp. 1965).

MAXWELL *v.* BISHOP.

mined—the jury turns to the wholly distinct issue of punishment. In a unitary trial, where guilt and punishment are decided at the same time by the same jury, the important question presented is whether a defendant receives that due process on this issue of punishment that is required by the Fourteenth Amendment.

I.

A defendant in a state criminal trial need not take the stand, for the Self-Incrimination Clause of the Fifth Amendment applicable by reason of the Fourteenth protects him. *Malloy v. Hogan*, 378 U. S. 1. As a corollary, his failure to take the stand may not be used against him by the prosecutor. *Griffin v. California*, 380 U. S. 609. This privilege against self-incrimination may be important. Yet if the defendant is to escape death, his testimony may be essential. If he takes the stand in a unitary trial, Arkansas permits searching cross-examination as to whether he ever committed "other crimes and immoralities." See *Skaggs* v. *State*, 234 Ark. 510, 511, 353 S. W. 2d 3, 4 (1962); *Rayburn* v. *State*, 200 Ark. 914, 141 S. W. 2d 532 (1940); *Bevis* v. *State*, 209 Ark. 624, 192 S. W. 2d 113 (1946), and a host of prejudicial questions. *Gaines* v. *State*, 208 Ark. 293, 186 S. W. 2d 154 (1945); *McGraw* v. *State*, 184 Ark. 342, 42 S. W. 2d 373 (1931). Once the question of his character is opened prior to the determination of guilt or innocence, there may be introduced every prejudicial occurrence, real or imagined, in the accused's history. *Amos* v. *State*, 209 Ark. 55, 189 S. W. 2d 611.

Unless the accused testifies or opens up the question, evidence of prior crimes is inadmissible. *Bonds* v. *State*, 240 Ark. 908, 403 S. W. 2d 52; *Alford* v. *State*, 223 Ark. 330, 266 S. W. 2d 804 (1954). Yet on the issue whether an accused should live or die, the jury, like the judge who imposes the sentence, *Williams* v. *New York*,

MAXWELL *v.* BISHOP.

337 U. S. 241, 247, may need to know much more about the accused than is likely or permissibly forthcoming on the trial of the issue of guilt. At times, his right of allocution may therefore be essential to the requirements of due process. See *Specht* v. *Patterson*, 386 U. S. 605, 610. *Hill* v. *United States*, 368 U. S. 424, 429. Yet a defendant can be subjected to the same withering cross-examination on character, misdeeds, reputation, and prior crimes, though he takes the stand in a unitary trial to tender mitigating circumstances. That is to say, though he uses his right of allocation in at attempt to obtain mercy rather than complete exoneration, his efforts to obtain a lesser punishment may only worsen his position on the issue of guilt. The law, as it developed, made taking the stand the great divide between immunity from atack on collateral matters that reflect on character or reputation on the one hand and relentless pursuit on the other. Yet crossing that great divide may indeed afford the only possible choice of obtaining a fair trial on the issue of punishment.

It may be that only by presenting his mitigating evidence may an accused make an impact on the jury's determination of the penalty. Yet he may not dare exercise his right of allocution at the unitary trial, lest he suffer irreparable harm on the guilt issue. He thus purchases a fair trial on the issue of guilt at the cost of sacrificing his right to a fair trial on the issue of punishment.

A unitary trial does not accommodate both the right of allocution and the right to silence; it forces the defendant to choose between them. In doing so, it is "inherently coercive," and "impose[s] an impermissible burden upon the assertion of a constitutional right." *United States* v. *Jackson*, 390 U. S., at 583.

MAXWELL *v.* BISHOP.

II.

And so we reach the *second* question whether lodging in a jury or in a judge an unlimited discretion that a defendant should live or die comports with the Fourteenth Amendment.

The law normally gives a jury guidelines:

Which party is at fault in an automobile accident?

Was the decedent insane when he made his will?

Was homicide justified because of self-defense?

The grant to a judge or a jury of an undefined and unreviewable discretion without any effective or practical opportunity to confine it is telling the judge or jury to send whomsoever they chose to death. That is lodging in its hands "a naked and arbitrary power," *Yick Wo.* v. *Hopkins,* 118 U. S. 356, 366, a power struck down in that case under the Equal Protection Clause because it permitted racial discrimination in the issuance of licenses to run a laundry. Our cases dealing with the Equal Protection Clause and economic issues give leeway where there is a rational foundation for discrimination. See *Loving* v. *Virginia,* 388 U. S. 1, 9. But we have been much stricter when "fundamental rights and liberties" are at issue. See *Harper* v. *Virginia Board,* 383 U. S. 663, 670. And there is, of course, no right more fundamental than the right to live.

In *Skinner* v. *Oklahoma,* 316 U. S. 535, a State sterilized those who robbed banks from the outside, exempting those who robbed banks from the inside; and we held the law to be violative of equal protection:

> "When the law lays an unequal hand on those who have committed intrinsically the same probity of offense and sterilizes one and not the other, it has made as . . . insidious discrimination as if it had selected a particular race or nationality for oppressive treatment." 316 U. S. 540–541.

MAXWELL v. BISHOP.

A law, such as Arkansas', may in operation seriously implicate the Equal Protection Clause.

The Due Process Clause of the Fourteenth Amendment is also involved, as indicated by *Graccio v. Pennsylvania*, 382 U. S. 399, an opinion of the Court written by Mr. Justice Black. The case involved a Pennsylvania prosecution in which the defendant was found not guilty. Pursuant to a Pennsylvania statute the jury was directed to determine whether the defendant or the other side should pay the costs. The jury made the assessment against the defendant. We set it aside, saying that a law fails to meet the requirements of due process if it "leaves judges and jurors free to decide, without any legally fixed standards, what is prohibited and what is not in each particular case." [3] *Id.*, 402–403. We said:

> "Certainly one of the basic purposes of the Due Process Clause has always been to protect a person against having the Government impose burdens upon him except in accordance with the valid laws of the land. Implicit in this constitutional safeguard is the premise that the law must be one that carries an understandable meaning with legal standards that courts must enforce. This state Act as

---

[3] We held that the instructions given to this jury did not cure the "void for vagueness" defect in the statute:

"It may possibly be that the trial court's charge comes nearer to giving a guide to the jury than those that preceded it, but it still falls short of the kind of legal standard due process requires. At best it only told the jury that if it found appellant guilty of 'some misconduct' less than that charged against him, it was authorized by law to saddle him with the State's costs in its unsuccessful prosecution. It would be difficult if not impossible for a person to prepare a defense against such general abstract charges as 'misconduct,' or 'reprehensible conduct.' If used in a *statute* which imposed forfeitures, punishments or judgments for costs, such loose and unlimiting terms would certainly cause the statute to fail to measure up to the requirements of the Due Process Clause. And these terms are no more effective to make a statute valid which standing alone is void for vagueness." 382 U. S., at 404.

MAXWELL v. BISHOP.

written does not even begin to meet this constitutional requirement." *Id.*, 403.

In a footnote we said "In so holding we intend to cast no doubt whatever on the constitutionality of the settled practice of many States to leave to juries finding defendants guilty of a crime the power to fix punishment within legally prescribed limits." *Id.*, 405, n. 8. Some courts have relied on that footnote as sanction for granting the jury complete discretion to exercise the death or life choice.[4] But we read it as doing no more than reserving the important constitutional question now tendered, what are "legally prescribed limits" in capital cases?

Under Arkansas law those who should receive death and those who should not are undefined. There is no classification whatsoever, the choice being left completely to the discretion of the jury.

Where there are no guidelines or relevant evidence one jury may decide that one defendant is not "fit to live." *Witherspoon* v. *Illinois*, 391 U. S. 510, 521, n. 20, because he is a black who raped a white woman, while another defendant is "fit to live" because he is a white who raped a black.[5] Or whatever the race of the defendant one jury may be seized by the spirit of the mob, while another, dealing with the same quality of offense, may be more reasoned and compassionate. As Attorney General Ramsey Clark recently said:[6]

"A small and capricious selection of offenders have been put to death. Most persons convicted of the

---

[4] The Death Penalty Cases, 56 Calif. L. Rev. 1268, 1416 *et seq.* (1968).

[5] Between 1930 and 1962, when petitioner was sentenced to die, 446 persons were executed for rape in this country. For the distribution of the cases by States and by race see United States Department of Justice, Bureau of Prisons, National Prisoner Statistics, No. 32, Execution 1962 (April 1963), Table 2.

[6] Hearings, Subcommittee on Criminal Laws and Procedures of the Senate Judiciary Committee on S. 1760, 1968.

MAXWELL *v*. BISHOP.

> same crimes have been imprisoned. Experienced wardens know many prisoners serving life or less whose crimes were equally, or more atrocious, than those of men on death row."

We know from our own observations that the death penalty is seldom suffered by the affluent member of society; it is reserved, in practice, for the indigent and those otherwise inferior or somehow incapacitated, whether by education or mental instability.

When the issue of punishment is resolved after guilt is determined, the defendant is free to testify without restraint and to offer any evidence, if there be such, that is of a mitigating character. In noncapital cases the presentence report to the judge covers early environment, religious training, education, employment record, and criminal history. Since the jury in the capital case performs the same function as the sentencing judge in the noncapital case, it is argued that the jury should have the same background information in some form or other.

The existence of standards and of a record makes possible at least a degree of judicial review.

The introduction of background evidence may help the defendant in some cases and hurt him in others.

If a State wants to leave to judges and juries discretion to take the life of a man who commits an offense, it must provide "legally fixed standards" lest the law become capricious or provide no understandable guidelines for the jury's or judge's decision.

What manner of men does a State want to execute? Is killing a policeman or a prison guard more heinous than killing a neighbor in an old feud? Is killing for a fee more monstrous than killing in a household quarrel?

The list of aggravating circumstances that one group thinks warrants imposition of the death penalty will be anathema to another group. There will likewise be a

MAXWELL *v.* BISHOP.

wide variety of opinions when it comes to mitigating circumstances.

Should the aggravating circumstances be those enumerated in § 201.6 (3) of the Model Penal Code of the American Law Institute?

"(a) The murder was committed by a convict under sentence of imprisonment.

"(b) The defendant was previously convicted of another murder or of a felony or felonies involving the use or threat of violence to the person.

"(c) At the time the murder was committed the defendant also committed another murder or murders.

"(d) The defendant knowingly created a great risk of death to many persons.

"(e) The murder was committed while the defendant was engaged or was an accomplice in the commission of, or the attempt to commit, or flight after committing robbery, rape by force or intimidation, arson, burglary or kidnaping.

"(f) The murder was committed for the purpose of avoiding or preventing a lawful arrest or effecting an escape from lawful custody.

"(g) The murder was committed for hire or pecuniary gain.

"(h) The murder was especially heinous, atrocious or cruel, manifesting exceptional depravity."

Should mitigating circumstances include those described in § 201.6 (4) of the Model Penal Code?

"(a) The defendant has no history of prior criminal activity.

"(b) The murder was committed while the defendant was under the influence of extreme mental or emotional disturbance.

MAXWELL *v.* BISHOP.

"(c) The victim was a participant in the defendant's homicidal conduct or consented to the homicidal act.

"(d) The murder was committed under circumstances which the defendant believed to provide a moral justification or extenuation for his conduct.

"(e) The defendant was an accomplice in a murder committed by another person and his participation in the homicidal act was relatively minor.

"(f) The defendant acted under duress or under the domination of another person.

"(g) At the time of the murder, the capacity of the defendant to appreciate the criminality of his conduct or to conform his conduct to the requirements of law was impaired as a result of mental disease or defect or intoxication.

"(h) The youth of the defendant at the time of the crime."

Should any substantial mitigating circumstances save the accused from the death penalty even if there are aggravating circumstances, as provided in § 201.6 (2) of the Model Penal Code?

The draft provides that the jury should be instructed that it may not impose the death sentence "unless it finds there was an aggravating circumstance" as defined in the draft and further that "there were no substantial, mitigating circumstances." *Id.,* p. 77.

Should evidence of the prospects of rehabilitating the defendant be admissible?

Should the prosecution be allowed to show that the defendant is a psychotic beyond the reach of any known therapy?

These considerations present profound questions. The task is not for this Court but for the local legislatures. Standards or guidelines are necessary for as Mr. Justice Black said in *Graccio* v. *Pennsylvania, supra,* a law

MAXWELL *v.* BISHOP.

which "leaves judges and jurors free to decide without
any legally fixed standards what is prohibitive and what
is not in each case" violates the Fourteenth Amendment.
382 U. S. 402–403. Without the guidance of standards,
the jury may unwittingly impose the death penalty for
reasons which the State considers impermissible.[7] Without standards, the appellate courts are precluded from
ensuring that the jury has performed its task. Without
standards to guide him in preparing his testimony, the
defendant has no notice of the reasons for which he may
live or die.[8]

III.

We reverse not on the issue of guilt but solely on
the infliction of capital punishment. That was the
effect of our reversal in *Witherspoon* v. *Illinois*, 391
U. S. 510, where we held that "a State may not entrust
the determination of whether a man should live or die
to a tribunal organized to return a verdict of death."
Id., at 521.

The state statute in that case[9] set the punishment
at death, life imprisonment, or imprisonment for 14
years. It was a unitary trial, the jury being directed to
"fix the punishment," once guilt was found.[10]

---

[7] Should "deterrence" be a standard? The California Supreme
Court has concluded that the *deterrence* rationale of capital punishment is "unproven and illegitimate," *People* v. *Ketchel*, 59 Cal. 2d
503, 537–539, 381 P. 2d 394, 412–413 (1963). It therefore prohibits
counsel from allowing the penalty jury to consider that standard.

[8] In Arizona, the jury is precluded from considering evidence concerning the defendant's background, character, or prior criminal
record, because the State has determined that the jury should punish
the *crime* rather than the *criminal*. Accordingly, the defendant has
notice that he will not be prepared to present evidence of "mitigating"
circumstances. *State* v. *Narten*, 99 Ariz. 116, ——, 407 P. 2d 81
86 (1965).

[9] Ill. Rev. Stat., c. 38, §§ 3360, 801 (1959).

[10] § 360, n. 3, *supra*.

MAXWELL *v.* BISHOP.

In the present case we follow the *Witherspoon* precedent and reverse on the issue of punishment only. Were this a case where guilt determination was prejudiced by a unitary trial, as where the accused waived his Fifth Amendment right to assert his right of allocution, a reversal on the finding of guilt would also be necessary. But Maxwell did not take the stand and no other evidence in the record suggests that the guilt determination was prejudiced by the unitary procedure.

This is a federal habeas corpus proceeding involving the constitutional rights of one convicted under a state law. The federal Act gives the District Court power to "dispose of the matter as law and justice require." 28 U. S. C. § 2243. See *Fay* v. *Noia,* 372 U. S. 391, 397, 438; *Sheppard* v. *Maxwell,* 384 U. S. 333, 363; *Jackson* v. *Denno,* 378 U. S. 368, 396; *Rogers* v. *United States,* 378 U. S. 549.

We reverse the judgment of the Court of Appeals and direct that the cause be remanded to the District Court for disposition in conformity with this opinion.

It is so ordered.

SUPREME COURT OF THE UNITED STATES

From: Stewart,
AP
Circulated:___

No. 622.—October Term, 1968.

William L. Maxwell, Petitioner, | On Writ of Cer̶t̶i̶o̶r̶a̶r̶i̶
v. | to the United States
O. E. Bishop, Superintendent, | Court of Appeals for
Arkansas State Penitentiary. | the Eighth Circuit.

Recirculated:___

[April —, 1969.]

Mr. Justice Stewart.

This case was tried long before the Court's decision in *Witherspoon* v. *Illinois*, 391 U. S. 510. It appears clear from even a cursory look at the trial record that several prospective jurors were removed from the panel upon grounds held impermissible in the *Witherspoon* case.

One prospective juror, for example, was successfully challenged for cause solely on the basis of the following interchange:

> "Q. If you were convinced beyond a reasonable doubt at the end of this trial that the defendant was guilty and that his actions had been so shocking that they would merit the death penalty do you have any conscientious scruples about capital punishment that *might* prevent you from returning such a verdict?
>
> "A. I *think* I do." (Emphasis supplied.)

Another venireman was removed from the jury on the basis of the following question and answer:

> "Q. Do you entertain any conscientious scruples about imposing the death penalty?
>
> "A. Yes, I am afraid I do."

Still another member of the panel was dismissed after the following colloquy:

> "Q. Mr. Adams, do you have any feeling concerning capital punishment that would prevent you

---

* JMHP.

MAXWELL *v.* BISHOP.

or make you have any feelings about returning a death sentence if you felt beyond a reasonable doubt that the defendant was guilty and that his crime was so bad as to merit the death sentence?

"A. No, I don't believe in capital punishment." (Emphasis supplied.)

As was made clear in *Witherspoon* and recently reaffirmed in *Boulden* v. *Holman,* —— U. S. ——, "a sentence of death cannot be carried out if the jury that imposed or recommended it was chosen by excluding veniremen for cause simply because they voiced general objections to the death penalty or expressed conscientious or religious scruples against its infliction." 391 U. S., at 522. There is no reason to suppose that such people as jurors would not be able "to follow conscientiously the instructions of a trial judge and to consider fairly the imposition of the death sentence in a particular case." *Boulden* v. *Holman, supra,* at ——. "Unless a venireman states unambiguously that he would automatically vote against the imposition of capital punishment no matter what the trial might reveal, it simply cannot be assumed that is his position." *Witherspoon* v. *Illinois, supra,* at 516 n. 9.

> "The most that can be demanded of a venireman in this regard is that he be willing to *consider* all of the penalties provided by state law, and that he not be irrevocably committed, before the trial has begun, to vote against the penalty of death regardless of the facts and circumstances that might emerge in the course of the proceedings. If the voir dire testimony in a given case indicates that veniremen were excluded on any broader basis than this. the death sentence cannot be carried out . . . ." *Id.,* at 522. n. 21.

It appears, therefore, that the sentence of death imposed upon the petitioner cannot constitutionally stand

MAXWELL *v.* BISHOP.

under *Witherspoon* v. *Illinois.* I would not, however,
finally decide that question now. Instead, without now
reaching any other issues, I would vacate the judgment
of the Court of Appeals and remand the case to the
District Court where the *Witherspoon* issue can be fully
considered. See *Boulden* v. *Holman, supra,* at ——.

SUPREME COURT OF THE UNITED STATES

No. 622.—OCTOBER TERM, 1968.

William L. Maxwell, Petitioner, *v.* O. E. Bishop, Superintendent, Arkansas State Penitentiary.	On Writ of Certiorari to the United States Court of Appeals for the Eighth Circuit.

[April —, 1969.]

MR. JUSTICE BLACK, dissenting.

If this Court is determined to abolish the death penalty, I think it should do so forthrightly, and not by nibbles. See, *e. g., United States* v. *Jackson*, 390 U. S. 570, and *Witherspoon* v. *Illinois*, 391 U. S. 510. So far as I know, no opinion of the Court has ever suggested that any part of the Federal Constitution compels either the States or Federal Government to have bifurcated trials, that is, trials in which separate jury proceedings are held to determine guilt and punishment. This country has managed to get along without the constitutional requirement of such trials for around 180 years and it seems late in the day for this Court to announce such a constitutional rule.

So far as I am concerned, the question of whether the Fourteenth Amendment compels the States' to adopt a two-stage jury trial in capital cases or any others was convincingly answered just two Terms ago in our decision in *Spencer* v. *Texas*, 385 U. S. 554. In his opinion for the Court rejecting the argument that the Constitution should for the first time be construed as compelling the States to adopt such two-stage trials, MR. JUSTICE HARLAN concluded:

"To say that the two-stage jury trial in the English-Connecticut style is probably the fairest, as some commentators and courts have suggested, and with

---

MAXWELL *v.* BISHOP.

which we might well agree were the matter before us in a legislative or rule-making context, is a far cry from a constitutional determination that this method of handling the problem is compelled by the Fourteenth Amendment. Two-part trials are rare in our jurisprudence; they have never been compelled by this Court as a matter of law, or even as a matter of federal procedure. With recidivism the major problem that it is, substantial changes in trial procedure in countless local courts around the country would be required were this Court to sustain the contentions made by these petitioners. This we are unwilling to do. To take such a step would be quite beyond the pale of this Court's proper function in our federal system. It would be a wholly unjustifiable encroachment by this Court upon the constitutional power of States to promulgate their own rules of evidence to try their own state-created crimes in their own state courts, so long as their rules are not prohibited by any provision of the United States Constitution, which these rules are not." 385 U. S., at 568–569.

Since I thought that this statement was constitutionally correct when it was written and since I still adhere to it, I would affirm this conviction.

SUPREME COURT OF THE UNITED STATES

No. 622.—October Term, 1968.

William L. Maxwell, Petitioner, | On Writ of Certiorari
v. | to the United States
O. E. Bishop, Superintendent, | Court of Appeals for
Arkansas State Penitentiary. | the Eighth Circuit.

[April —, 1969.]

Mr. Justice Fortas.

I concur in the judgment of the Court and in Part I of its opinion.

I do not agree that we should rule, on the basis of the present state of our knowledge, that statutes which allow the judge or jury a choice of punishment to be imposed are unconstitutional unless explicit standards are prescribed to guide them in making the choice. I do not know, and the Court does not suggest, meaningful standards or a basis upon which a legislature could prescribe different punishments for the kaleidoscope of crime and the infinite variety of humans who commit them. Neither the refinement of moral criteria nor the progress of penology or of the arts of psychiatry, chemistry or environmental therapy enables me to envision the development of meaningful standards. In this area, we do not yet have the skills to produce words which would fit the punishment to the crime or to the criminal with more precision than would result if the judge or jury acted without standards. To assume otherwise, I think, is to delude ourselves and to insist upon a constitutional mandate which, at best, will be meaningless. The standards to be adopted will not really serve the purpose of administering justice more evenly, or more appropriately, or both better results. And I fear that insistence upon standards will cause legislatures to reduce the use of the flexible

* JMHP.

MAXWELL *v.* BISHOP.

or alternative penalties which most modern penologists
applaud, and to substitute for them more stringent,
mandatory penalties. I am not prepared to say that due
process of law requires these results.

On the other hand, I fully agree that due process
requires that the defendant be given an adequate opportunity to present to the sentencing authority—judge or
jury—material relevant to the sentence to be imposed.
In the case of jury sentencing at least, this means that
he is entitled to a bifurcated trial.

I think we should note that the thrust of the Court's
opinion may not be confined to capital cases, but may
apply in all cases involving major penalties, at least
where the jury has sentencing power and alternatives are
available to it.

SUPREME COURT OF THE UNITED STATES

From: Brenn

Circulated:

Recirculated

No. 622.—OCTOBER TERM, 1968.

William L. Maxwell, Petitioner, *v.* O. E. Bishop, Superintendent, Arkansas State Penitentiary.	On Writ of Certiorari to the United States Court of Appeals for the Eighth Circuit.

[May —, 1969.]

MR. JUSTICE BRENNAN, concurring.

I join the Court's opinion holding that the Constitution requires a separate penalty trial in cases where the death sentence is authorized. But this holding does not in my view suffice to dispose of the issues raised by the case before us. The separate penalty trial must itself be held in accordance with the requirements of due process. And, the most elementary requirement of due process is that judicial determinations concerning life or liberty must be based on pre-existing standards of law and cannot be left to the unlimited discretion of a judge or jury.

The Arkansas Legislature decided that not every defendant convicted of rape should be sentenced to death. It made no effort, however, to specify criteria for determining which persons convicted of rape should live and which should die. The life or death decision was left to be made by particular juries on a wholly ad hoc basis. No other legal decision is so completely left to the discretion of juries. As Chief Justice Traynor of the Supreme Court of California remarked from the bench in a case similar to this one:

> "We wouldn't turn it over to a jury, the determining of whether the father or the mother or whether the grandmother or a sister-in-law got the child, according to the absolute whim or caprice, or . . . the dis-

---

* JMHP.

MAXWELL *v.* BISHOP.

cretion of the jury. We wouldn't turn over to the whim of a jury the determination of whether a fox terrier belonged to the husband or the wife in a separation. We wouldn't let a jury determine that with absolute discretion. Any issue in the whole legal system that you can think of, rights, property rights, personal rights, are guided by precedents, by standards, and to leave to a jury the absolute discretion to determine whether a person lives or dies, without any guidance, or any compass or standard, principles or anything else, is foreign to the whole basic tradition of the Anglo-Saxon common law." [1]

The Arkansas Legislature might have chosen to adopt various standards or sets of criteria for determining who among those convicted of rape should be put to death. It might have decided that the life or death decision should turn on the nature of the crime committed. The crime of rape in Arkansas encompasses every variety of consummated sexual assault, regardless of the age of the victim, the brutality of the assault, or the previous relationship between assailant and victim. If the legislature wished to distinguish among those convicted of different types of rape, it could have done so; instead, it left to individual juries the choice of whether to adopt such a distinction and, if adopted, how to apply it. Perhaps the legislature would have decided that factors relating to the personal status of each defendant—*e. g.*, age, prior records of convictions, mental and emotional status at the time of the crime, mental and emotional status at the time of sentencing, possibility of rehabilitation, and so forth—should be determinative of the appropriate punishment. The legislature might have decided that

---

[1] Transcript of Proceedings in the Supreme Court of California, *In re Anderson*, Crim. No. 11, 572 (1968), pp. 107–108. Chief Justice Traynor joined in Justice Tobriner's dissent in *Anderson*, — Cal. 2d —, —, 447 P. 2d 117, 132 (1968).

MAXWELL *v.* BISHOP.

both types of considerations discussed above are relevant; it might have specified additional factors as relevant. It might have precluded the jury from considering certain factors, required findings of fact as to other factors, and given the jury discretion whether to consider still other factors.[2] It might have done all these things, and yet it chose to abdicate its decision-making role, leaving questions of general social policy to be answered by individual juries, indeed by individual jurors, since each jury member was left free to decide for himself which criteria are relevant, and no agreement on criteria need be made to reach a verdict of death. This delegation of responsibility from the legislature to the jury resulted in a decision-making process which cannot meet the test of due process.

The Fourteenth Amendment declares that no State may "deprive any person of life, liberty, or property without due process of law . . . ." With respect to determinations of guilt or innocence, due process has always been taken to require that judgments be based on pre-existing standards. Thus, a legislature may not authorize juries to convict any person whose conduct they consider blameworthy. Cf. *Giaccio* v. *Pennsylvania*, 382 U. S. 399 (1966). The substantive elements of criminal conduct must be precisely defined. Otherwise, no person would have adequate notice of what constitutes punishable conduct, and accused persons would be deprived of a full and fair hearing on the issue of their guilt and denied the essential benefit of the rule of law—equal and nonarbitrary treatment. That the Due Process Clause applies as well to determinations regarding punishment cannot be gainsaid, *Witherspoon* v. *Illinois*,

---

[2] The American Law Institute has formulated proposed standards for determining when the death penalty may be imposed in murder cases. ALI Model Penal Code (Proposed Official Draft 1962) § 210.6.

MAXWELL *v.* BISHOP.

391 U. S. 510 (1968); *Townsend* v. *Burke,* 334 U. S. 736 (1948); Cf. *Skinner* v. *Oklahoma,* 316 U. S. 535 (1942). The "basic requirements of procedural fairness [cannot] be ignored simply because the determination involved [in deciding whether the death penalty should be imposed] differs in some respects from the traditional assessment of whether the defendant engaged in a proscribed course of conduct." *Witherspoon* v. *Illinois, supra,* at 521, n. 20. And, analysis demonstrates that for all but one of the reasons that pre-existing standards are required for guilt determinations, due process requires pre-existing standards for penalty determinations.

Pre-existing standards for penalty determinations unlike standards for guilt determinations, do not serve to provide citizens notice of what constitutes criminal conduct. Without such standards, however, the separate penalty trial which the Court now requires could not conceivably afford a full and fair hearing for those faced with the possibility of a sentence of death. The convicted offender would be in the Kafkaesque situation of having his life at stake and not knowing which arguments will hurt him and which might save him. For example, should he bring to the jury's attention a mental or emotional disorder? Or would this persuade at least some of the jurors that he is a "perverted savage" who should be executed?[3] Should he point out that he committed the crime under the influence of alcohol or drugs? Or would there be jurors who consider these aggravating rather than mitigating circumstances? Should he stress his youth? Or would this only increase the fear

---

[3] A recent study of California's standardless penalty trial in capital cases indicates that an offender who unsuccessfully raised the insanity defense at the trial on guilt or innocence "stood a greater probability of receiving the death penalty than his counterpart who did not try an insanity defense." —————————————————, 21 Stan. L. Rev. ——, —— (1969).

MAXWELL *v.* BISHOP.

in some jurors that if he is spared execution he might someday be released from prison? Concededly, not all arguments concerning the appropriate punishment are two-edged. But even as to those arguments that are not, the convicted offender could not intelligently decide which to present and which to emphasize without any knowledge of the standards to be applied by the jury.

Moreover, without standards, the convicted offender is denied the traditional safeguard which the law provides against impermissible jury decisions. Without standards, there is nothing to prevent the jury from basing its life or death decision solely on, for example, the offender's race or on whether he testified at the trial of guilt. It is true that even with standards there can be no assurance that the jury will confine its consideration to legitimate issues. Nevertheless, when the imposition of a sentence must be supported by certain findings of fact, the leeway for impermissible sentencing decisions is reduced, since reviewing courts would be able to examine the sufficiency of the evidence underlying the jury's fact-findings.

More fundamentally, to sentence a man to death at a standardless penalty trial would be antithetical to the principle of the rule of law itself. The very essence of the rule of law is that no man's life, liberty, or property may be put in jeopardy of arbitrary governmental decisions—decisions not based on pre-existing legal standards:

> "When we consider the nature and the theory of our institutions of government, the principles upon which they are supposed to rest, and review the history of their development, we are constrained to conclude that they do not mean to leave room for the play and action of purely personal and arbitrary power . . . . [T]he very idea that one man may be compelled to hold his life, or the means of living, or any material right essential to the enjoyment of life, at the mere will of another, seems to be

MAXWELL *v.* BISHOP.

intolerable in any country where freedom prevails, as being the essence of slavery itself." *Yick Wo* v. *Hopkins,* 118 U. S. 356. 369–370 (1886).

Surely, these precepts are not suspended when the decision-making body is the jury.

The need for a full and fair penalty hearing and for unswerving adherence to the principle of the rule of law is magnified in case involving a life or death judgment. "It should be understood that much more is involved here than a simple determination of sentence. For the State . . . empowered the jury in this case to answer 'yes' or 'no' to the question whether this defendant was fit to live." *Witherspoon* v. *Illinois, supra,* at 521, n. 20. In *Skinner* v. *Oklahoma, supra,* we held that special examination need be made of a state scheme providing for the sterilization of a particular class of criminal offenders. There we found that a state legislature could not constitutionally distinguish between those convicted of grand larceny and those convicted of embezzlement where so drastic a personal deprivation is at stake. Certainly, a legislature could not circumvent this proscription by delegating to juries the power to make such a distinction. Yet, to authorize standardless death-penalty hearings would be to permit juries to choose which convicted offenders should live and which should die on the basis of even less substantial distinctions.

It is clear therefore that a separate penalty trial without pre-existing standards of law could not meet the requirements of due process. Still there are those who suggest that the clear dictates of due process be ignored in light of possible adverse practical consequences of requiring standards. We are told, for example, that promulgation of standards will reduce desired flexibility in sentencing. But flexibility is not reduced by legislative formulation of sentencing goals. Such a formulation merely makes sentencing a more rational and less

MAXWELL *v.* BISHOP.

mystical process. I agree with petitioner that "[t]o concede the complexity and interrelation of sentencing goals . . . is no reason to sustain a procedure which ignores them all." [4]

It is also suggested that requiring States to provide standards will likely result in greater legislative imposition of mandatory death penalties and hence more executions. This, of course, is sheer speculation. But, in any event, so long as the death penalty is constitutional, it is not a proper concern of this Court whether States will impose the death penalty more or less frequently. Our sole concern is to declare the relevant constitutional principles which govern the imposition of the death penalty by the States.

---

[4] Brief for Petitioner, p. 65.

MAXWELL V. BISHOP

No. 13

MR. JUSTICE HARLAN, concurring in the result.

Until 1915, one convicted of rape in Arkansas was automatically sentenced to death. In that year, a statute gave
the jury discretion to impose instead a sentence of life
imprisonment at hard labor. See Ark. Stat. Ann. § 43–
2153. Arkansas' reform was part of a nationwide dissatis-
faction with mandatory death penalties, which eventu-
ated in the repeal of all such provisions.

The State of Arkansas acknowledges that, due to the
statutory bestowal of sentencing discretion upon the jury,
there is at issue in an Arkansas capital case "something
more than the guilt or innocence of the accused . . . ;
the jury must decide whether the convicted will live or
die." Once it is recognized that the jury may have to make
this second, distinct decision, it becomes apparent that a
capital defendant has the strongest imaginable interest in
being accorded a hearing at which he may put before the
jury in an effective manner any evidence which might
operate to mitigate his punishment.

When the issue in a criminal trial is that of guilt or
innocence, this Court has held that "[a] person's right
to . . . an opportunity to be heard in his defense—a right
to his day in court—[is] basic to our system of jurisprudence," and has stated that "there are certain im-
mutable principles of justice which inhere in the very
idea of a free government which no member of the Union
may disregard, as that no man shall be condemned in his
person or property without . . . an opportunity of being
heard in his defense." In a variety of cases involving administrative tribunals, this Court has consistently held
that when one's liberty or property is significantly affected
by an adjudicative decision, "due process of law requires

---

* JMHP. The original is a typed manuscript.

CONCUR, DRAFT 2

that at some stage of the proceedings . . . [he] shall have an opportunity to be heard," and that in such instances" a hearing in its very essence demands that he who is entitled to it shall have the right to support his allegations by argument, however brief, and, if need be, by proof, however informal."

No administrative or judicial decision could possibly have greater significance for a party than the determination of a jury whether he is to live or to die. I would hold that the principle of the foregoing cases does apply to capital sentencing when performed by a jury, and would hold that a capital defendant has a right, assured by the Due Process Clause of the Fourteenth Amendment, to present to the jury evidence in mitigation of his punishment. I would hold that the right encompasses not only the giving of personal testimony but the presentation of evidence by the testimony of other witnesses, by documents, and by physical exhibits.

I find no conflict between the existence of such a right and my view that, for reasons which appear *infra*, at _____-_____, a State is not constitutionally required to promulgate specific standards to govern jury sentencing. My Brother BRENNAN argues that unless a State has established such standards a defendant will never be able effectively to exercise his right to present mitigating evidence, since otherwise he will not know what evidence is relevant. I think this objection ephemeral. Some States have gone part way toward establishing standards by decreeing that certain types of mitigating evidence are inadmissible. I find this perfectly proper, so long as the distinction between admissible and inadmissible evidence is not wholly arbitrary. In my view, a capital defendant in such a State would have a constitutional right to present all mitigating evidence which is relevant under the State's own criteria.

On the other hand, some States have ruled that the

CONCUR, DRAFT 2

sentencing decision is to be within the jury's "absolute discretion." I take this to mean that the jury may fix the defendant's punishment on the basis of any or all evidence which seems to it relevant, in light of their own or the community's conceptions of punishment. In such a State, I would hold that the defendant has a constitutional right to introduce, within very broad limits, whatever evidence he thinks might induce the jury to mitigate his punishment. Exercise of the right would in no way contravene the State's policy of permitting the jury "absolute discretion" in sentencing—the only result would be that the jury would have more evidence upon which to base its discretionary decision.

According to *The Brethren, Maxwell* v. *Bishop* was ultimately left undecided because Justice Douglas "circulated a sweeping opinion. Harlan had had difficulty with Douglas's opinion; it went too far, calling into question sentencing procedures, not only in death cases but in all criminal cases."[23] Justice Harlan is said to have switched his vote, and "the comfortable 6-to-3 majority had become a very close 5-to-4. Before the opinion could be issued, Fortas had resigned, leaving the Court deadlocked, 4 to 4."[24]

This account is inaccurate. One who reads the Douglas draft opinion of the Court reprinted on page 412 can see that it is anything but sweeping. It is confined to the case before the Court and strikes down only the procedure under the Arkansas death penalty law. It does not call "into question sentencing procedures . . . in all criminal cases." Nor was the Douglas draft prevented from coming down as the opinion of the Court because Justice Harlan switched his vote. As the Harlan draft concurrence reprinted on page 438 shows, Justice Harlan then agreed with the Douglas view on bifurcation, but he wanted to issue his own opinion on the matter.

After Justice Fortas's resignation, Justice Harlan wanted more time to polish his admittedly rough draft. Justice Douglas, now unable to muster five votes for his opinion, also agreed to delay. In addition, Justice Stewart, still stubbornly adhering to the *Witherspoon* ground, pushed for reargument. In these circumstances, the Justices decided to hold off the decision and, on May 26, 1969, the Court set the case for reargument in the following term.[25]

But the Court that dealt with the case in the new 1969 term was a different Court. With Chief Justice Warren and Justice Fortas off the bench, two crucial votes for reversal on bifurcation were gone.

The new Chief Justice approached the case differently than Chief Justice Warren had done. At the conference after the reargument, Chief Justice Burger said that he saw "no way of shaping standards." In his view, "the sum total of the life experience of the jurors is the best you can do. You can't read [standards] into due process or any other clause of the Constitution." On bifurcation, the new Chief Justice asserted that he was "not sure it's a useful device or even helpful to defendants. I can't see it as a component of due process."

Justice Harlan's position at the conference is of particular interest, in view of the assertion in *The Brethren* that the Justice now led the fight against reversal on bifurcation.[26] Notes taken at the conference indicate that Justice Harlan not only still adhered to his vote against the unitary trial, but stated it in much stronger terms than he had the year before, using such language as, "This is one of the clearest cases of denial of fundamental fairness" and "I cannot imagine a more flagrant violation of due process."

The Brethren is incorrect in its statement that the vote in *Maxwell* v. *Bishop* after the reargument was five to three to uphold the Arkansas law.[27] It is true that this was the division on the standards issue (with Chief Justice Burger and Justices Black, Harlan, Stewart, and White for affirmance and Justices Douglas, Brennan, and Marshall for reversal). But the conference divided four to four on bifurcation (with the Chief Justice and Justices Black, Stewart, and White for affirmance and Justices Douglas, Harlan, Brennan, and Marshall for reversal). With the eight-man Court so closely divided on the standards and bifurcation issues, the Justices decided to dispose of *Maxwell* v. *Bishop* on the *Witherspoon* ground urged unsuccessfully the year before by Justices Stewart and White. There was a six-to-two majority for a *Witherspoon*-based reversal, with only the Chief Justice and Justice Black voting the other way.

On June 1, 1970, the Court issued a *per curiam* drafted by Justice Stewart, which held that the case should be remanded because a prospective juror had been removed after stating scruples about capital punishment.[28] This was a makeweight decision, designed to avoid a decision on the bifurcation and standards issues while the Court remained without a majority on them.

Justice Black alone dissented from the *Witherspoon* resolution of *Maxwell* v. *Bishop* (at the conference he had asserted, "This is any way only a fight to abolish capital punishment. That's for the legislature, not the courts."). The final vote on the case was six to one, since Chief Justice Burger (who had said at the conference that he saw no merit in the *Witherspoon* claim) ultimately went along with the majority, and Justice Marshall was reported as taking no part in the decision (although, in the conference notes on which my reconstruction is based, he is listed as voting).

By the 1970 term, a clear majority on the standards and bifurcation issues had been secured, but against the view expressed in the Douglas draft opinion of the Court in *Maxwell* v. *Bishop*. Two factors converted the original *Maxwell* majority into a three-Justice minority in *McGautha* v. *California*, where the Court upheld a statute permitting the jury to impose the death penalty in a unitary trial without governing standards.[29] In the first place, the new Chief Justice (as seen from his statement at the *Maxwell* v. *Bishop* conference after the reargument) strongly supported rejection of the constitutional claims to a bifurcated trial and standards. In an April 13, 1971, letter to Justice Harlan, headed "Personal," Chief Justice Burger wrote, "There is indeed a superficial or surface appeal to the claim for standards, but as a constitutional claim it is for me essentially a *plausible* claim for what might arguably be a *better* system. . . . it would take much more than the arguments presented to lift this claim above plausibility."[30] Justice Blackmun, newly appointed to the Court, agreed with Chief Justice Burger and voted with him and Justices Black, Stewart, and White to affirm the *McGautha* conviction.

So, also, did Justice Harlan, and his switched vote (changed from that in the *Maxwell* v. *Bishop* conferences and his draft concurrence, supra page 438) was the second factor making for the new majority in *McGautha*. With Justice Harlan writing the opinion, the Burger Court held that a defendant's constitutional rights were not violated by the jury's imposition of the death penalty in the same unitary proceeding that determined the issue of guilt or by permitting the jury to impose the death penalty without governing standards.

Justice Douglas used much of his *Maxwell* v. *Bishop* draft opinion in his *McGautha* dissent, joined by Justices Brennan and Marshall.[31] Justice Brennan, joined by Justices Douglas and Marshall, also issued a strong *McGautha* dissent.[32] Justice Brennan had originally planned to use his *Maxwell* draft concurrence in *McGautha*. "I had hoped," he wrote to Justice Harlan on March 1, 1971, "I could rest on what I circulated two years ago but, in light of your treatment, I think I'll have substantially to expand what I then said."[33] Justice Brennan's *McGautha* dissent is an expanded version of his draft *Maxwell* concurrence reprinted on page 431.

The morning before the Brennan dissent was circulated, the Justice was reading a copy of it on the bench when Justice Douglas was heard to ask what it was. He was told and then asked, "Do you want me to join it now?" At this Justice Brennan replied, in mock horror, "So this is the way we get the benefit of your thirty years' experience." Justice Douglas then promised at least to read the draft before joining it. The next day he sent Justice Brennan a note asking to join the opinion.

Resolution of the *Maxwell* v. *Bishop* issues does not, however, end with *McGautha* v. *California*. The *McGautha* decision on the validity of a unitary trial is probably still good law.[34] But the same is not true of the *McGautha* decision holding that death sentences may be imposed under statutes that leave juries with untrammeled discretion to impose or withhold the death penalty.[35] The 1972 decision in *Furman* v. *Georgia* struck down death penalty laws under which death may be imposed in an arbitrary and capricious manner. Such laws must be carefully drafted to ensure that the sentencing authority is given adequate information and guidance.[36] *Furman* did not overrule *McGautha*, yet there is clearly substantial tension between the two decisions.[37] As a more recent opinion has expressed it, *Furman* is a "determination that where the ultimate punishment of death is at issue a system of standardless jury discretion violates the Eighth and Fourteenth Amendments,"[38] a determination inconsistent with the *McGautha* holding on standards.

One interested in the "might have been" in Supreme Court jurisprudence cannot help but wonder what would have happened if Justice Goldberg had used his memorandum, reprinted on page 401, as the basis for a dissent challenging the constitutionality of the death penalty as such. The Bar would then have been alerted to the fact that at least one Justice doubted the constitutionality of the death penalty. Counsel in capital cases might then have been willing to raise the Eighth Amendment point in their appeals. *Maxwell* v. *Bishop* might have challenged the constitutionality of the death penalty as such. By then, the issue would have been one about which the Justices and the profession would have thought for several years. The Eighth Amendment issue might have been decided by the Warren Court instead of its successor.

Notes

1. Woodward and Armstrong, *The Brethren: Inside the Supreme Court* 205–206 (1979).
2. 398 U.S. 262 (1970).
3. 408 U.S. 238 (1972).
4. *Trop* v. *Dulles*, 356 U.S. 86, 99 (1958).
5. Powell, J., dissenting, in *Furman* v. *Georgia*, 408 U.S. at 428.
6. *Walker* v. *Nevada*, 375 U.S. 882 (1963); *Arnold* v. *North Carolina*, 376 U.S. 773 (1964); *Snider* v. *Cunningham*, 375 U.S. 889 (1963); *White* v. *Washington*, 375 U.S. 883 (1963); *Rudolph* v. *Alabama*, 375 U.S. 889 (1963); *Smith* v. *Bomar*, 376 U.S. 915 (1964).

    These are the cases listed in note 1 of Justice Goldberg's memorandum reprinted on page 401. On his copy of this memo, Justice Clark added in the margin "*Smith* v. *Heard*, 375 U.S. 883 (1963)." TCCT.
7. In *Furman* v. *Georgia*, supra note 3.
8. 356 U.S. 86, 101 (1958).
9. Goldberg memorandum, supra page 401.
10. 375 U.S. 889 (1963).
11. Ibid.
12. Supra note 3.
13. 428 U.S. 153 (1976).
14. See Schwartz, *Super Chief: Earl Warren and His Supreme Court—A Judicial Biography* 739 (1983).
15. JMHP.
16. 391 U.S. 510 (1968).
17. 398 U.S. 262 (1970).
18. Loc. cit. supra note 1.
19. See Schwartz, op. cit. supra note 14, at 740.
20. Ibid.
21. Id. at 741.
22. It is headed "Draft 2."
23. Woodward and Armstrong, op. cit. supra note 1, at 206.
24. Ibid.
25. 395 U.S. 918 (1969).
26. Woodward and Armstrong, op. cit. supra note 1, at 206.
27. Ibid.
28. 398 U.S. 262 (1970).
29. 402 U.S. 183 (1971).
30. JMHP (emphases in original).
31. 402 U.S. at 226.
32. Id. at 248.
33. JMHP.
34. See *Lonberger* v. *Jago*, 635 F.2d 1189, 1193 (6th Cir. 1980).
35. Compare *Gregg* v. *Georgia*, 428 U.S. at 196, n. (1976).
36. Id. at 195.
37. Id. at 196, n.; *Furman* v. *Georgia*, 408 U.S. at 248, n. 11.
38. *Gregg* v. *Georgia*, 428 U.S. at 196, n.

11

Brown v. Board of Education (1954, 1955): The Drafting Process in a Landmark Case

Brown v. *Board of Education*[1] stands at the head of the cases decided by the Warren Court. In many ways, *Brown* was the watershed constitutional case of this century. Justice Reed, who participated in the *Brown* decision, told one of his clerks that "if it was not the most important decision in the history of the Court, it was very close."[2] When *Brown* struck down school segregation, it signaled the beginning of effective enforcement of civil rights in American law.

Brown I (1954)

As much as any case, *Brown* illustrates the "might have been" in Supreme Court jurisprudence. *Brown* first came before the Court when Chief Justice Fred M. Vinson sat in its center chair. When the Justices discussed the case on December 13, 1952, Vinson stated that he was not ready to overrule *Plessy* v. *Ferguson*[3]—the 1896 case that had upheld a state law requiring "equal but separate accommodations for the white and colored races." The subsequent structure of racial discrimination in much of the country was built on the "separate but equal" doctrine approved in *Plessy* v. *Ferguson*.

At the December 13 conference[4] Vinson stressed the cases following *Plessy* v. *Ferguson*. There was, he declared, a whole "body of law back of us on separate but equal" and the Court should not overrule this substantial jurisprudence. What was needed, according to Vinson, was time to deal with the racial problem. "We can't," he said, "close our eyes to the seriousness [of the problem] in various parts of the U.S. We face the complete abolition of the public school system in the South."

With the Chief Justice indicating his own inclination in favor of up-holding segregation, the Vinson Court was far from ready to issue a ring-ing pronouncement in favor of racial equality. Indeed, had Vinson pre-sided over the Court that decided *Brown*, the result would have been a sharply divided decision. In a May 20, 1954, letter to a colleague three days after the unanimous *Brown* decision was announced, Justice Frank-furter wrote,[5] "I have no doubt that if the *Segregation* cases had reached decision last Term there would have been four dissenters—Vinson, Reed, Jackson and Clark—and certainly several opinions for the majority view. That would have been catastrophic."[6]

The "catastrophe" was avoided when *Brown* was set for reargument in the next Court term and, in the interim, Chief Justice Vinson suddenly died. "This is the first indication that I have ever had that there is a God," Frankfurter caustically remarked to two former law clerks when he heard of Vinson's death. The Justice must have felt confirmed in his comment when Warren was appointed as Vinson's successor. For, under the new Chief Justice, the Court was able to issue its landmark ruling striking down segregation and to do so unanimously, without a single concurring or dissenting voice to detract from the forthrightness of the decision.

Both the decision and the unanimity were attributable directly to Warren's leadership. A few days before the *Brown* decision was an-nounced, Justice Burton wrote in his diary, "It looks like a unanimous opinion—a major accomplishment for his [Warren's] leadership."[7] And, just after the *Brown* opinion was read, Burton wrote to Warren, "To you goes the credit for the character of the opinions which produced the all important unanimity."[8]

The new Chief Justice led the Court to its unanimous decision by first setting a completely different conference tone from that of his pre-decessor. Warren began his first *Brown* conference on December 12, 1953,[9] with a strong statement on the unconstitutionality of segregation: "I don't see how in this day and age we can set any group apart from the rest and say that they are not entitled to exactly the same treatment as all others. To do so would be contrary to the Thirteenth, Fourteenth, and Fifteenth Amendments. They were intended to make the slaves equal with all others. Personally, I can't see how today we can justify segregation based solely on race."

As far as *Plessy* v. *Ferguson* was concerned, said Warren, "the more I've read and heard and thought, the more I've come to conclude that the basis of segregation and 'separate but equal' rests upon a concept of the inherent inferiority of the colored race. I don't see how *Plessy* and the cases following it can be sustained on any other theory. If we are to sus-tain segregation, we also must do it upon that basis." Warren then asserted that "if the argument proved anything, it proved that that basis was not justified."

Warren's conference presentation put the proponents of *Plessy* in the awkward position of appearing to subscribe to racist doctrine. Justice

Reed, who spoke most strongly in support of *Plessy*, felt compelled to assert that he was not making "the argument that the Negro is an inferior race. Of course there is no inferior race, though they may be handicapped by lack of opportunity." Reed did not, however, suggest any other ground on which the Court might rely to justify segregation now.

When the conference was finished, it appeared that Warren had six firm votes for his view that segregation should be ruled invalid. Two Justices, Jackson and Clark, indicated that they would vote the same way if an opinion could be written to satisfy them. Only Reed still supported the *Plessy* doctrine.

Warren now devoted all his efforts to eliminate the danger of dissenting and concurring opinions. During the months that followed, he met constantly with his colleagues on the case, most often talking to them informally in their chambers. From all we know about Warren, he was most effective when he was able to operate in a one-on-one setting. That was the way he had been able to accomplish things back in California. The result in *Brown* showed that he had not lost any of his persuasive powers in the Marble Palace.

Despite the Chief Justice's efforts, there are indications that Reed persisted in voting to uphold segregation until the end of April 1954. By then, however, the Justice stood alone and Warren continued to work on him to change his vote, both at luncheon meetings and in private sessions. Then, toward the end, the Chief Justice put it to Reed directly: "Stan, you're all by yourself in this now. You've got to decide whether it's really the best thing for the country."[10] As described by Reed's law clerk, who was present at the meeting, Warren was typically restrained in his approach. "Throughout the Chief Justice was quite low-key and very sensitive to the problems that the decision would present to the South. He empathized with Justice Reed's concern. But he was quite firm on the Court's need for unanimity on a matter of this sensitivity."[11]

Ultimately, Reed agreed to the unanimous decision. He still thought, as he wrote to Frankfurter, that "there were many considerations that pointed to a dissent." But, he went on, "they did not add up to a balance against the Court's opinion. . . . the factors looking toward a fair treatment for Negroes are more important than the weight of history."[12]

At the conference that took the vote to strike down segregation, it was agreed that the opinion should be written by the Chief Justice.[13] The writing of the *Brown* opinion was done under conditions of even greater secrecy than usual. The extreme secrecy was extended to the entire deliberative process in the segregation case. Thus, the covering note to a Frankfurter memorandum on the fashioning of a decree in the case stated at the end: "I need hardly add that the typewriting was done under conditions of strictest security."[14] The Justices also took steps to ensure that the way they voted would not leak out. No record of actions taken in *Brown* was written in the docket book that was kept by each Justice and was available to his clerks. Warren tells us that, at the conference at which the opinion was assigned, "the importance of secrecy was discussed. We agreed that only my law clerks should be involved, and that any writing between my office and those of the other Justices would be delivered to the Justices personally. This practice was followed throughout and this was the only time it was required in my years on the Court."[15]

Toward the end of April, after he had secured Reed's vote, the Chief Justice was ready to begin the drafting process. On April 20, Justice Burton wrote in his diary, "After lunch the Chief Justice and [I] took a walk around the Capitol then went to his chambers where he uttered his preliminary thoughts as to author segregation cases."[16] Soon thereafter Warren went to work on the *Brown* draft opinion.

Warren's normal practice was to leave the actual drafting of opinions to his law clerks. He would usually outline verbally (though in important cases he would dictate the outline to Mrs. Margaret McHugh, his executive assistant) the way he wanted the opinion drafted. The outline would summarize the facts and how the main issues should be decided. The Chief Justice would rarely go into particulars on the details involved in the case. That was for the clerk drafting the opinion, who was left with a great deal of discretion, particularly on the reasoning and research supporting the decision.

It has been assumed that this procedure was also followed in the *Brown* drafting process. However, the draft opinion printed on p. 451 shows that it was Warren himself who wrote the first *Brown* draft. Headed simply "Memorandum" and undated, the original, in Warren's handwriting, is in pencil on nine yellow legal-size pages.

Certain things about Warren's first *Brown* draft stand out. First, it definitely set the tone for the final opinion. It was written in the typical Warren style: short, nontechnical, well within the grasp of the average reader. The language is direct and straightforward, illustrating the point once made to me by one of his law clerks: "He had a penchant for Anglo-Saxon words over Latin words and he didn't like foreign phrases thrown in if there was a good American word that would do."

Warren's own draft was based on the two things he later stressed to Earl Pollock, the clerk primarily responsible for helping on the *Brown* opinion: the opinion should be as brief as possible, and it was to be written in understandable English, avoiding legalisms. The Chief Justice told Pollock he wanted an opinion that could be understood by the layman. This was repeated in Warren's May 7 memorandum transmitting the draft opinion to the Justices. The draft, wrote the Chief Justice, was "prepared on the theory that the opinions should be short, readable by the lay public, non-rhetorical, unemotional and, above all, non-accusatory."[17]

Even more important is the fact that the Warren draft opinion is basically similar to the final *Brown* opinion. Changes were, to be sure, made in the draft—both by the Chief Justice and his clerks, as well as other Justices. In particular, supporting authority was supplied by the clerks, both in the text and in fleshing out the opinion with footnotes. But the essentials of the *Brown* opinion (and most of its language) were contained in the draft Warren wrote out in his own forcefully legible hand at the end of April 1954. As we shall see, the only important change made, primarily by two of the clerks, did anything but improve the final opinion.

The Warren draft contains two of the three most famous passages in the *Brown* opinion. First, after referring to the decision facing the Court, the draft states, "In approaching it, we cannot turn the clock of education back to 1868, when the Amendment was adopted, or even to 1895 when *Plessy* v. *Ferguson* was decided."

The Warren draft also contains *Brown*'s striking passage on the baneful effect of segregation on black children: "To separate them from others of their age in school solely because of their color puts the mark of inferiority not only upon their status in the community but also upon their little hearts and minds in a form that is unlikely ever to be erased."

Concern with the impact of segregation on the "hearts and minds" of black children was typical of the Warren approach. In the case of segregation, this view had roots in Warren's contact with Edgar Patterson, his black driver while he was Governor of California. Patterson later recalled how he used to talk to the Governor about his early years. Warren would ask, "Tell me about how you felt when you were a little kid, going to school. And then I used to tell him about some of the things that happened in New Orleans, the way black kids felt." Patterson thought that the *Brown* opinion "almost quoted the ideas that he and I used to talk about on feelings . . . things that he picked up as he was asking questions about how the black man felt, how the black kid felt." Just before Warren's death, Patterson visited him in Georgetown University Hospital and told him his *Brown* decision "seemed to be based on our discussion of my early school life in New Orleans." Warren laughed and indicated that many other factors had entered into the decision.[18]

In addition, it was the Warren draft that stressed the changed role of education in the contemporary society, as contrasted with the situation when the Fourteenth Amendment was adopted ("No child can reasonably be expected to succeed in life today if he is deprived of the opportunity of an education") and also posed the crucial question presented to the Court: "Does segregation of school children solely on the basis of color, even though the physical facilities may be equal, deprive the minority group of equal opportunities in the educational system?"—as well as its answer: "We believe that it does."

The only part of the Warren draft that was not used in the final *Brown* opinion was its characterization of *Plessy* v. *Ferguson:* "In that case, the Court with results customary in such circumstances, attempted to serve two masters—(1) the master of equality under the laws; and (2) the master of racial concept as it existed at that time in the Southern States of the Union. It endeavored to retain both the philosophy of the *Dred Scott* case and the principle of the Fourteenth Amendment." This passage is interesting because it reveals the emotional disdain felt by the Chief Justice toward the decision upholding segregation. It was, however, best omitted from an opinion intended to meet the "unemotional" desideratum stated in Warren's already quoted May 7 memorandum.

An early draft of the memorandum transmitting the *Brown* draft to the Justices declared, "On the question of segregation in education, this should be the end of the line."[19] If that was true, it was mainly the Chief Justice's doing—even more than commentators on *Brown* have realized. The Warren *Brown* draft shows us that the Chief Justice was primarily responsible not only for the unanimous decision, but also for the opinion in the case. This was one case where the drafting was not delegated.[20] The opinion delivered was essentially the opinion produced when Warren himself sat down and put pencil to paper.

MEMORANDUM*

These cases come to us from the States of Delaware, Virginia, Kansas and South Carolina and from the District of Columbia. They are premised on different facts and different local and state conditions, which under the equity powers of this Court call for separate and even different decrees, but the basic law involved in their decision is identical to the point that they can on principle properly be considered together in this opinion.

In each of the cases a minor of the Negro race, through his legal representative, seeks the aid of the courts in obtaining admission to the public schools of his State on the same basis as white children of the community in which he lives. In each instance, he has been denied that right by the Board of Education under State laws requiring or permitting segregation merely because of color. In each State case, except the Delaware case, the courts have decided against him on the so-called "separate but equal" doctrine announced by this Court in *Plessy* v. *Ferguson*, 163 U.S. 537. In the Delaware case, the court below adhered to that doctrine, but granted respondents injunctive relief on the ground that the school facilities for colored children were not equal to those maintained for white children. From this judgment, the members of the School Board appealed. In the District of Columbia case, the Board and United States District Court relied upon congressional authorization to accomplish segregation.

The original plaintiffs in all these cases contend that the "separate but equal" doctrine denies them of due process and of equal protection of the laws, and that the school facilities afforded them are not in fact and cannot be made equal under any segregated system. In none of the cases did the court below find that the facilities complained of were equal. In some, the court specifically found that the plaintiff suffered from inequality in some form or

---

* Original in Chief Justice Warren's handwriting. Earl Warren Papers, Library of Congress.

MEMORANDUM

other. Because of the importance of the problem and the Constitutional question involved, this Court took jurisdiction. The basic question may be stated as follows:

[Quote]

At the request of the Court, the Government appeared and ably answered certain questions propounded by the Court as basic to a decision.

All parties thoroughly discussed the legislative history of the Fourteenth Amendment and the contemporary views of proponents and opponents concerning its purpose and scope. The Government was particularly helpful in this regard. It concluded that both the legislative history and the contemporary statements concerning the scope of the Amendment as they apply to these cases were inconclusive. This is not surprising because neither the Constitution itself nor any of its Amendments have been adopted under circumstances comparable to those in 1868 surrounding the adoption of the Fourteenth Amendment. The country had but recently emerged from four years of fratricidal warfare revolving around the status of the Negro in American life. In 1868, there had been 37 states admitted to the Union, _____ of them since the war. They were almost evenly divided during the war. In 1868, there was still intense emotion on both sides. The Congress, which submitted the Amendment, did not have representation from the Southern States, and the latter, 17 in all, gave approval to it only as a condition of restoration to full participation in the Federal Government. These states were, of course, opposed to both the letter and spirit of the Amendment. On the other hand, those who were most active in its adoption unquestionably intended that it, together with the Thirteenth and Fifteenth, should eradicate all differences under the laws of the states between ". . . all persons born or naturalized in the United States, and subject to the jurisdiction thereof . . ." (14th Amend-

MEMORANDUM

ment). What others in Congress and in the State Legislatures not included in either of these groups had in mind cannot be ascertained. The record of Congress is not adequate for this purpose and in many of the Legislatures, the adoption was accomplished with little or no formal discussion. Particularly is that true in the Southern States.

The idea of "separate but equal" was not current at that time. It first made its appearance in this Court in 1895 in the case of *Plessy* v. *Ferguson, supra.* In that case, the Court with results customary in such circumstances, attempted to serve two masters—(1) the master of equality under the laws; and (2) the master of racial concept as it existed at that time in the Southern States of the Union. It endeavored to retain both the philosophy of the *Dred Scott* case and the principle of the Fourteenth Amendment. This Court has since labored with the doctrine for more than a half century. In the field of education alone with which we are here concerned, _____ cases prior to these have found their way to this Court. In each of them, the "separate but equal" doctrine has been attacked as being per se unconstitutional, and as not being capable of implementation in the field of education. In none of them has the Court been able to apply the doctrine. In each case, on its own facts, it was held that equality was absent.

These cases bring us to the elementary and high school level. If we decide that segregation, as reflected in these cases, is violative of the constitutional rights of plaintiffs below and of other persons so situated, we will have run the gamut of the public educational system without finding any instance to which the doctrine can be applied and that in education it must, therefore, be abandoned.

We have no doubt that we are presently faced with this residuary decision. In approaching it, we cannot turn the clock of education back to 1868, when the Amendment

MEMORANDUM

was adopted, or even to 1895 when *Plessy* v. *Ferguson* was decided. We must consider public education in the light of the present-day concept, the place of public education in American life and the mutual relationships of pupils, parents and government. Only in this way can it be determined if segregation in the school system abridges the privileges of American citizens, denies them due process or of equal protection of the laws.

In 1868, public education was not an accepted fact throughout the Union, particularly in the Southern States. In some of the States, public schools were only for the needy. And until 1864, it was a crime in the Southern States to teach Negroes even to read or write. In some States, a special extra tax was levied on Negroes for their own education. In Washington, D.C., separate schools for Negroes were maintained by authorization of Congress, but not on the "separate but equal" theory. There, as in the states which require or permit segregation, separate schools were maintained on the basis of Negro inferiority until *Plessy* v. *Ferguson* announced its rationalization.

Now the public schools represent a major function and expense of local and, in most states, state government. There are reciprocal rights and responsibilities between parents, pupils and government. Children are required by law to attend school to a specified age. For non-attendance, they are subject to juvenile discipline and their parents to fine and imprisonment. State and local governments, mostly by constitutional mandate, undertake to give every child a sound, basic education, sufficient to equip him for a place in local and national life. The United States Government spends large sums annually to implement the program (school lunches, construction, schools on military reservations, etc.). No child can reasonably be expected to succeed in life today if he is deprived of the opportunity of an education. He must even meet educational standards to serve his country in the armed

MEMORANDUM

forces. It is a right which he is entitled to share equally with every other child in his state and community. It must, therefore, follow that anything which arbitrarily sets him apart from other children and circumscribes his right to such an education abridges his privileges and denies him the equal protection of the laws. This question then propounds itself:

Does segregation of school children solely on the basis of color, even though the physical facilities may be equal, deprive the minority group of equal opportunities in the educational system? We believe that it does. We believe that it applies particularly to children of tender age, and that the reasons stated for striking down segregation in the college cases apply with added force to children in the grade and high schools. To separate them from others of their age in school solely because of their color puts the mark of inferiority not only upon their status in the community but also upon their little hearts and minds in a form that is unlikely ever to be erased. We believe that it has many other divisive results not necessary to enumerate here but which, in the aggregate, make the doctrine of "separate but equal" inapplicable to education.

We, therefore, hold that in each of the cases here under review the plaintiff below, and others similarly situated for whom the action may have been brought, are, by reason of the segregation complained of, deprived of their constitutional rights and are entitled to the relief sought.

Because these are class actions and because many thousands of other people are affected by this decision, under widely different local conditions, and because the relief phase of the cases was submerged by the argument concerning the basic issue of segregation, the question of appropriate decrees is continued to the next Term of Court for further argument in accordance with questions to be propounded by the Court. The Government is again requested to assist the Court as it did so ably this Term.

"An opinion in a touchy and explosive litigation . . . is like a soufflé—
it should be served at once after it has reached completion." The *Brown*
drafting process, after Warren had penciled the draft opinion reproduced
on p. 451, showed that the Chief Justice agreed with this sentiment contained in a May 15, 1954, note to him from Justice Frankfurter.

As soon as Warren had finished his *Brown* draft and had it typed, he
called in his three law clerks and told them the decision of the Court was
to overturn *Plessy*, and that the decision was unanimous. He enjoined
them to the strictest secrecy, saying that he had not told anyone outside
the Justices what the decision was—not even his wife. The Chief Justice
asked all three clerks to write drafts based on his own draft opinion. It
was now the end of April, and the clerks worked the entire weekend in
order to have their drafts ready on Monday, May 3. Earl Pollock, in particular, recalls working straight through the weekend on his draft—virtually without sleep. Pollock was the clerk with primary responsibility
for the case, since he had written the *Brown* bench memo. Such a memo
is prepared for each Justice after the Court votes to hear a case.

The clerks' three drafts were finished on Monday, May 3. Of the
three, Pollock's was the most important, for he made the only significant
changes in the Chief Justice's draft. The most important change was the
separation of the companion case of *Bolling* v. *Sharpe*[21] from the *Brown*
case itself. The segregation cases presented to the Court involved schools
in four states and the District of Columbia. Warren's *Brown* draft had
dealt with all these cases together, as shown by its opening sentence:
"These cases come to us from the States of Delaware, Virginia, Kansas
and South Carolina and from the District of Columbia." The Warren
draft went on to say that, though they were separate cases, "the basic
law involved in their decision is identical to the point that they can on
principle properly be considered together in this opinion."

In treating the state and D.C. cases together, the Warren draft was
making a legal mistake. The rationale for striking down segregation in
the states cannot be used to reach that result in Washington, D.C. The
state action in *Brown* was invalidated under the Equal Protection Clause
of the Fourteenth Amendment. Yet that amendment is binding only on
the states, not the Federal Government. The latter is bound by the Fifth
Amendment, which contains a Due Process Clause, but no requirement
of equal protection. Obviously, the Court would not decide that the states
could not have segregated schools, while the District of Columbia could.
But the result had to be reached in terms of due process, rather than
equal protection, analysis.

Following the example set in Warren's draft, the three law clerks
dealt with the state and D.C. cases together in their drafts. However, in
the May 3 covering memorandum attached to his draft, Pollock indicated
that this was not the proper approach. Pollock stated that his draft was
"along the lines of your memo of last week. Like the memo, this draft
covers all five cases in one consolidated opinion." Pollock then wrote, "I

am inclined to think, however, that the District of Columbia case should be treated independently in a short, separate opinion accompanying the other one. . . . The material relating to the equal protection clause of the 14th Amendment has no direct relevance to the District of Columbia case, which, of course, is based primarily on the due process clause of the 5th Amendment." "In short," the Pollock memo concluded, "the legal problem in the states and the legal problem in the District are different and require somewhat different treatment. For the sake of clarity, a short, separate opinion in the District case is recommended."

Warren accepted this suggestion, and the details of the legal theory underlying the D.C. case were worked out by the other two clerks, William Oliver and Richard Flynn. They also drafted the separate short opinion delivered in the case.

In addition to the May 3 drafts of the clerks, there were further *Brown* drafts on May 5 and 7, before the draft opinion was ready to be circulated to the Justices, together with the draft in the D.C. case. This typed *Brown* draft, composed of nine legal size pages, was titled "MEMO-RANDUM ON THE STATE CASES." The draft in *Bolling* v. *Sharpe*, four typed pages, was titled "MEMORANDUM ON THE DISTRICT OF COLUMBIA CASE." The draft opinions were then delivered personally to the Justices on Saturday, May 8. Justice Burton's diary entry for that date notes: "In AM the Chief Justice brought his draft of the segregation cases memoranda. These were in accord with our conversations."[22] Warren himself took the printed drafts to the Justices who were in their chambers. His clerks brought copies to the others. Justice Black's copy was brought to him on the tennis court at his home in Alexandria, Justice Minton's at his Washington apartment.

As indicated in my discussion before the text of the *Brown* draft opinion, few significant alterations were made in the Warren draft. The Justices themselves made only minor stylistic changes.[23] The only one of these worthy of note was the Frankfurther suggestion for the Warren "hearts and minds" passage—that of changing "puts the mark of inferiority" to "generates a feeling of inferiority." But the sentence in the final version was essentially the one Warren had originally written.

In the Warren chambers, the further drafts were prepared by Pollock who also made numerous cosmetic alterations in the Chief Justice's draft. There were only two important changes. The first was a discussion of the post-*Plessy* v. *Ferguson* education cases. This added some legal meat to the opinion, but did not really add anything of substance to it.

The second change was more significant, particularly when we add the contribution made to it by a second law clerk. After Warren's "hearts and minds" sentence on the baneful effect of segregation, Pollock's first draft of May 3 added the passage from the opinion of the lower court in the Kansas case that now appears in the *Brown* opinion. The Pollock draft then asserted, "Whatever may have been the state of psychological knowledge when *Plessy* v. *Ferguson* was decided, this finding is amply

supported by modern authority. To the extent that there is language in
Plessy v. *Ferguson* to the contrary, and to the extent that other decisions
of this Court have been read as applying the 'separate but equal' doctrine
to education, those cases are overruled."

This statement was accepted by the Chief Justice and repeated in the
drafts of May 5, 7, and 8. The passage was put into its final form by written corrections in Pollock's writing in the draft of May 12, the final draft
in the case.

In a recent interview Pollock told me that he had been greatly troubled by the *Plessy* v. *Ferguson* opinion. "It seemed to me," he went on,
"that the most noxious part of *Plessy* was the notion that, if Negroes
found segregation a 'badge of inferiority,' that was sort of in the eye of
the beholder. I was looking for a way to part company and to say that,
whatever the situation was in the 1890's, we know a lot more about law
in society than we did then."

It was this approach that was responsible for the most controversial
part of the *Brown* opinion—that relying not on law but "psychological
knowledge." In *The New York Times* of May 18, 1954, James Reston
analyzed *Brown* in a column headed, "A Sociological Decision." According to Reston, the Court had relied "more on the social scientists than on
legal precedents. . . . The Court's opinion read more like an expert paper
on sociology than a Supreme Court opinion."[24]

The Reston characterization was based on the assertion that the
Brown opinion rested, not so much on legal reasoning, as on the Pollock
statement on "psychological knowledge . . . amply supported by modern authority." Even more suggestive to commentators was the fact that
the statement was backed by a footnote—the celebrated footnote 11,
which soon became the most controversial note in Supreme Court history.

Footnote 11 listed seven works by social scientists, starting with an
article by Kenneth B. Clark and concluding with the massive two-volume
study by Gunnar Myrdal, *An American Dilemma*.[25] Both supporters and
critics of the Court have assumed, like Reston, that footnote 11 means
that the *Brown* decision was based on the work of the social scientists
cited. As Kenneth Clark, the first mentioned in the footnote, summarized
it, "the Court . . . appeared to rely on the findings of social scientists in
the 1954 decision."[26] A plethora of learned commentary followed, analyz-
ing in amazing detail the works cited, the significance of the order of
citation, and the fact that other relevant writings were not cited—as well
as the whole subject of using the methods and products of social science
in deciding controversial legal issues. Even supporters of the decision have
shown how vulnerable the studies and tests relied on in most of the cited
works really were.

Those who have focused so intensively on the controversial footnote
have acted out of ignorance of the manner in which Supreme Court opinions are prepared. Warren himself stressed that it was the decision, not
the citations, that were important. "It was only a note, after all," he de-

clared to an interviewer.[27] Warren normally left the citations in opinions to his law clerks. He considered them among the minutiae of legal scholarship, which could, in the main, be left to others.

In the *Brown* case, the fleshing out of the opinion with footnotes was left primarily to one of Warren's clerks, Richard Flynn. As he recalls it, there was no specific method in the organization of footnote 11. When it came time to cite supporting authority, the works listed (particularly those by Myrdal and Clark) were, to Flynn, the "obvious" things to list. When asked by me if there was any method in the way he organized the note, he answered, "I don't recall any, that's just the way it fell."

It has been said that footnote 11 provoked concern among several Justices, particularly in the gratuitous citation of the Myrdal work, which had, in the decade since its publication, become a red flag to the white South. In 1971, Justice Clark, then retired from the Court, told an interviewer, "I questioned the Chief's going with Myrdal in that opinion. I told him—and Hugo Black did, too—that it wouldn't go down well in the South. And he didn't need it."[28]

Clark's recollection appears now to have been inaccurate. Over the years, he may have come to feel that, in view of the storm in the South caused by the Myrdal citation, he should have said something at the time, which may, years later, have become a blurred recollection that he and Black had expressed concern. But, in all likelihood, if Justices Black and Clark had objected, the Myrdal reference would have been taken out. The citation was just not important enough to Warren to withstand even a mild expression of concern by any of the Justices.

Justice Clark did suggest one correction in footnote 11 that was speedily accepted by the Chief Justice—which indicates that the same thing might well have happened if Clark had asked for the Myrdal to be removed. In the draft of the *Brown* opinion originally delivered to the Justices, the footnote began with the citation: "Clark, Effect of Prejudice and Discrimination on Personality Development (Midcentury White House Conference on Children and Youth, 1950)."[29] Justice Clark objected that this did not sufficiently identify the Clark who had written the article cited. He did not want people, particularly in his own South, to think that the Court was citing an anti-segregation article that he—Tom Clark—had authored. He, therefore, asked that the citation be changed to "K. B. Clark," so that no one would confuse the Justice with the author. In the final opinion, the name of the first author cited appears with initials, as Justice Clark had suggested—the only author in the footnote not identified solely by last name.

There was thus no "psychological knowledge"—footnote 11 controversy in the Court itself. So far as we know, the draft *Brown* opinion was speedily approved by the Justices—and without significant changes. The general attitude among Warren's colleagues was expressed in a handwritten note by Justice Douglas: "I do not think I would change a single word. . . . You have done a beautiful job."[30]

The final *Brown* draft was circulated on May 13 in printed form. The next day, Saturday, May 15, was a conference day. At lunch, the Justices were entertained by Justice Burton, with a large salmon provided by Secretary of the Interior Douglas McKay. Just before, Burton wrote in his diary, the "conference finally approved Segregation opinions and instructions for delivery Monday—no previous notice being given to office staffs etc so as to avoid leaks. Most of us—including me—handed back the circulated print to C.J. to avoid possible leaks."[31]

When the *Brown* opinion was delivered, the Justices were well aware that they had participated in what Justice Frankfurter termed "a day that will live in glory."[32] A few days earlier, in a note to Warren joining the opinion, Frankfurter wrote: "When—I no longer say 'if'—you bring this cargo of unanimity safely to port it will be a memorable day no less in the history of the Nation than in that of the Court. You have, if I may say so, been wisely at the helm throughout this year's journey of this litigation. *Finis coronat omnia*."[33]

Brown II (1955)

The *Brown* case presented two principal questions: (1) Was school segregation constitutional?; (2) If it was not, what remedy should the Court decree? The Court's decision on May 17, 1954, answered the first of these questions in the negative. The Warren opinion of the Court, based upon the Chief Justice's draft, which is reprinted on p. 451, ruled only that school segregation violated the rights of plaintiff black children. It did not, however, make any provision for enforcement.

There is an undated note, written on a Supreme Court memo pad in Justice Frankfurter's handwriting, that reads, "It is not fair to say that the South has always denied Negroes 'this constitutional right.' It was NOT a constitutional right till May 17/54."[34]

The May 17, 1954, opinion declared the right against segregation, but it made no provision for vindication of the new right. Instead, acting on a suggestion made by Justice Jackson at Warren's second *Brown* conference on January 16, 1954,[35] the Chief Justice's opinion concluded by announcing that the Court was scheduling further argument on the question of appropriate relief. Thus, although the May 17 decision settled the issue of constitutionality, the Supreme Court still had another round to go in the *Brown* litigation. The situation was summarized in *The New York Times* account of the *Brown* decision: "when it returns in October for the 1954–1955 term [the Court] will hear rearguments then on the question of how and when the practice it outlawed today may finally be ended."[36]

The theme for the second *Brown* decision and opinion was set by the Chief Justice himself at the conference that met on Saturday, April 16, 1955, following the oral reargument on the terms of the decree earlier in the week. Warren's presentation opening the conference[37] stated the main lines of what became the Court's enforcement decision. First, the Chief Justice rejected various proposals that had been discussed in the Court: appointment of a master (a lawyer chosen to work out the terms of an enforcement decree), fixing of a date for completion of desegregation, requiring specific desegregation plans from defendant school districts, and imposing of procedural requirements—all of which were also rejected by the Court's decision. Then he emphasized that the Court should furnish guidance to the lower courts: "the opinion ought to give them some guidance. It would make it much easier and would be rather cruel to shift it back to them and let them flounder." The guidance should be in an opinion listing the factors to be taken into account, rather than a formal decree: "I think there should be an opinion with factors for the courts below to take into account rather than a formal decree." The opinion-not-decree approach had the advantage of less formal precision and hence greater flexibility. Flexibility in enforcement was also the keynote of the "ground rules" Warren suggested to guide the enforcement process.

Once again, Warren's presentation set the theme both for the conference and the decision. With one exception, the others at the conference indicated agreement with the Warren approach. The exception was Justice Black. "I differ from your views," he told the Chief. "How to say and do as little as possible is my present desire. I was brought up in an atmosphere against federal officials, which is rooted in the race question. . . . The South would never be a willing party to Negroes and whites going to school together. There's no more chance to enforce this in the deep South than Prohibition in New York City. Nothing is more important than that this Court should not issue what it cannot enforce." Black wanted the decree to be "as narrow as possible."

As Warren's own conference notes quote him, Black said, "Would write a decree and quit. The less we say the better off we are."[38] Black concluded his presentation by asserting that, at best, there would be only "glacial movement" toward desegregation. "It is futile to think that in these cases we can settle segregation in the South."

Fortunately, Black agreed that it was vital for the Court to remain unanimous in the enforcement decision. "If humanly possible," he said at the conference, "I will do everything possible to achieve a unanimous result." Despite his different views, he ultimately went along with the *Brown II* decision and opinion.

Once again the conference agreed that the unanimous opinion should be written by the Chief Justice. Warren stressed to his clerks that the opinion should be as short as possible and cover the main points he had made at the conference: that enforcement be flexible, under accepted equity principles, and that it take into account various factors to be briefly listed to serve as "ground rules" for the lower courts.

As was true in *Brown I*, the drafting of the *Brown II* opinion was primarily by the Chief Justice himself. On April 28, 1955, Warren dictated an outline to Mrs. McHugh listing the points to be covered in the opinion. All the main points dealt with in the *Brown II* opinion were included in this outline. The outline was revised by Gerald Gunther, one of the Warren law clerks, on May 18. It is fair to say that the revisions were minor.

Warren then once more put pencil to paper and produced the draft opinion reproduced on p. 463. The original is again in pencil in the Chief Justice's handwriting on six yellow legal size pages and headed "*Memo.*"[39] As was true of Warren's *Brown I* draft, this *Brown II* draft is essentially similar to the final *Brown II* opinion and contains most of the latter's language. As we shall see, some nonstylistic changes were made, both by the Chief Justice and others. But they did not necessarily improve the final product.

MEMO*

These cases were decided on May 17, 1954, when we held racial discrimination in public education unconstitutional. The opinions of that date, which are incorporated herein by reference, declared the governing constitutional principles. In this opinion we designate the manner in which these principles and the rights of the parties are to be made effective.

Because the effectuation of these principles must take place under different local conditions, with a resulting variety of local problems, we requested the assistance of the parties through further arguments on the question of relief. In view of the nationwide importance of the decision, we invited the Attorney General of the United States and the Attorneys General of all states requiring or permitting racial discrimination in public education to present their views on the formulation of the decrees. The parties, the United States and the States of Florida, North Carolina, Arkansas, Oklahoma, Maryland and Texas filed briefs and impressively presented their views orally.

These briefs and arguments were both informative and helpful to the Court in its consideration of the problems arising from the transition to a non-discriminatory system of public education. The arguments also demonstrated that substantial steps to eliminate racial discrimination in public education have already been taken in some of the communities in which these cases arose, in some of the states appearing as amicus curiae, and in other states as well. Such progress has been made in the District of Columbia and in the communities in Kansas and Delaware involved in this litigation. Because of this fact formulation of decrees in the cases coming from these jurisdictions presents no complex problems. The defendants in the cases coming to us from South Carolina and

* Original mostly in Chief Justice Warren's handwriting. Earl Warren Papers, Library of Congress.

MEMO

Virginia are awaiting the decision of this Court concerning relief.

Recognizing that full implementation of the applicable constitutional principles may require solution of varied local school problems which have not yet been judicially considered, and because in the determination of them, the taking of testimony may be required as well as contact retained with the local boards of education which have the primary responsibility for elucidating, assessing and solving school problems, we conclude that such judicial consideration can best be given with the assistance of the parties, and progress made in the light of local conditions, by the lower courts which originally heard these cases. The situation then calls for a remand of the cases to them for appropriate decrees not inconsistent with this opinion.

In fashioning the decrees and supervising their enforcement, the lower courts will be guided by general equitable principles. Equity has traditionally been characterized by a practical flexibility in the shaping of its remedies, *Addison* v. *Holly Hill Co.,* 322 U.S. 607, 622, and by a facility for adjustment and reconciliation of public interest and private needs as well as between competing private claims. *Hecht Co.* v. *Bowles* 321 U.S. 321, 329-330. These cases call for the exercise of these traditional attributes of equity.

Thus, there is on the one hand the personal interest of these plaintiffs and those similarly situated in their respective school districts in admission to public schools on a non-discriminatory basis. Yet these cases call for elimination of a variety of obstacles involved in making the transition to school systems operated in accordance with constitutional principles. Courts of equity may, therefore, properly take into account the public interest in accomplishing this transition in an orderly, effective manner.

In acting under these equitable principles and giving weight to the public as well as private considerations, the

MEMO

lower courts will of course require that the defendants make a prompt and reasonable start toward full compliance with our May 17, 1954, ruling. They will also consider the adequacy and effectiveness for the purposes of these cases of any plans which the defendants may propose for transition to a non-discriminatory school system.

Once the required prompt, reasonable start has been made, the courts may find that additional time is necessary to implement the newly defined constitutional rights fully and in an effective, orderly manner. The burden rests upon the defendants to establish that such additional time to overcome the relevant local problems is necessary in the public interest and for good faith compliance at the earliest practicable date. To that end, the courts may consider such problems related to administration as those arising from:

> the physical condition of the school plant;
> the school transportation system;
> financing;
> personnel;
> revision of school districts and attendance areas into compact units to achieve a system of determining admission to the public schools on a non-racial basis,
> and revision of local laws and regulations which may be necessary in solving the foregoing problems.

The judgments of the Courts of Appeal are accordingly reversed (except Delaware) and the causes are remanded to the District Courts to take such proceedings and enter such orders and decrees consistent with this opinion as are necessary and proper to admit plaintiffs and those similarly situated in their respective school districts to the public school system on a non-discriminatory basis at the earliest practicable date.

Reversed and Remanded

The *Brown II* draft was circulated to the Justices on May 26. The memorandum transmitting the draft noted that "minor changes, largely stylistic, have been made to conform to suggestions of several members of the Court." It also suggested that "if agreeable, we will discuss it at the Conference tomorrow."[40] The conference on May 27 considered the proposed *Brown II* opinion in detail. The one discordant note was a suggestion by Justice Frankfurter (made privately a few days earlier to some of the Justices) that the opinion should be an unsigned per curiam. The Court voted eight-to-one that the opinion should be by the Chief Justice, as originally decided. The Conference also agreed that the decision should be announced on May 31—the last day of the 1954 term.

The conference made only one substantial change in the draft *Brown II* opinion. The Warren draft stated that the district courts were to enter such orders and decrees as to ensure the nondiscriminatory admission to public schools of "plaintiffs and those similarly situated in their respective school districts." This wording would have converted *Brown* into a virtual class action, allowing not only the actual parties, but also those similarly situated, to obtain the relief ordered. At the April 16 conference, Warren had stated the view that "these are class actions and not only the named plaintiffs" would come within whatever decree was issued. Although several Justices agreed, Justices Black and Douglas were opposed and insisted that relief should be restricted to the named plaintiffs only. Their opposition prevailed at the May 27 conference, and the final version ordered the district courts to enter such decrees as were necessary to admit to public schools "the parties to these cases."

Two other changes of interest were made in the Warren draft. The first was the insertion of a sentence called forth by a dramatic incident during the *Brown II* reargument. It occurred when S. Emory Rogers led off the Southern case on April 12. Rogers, a short, florid scion of the plantation district involved, asserted, in answer to the *Brown I* opinion statement that the clock could not be turned back to 1868, when the Fourteenth Amendment was adopted, or 1896, when *Plessy* v. *Ferguson* was decided, "I do not believe that . . . we can push the clock forward abruptly to 2015 or 2045." He then asked for an "open decree"—one that sent the cases back without instructions specifying when and how the schools had to be desegregated. Then came one of the sharpest exchanges in a Supreme Court argument, which started with Warren's question:

"Is your request for an open decree predicated upon the assumption that your school district will immediately undertake to conform to the opinion of this Court of last year to the decree, or is it on the basis—"

Warren could not finish the question. Rogers interrupted, "Mr. Chief Justice, to say we will conform depends on the decree handed down. I am frank to tell you, right now in our district I do not think that we will send—the white people of the district will send their children to the Negro schools. It would be unfair to tell the Court that we are going to do that. I do not think it is. But I do think that something can be worked out. We hope so."

To Warren this was legal heresy. The parties did not "work out something" with Supreme Court decrees; they obeyed them. Warren looked down on the Southern attorney: "It is not a question of attitude, it is a question of conforming to the decree. Is there any basis upon which we can assume that there will be an immediate attempt to comply with the decree of this Court, whatever it may be?"

Rogers replied that the question of compliance should be left to the lower court. Warren insisted on the question of compliance: "But you are not willing to say here that there would be an honest attempt to conform to this decree, if we did leave it to the district court?"

"No, I am not," answered Rogers. And, raising his forefinger toward the bench, he declared, "Let us get the word 'honest' out of there."

"No," countered the Chief Justice, by now quite flushed, "leave it in."

The Southerner was not repressed. "No," he came back, "because I would have to tell you that right now we would not conform—we would not send our white children to the Negro schools."[41]

It looked for a moment as though Warren, bristling at the attorney's presumption, might take strong measures. "We thought he might charge Rogers with contempt," recalled Virginia Attorney General J. Lindsay Almond.[42] But Warren was able to keep his temper under control. The exchange was cut short by the Chief Justice's steely "Thank you." Still, Warren was plainly angry at the Rogers argument. When his *Brown* draft was revised, he added a sentence because of his acrimonious exchange with Rogers: "But it should go without saying that the validity of these constitutional principles cannot be allowed to yield simply because of disagreement with them."

But the most noted change in Warren's *Brown II* opinion was made at Justice Frankfurter's urging. The Chief Justice had closed his original draft: "The judgments of the Courts of Appeal are accordingly reversed (except Delaware) and the causes are remanded to the District Courts to take such proceedings and enter such orders and decrees consistent with this opinion as are necessary and proper to admit plaintiffs and those similarly situated in their respective school districts to the public school system on a non-discriminatory basis *at the earliest practicable date.*"[43]

In the final *Brown II* opinion, this was changed to: "The judgments below, except that in the Delaware case, are accordingly reversed and the cases are remanded to the District Courts to take such proceedings and enter such orders and decrees consistent with this opinion as are necessary and proper to admit to public schools on a racially nondiscriminatory basis *with all deliberate speed* the parties to these cases."[44]

When the *Brown II* opinion declared that the lower courts were to ensure that blacks were admitted to schools on a nondiscriminatory basis "with all deliberate speed," it led to learned controversy on the origins of that phrase—itself so untypical of the normal Warren mode of expression. The phrase itself comes from Justice Holmes. But it was used before him by the British poet Francis Thompson in an 1892 poem, *The Hound of Heaven.* After a newspaper account credited Justice Frankfurter with suggesting the term in *Brown II*, several correspondents wrote asking whether he had gotten it from Thompson. The Justice replied, pointing out that "the phrase has a legal lineage older than Thompson's use of it. In a letter dated March 7, 1909, Mr. Justice Holmes wrote to his friend, Sir Frederick Pollock, 'in your chancery's delightful phrase, with all deliberate speed.' . . . Again, in his opinion in *Virginia* v. *West Virginia*, 222 U.S. 17, 20, he stated 'in the language of the English Chancery, with all deliberate speed.' "[45]

Frankfurter wrote other correspondents, "I have made the most assiduous search to find Holmes's authority for saying this was a Chancery phrase"—but "all to no avail."[46] Nor has anyone else succeeded in tracing it to its alleged English legal derivation. "Yet," as Frankfurter insisted, "it cannot be that Holmes pulled it out of the air."[47]

But, if we remain uncertain where Holmes obtained the phrase, what is certain is that Frankfurter got it from Holmes and the *Brown II* opinion got it from Frankfurter. It is true that commentators on *Brown II* have all assumed that this was the case; but they have had to support the assumption by largely circumstantial evidence. However, two letters by Frankfurter to the Chief Justice enable us to confirm definitely that the Justice was responsible for the "all deliberate speed" language.

These letters show that Warren had discussed the opinion with Frankfurter even before his draft opinion was circulated and the Justice had then suggested the Holmes phrase. On May 24, Frankfurter wrote that he had read the draft "and I am ready to sign on the undotted line." But, Frankfurter went on, "I still think that 'with all deliberate speed,' *Virginia* v. *West Virginia*, 222 U.S. 17, 22, is preferable to 'at the earliest practicable date' (p. 4). The reference to *Virginia* v. *West Virginia* is, from my point of view, all to the good. That, too, involved constitutional rights—the right of a State to have this Court enforce its just claims against another State. And if the Virginia litigation may suggest that it takes time to get enforcement, that is a good intimation."

Warren did not make the change in his circulated draft. So Frankfurter sent him a May 27 letter repeating the suggestion: "I still strongly believe that 'with all deliberate speed' conveys more effectively the process of time for the effectuation of our decision. . . . I think it is highly desirable to educate public opinion—the parties themselves and the general public—to an understanding that we are at the beginning of a process of enforcement and not concluding it. In short, I think it is far better to habituate the public's mind to the realization of this, as both the phrase 'with all deliberate speed' and the citation of *Virginia* v. *West Virginia*, are calculated to do."

Warren did, of course, finally accept the Frankfurter suggestion and the "all deliberate speed" phrase remains the most striking one in the *Brown II* opinion. More important was the two-edged nature of the phrase. It ensured flexibility by providing time for enforcement; but it also countenanced delay in vindicating constitutional rights. "All deliberate speed" may never have been intended to mean indefinite delay. Yet that is just what it did mean in much of the South.

Some of the Justices, including the Chief Justice, later indicated that it had been a mistake to qualify desegregation enforcement by the "all deliberate speed" language. Justice Black's son quotes him as saying, "It tells the enemies of the decision that for the present the status quo will do and gives them time to contrive devices to stall off segregation."[48] This Black statement is inconsistent with what he said at the April 16, 1955, conference on the *Brown* enforcement question. As already seen, the Justice then had indicated that the Court should not try to settle the segregation issue too rapidly. If it attempted to do so, its decree "would be like Prohibition." Black, in fact, was the one Justice who predicted that the movement toward desegregation in the South would, at best, be only "glacial."

The Chief Justice, too, came to believe that it had been a mistake to accept the "all deliberate speed" language. In his later years Warren concluded that he had been sold a bill of goods when Justice Frankfurter induced him to use the phrase. It would have been better, he later said, to have ordered desegregation forthwith. By then, however, Justice Black's prediction of the "glacial" pace of desegregation had proved, if anything, overoptimistic. The Justices had, to be sure, not expected enthusiastic compliance by the South. But the extent of opposition was something that had not been foreseen. Looking back, Warren, at least, felt that much of the defiance could have been avoided if the South had not been led to believe that "deliberate speed" would countenance indefinite delay. When a comparable problem arose in 1964 in connection with enforcement of the "one man-one vote" principle in legislative apportionments, the Chief Justice did not hesitate to urge immediate enforcement, regardless of the problems in individual states in adapting to the new rule.[49]

Notes

1. 347 U.S. 483 (1954); 349 U.S. 294 (1955). Unless otherwise stated, all documents quoted in this chapter are in the Earl Warren Papers, Library of Congress.
2. Kluger, *Simple Justice: The History of Brown v. Board of Education and Black America's Struggle for Equality* 709 (1976).
3. 163 U.S. 537 (1896).
4. The quotes from this conference are from Justice Burton's notes. HHBLC.
5. FF-SR, May 20, 1954. FFH.
6. According to Justice Douglas, the vote would have been 5–4 in favor of segregated schools. Douglas, *The Court Years 1939–1975* 113 (1980).
7. Burton Diary, May 12, 1954. HHBLC.
8. May 17, 1954. HHBLC.
9. There are detailed notes on the conference by Justice Burton, as well as sketchy ones by Justice Frankfurter. HHBLC, FFLC. Quotations are from these notes.

10. Kluger, op. cit. supra note 2, at 698.
11. Ibid. The clerk in question confirmed this statement to me.
12. SR, May 21, 1954. FFH.
13. *The Memoirs of Earl Warren* 285 (1977).
14. FF, "Dear Brethren," January 15, 1954. HHBLC.
15. Loc. cit. supra note 13.
16. Burton Diary. HHBLC.
17. EW, To the Members of the Court, May 7, 1954. TCCT.
18. Patterson interview. Earl Warren Oral History Project, Bancroft Library, University of California, Berkeley.
19. 5/5/54-II. The first draft of this memo is also in Warren's writing.
20. A comparison with Earl Pollock's bench memo in *Brown* also shows that the Warren draft was not in any way based on that memo.
21. 347 U.S. 497 (1954).
22. Burton Diary. HHBLC.
23. These are discussed in Schwartz, *Super Chief: Earl Warren and His Supreme Court—A Judicial Biography* 97–98 (1983). There is also a note suggesting a few stylistic changes in Reed's writing in the Warren Papers.
24. May 18, 1954, quoted in Kluger, op. cit. supra note 2, at 713.
25. 347 U.S. at 494, note 11.
26. Argument: The Oral Argument before the Supreme Court in *Brown* v. *Board of Education of Topeka*, 1952–55, XXXVII (Friedman ed. 1969).
27. Kluger, op. cit. supra note 2, at 706.
28. Ibid.
29. Memorandum on the State Cases, May 7, 1954. HHBLC.
30. WOD-EW, May 11, 1954.
31. Burton Diary. HHBLC.
32. FF-EW, May 17, 1954.
33. FF-EW, May 13, 1954.
34. HHBLC.
35. See Schwartz, op. cit. supra note 23, at 93.
36. May 18, 1954, p. 18.
37. Notes of the April 16 conference are in HHBLC and FFLC.
38. There are sketchy conference notes in Warren's writing in his papers, Library of Congress.
39. At the upper right is written, in another hand, "Chief Justice's draft—5/23/55/." Page 5 of this draft is typed. It has "5/18/55" at its upper right corner.
40. EW, Memorandum for the Conference, May 26, 1955. HHBLC.
41. Op. cit. supra note 26, at 414.
42. Kluger, op. cit. supra note 2, at 752.
43. Emphasis added.
44. Emphasis added.
45. FF-Mr. Hennessy, September 8, 1958. FFLC.
46. FF-Mark de Wolfe Howe, May 5, 1958. FFLC.
47. FF-Paul A. Freund, July 22, 1958. FFLC.
48. Hugo Black, Jr., *My Father: A Remembrance* 209 (1975).
49. *Reynolds* v. *Sims*, 377 U.S. 533 (1964). See Schwartz, op. cit. supra note 23, at 505–506.